A FUNDAMENTAL THEOLOGY OF THE PRIESTHOOD

A FUNDAMENTAL THEOLOGY OF THE PRIESTHOOD

Proceedings of the Symposium Sponsored by the Center for Research and Anthropology of Vocations

Volume 1

EDITED BY
Cardinal Marc Ouellet

Paulist Press
New York / Mahwah, NJ

Scripture quotations vary as they have been taken or translated from the original presentations by each of the contributors who provided either their own translation or drew from various sources.

Cover images: Front--Christ Pantocrator, Cathedral of Santa Maria Nuova (Monreale) © Gérard Holden, CRAV. Used with permission. Back--Pope Francis and Cardinal Marc Ouellet © Tamino Petelinse
Cover and book design by Lynn Else

First published in 2023 in Italian as *Per Una Teologia Fondamentale del Sacerdozio* by Editrice Libreria Vaticana, Vatican City. This edition published by arrangement with the Centre de Recherche et d'Anthropologie des Vocations, Saint-Cloud, France.

Library of Congress Control Number: 2023933689

ISBN 978-0-8091-5674-0 (paperback)
ISBN 978-0-8091-8836-9 (e-book)

Published by Paulist Press
997 Macarthur Boulevard
Mahwah, New Jersey 07430
www.paulistpress.com

Printed and bound in the
United States of America

CONTENTS

Cardinal Marc Ouellet
Prefect of the Congregation for Bishops

OPENING SPEECH OF THE SYMPOSIUM

"For a Fundamental Theology of the Priesthood"

Beloved Holy Father,
Your Eminences, Your Excellencies,

Dear symposium participants,

"Ask the Lord of the harvest to send laborers to his harvest!" Our Lord calls laborers of every kind to work in his vineyard. Some are hired at the first hour, others at midday, and still others at the last hour. All of them receive a fair wage, not in hard cash, according to the criteria of this world, but in communion with the Master whose goodness does not let itself be outdone in generosity.

What can be expected of a "fundamental theology of the priesthood" in the current context, convulsed by the clerical sex abuse crisis? Would it not be better to refrain from talking about the priesthood, now that the sins and crimes of unworthy ministers are front-page news in the international press for having betrayed their commitment or shamefully covered up those guilty of such depravity? Would it not be better to keep quiet, repent, and seek the causes of those disastrous faults?

We are broken and humbled by these crucial questions, which are daily before us as members of Jesus Christ's Church. This is a good opportunity for us to give expression to our sincere grief and ask for forgiveness from the victims of all sorts who are suffering, their lives having been wrecked by abusive, criminal acts that for so long remained hidden and were treated lightly by those who protected the institution and the culprits instead of the victims. This symposium fully recognizes the popular outcry and anger that afflict us; we join our voices to those who seek truth and justice, adding our prayer to the Lord of the harvest to grant us the grace to respond adequately to the challenges posed by the crisis of the priesthood in our times.

In this regard, I feel it will possibly be necessary to organize an event similar to this one to take stock of current sociological research and analyze the historical, cultural, and even theological causes at the root of what Pope Francis calls "clericalism." Clericalism is a general but nonetheless specific term designating a whole set of abuses of power, spiritual abuse, and abuses of consciences, of which sex abuse is only the tip of the iceberg—a visible, perverted one—emerging from deeper deviances that must be identified and unmasked.

Dear friends, we are not yet equipped for that painful but necessary exercise, that theological, spiritual, and pastoral examination of conscience. We will need to prepare for it by various stages of reflection, which will first reconstruct the overall scope of the priesthood and the complementary dimensions of its mediation; because at the base of the phenomena mentioned above there is an imbalance: undue value is given to one form of the priesthood at the expense of the other form, the baptismal form, which has, alas, almost been forgotten in the Catholic world. The doctrinal defense of the ministerial priesthood in the face of the Protestant Reformation meant that its other, no less essential, dimension was left in the shadows, while a clerical power mentality and an attitude of excessive control by the clergy over the whole of the ecclesial community was reinforced. Current synodal research offers hope of a new balance.

The aim of this symposium is to go deeper into the overall scope of the priesthood of Christ, shared firstly with the baptized, and then with ordained ministers, so that the specific connections between the different members of the people of God can be actively set within the framework of an ecclesiology of communion, with a fundamental, many-sided commitment to a synodal Church. The Holy Spirit is calling the Church of the third millennium to be synodal, and thus to universalize her mission by announcing the good news as a people journeying through history, as an organic body that counts on each of its members to offer the gospel to all mankind.

Rediscovering the overall scope of the priesthood in its two modes of participation—baptismal and ministerial—in the one priesthood of Christ is a necessary precondition for a complete theological analysis of the abuse crisis. It will also enable us to take up once again the question of the place of women in the Church, in a more open way, more sensitive to communities' charismatic dimension. That will moreover encourage and sustain enthusiasm for all vocations, by offering an attractive view of their communion. In a world that is saturated with bad news, why should we not be able to make room for the joy of a new vocational enthusiasm in following Christ?

We are extremely honored and encouraged, dear Holy Father, by your presence at the opening of this event, which you have supported from the outset. Thank you, with all my heart. I also thank and offer a warm welcome to those who have signed up for this symposium in spite of the uncertainties of the pandemic. I also greet all those who will be following these sessions virtually. Dear Holy Father, we are looking forward to hearing you, and to letting ourselves be spurred forward in the direction of your discernment of the Holy Spirit at work today for a missionary conversion of the Church. Together with you, we pray to the Lord of the harvest to send laborers to his harvest.

Paul VI Hall
February 17, 2022

ADDRESS OF HIS HOLINESS POPE FRANCIS

Dear brothers, good day!

I am grateful to have the opportunity to share with you this reflection on some things that the Lord has gradually helped me to realize over the more than fifty years of my priesthood. In this grateful remembrance, I wish to include all those priests who, by their life and witness, showed me from my earliest years what it means to reflect the face of the Good Shepherd. In thinking about what to share concerning the life of the priest today, I concluded that the best thing is to speak of the witness I have received from so many priests over the years. What I now offer is the fruit of my thoughts about them, and my recognition and appreciation of what it was that distinguished them and gave them singular strength, joy and hope in their pastoral mission.

At the same time, I should also speak of those brother priests whom I have had to accompany because they had lost the flame of their first love and their ministry had become barren, repetitive and almost meaningless. There are different times and situations in the life of every priest. I personally have passed through a variety of times and situations and, in "ruminating" on the movements of the Spirit, I have come to realize that in some of those situations, which included moments of trial, difficulty, and desolation, somehow there always remained a sense of peace in my life. I realize we can talk and speculate endlessly on the priesthood, but today I want to share with you this "little album," so that today's priests, wherever they find themselves, can experience the peace and fruitfulness that the Spirit desires to bestow. It may be that these reflections are the "swan song" of my own priestly life, but I can assure you that they are the fruit of my own experience. I am speaking about what I have experienced, not any theory.

The times we are living in require us not only to experience change, but to accept it in the realization that ours is a time of epochal change—I have said this many times. If we had any doubts about this, COVID has made it amply evident: indeed, the outbreak of the virus cannot be restricted to a question of medicine and health care; it is much more than a cold.

We can respond in many ways to the challenge of change. The problem is that while many actions and attitudes can be helpful and good, not all of them have the flavor of the gospel. Here is the crux of the matter: discerning whether changes and actions have the flavor of the gospel or not. For example, seeking established ways of doing things, very often anchored in the past, that "guarantee" a sort of protection from risks, sheltering us in the world or a society that no longer exists (if it ever did), as if this determined order could quell the conflicts that history sets before us. That is the crisis of going backward in order to find shelter.

Another attitude might be that of exaggerated optimism—"Everything will be all right"—moving too far forward without discernment and without taking necessary decisions. This optimism ends up ignoring the pain involved in this transformation and failing to accept the tensions, complexities, and ambiguities of the present time, "consecrating" the latest novelty as the ultimate reality and thereby dismissing the wisdom of the years.

Both are a kind of flight. They are the response of the mercenary who sees the wolf coming and runs away: either toward the past or toward the future. Neither can lead to mature solutions. The concrete reality of the present time is where we must stay, there in today's concrete reality.

I prefer the response born of a trusting acceptance of reality, anchored in the wise and living Tradition of the Church, which enables us to put out into the deep *without fear*. At this moment of history, I feel that Jesus is once more inviting us to "put out into the deep" (cf. Luke 5:4) trusting that he is the Lord of history and that, with his guidance, we will discern the direction to take. Our salvation is not "aseptic," the product of a laboratory or a disembodied spiritualism:

this is always the temptation of Gnosticism, one that is contemporary, that is current. *Discerning the will of God* means learning to view realities with the Lord's own eyes. It means not evading the realities that our people are experiencing, or anxiously seeking a quick and quiet exit provided by the ideology of the moment or prefabricated answers. Neither of these can deal with the more difficult and even dark moments of our history. These two paths would lead us to deny "our history as a Church, which is glorious precisely because it is a history of sacrifice, of hopes and daily struggles, of lives spent in service and fidelity to work" (*Evangelii Gaudium* 96).

These challenges are also affecting the lives of priests; a symptom of this is the vocations crisis experienced by our communities in several places. Often, however, this is due to the absence within communities of a contagious apostolic zeal, with the result that they lack enthusiasm and attractiveness: communities, for example, that function and are well organized yet without enthusiasm, where everything is in place yet without the fire of the Spirit. Where there is life and fervor, and a desire to bring Christ to others, genuine vocations spring up. Even in parishes whose priests are not particularly engaged and joyful, the active and fraternal life of the community can awaken a desire to consecrate one's life entirely to God and to the preaching of the gospel. This is especially the case if that community prays insistently for vocations and has the courage to propose to its young people a path of special consecration. When we fall into functionalism or pastoral organization—if this becomes the only thing—that does not attract at all. Instead, when the priest or the community has a Christian baptismal fervor, this attracts new vocations.

The life of a priest is above all the salvation history of one baptized person. Cardinal Ouellet has spoken of the distinction between the ministerial priesthood and the baptismal priesthood. At times we forget about baptism, and the priest then becomes a functionary, and the danger of functionalism sets in. We should never forget that each specific vocation, including that of holy orders, is a completion of baptism. It is always a great temptation to live *a priesthood without baptism*—and there are some priests "without baptism"—in other words, forgetting that our primary vocation is to holiness. To be holy means to conform ourselves to Jesus, letting our hearts thrill with his same sentiments (cf.

Phil 2:15). Only when we strive to love others as Jesus does, do we make God visible and fulfil our vocation to holiness. Quite rightly, St. John Paul II reminded us that "the priest, like every other member of the Church, ought to grow in the awareness that he himself is continually in need of being evangelized" (*Pastores Dabo Vobis* 26). And when you say to some bishops or priests that they need to be evangelized, they don't understand. This happens, this is a tragedy nowadays.

Each specific vocation must be submitted to this kind of discernment. Our vocation is before all else a response to the One who loved us first (cf. 1 John 4:19). This is the source of our hope, for even amid crises, the Lord never ceases to love us and to call us. Each of us can testify to this: one day the Lord found us, where we were and as we were, in uncertain circumstances or complex family situations. I like to re-read Ezekiel 16 and at times see myself: the Lord found me there, he found me in that state, and he led me forward. Yet this did not discourage him from using each of us to write the history of salvation. So it was from the beginning—we can think of Peter, Paul, and Matthew, just to name a few. Jesus did not choose them because they were perfect, but because he was concretely committed to each of them. In looking at his own humanity, his own history, his own personality, each of us should ask, not if responding to a vocation is agreeable or not, but whether, in conscience, that vocation brings to light within us the potential for love that we received on the day of our baptism.

In these changing times, many questions have to be faced and many temptations will arise. In these remarks, I will simply speak about what I consider decisive for the life of a priest today. St. Paul tells us that "in Christ, the whole structure is joined together and grows into a holy temple in the Lord" (Eph 2:21). Growing in a well-ordered way means growing in harmony, and growth in harmony is something only the Holy Spirit can bring about, for as St. Basil says so beautifully, "He himself is harmony" (*Ipse harmonia est*; *Treatise on the Holy Spirit*, 38). Every structure, to keep standing, needs solid foundations. For this reason, I would like to speak of the attitudes that sustain us as priests. You have heard of these attitudes already, but I will repeat them once more. I will refer to those four pillars of our priestly life as "four forms of closeness," since they imitate God's own "style," which is essentially that of closeness (cf. Deut 4:7). God defines himself this way to his people: "For what great nation is there that has a god so near to it as I am to you?" God's style is closeness, a special, compassionate, and tender closeness. These are three words that define the life of a priest, and of a Christian as well, because they are taken precisely from God's style: closeness, compassion, and tenderness.

I have mentioned these in the past, but today I would like to discuss them more fully because, more than recipes or theories, priests need concrete tools for exercising their ministry, their mission and their daily activity. St. Paul exhorted Timothy to rekindle the gift of God that he had received through the laying on of his hands: a spirit not of fear, but of strength, love, and self-discipline (cf. 2 Tim 1:6–7). I am convinced that these four pillars, these four "forms of closeness" that I will speak of now can help us in a practical, concrete and hope-filled way to rekindle the gift and the fruitfulness that were once promised to us, to keep that gift alive.

First, closeness to God. Four forms of closeness, the first of which is closeness to God.

CLOSENESS TO GOD

First, closeness to God, that is, to the Lord of closeness. "I am the vine, you are the branches." These words occur when John's Gospel speaks about "remaining." "Those who abide in me, and I in them, bear much fruit, because apart from me you can do nothing. Whoever does not abide in me is thrown away like a branch and withers; such branches are gathered, thrown into the fire and burned. If you abide in me, and my words abide in you, ask for whatever you wish, and it will be done for you" (John 15:5–7).

A priest is called above all to cultivate this closeness, this intimacy with God, and from this relationship, he will be able to draw all the strength needed for his ministry. Our relationship with God is, so to speak, what "grafts" us to him and makes us fruitful. Without a meaningful relationship with the Lord, our ministry will prove fruitless. Closeness to Jesus and daily contact with his word enables us to measure our life against his, learning not to be scandalized by whatever befalls us and protecting ourselves from "stumbling blocks." Like the

Master, you will experience joy, wedding feasts, miracles and healings, multiplications of loaves and repose, moments of praise. But you will also experience ingratitude, rejection, doubt, and solitude, to the point of crying out, "My God, my God, why have you forsaken me?" (Matt 27:46).

Closeness to Jesus makes us unafraid of those times—not because we rely on our own strength but because we look to him, cling to him, and cry out, "Lord, keep me from falling into temptation! Make me realize that I am experiencing a critical moment in my life and that you are with me, to test my faith and my love."* This closeness to God can sometimes take the form of a struggle: a struggle with the Lord, especially in those moments when his absence is most felt in our own lives and in the lives of the persons entrusted to us. A struggle that lasts through the night, and during which we ask his blessing (cf. Gen 32:25–27), which will be a source of life for many. At times this is a struggle. A priest who works here in the curia—he is young and has a difficult job, keeping track of things—said to me that he returned home tired, but he took a little rest in front of Our Lady with his rosary in hand before going to bed. This curial official, this Vatican employee, needed that closeness. To be sure, sometimes people in the curia are much criticized, but I can also say and bear witness that there truly are saints in the curia.

Many crises in the priesthood originate precisely in a poor life of prayer, a lack of intimacy with the Lord, the reduction of the spiritual life to mere religious practice. I want to point this out even in formation: the spiritual life is one thing; religious practice is another. "How is your spiritual life going?" "Good, good. I make my meditation in the morning, I pray the rosary, I pray the breviary and all the rest. I'm doing everything." No, this is religious practice. But how is your spiritual life going? I can think of important moments of my own life, where closeness to the Lord proved decisive in sustaining me, sustaining me in dark moments. The intimacy born of prayer, the spiritual life, concrete closeness to God through listening to his word, the celebration of the Eucharist, the silence of adoration, entrustment to Mary, the wise accompaniment of a guide and the sacrament of Reconcilia-

* C. M. Martini, *Perseverance in Trial: Reflections on Job* (Collegeville, MN: Liturgical Press, 1992).

tion.... Without these concrete "forms of closeness," a priest is merely a weary hireling who has none of the benefits of the Lord's friends. In my former diocese, I liked to ask priests, "Tell me,"—they told me about all their work—"Tell me, how do you go to bed?" They did not understand. "Yes, yes, at night, how do you go to bed?" "I come home tired, I have a bite to eat, and I go to bed, but before bed, a little television." "Ah, good! But you don't stop before the Lord, at least to tell him good night?" This is the problem. A lack of closeness. Being tired from work is normal, going to rest and watching television are legitimate, but without the Lord, without this closeness? Praying the rosary, praying the breviary, but without intimacy with the Lord. Feeling no need to say to the Lord, "Goodbye, until tomorrow, many thanks!" These are little acts that reveal the attitude of a priestly soul.

All too often, for example, in the life of priests, prayer is practiced only as a duty; we forget that friendship and love do not come from following rules, but are a fundamental choice of the heart. The priest who prays remains, ultimately, a Christian who has come to appreciate fully the gift received at baptism. A priest who prays is a son who constantly remembers that he is such, and that he has a Father who loves him deeply. A priest who prays is a son who keeps close to the Lord.

None of this is easy, however, unless we are accustomed to find moments of silence throughout our day and to set aside the activism of Martha to learn the quiet contemplation of Mary. We find it hard to give up that activism—and very often activism can be an escape—because once we stop running around, what we immediately feel is not peace but a kind of emptiness; and in order to keep from feeling that, we are unwilling to slow down. Work is a distraction, in order not to enter into desolation. Yet desolation is a little point of encounter with God. Once we accept the desolation that is born of silence, fast from our activities and words, and find the courage to take a sincere look at ourselves, everything takes on a light and peace no longer based on our own strengths and abilities. We need to learn to let the Lord bring his work to fulfilment in each of us and to "prune" all that is unfruitful, barren, or unworthy of our calling. Perseverance in prayer is more than simply remaining faithful to its practice: it means not running away in those times when prayer draws us into the desert. The way of the desert is the way that leads to intimacy with God, provided we do not run away or find ways to avoid this encounter. In the desert "I will speak tenderly to her," says the Lord to his people through the words of the prophet Hosea (Hos 2:14). This is something that a priest must ask himself: if he is able to let himself be led into the desert. Spiritual guides who accompany priests have to understand and help them and pose this question: Are you able to let yourself be drawn into the desert? Or do you go right away to the oasis of television or something else?

Closeness with God enables the priest to touch the hurt in our hearts, which, if embraced, disarms us even to the point of making possible an encounter. The prayer that, like fire, stirs up our priestly life is the plea of a contrite and humble heart, which, as the Scripture tells us, the Lord does not disdain (cf. Ps 51:17). "They call and the LORD hears and rescues them from their distress. The LORD is close to the brokenhearted; those whose spirit is crushed he will save" (Ps 34:17–18).

A priest needs to have a heart sufficiently "enlarged" to expand and embrace the pain of the people entrusted to his care while, at the same time, like a sentinel, being able to proclaim the dawning of God's grace revealed in that very pain. Embracing, accepting, and showing his own impoverishment in closeness to the Lord is the best means to learn gradually how to embrace the neediness and pain that he encounters daily in his ministry, and thus to be conformed ever more closely to the heart of Christ. That, in turn, will prepare the priest for another kind of closeness: closeness to the people of God. In closeness to God, the priest grows in closeness to his people; and conversely, in closeness to his people, he experiences closeness to his Lord. And this closeness to God—this gets my attention—is the first task of bishops, for when the apostles "invented" deacons, Peter explained their role and said, "But we"—the bishops—"will devote ourselves to prayer and to the ministry of the word" (cf. Acts 6:4). In other words, the first task of a bishop is to pray; and a priest must take this up as well: to pray.

In the words of St. John the Baptist, "He must increase, but I must decrease" (John 3:30). Intimacy with God makes all this possible, for in prayer we realize that we are great in his eyes, and so, for priests close to the Lord, it is easy to become small in the eyes of the world. There, in that closeness, we no longer fear to be configured to the crucified Jesus, as is demanded of us in the Rite of Priestly Ordination. This is very beautiful, yet we often forget it.

Let us turn now to the second form of closeness, which will be briefer than the first.

CLOSENESS TO THE BISHOP

This second form of closeness has long been interpreted in a one-sided way. As Church, all too often, even today, our view of obedience is far from the sense of the gospel. Obedience is not a disciplinary attribute but the deepest sign of the bonds uniting us in communion. To obey, in this case obeying the bishop, means to learn how to listen, to remember that no one "owns" God's will, which must be understood only through discernment. Obedience is thus attentive listening to the will of God, which is discerned precisely in a bond, a relationship with others. Such an attitude of attentive listening makes us come to realize that none of us is the beginning and the end of life, but that each of us must necessarily interact with others. The "internal logic" of closeness—in this case with the bishop, but with others too—enables us to conquer all temptations to closedmindedness, self-justification and living our lives as "bachelors." When priests close themselves off, they end up as "bachelors," with all the quirks of "bachelors" and this is not good. Instead, this closeness invites us to listen to others, to find the way that leads to truth and life.

The bishop is not a school superintendent or supervisor; he is a father and must show this closeness. The bishop must try to behave this way because otherwise he pushes his priests away, or he comes near only to the ambitious ones. The bishop, whoever he may be, remains for each priest and for every particular Church a bond that helps discern the will of God. Yet we should not forget that the bishop himself can be a means for this discernment only if he is himself attentive to the lives of his priests and of the holy people of God entrusted to his care. As I wrote in *Evangelii Gaudium*,

> We need to practice the art of listening, which is more than simply hearing. Listening, in communication, is an openness of heart that makes possible that closeness without which genuine spiritual encounter cannot occur. Listening helps us

> to find the right gesture and word which shows that we are more than simply bystanders. Only through such respectful and compassionate listening can we enter on the paths of true growth and awaken a yearning for the Christian ideal: the desire to respond fully to God's love and to bring to fruition what he has sown in our lives. (171)

Not by chance does evil, in order to destroy the fruitfulness of the Church's work, seek to undermine the bonds that establish and preserve us in unity. To defend the bonds of a priest with his Church, with the Institute to which he belongs, and with his bishop, makes priestly life trustworthy and sure. To defend the bonds. Obedience is the fundamental decision to accept what is asked of us, and to do so as a concrete sign of that universal sacrament of salvation which is the Church. Obedience can also be discussion, attentive listening, and in some cases tension, but not a rupture. This necessarily demands that priests pray for their bishops and feel free to express their opinions with respect, courage and sincerity. It likewise demands that bishops demonstrate humility, an ability to listen, to be self-critical, and to let themselves be helped. If we can preserve this bond, we will advance securely on our way.

I think this is enough about closeness to the bishop.

CLOSENESS TO OTHER PRIESTS

The third form of closeness. Closeness to God, closeness to the bishop, and closeness to other priests. It is precisely on the basis of communion with the bishop that a third form of closeness emerges, the closeness of fraternity. Jesus is present wherever there are brothers and sisters who love one another: "For where two or three are gathered in my name, I am there among them" (Matt 18:20). Fraternity, like obedience, cannot be a moral imposition from without. Fraternity means choosing deliberately to pursue holiness together with others, and not by oneself. As an African proverb, which you know well, says, "If you want to go fast, go alone; if you want to go far, go with others." Sometimes it seems that the Church is slow, and that is true. Yet I like to think of it as the slowness of those who have chosen to walk in fraternity. Also accompanying those who are least, but always in fraternity.

The signs of fraternity are those of love. St. Paul, in the First Letter to the Corinthians (chapter 13), has left us a clear "road map" of love and, in a certain sense, has pointed out the goal of fraternity. Before all else, to learn *patience*, the ability to feel responsible for others, to bear their burdens, to suffer in some way with them. The opposite of patience is indifference, the distance we create with others, so as not to get involved in their lives. Many priests experience the drama of solitude, of loneliness. We can feel undeserving of patience or consideration. Indeed, it can appear that from others we can expect only judgment, not goodness or kindness. Others seem unable to rejoice in the good things happening in our lives, or we ourselves seem unable to rejoice when we see good things happening in the lives of others. This inability to rejoice in the good of others—and I want to emphasize this—is *envy* that is very present in our circles; it is an obstacle to the pedagogy of love, not merely a sin to be confessed. Sin is the end result; it comes from an attitude of envy. Envy is very present in priestly communities. God's word tells us that it is a destructive attitude: through the envy of the devil, sin entered the world (cf. Wis 2:24). Envy is the door for destruction. We must speak clearly about this: envy exists in our presbyterates. It is not that everyone is envious, no, but the temptation to envy is there at hand. We need to be attentive, for from envy comes gossip.

To feel part of the community or "group," there is no need to put on masks to make ourselves more attractive to others. We have no need, in other words, to be *boastful*, much less to *be inflated* or, worse yet, to be arrogant or rude, *lacking respect* for our neighbor. There are also clerical forms of bullying. If there is one thing a priest can boast about, it is the Lord's mercy. For conscious of his own sinfulness, weakness, and limitations, he knows from experience that where sin abounds, love abounds even more (cf. Rom 5:20). This is the first and most reassuring message that he brings. A priest who keeps this in mind is not, and cannot be, envious.

Fraternal love *does not insist on its own way*, or yield to *anger* or resentment, as if my brother or neighbor had somehow cheated me of something. When I encounter the meanness of others, I choose *not to harbor a grudge*, to make that my sole basis of judgment, even perhaps to the point of *rejoicing over evil* in the case of those who have caused me suffering. True love *rejoices in the truth* and considers it a grave sin to offend truth and the dignity of our brothers and sisters through slander, detraction, and gossip. These originate in envy, to the point even of slander in order to get a position. And this is very sad. When we ask for information to appoint someone a Bishop, many times we receive information poisoned by envy. This is a sickness of our presbyterates. Many of you are formators in seminaries; you should bear this in mind.

We should never, on the other hand, allow fraternal love to be considered utopian, much less a trite phrase useful for awakening warm feelings or stilling disagreements. No! All of us know how difficult it can be to live in community, or in a presbyterate—a saint once said that community life was his penance—yet how difficult it is to live alongside those we have chosen to call our brothers and sisters. Fraternal love, provided we do not make it saccharine, redefine it or diminish it, is the "great prophecy" that we are called to embody in today's throwaway society. I like to think of fraternal love as a "gymnasium of the spirit," where we daily take stock of our progress and check the temperature of our spiritual life. Today the prophecy of fraternity has not faded, but it does need heralds, men and women who, while conscious of their own limitations and challenges, let themselves be touched, challenged and moved by the words of the Lord: "By this everyone will know that you are my disciples, if you have love for one another" (John 13:35).

Fraternal love, for priests, cannot be restricted to a small group, but finds expression in pastoral charity (cf. *Pastores Dabo Vobis*, 23), which inspires us to live that love concretely as mission. We can say that we love only if we learn to express love in the way that St. Paul describes. Only the one who seeks to love remains secure. Those who live with the syndrome of Cain, convinced that they are incapable of loving others because they themselves feel unloved and unappreciated, end up living always as restless wanderers, never feeling quite at home, and precisely for this reason all the more exposed to evil: hurting themselves and hurting others. This is why love among priests has the role of safeguarding, of safeguarding each other mutually.

I would also add that when priestly fraternity, closeness among priests, thrives and bonds of true friendship exist, it likewise becomes possible to experience with greater serenity the life of celibacy. Celibacy is a gift that the Latin Church preserves, yet it is a gift that, to be lived as a means of sanctification, calls for healthy relationships, relationships of true esteem and true goodness that are deeply rooted in Christ. Without friends and without prayer, celibacy can become an unbearable burden and a counter-witness to the very beauty of the priesthood.

We come now to the fourth and last form of closeness, closeness to the holy people of God. We would do well to read *Lumen Gentium* 8 and 12.

CLOSENESS TO PEOPLE

I have often emphasized how our relationship with the holy people of God is for each of us not a duty but a grace: "Loving others is a spiritual force drawing us to union with God" (*Evangelii Gaudium* 272). For this reason, the proper place of every priest is in the midst of people, in close relationship to others. In *Evangelii Gaudium*, I stressed that

> to be evangelizers of souls, we need to develop a spiritual taste for being close to people's lives and to discover that this is itself a source of greater joy. Mission is at once a passion for Jesus and a passion for his people. When we stand before Jesus crucified, we see the depth of his love which exalts and sustains us, but at the same time, unless we are blind, we begin to realize that Jesus' gaze, burning with love, expands to embrace all his faithful people. We realize once more that he wants to make use of us to draw closer to his beloved people. Jesus wants to make use of priests to draw closer to the holy faithful People of God. He takes us from the midst of his people and he sends us to his people; without the sense of belonging we cannot understand our deepest identity. (268)

Priestly identity cannot be understood without this belonging to the holy faithful People of God.

I am convinced that, for a renewed understanding of the identity of the priesthood, it is important nowadays to be closely involved in people's real lives, to live alongside them, without escape routes.

> Sometimes we are tempted to be that kind of Christian who keeps the Lord's wounds at arm's length. Yet Jesus wants us to touch human misery, to touch the suffering flesh of others. He hopes that we will stop looking for those personal or communal niches which shelter us from the maelstrom of human misfortune and instead enter into the reality of other people's lives and know the power of tenderness. Whenever we do so, our lives become wonderfully complicated and we experience intensely what it is to be a people, to be part of a people. (270)

"A people" is not a logical category, no; it is a mythic category. To understand this, we must approach it as we approach a mythic category.

Closeness to the people of God, a closeness that, enriched by those three other forms of closeness, invites and indeed demands that we imitate the Lord's own "style." That style is one of closeness, compassion, and tenderness, in which we act not as judges, but as Good Samaritans who acknowledge the wounds of our people, their silent sufferings, the self-denial and sacrifices made by so many fathers and mothers to support their families. Who acknowledge, too, the effects of violence, corruption, and indifference that, in their wake, seek to stifle all hope. A style of closeness that allows us to pour balm upon wounds and to proclaim a year of favor from the Lord (cf. Isa 61:2). It is imperative to remember that the people of God are hoping to find *shepherds* in the style of Jesus. Not "clerical functionaries" or "professionals of the sacred"—let's recall that period in France, the time of the Curé of Ars: he was a curate, but there was also "monsieur l'abbé," a clerical functionary. Today, too, people are asking us to be shepherds of the people and not "professionals of the sacred," shepherds filled with compassion and concern. Men of courage, ready to draw near to those in pain and lend a helping hand. Contemplative men, whose closeness to people enables them to proclaim before the wounds of our world the power of the resurrection even now at work.

One of the distinctive marks of this, our society of "networks," is people's growing sense of being "orphaned," a current phenomenon. Though connected to everybody and everything, we lack the feeling of belonging, which is something more than mere connectivity. The closeness of a pastor makes it possible to gather a community and foster the growth of that sense of belonging. For we belong to God's holy and faithful people, which is called to be a sign of the breaking of the kingdom of heaven into the here and now of history. If their shepherd strays or withdraws, the sheep will scatter and be at the mercy of any and every wolf.

This sense of belonging will in turn prove an antidote to the distortion of vocation that happens whenever we forget that the priestly life is owed to others—to the Lord and to the persons he has entrusted to us. Forgetting this is at the root of clericalism—what Cardinal Ouellet spoke of—and its consequences. Clericalism is a distortion, as is one of its signs, rigidity. Clericalism is a distortion because it is based not on closeness but on distance. This is strange: not closeness, but the opposite. When I think of clericalism, I also think of the clericalization of the laity: the creation of a small élite around the priest who end up betraying their own essential mission (cf. *Gaudium et Spes* 44), the mission of the laity. Many laypersons are clericalized: "I belong to that association; we are there in the parish." The lay clericalized "elect" is a great temptation. Let us remember that

> my mission of being in the heart of the people is not just a part of my life or a badge I can take off; it is not an "extra" or just another moment in life. Instead, it is something I cannot uproot from my priestly being without destroying my very self. *I am a mission* on this earth; that is the reason why I am here in this world. We have to regard ourselves as sealed, even branded, by this mission of bringing light, blessing, enlivening, raising up, healing and freeing. (*Evangelii Gaudium* 273)

I would like to relate this closeness to the people of God with closeness to God, since the prayer of a shepherd is nurtured and becomes incarnate in the heart of God's people. When he prays, a pastor bears the marks of the sorrows and joys of his people, which he presents in silence to the Lord, to be anointed by the gift of the Holy Spirit. Such is the hope of every shepherd who trustingly and tirelessly works so that the Lord may bless his people.

St. Ignatius teaches that "it is not knowing much but realizing and relishing things interiorly that contents and satisfies the soul" (*Spiritual Exercises*, Annotations, 2, 4). Bishops and priests would do well to ask, "How am I practicing these forms of closeness? How am I living these four aspects that intersect and shape my priestly heart, enabling me to deal with the tensions and imbalances that we experience daily?" Those four forms of closeness are good training for "playing on an open field," where the priest is called to be present without fear or rigidity, without reducing or impoverishing his mission.

A priestly heart knows about closeness, because his primary form of closeness is with the Lord. May Christ visit his priests in their prayer, in their bishop, in their brother priests and in their people. May he upset our routine, disrupt our lives and disquiet us—as at the time of our first love—and lead us to employ all our talents and abilities to ensure that our people may have life and life in abundance (cf. John 10:10). The forms of closeness that the Lord demands—closeness with God, closeness with the bishop, closeness among us priests and closeness with the holy faithful people of God—are not an added burden: they are a gift that he gives to keep our vocation alive and fruitful. If we are tempted to get caught up in interminable speeches, discussions about the theology of the priesthood or theories about what the priesthood should be, the Lord for his part simply looks upon us with tenderness and compassion. He shows priests the signposts that point the way to appreciating and rekindling their missionary zeal: closeness that is compassionate and tender, closeness to God, to the bishop, to brother priests and to the people entrusted to their care. A closeness in the "style" of God himself, who is ever close to us, with compassion and tender love.

Thank you for your closeness and patience, thank you, thank you very much! I wish all of you well in your work. I am going to the library because I have many appointments this morning. Please pray for me and I will pray for you. I wish you all good work!

DAY ONE

TRADITION AND NEW HORIZONS

February 17, 2022

1

RELIGION AND PRIESTHOOD

A Basic Anthropological Factor

FATHER SERGE-THOMAS BONINO, OP

SHOULD THE FIGURE of the priest be desacralized? This question has been raised recently in the painful context of the clerical sex abuse crisis; and more generally, in criticisms leveled at the errors of "clericalism." Such criticisms assert that the sacralization of priests—particularly accentuated, it is claimed, after the Gregorian reforms, and especially in the Tridentine view of the priestly ministry—is one of the structural, "systemic" causes of the abuse crisis. From one angle, it is stated, the sacred character attributed to priests tends to make them a figure set apart, participating in some way in God's own authority, and this can numb the critical faculties of members of the faithful who are psychologically fragile. They are caught in the sacred aura—*fascinosum et tremendum*—of the priest, like a rabbit frozen in the glare of headlights. From another angle, it is alleged that what is sacred is seen as untouchable, outside the scope of common law, so that the sacred institution of the priesthood must, so to speak, be above the laws of human justice. To remedy the dysfunctional behavior, some people suggest that the figure of the priest must be desacralized; priests should be seen as mere men like everyone else, Christians like other Christians, only distinguished by exercising certain functions in the service of the community. Furthermore, according to some theologians, the projected desacralization is even more commendable in that it would enable us to recover a more authentically Christian view of the Church's ministry, freed from the accumulated deformations caused—regrettably—by forgetting the radical newness of Christianity within the religious sphere. Indeed, the sacralization of ordained ministers is said to be the product not only of a relatively late sacerdotalization of the Christian ministry, but also of an unfortunate regression toward the Old Testament, "Levitical" notion of the priesthood as a specialized caste of servants of cultic acts, or even of a regression toward the religious forms of archaic pagan worship. In each case, according to this view, the specifically christological form of Church ministry is short-circuited or undervalued. Now, is it not starting from, and in function of, Jesus Christ and Jesus Christ alone that the Christian ministry, and specifically the priesthood, need to be rethought?

The ministerial priesthood and the common priesthood of the faithful are indeed two distinct ways of participating in the one, definitive priesthood of Jesus Christ. A process of recentering on the christological form of the priesthood is therefore essential. But the question immediately arises: How should the priesthood of Jesus Christ be conceptualized?

There are two possible ways forward. The first is the dialectic way. This defines Christ's priesthood by contrasting it with all the forms of priesthood found either in the old dispensation or in religious structures that grew up outside the current of Judeo-Christian revelation. The latter are the application of a "natural" religious sense that is generally held suspect by partisans of the dialectic way, which rests on the opposition between faith and religion. But faced with the risk of equivocation that threatens the dialectic approach—since it holds that the priesthood of Christ has nothing in common with the institution known as priesthood in religious anthropology—the second way has recourse instead to analogy. The priesthood of Jesus Christ assumes, purifies, recapitulates, and brings to unexpected perfection the imperfect forms of priesthood that are present in most religions, and that express, with differing degrees of success, a constitutive aspect of religious anthropology in its communitarian aspect. In this regard it is significant that in the *Summa Theologiae*, on coming to the question of whether Jesus Christ is truly a priest—or rather, of finding a theological justification for the *revealed* attribution to Jesus Christ of the quality of priesthood—St. Thomas Aquinas begins (can it be done otherwise?) by describing in general terms the *officium sacerdotis*, the priestly function. To this end, he sets out a general concept, that is both flexible and analogical, of the priesthood,[1] totally centered on the theme of mediation.[2] He next proceeds to show how Jesus Christ fulfils this concept truly and in an eminent way: *Hoc maxime convenit Christo*.[3] We need to understand this properly: it is not about persuading or forcing Christ's priesthood into a preestablished framework, that is, subsuming it under an a priori, univocal, closed concept of the priesthood, but of drawing up, in the combined light of reason and faith, an analogical, flexible, "open" notion of the priesthood that Christ both fulfills and brings to its own fulfillment, thus unveiling the ultimate meaning of something that other kinds of priesthood attain only very imperfectly. God really does speak in human language, and we would be unable to hear the revelation of Jesus Christ's priesthood if it did not rest on (while deeply transforming it though without destroying it) a common notion of priesthood, which was moreover prophetically oriented toward Christ in the form it took in the Old Testament priesthood. The Letter to the Hebrews proceeds along this same line.[4]

Jesus Christ, High Priest of the of the new and eternal covenant, fulfills and surpasses not only the priesthood of the first covenant, which was directly ordered toward him as a prophetic figure, but also the priesthood as a "natural religious institution," that is, as a constitutive element of the communitarian form that expresses the religious sense inherent in human nature. This analogical way offers a clearer notion of the sacred character that Church Tradition recognizes in those who, through the consecration of the sacrament of holy orders, participate ministerially in Christ's priesthood, namely, bishops and priests. The first part of this study will aim to specify the nature of this sacred element. The second part will consider how this "sacredness" of the priesthood has undergone a crisis in the context of our disenchanted and secularized cultures.

THE SACRED DIMENSION OF THE PRIESTLY MINISTRY

Today, because of the crisis of the religious dimension, which was always its natural home, the concept of sacredness has tended to fall back on ethics and ethical values. This is part of the general (but inadequate) movement to reduce religion to ethics. Such approaches consider "sacred" as that which is inviolable, indispensable, not subject to human manipulation. Accordingly, it is the human person that is, in the best cases, associated with sacredness, as the clearest way of upholding human dignity. But the very persistence of religious-type terminology suggests that the dignity of the human person implicitly refers back to a religious basis. In fact, it is human beings' unique relationship with God, their principle and their last end—their status as the "image of God" (Gen 1:26) called to be like him—which, in the final analysis, gives each human being his or her sacred value.

Sacredness, in fact, concerns the intrinsically religious dimension of the human condition, that is, the fact that man, like every created being, is metaphysically connected to God as his first transcendent cause. More precisely, sacredness is a category related to worship, the complex activity whereby men and women, according to the First Commandment, render to God the honor and glory that are due to him, showing that they recognize him as their principle and last end. In so doing they place themselves in the correct attitude toward their Creator.[5] St. Thomas Aquinas makes worship the subject of a moral virtue, one that is somewhat neglected and nevertheless essential to the present argument: the virtue of religion, which he connects with the cardinal virtue of justice.[6] Religion is a virtue that straddles the natural and the supernatural orders. On the one hand the virtue of religion is called to unify the whole of the "natural" moral life by giving it a fundamentally religious orientation. Thus religion, mutatis mutandis, is in the natural moral order what charity is in the supernatural order: its unifying form. On the other hand, the virtue of religion ensures mediation between (a) the structural moral demands flowing from our intrinsic condition as created beings, and (b) the forms of our supernatural, "theological" life as sons and daughters of God, sharers in the divine nature; not forgetting that adoption as God's children does not in any sense cancel out our metaphysical condition as creatures. The theological virtues open up to religion a new horizon and new modalities for glorifying God, while religion confers a specific tone on the "theological" life.

Worship activity is extremely diverse by reason of the complexity of our human nature. It ranges from the most internal actions—such as prayer of petition, which is an act of confessing God's sovereignty—to the most external, as required by the corporal roots and the social and communitarian dimensions of our being. This external public worship is totally ordered toward internal worship. Its aim is to arouse it and nourish it, or else to express it, but—and this is the essential point—external worship is not absorbed back into internal worship. External, liturgical worship is not a mere temporary scaffold that I can and even should dispense with once I have settled into the rarefied atmosphere of purely internal worship. No: even when it is finalized by internal worship, external worship preserves its own specific consistency and its own specific value: it is the whole human being, in all his or her dimensions, that needs to glorify God "in spirit and in truth."

It is precisely in the sphere of external worship that the notion of sacredness finds its primary signification. External, social worship is a language—a system of symbolic or conventional signs by which the community that celebrates an act of worship tells itself first who the God is that it is referring itself to, and second what type of relationship it has with him. This system of signs, it goes almost without saying, varies considerably depending on times and locations, in other words, depending on the different cultures. Nevertheless, it obeys a general "grammar," and an essential aspect of this is the principle of consecration or being set apart as sacred. The community removes certain items or persons from common use and transfers them symbolically to the domain of God.[7] These "consecrated" realities then become the sign of the presence of a transcendent, holy, separate God who is not "disposable" or manipulable, but who himself disposes all things according to his own free will. The principle of consecration culminates in the supreme act of external worship, which is sacrifice. As indicated by its etymology (*sacrum facere*), sacrifice is a radical, irreversible consecration or setting apart—which is perhaps the primary reason for the destruction inherent in sacrifice—that attests the sovereignty of God's domain.[8] Around sacrifice, a whole signifying system of consecrations of places, times, objects and persons is put in place.[9] This is where the priesthood as an institution appears. Within the worshiping community, which is itself consecrated and identified by means of initiation rites, certain people—priests—are set apart and consecrated to offer the sacrifice of the community and distribute its fruits to all.[10] This consecration implies for priests a specific way of life that is visible as such to others, and that recalls, in the very heart of society, the primacy of the religious and worship dimension in human life.

The Christian priesthood takes up after its own fashion, analogically, this dimension of the sacred that belongs to the priesthood as a natural religious institution.[11] To understand this properly, we need to specify the status of "nature" in Christianity. Human nature is not a static, closed set of elements that are always and everywhere the same in all individuals. Rather, it designates an open collection of basic dynamisms that are still largely indeterminate, and therefore need to be incarnated in historically determined cultural realizations. Human nature as such demands culture. Admittedly, nature shows that there are certain analogical constants to be observed in the diversity of human cultures, but natural religious demands are fulfilled in very diverse ways in the course of history.[12] And when that history is a holy history, when it is the place where the mystery is progressively accomplished, namely the Father's benevolent desire to restore all things in his Son, then natural religious structures are taken up and refashioned in depth by the life of grace.

Thus worship (and hence the priesthood), while retaining its fundamental religious value, takes on specific modalities corresponding to the historic-theological system in which it is set. Therefore, there is a specifically Christian system of worship—*cultus Dei secundum ritum Christianae religionis*, to use St. Thomas's expression, which has the merit of underlining both the continuity of the natural demand (*cultus Dei* = the worship of God) and the newness bestowed by the determination of grace (*secundum ritum Christianae religionis* = according to the rite of the Christian religion).[13] This Christian system of worship has two very particular characteristics.

First, in the natural order, the virtue of religion fulfills an architectural role. It shapes the totality of the moral life, orienting it to the service of God, Creator and Last End. By contrast, in the Christian system, religion—the virtue of religion—is no longer the final word in our relationship with God. It is, so to speak, overtaken by the theological life of faith, hope, and charity through which believers truly share in the depths of the communion of the Trinity. That said, just as grace does not destroy nature, the theological life does not consume the religious life, nor does it supplant it. A symbiosis is set up between the theological life and the (supernatural) virtue of religion.[14] In this configuration, the acts proper to the virtue of religion pass into the service of the theological life. While retaining all their own value, they additionally become the expression, the manifestation, of the life of grace of the children of God.[15] For example, the prayer of petition, which in fact is an act of religion, also acquires in the Christian system the value of an act of faith and manifestation of hope.

The eucharistic sacrifice is the summit of Christian worship because it makes present the passion, by which, as Aquinas says, Christ "inaugurated the rite of the Christian religion by 'offering himself as an oblation and victim to God' (Eph 5:2)."[16] In the eucharistic sacrifice, then, three hierarchically ordered dimensions, three necessary "values," are to be found, none of which cancels the others but each strengthens and permeates the others. The eucharistic sacrifice is, first, an external, public act of worship accomplished by priests who are consecrated in order to carry out that sacred action; this action, second, is finalized by the interior worship of the participants, namely the priests themselves and all the members of the worshiping community (an interior act of the virtue of religion), and, third, this religious worship, inseparably exterior and interior, is an expression of the theological life of faith and love by which each participant is configured by grace to the mystery of the charity of Christ offering himself for God's glory and our salvation.

Second, the Christian liturgy, like all exterior and social worship, is a symbolic system, through which the community tells itself who its God is and what its relationship is to this God. Now, this God is the One who, in Jesus Christ, came and does not cease to come before humanity, unite us to himself, and introduce us into the trinitarian communion; in short, to make us holy as he himself is holy. Christian worship is therefore a *sanctifying* worship: through means of the rites, which gravitate around the sacraments instituted by Christ—because Christian worship is essentially a *usus sacramentorum*—God, through

Christ, bestows grace, which is a real participation in the fullness of life of the incarnate Son.[17] The sacred realities always signify something about God, but in Christian worship this God is a God who freely communicates himself, so that they contain and cause what they signify, whence their sanctifying value. The very notion of the sacred, without losing its meaning, is here profoundly modified. On the one hand, to its intrinsic meaning of a sign of the transcendence of the holy God, is added the meaning of a sign of the closeness of this God, who becomes still closer in Jesus Christ in order to sanctify us, that is, to introduce the "profane," all of it, into the sphere of the divine, to imbue it with the divine. This is the paradox of the Christian God, who is both the furthest away, as the most transcendent, ontologically beyond the whole order of creation; and the closest, being deeper within me than my inmost self as the permanent source of my being and communicating himself still more to me in grace. And on the other hand, in sacramental worship the sacred is taken to its maximum degree of ontological realism. It really participates in what it signifies. In the sacrament of the Eucharist, it is the risen Christ in person, that is, the source of all grace, who makes himself sacramentally present. Thus, in Christian sacramental worship the consecrations, however symbolic and however functional they are, have as a consequence an intensely real, "ontological" scope, as M.-D. Chenu underlines:

> [Religion in the Christian system] is undoubtedly the virtue of worship, demanded in justice towards the transcendent and tremendous God; but this moral obligation, with its own values, proceeds henceforth from a faith, hope and charity whose object is the Messiah, and which establish us in physical communion with the Man who is God. Worship, sacrifice, priesthood, liturgy, without being detached from their "natural" context, take on a significance that transmutes their content into acts, and into the presence of Christ, in the Community of his Body, living by these "sacraments."[18]

It follows from this that the celebration of Christian worship, centered on the offering of the eucharistic sacrifice, requires of participants a real consecration, with an ontological effect, which qualifies both ministers and the community as such for the exercise of that worship. This consecration implies the presence of a real ontological principle in the consecrated person that adapts him to the nature of the worshiping action that he is to exercise. Tradition gives this principle the name *character*:

> The sacramental character is a certain participation in the priesthood of Christ by his faithful. Thus, just as Christ possesses the fullness of the power of the spiritual priesthood, so too his faithful are configured to him in so far as they share in some spiritual power relative to the sacraments and the things that have to do with divine worship.[19]

It is in this context that the sacred character marking Christ's priests should be considered. It is a result of their real participation in Christ's own priesthood, a participation that enables them to offer the eucharistic sacrifice of the whole Church *in persona Christi*.[20] This "sacredness" is not the same thing as moral holiness (and obviously, neither does it exclude it; in fact, it calls for it!) and it is totally referred to Christ.

How is this "sacredness" of the priest applied and lived out in practice? On the part of the priest himself, by reason of his intrinsic reference to Christ, it can only be lived out in a spirit of service modeled on Christ. Furthermore, it would be profitable for the priest to meditate regularly on La Fontaine's fable about the donkey carrying relics:

> An Ass, with relics loaded, thought the crowd
> Knelt down to him, and straightway grew so proud
> He took to his own merit, without qualms,
> Even the incense and loud-chanted psalms....

Regarding the "separating" or "setting apart" implied by all consecration, it must necessarily be combined with real pastoral closeness to the faithful in the community under his care. It will be shown above all in a way of life that shows the priority given to his relationship with God, including in its strictly "religious" aspect; together with a certain distance from activities arising from purely worldly affairs and the temporal order. As for the lay faithful, the sacred respect they show to priests as priests is directed to Christ alone, regardless of the esteem they may or may not feel for the man who is their pastor. In his Second Letter to the Corinthians St. Paul speaks of Titus's joy on recalling how the Corinthians received him with "fear and trembling" (2 Cor 7:15). Fear and trembling, in biblical terms, have nothing to do with the fear that paralyzes or the fascination that infantilizes and robs people of their critical sense. They express the joyous, respectful recognition of the sacramental presence of God himself in a place, a situation, or a person.

THE SACRED DIMENSION OF THE PRIESTLY MINISTRY IN A SECULARIZED CULTURE

As the sacred is originally a religious category, and religion is defined as being marginalized in secularized cultures, the way the sacred dimension of the priestly ministry is perceived, received, and put into practice is necessarily affected. This is also the case within the ecclesial community, whose members cannot fail to share at least to some extent in the prevailing tendencies and cultural perceptions of the societies in which they are called to live out their faith.

Today the recognition of the sacred character of the priest suffers from the general crisis affecting the notion of hierarchy in the broad sense. As its etymology suggests, hierarchy refers to the idea that a community is structured by a sacred (*hieros*) principle or power (*arkhê*). The need for a principle of order—or unity—to structure a community is not contested. But for this principle to be "sacred," in other words, for it to participate in the domain and authority of God and consequently be ruled from outside (heteronomous) instead of being autonomous, its authority given from above and not produced from below, is a terrible stumbling-block for contemporary thought. Now, the Church is received entirely from Christ the head, the supreme sacred principle, and Christ's constitutive action of gathering and sanctifying his Church is rendered sacramentally present by the ordained ministry. The sacred power of the priest, who acts in the name of Christ the head especially in the liturgy, attests to this constitutive heteronomy of the ecclesial community. But this hierarchical structure of the ecclesial community conflicts head-on with the contemporary mentality, the social and cultural worldview that is so deeply imbued with the notion of the nontransferable hegemony of the principle of immanence.

In very general terms, the principle of immanence consists of explaining something by its constituent parts or by causes belonging to the same order of reality. Applied to the knowledge of the world or the understanding of history, the principle of immanence explains the working of nature or the march of history by using solely physical or sociological laws, without reference to any external, transcendent principle. This procedure is perfectly legitimate, as long as it does not exclude the possibility, even the necessity, of another type of explanation on a different level—that of metaphysical inquiries into underlying realities—which in the final analysis leads to the action of a first transcendent cause. It is also true that the mentality produced by the principle of immanence is constantly threatened by the temptation to reductionism.

This mentality receives a sort of social confirmation (which, in return, it helps to sustain) from the predominance of the democratic way of organizing the life of society. Indeed, democracy is today much more than a legitimate and desirable mode of government of the people by the people for the people. It represents, more deeply, a way of understanding, through the principle of immanence, the very nature of human society as instituting itself in a sovereign way. That implies a determined rejection of all heteronomy, beginning with the religious kind, and consequently of all "hierarchical" structuring. The French philosopher Marcel Gauchet sees in this switch from the heteronomous or hierarchical structuring of human societies to autonomous structuring, a major turning point for civilization. It marks the entry into modernity, which is defined as an "exit from religion," meaning not the beliefs of individuals but religion as a principle of the organizing of society.[21] In heteronomous (and hence premodern) structuring, the principle that organizes society is not the product of self-determination; it is "sacred." It may be the immemorial tradition of the ancients, or a divine law that has come down from heaven. And this foundational "sacredness" is incarnated in certain figures who, within the society, act as mediators of the sacred principle, making it present, and are therefore set above others, in a natural or functional inequality. That, then, is a hierarchical society.[22]

That is the structuring that the democratic principle aims to abolish in the name of the "sovereignty" of the people, understood as the capacity for deciding for themselves the norms that rule the life of society. This self-determination may apply solely to how the objective values that precede and form the basis of a society should be put into practice in concrete historical circumstances. Then it is a "substantial" democracy whose principles (e.g., the equal dignity of persons, the inviolability of the rights of conscience, the right to life) are in themselves unquestionable, in some way "sacred." In that case self-determination is exercised within a sphere that is not itself the product of that self-determination but expresses basic norms fundamental to the society (for example the natural law). But the principle of sovereignty today tends to operate ever more radically: self-determination is applied at the very foundations of society, which, reduced to mere conventions, are thereby desacralized. One of the consequences of this is the crisis of mediation and of authority, insofar as the mediator is the person who makes the foundations present within the social community. Radical individualism, the passion for equality, and ethical relativism steadily diminish the role of such institutional mediation. We can see the signs of this in the current crisis of representational parliamentary democracy, which people want to replace with direct democracy, or in the crisis of the authority of the mass media, which are contested by the horizontal operation of social networks.

We need to take account of the extreme tension produced within the ecclesial community by this broad movement at the level of our civilization. The "hierarchical constitution of the Church" (and the priest's role as mediator) is out of step with the principle of immanence that permeates common democratic civilization.[23] Admittedly, one can simply proclaim that the nature of the ecclesial community is entirely different from human communities. But arguments that exacerbate contradictions between nature and grace are never a good idea. If one wishes instead to reduce tension, though without ignoring the differences, there are two possibilities, which in no way conflict with one another. The first is at work today, with the rediscovery of synodality. This consists of according due value to the active participation of all the baptized in the life of the ecclesial community. It is not a matter of introducing democracy, or a dose of democracy, in worldly terms, into the Church, but of recognizing the fact that all the baptized, each in accordance with their own charism and mission, share in the Spirit of the sacred principle who structures the community, Christ himself. The second possibility is to witness humbly, and actually for the benefit of human societies threatened by radical immanence, to the irreducible portion of heteronomy that structures not only the Church but also every human community. Religion's sense of otherness guarantees a just perception of the irreducible "hierarchical" dimension of all community life. This dimension is incarnated, and may be glimpsed, in the sudden rays of transcendence and sacredness represented by, for instance, the structuring authority of parents with regard to their children, or the moral authority of "the just"—those men and women who, at the very heart of social life, show and make lovable the basic rule of natural law by incarnating it in their virtuous behavior.[24] At another level, the sacred character of the priest, his otherness, incarnates and renders visible in the Church, but also, indirectly, by refraction, for the benefit of the civic community, the presence of that Other who alone gives human life all its meaning.

NOTES

1. Thomas Aquinas, *Summa Theologiae* [*STh.*], *IIIa*, q. 22, a. 1: "The function of the priest is to be a mediator between God and the people, in so far as he transmits divine things to the people and offers to God the prayers of the people and makes satisfaction to God in some way for their sins (Officium sacerdotis est esse mediatorem inter Deum et populum, inquantum scilicet divina populo tradit...et iterum inquantum preces populi Deo offert, et pro eorum peccatis Deo aliqualiter satisfacit)." The etymology of "priesthood" refers back, according to St. Isidore, to this mediating function of the priest in the order of the sacred. Cf. Isidore of Seville, *Etymologiarum sive originum libri XX*, VII, xii: "Sacerdos autem nomen habet compositum ex Graeco et Latino, quasi sacrum dans; sicut enim rex a regendo, ita sacerdos a sacrificando vocatus est....Ideo autem et presbyteri sacerdotes vocantur, quia sacrum dant." This text, taken up by Peter Lombard, *Sententiae*, IV, d. 24, c. 11 (*De presbyteris*), 2, runs like a stream through all mediaeval thought. St. Thomas applies this etymology principally to descending mediation (cf. *Scriptum super libros Sententiarum*, IV, d. 24, q. 1, a. 3, qla 3, ad 1; *STh.*, *IIIa*, q. 22, a. 1) but he does also apply it to ascending mediation. Cf. *Scriptum super libros Sententiarum*,

IV, d. 22, q. 2, a. 2, qla 2, arg. 1: "Sacramentum a sacrando dicitur.…Sed consecrare sacerdotis est, quia ex hoc sacerdos dicitur quod sacra dat."

2. Priestly mediation is both ascending and descending. Cf. Thomas Aquinas, *STh.*, *IIa-IIae*, q. 86, a. 2: "The priest is in some way established as mediator and intermediary between the people and God, according to what is said of Moses in *Deut* 5. This is because it belongs to him to transmit the divine teachings and the sacraments to the people, and also the things of the people—prayers, sacrifices and oblations—must be presented to God by him, according to what the Apostle says in *Heb* 5: 'every high priest chosen from among men is appointed to act on behalf of men in relation to God, to offer gifts and sacrifices for sins' (Sacerdos quodammodo constituitur sequester et medius inter populum et Deum, sicut de Moyse legitur Deut 5. Et ideo ad eum pertinet divina dogmata et sacramenta exhibere populo; et iterum ea quae sunt populi, puta preces et sacrificia et oblationes, per eum Domino debent exhiberi; secundum illud Apostoli ad Heb. 5: 'Omnis pontifex ex hominibus assumptus pro hominibus constituitur in his quae sunt ad Deum, ut offerat dona et sacrificia pro peccatis')." Cf. S.-T. Bonino, "Le sacerdoce comme institution naturelle," in *Études thomasiennes* (Paris, 2018), 441–68. Here more than elsewhere a christological recentering is essential. In Christianity there is only one single Mediator through whom we alike have free access to the Father, in one same Spirit (Eph 2:18). The gospel sweeps the path between humanity and God free of all other mediations, cosmological, angelical, or priestly. All mediation is concentrated in the person of Jesus Christ. The ordained minister does not therefore stand as a mediator beside Christ, nor is he a mediator giving access to the Mediator. He is the sacrament of the one mediation of Christ.

3. *STh.*, *IIIa*, q. 22, a. 1.

4. Cf. Id., *Lectura super epistolam ad Hebraeos*, c. 5, lect. 1 (Cai [ed.], Marietti, No. 239): "[The Apostle] shows first that Christ is a priest.…To do this he does two things. First he shows what is required for priesthood. Second, he shows that all this comes together in Christ, and so concludes that Christ is a priest. (Primo ostendit Christum esse pontificem.…Adhuc circa primum duo facit. Primo ostendit, quae requirantur ad pontificem; secundo ostendit illa convenire Christo et sic concludit ipsum esse sacerdotem)."

5. Cf. *STh.*, *IIa-IIae*, q. 81, a. 3: "It belongs to religion to render honour to the one God, for the single reason that he is the first beginning of the creation and government of things. Thus he himself says at Mal 1: 'If I am Father, where is my honour?' (Ad religionem autem pertinet exhibere reverentiam uni Deo secundum unam rationem, inquantum scilicet est primum principium creationis et gubernationis rerum, unde ipse dicit, Malach. I, 'Si ego pater, ubi honor meus?')"; a. 4: "The good to which religion is ordered is to render to God the honour that is due to him. Honour is owed to someone by reason of their excellence. Singular excellence belongs to God, in that he infinitely transcends all things by surpassing

them all in every way. Hence special honour is owed to him (Bonum autem ad quod ordinatur religio est exhibere Deo debitum honorem. Honor autem debetur alicui ratione excellentiae. Deo autem competit singularis excellentia, inquantum omnia in infinitum transcendit secundum omnimodum excessum. Unde ei debetur specialis honor)."

6. Cf. *Catechism of the Catholic Church*, nos. 2095ff; M.-M. Labourdette, *La Religion*, "Grand cours" de théologie morale/13, Bibliothèque de la Revue thomiste, Paris, Parole et silence, 2018.

7. Cf. I. Menessier, "L'idée de 'sacré' et le culte," *Revue des Sciences philosophiques et théologiques* 19 (1930): 63–82 [p. 74]: "[The sacred] is that which receives a certain specialisation for the use of worship, symbolising through its restricted use a transcendent, unchangeable majesty and thus eliciting very special inner feelings of respect and veneration."

8. The expiatory value of sacrifice is always subordinated to its latreutic value. The expiatory value only appears within the context of a religious economy historically marked by sin, while the latreutic value belongs to natural law. On sacrifice as a requirement of natural law, cf. *STh.*, *IIa-IIae*, q. 85, a. 1.

9. Cf. *STh.*, *Ia-IIae*, q. 101, a. 4: "The ceremonial precepts are ordained to the worship of God. In this worship, the worship itself, the worshippers, and the instruments of worship may be considered. The worship consists specially in sacrifices, which are offered for the reverence of God. The instruments of worship refer to sacred things, such as the tabernacle, the vessels and other things of this kind. With regard to the worshippers two points may be considered. Namely: their investiture for divine worship, which is effected by a certain consecration either of the people or of the ministers; and this is the role of the sacraments. And secondly, their particular way of living, whereby they are distinguished from those who do not worship God: and to this pertain observances, for instance, in matters of food, clothing, and so forth (Caeremonialia praecepta ordinantur ad cultum Dei. In quo quidem cultu considerari possunt et ipse cultus, et colentes, et instrumenta colendi. Ipse autem cultus specialiter consistit in sacrificiis, quae in Dei reverentiam offeruntur. Instrumenta autem colendi pertinent ad sacra, sicut est tabernaculum, et vasa, et alia huiusmodi. Ex parte autem colentium duo possunt considerari. Scilicet et eorum institutio ad cultum divinum, quod fit per quandam consecrationem vel populi, vel ministrorum, et ad hoc pertinent sacramenta. Et iterum eorum singularis conversatio, per quam distinguuntur ab his qui Deum non colunt, et ad hoc pertinent observantiae, puta in cibis et vestimentis et aliis huiusmodi)."

10. Cf. Exod 28—29; Lev 8—10; etc.

11. The priesthood is a *natural* institution in that it is a universal social structure connected with worship that flows from human nature as such. It is a natural *institution* in that the particular form taken by the priesthood is determined by contingent historical settings.

12. In humankind, marked as it is by sin, the natural religious sense can go astray in perverted ways and has done so in history (human sacrifice, superstition, ritualism, *do ut des*, etc.). But Catholicism normally rejects the temptation of reducing historical religions to being merely the expression of the sinful condition of man who uses religion to shut himself off from the grace of God and protect himself from the demands of the gospel.

13. *STh., IIIa*, q. 63, a. 2.

14. With regard to the relationship between the ritual consecrations that belong to the life of worship, and the holiness of the moral and theological life, Cardinal Journet describes Catholic teaching as a road along a crest between two errors. On one side, paganism tends to prioritize consecration for worship over moral holiness, thus risking falling into magic and a religion that is entirely ritual and formal. On the other side, Protestantism, "trying, by an error directly contrary to that of paganism, to eliminate the notion of consecration and replace it with that of moral holiness, seriously mistook the essence of Christianity, which, far from setting them in opposition, divinely reconciles in itself the notions of ritual worship and morality...of consecration and holiness." Cf. C. Journet, *L'Église du Verbe incarné. Essai de théologie spéculative, I. La hiérarchie apostolique* (Paris: Editions Saint-Augustin, 1941), 99–101: "Consécration cultuelle et sainteté morale."

15. Cf. *STh., IIa-IIae*, q. 81, a. 5, ad 1: "The power or virtue which operates with regard to an end always moves by its command the power or virtue which operates with regard to means directed to that end. Now the theological virtues, faith, hope and charity have an act in reference to God as their proper object. Therefore, by their command, they cause the act of religion, which performs certain deeds directed to God. And so Augustine says that God is worshipped by faith, hope and charity. (Semper potentia vel virtus quae operatur circa finem, per imperium movet potentiam vel virtutem operantem ea quae ordinantur in finem illum. Virtutes autem theologicae, scilicet fides, spes et caritas, habent actum circa Deum sicut circa proprium obiectum. Et ideo suo imperio causant actum religionis, quae operatur quaedam in ordine ad Deum. Et ideo Augustinus dicit quod 'Deus colitur fide, spe et caritate')."

16. *Ivi, IIIa*, q. 62, a. 5: Similiter etiam per suam passionem initiavit ritum Christianae religionis, 'offerens seipsum oblationem et hostiam Deo.' ut dicitur Ephes.V."

17. Cf. *STh., IIIa*, q. 60, a. 5: "Two things may be considered in the use of the sacraments: the worship of God and the sanctification of man. The first concerns man in his relationship to God, while the second concerns God in his relationship to man (In usu sacramentorum duo possunt considerari, scilicet cultus divinus, et sanctificatio hominis, quorum primum pertinet ad hominem per comparationem ad Deum, secundum autem e converso pertinet ad Deum per comparationem ad hominem)."

18. M.-D. Chenu, *Saint Thomas d'Aquin, l'homme chrétien* (Paris: Éditions du Cerf, 1965), 249.

19. *STh., IIIa*, q. 63, a. 5: "Character sacramentalis est quaedam participatio sacerdotii Christi in fidelibus eius, ut scilicet, sicut Christus habet plenam spiritualis sacerdotii potestatem, ita fideles eius ei configurentur in hoc quod participant aliquam spiritualem potestatem respectu sacramentorum et eorum quae pertinent ad divinum cultum. Et propter hoc etiam Christo non competit habere characterem, sed potestas sacerdotii eius comparatur ad characterem sicut id quod est plenum et perfectum ad aliquam sui participationem." Cf. also *ivi*, a. 3: "The whole rite of the Christian religion is derived from the priesthood of Christ. And therefore, it is plain that the sacramental character is especially the character of Christ, to whose priesthood the faithful are configured according to the sacramental characters, which are nothing other than certain participations in the priesthood of Christ, deriving from Christ himself" (Totus autem ritus Christianae religionis derivatur a sacerdotio Christi. Et ideo manifestum est quod character sacramentalis specialiter est character Christi, cuius sacerdotio configurantur fideles secundum sacramentales characteres, qui nihil aliud sunt quam quaedam participationes sacerdotii Christi, ab ipso Christo derivatae)."

20. It will be objected that this sacredness of the priest is after all limited, or even marginal, since in Christianity the ordained ministry, even though it is, in bishops and priests, a participation in Christ's priesthood, embraces much more than the celebration of worship. It is true that the ordained minister is configured to Christ the Head edifying his Church by the integrated exercise of the *tria munera*. But it is also true that the ministry is ordered to and unified around worship, in the sense that the eucharistic sacrifice is "the source and summit of the whole Christian life" (Vatican II, Dogmatic Constitution *Lumen Gentium* 11) and that it is the place where the sacred charge of the minister is expressed in the highest degree. Cf. *ivi*, 28: "They exercise their sacred function especially (*maxime*) in the Eucharistic worship or the celebration of the Mass, by which, acting in the person of Christ and proclaiming His Mystery they unite the prayers of the faithful with the sacrifice of their Head and renew and apply in the sacrifice of the Mass until the coming of the Lord (cf. *1 Cor* 11:26) the only sacrifice of the New Testament, namely that of Christ offering Himself once for all a spotless Victim to the Father (cf. *Heb* 9:11-28)." Preaching (*munus docendi*) prepares for the Eucharist and leads to the Eucharist, which through governing the community (*munus regendi*) the ordained minister then makes fruitful in service to others and the actual life of the communities.

21. It remains true that the exit from religion as a principle of social organization necessarily affects the way personal religious belief is experienced and practiced. Cf. M. Gauchet, *La Religion dans la démocratie, Parcours de la laïcité* (Paris: Gallimard, 1998), 140–51 : "Une révolution du croire."

22. Gauchet defines hierarchy as follows: "A type of bond holding people together by their inequality of nature, by the mutual attachment of the inferior to the superior at every level of collective life, from the humblest to the highest, from the father who is the head of the family, to the supernatural Sovereign. An inequality of nature that echoes in the substance of social relations the supreme difference between the 'beyond' that commands and the 'here below' that obeys" ("Sécularisation ou sortie de la religion?" in *Droits. Revue française de théorie, de philosophie et de culture juridiques* 59 (2014): 3–10 [7]).

23. It is very significant that in the nineteenth century the bitter conflict between the Church and the "modern world" crystalized around an opposition—felt at the time to be irreconcilable—between the principle of authority incarnated by the Church (which often extended it to the political sphere) and the principle of democracy.

24. Cf. S.-T. Bonino, "Vertus sociales et sens de Dieu," in *Études thomasiennes*, 423–37.

2

THE BIBLICAL FOUNDATION OF THE RELATIONSHIP BETWEEN THE PRIESTHOOD OF ALL THE BAPTIZED AND THE APOSTOLIC OFFICE

Father Robert Vorholt

THE NEW TESTAMENT recognizes a wide range of offices and ministries besides apostolic leadership. This variety of services is a reflection of the variety of charisms brought about through the Holy Spirit in order to build communities. All the baptized build the one church of Jesus Christ and bear the responsibility of sending this church into the world. Corresponding to this basic ecclesiological idea of the common priesthood of all the baptized is the development of a theology of the people of God, which becomes clear in the New Testament, especially in the First Letter of Peter.

THE THEOLOGY OF THE PEOPLE OF GOD IN THE FIRST LETTER OF PETER

The New Testament dares to start a salvation history transition process when it takes the term "people of God" from the Septuagint, where it was exclusively reserved for Israel, and transfers it to the Christian

Ekklesia.[1] As the early Church consisted of believers of Jewish as well as pagan provenance, the previous Old Testament concept of the people of God was expanded, as now the pagans also needed to be included.[2] The author of the First Letter of Peter—let us simply call him Peter on this isolated occasion[3]—draws from the tradition of the Book of Exodus and the prophetic books of Hosea and Isaiah in order to assign a particular place in salvation history to the communities he was addressing (see 1 Pet 1:1) predominantly composed of Gentile Christians.

The central text reads (1 Pet 2:9–10), "But you are a chosen race, a royal priesthood, a holy nation, God's own people, in order that you may proclaim the mighty acts of him who called you out of darkness into his marvelous light. Once you were not a people, but now you are God's people; once you had not received mercy, but now you have received mercy."

Just a few verses before, the author of the First Letter of Peter had focused on the community that believed in Jesus Christ as a whole and told every individual believer as a member of the one *Ekklesia*: "Like living stones, let yourselves be built into a spiritual house, to be a holy priesthood, to offer spiritual sacrifices acceptable to God through Jesus Christ" (1 Pet 2:5).

It is unmistakably clear how the First Letter of Peter recognized the young *Ekklesia* of Jewish and Gentile Christians as the holy people of God (see Lev 11:44; 20:6), chosen by him, his exalted possession. The election that the prescript of the First Letter of Peter judges as the "prognosis" of God the Father (1 Pet 1:2), is an election to a "genos"; that is, into a lineage and thus into a fellowship. Together, the believers have access to the mystery of God.[4]

Of particular importance in the context of the topic of this contribution is the designation of the people of God as a "royal priesthood." The First Letter of Peter takes this honorific from the Torah of Israel, in particular, from the Book of Exodus (Exod 19:6 LXX). Here it reads: "You shall be for me a priestly kingdom and a holy nation."

In the Pentateuch, Exodus 19 begins the recollections of the events of Sinai, which allowed Israel to become, eminently, the people of Adonai.[5] Israel would be set apart from the peoples by Adonai, the Holy One of Israel; in other words, it would be sanctified as a nation living in the holy sphere of salvation. Fundamental to the understanding in Exodus 19:6 is the idea of being chosen by God, which here correlates to the Old Testament concept of holiness (particularly prominent in the Book of Leviticus). The act of election is a process of exhumation: holiness is the consequence of the election.[6] The honorific "royal priesthood" clarifies, in ritual language, the high quality of vocation bestowed upon the entire people of God. Mirroring the tradition of Exodus, the priestly functions are not emphasized, but rather the priestly character of the people of God. It is not chiefly about doing (function) but about being (character).

The comparison between the Septuagint version of Exodus 19:6 with the Masoretic text of the Hebrew Bible brings an interesting nuance to light. Unlike in Exodus 19:6 MT, in the Septuagint there are two terms independent from each other, "royal house" and "priesthood," that are only brought into a common horizon of meaning with a further predication ("holy nation"). The Masoretic text emphasizes the cooperative moment. The Septuagint supplements it with a functional aspect: Israel, the people of God, should, because of their own election, take up the priestly task of witnessing to the one unique God of Israel to the peoples: "By being holy and obedient to Yahweh, they mediate God to the nations and thus fulfill their priestly role."[7] Election, selection, and dignity would no longer be seen only in the relationship of Israel with their God but is now also seen in the sense of a duty to priestly service to the people. It no longer only deals with being (character) but also doing (function). But this function of priestly service to the priestly service of the whole people of God refers not to a sacramental intermediation between God and his people, but rather to prophetic witness and preaching the love of God to the people of the whole world. Israel is God's kingdom and God's royal house. His holiness must be witnessed before the world—through prayer and worship, and equally through loving one's neighbors as well as one's enemies.

The First Letter of Peter moves along the channels indicated by the Septuagint in its reception of Exodus 19:5. These channels are the infrastructure of his theological argument.[8] The designation of the people of God as a "royal priesthood" serves as the cipher of the election for Peter.[9] The Letter describes the *Ekklesia* by drawing from the titles of the Book of Exodus, representing the new Israel (without displacing the old) as a holy people of which Adonai is the king. But this so excellent people, the Church, does not only live the character of its holiness in immediate nearness to God, but is simultaneously called out of it to exercise a priestly service for the world, by—like a good minister—testifying to the love of God in all its immensity before the world and in the world.

The faithful gain the title of the election to a holy priesthood (1 Pet 2:5.9) in the event of the rebirth that the First Letter of Peter considers the soteriological fruit of Jesus Christ's crucifixion and resurrection. Therefore, the holy and royal priesthood of the faithful is a community in love, but in two ways: first, because it was born of God's strong salvific will; it is also where she gives her response to God's election and where her saintly transformation assumes a visible and concrete form. The life of the *Ekklesia* as a holy and royal priesthood does not exhaust itself in the acquisition of merit in salvation history but requires the ratification and actualization of this election within the world. It is no coincidence that the First Letter of Peter paranetically frames the reference to the faithful as a royal priesthood whose reason for existence is God's mercy (1 Pet 1:22—2:3; 2:11ff.). The explicit mission of all believers is expressed in the same way, relating to the political, social, and familial aspects of shared social life. The author of the First Letter of Peter is convinced that a consistent life according to the Gospels—provided it remains free of eccentricity and rigor—is attractive in the long run through its simplicity, through its solidarity, through its charitable engagements, and not least through its worship.[10]

Significantly and emphatically, the First Letter of Peter keeps itself from conveniently remaining within the internal perspective of ecclesiology. Instead, it is about entering into relationship with the world and confidently nurturing this relationship. All the faithful are encouraged in the development of an "'attraction model,' rooted in the daily life and involvement of Christian communities and each of their members."[11] This is why the persuasive strength of the lifestyle of all the faithful is invoked (see 1 Pet 2:11–12, 15; 3:16) and their willingness to enter into dialogue as an unmistakable witness to hope is required (1 Pet 3:15–16). Even the judgment of non-Christians is important here, as the task of the whole church depends on being welcoming.[12]

THE APOSTOLIC OFFICE

In addition to—and in no way contrary to—the theological idea of the common priesthood of all the faithful, the New Testament also establishes the ecclesiological concept of apostolic service. The apostolic office is ordered to and is also distinct from the variety of the services of the common priesthood. No one has come close to describing it as clearly as the Apostle Paul.

In his letter, Paul presents himself as an apostle of Jesus Christ, called by God and sent to the pagans by Jesus Christ (see 1 Cor 1:1; 9:1; 15:8, 10; 2 Cor 1:1; Gal 1:1; Rom 11:13). He takes the title of apostle for himself—contrary to Luke's understanding—not claiming to be an eyewitness of Jesus and "man of the first hour,: but by virtue of the apostolic vocation granted to him through God's grace (see Gal 1:15–16). The theological center of his mission is the knowledge of God's call that was revealed to him in the encounter with the risen Kyrios on the road to Damascus. The goal of his call is the proclamation of the gospel among the peoples and the founding of the *Ekklesia* (see 1 Cor 3:10–17). The constitutive foundational paradigm of apostolic existence is the appearance of the resurrected Christ, whence derives the mission and task of witnessing to him. The apostolate is substantially related to the Church as a whole, just as, conversely, the Church is characterized by the apostles. The apostolate derives from the grace of God because it springs from God's will of salvation. It is authorized (see 2 Cor 10:8; 13:10; Phil 8), insofar as the apostle expresses and brings God himself to light in word and deed (see 1 Cor 2:4–5; Rom 15:19). At the same time, it is a service (Rom 11:13; 2 Cor 3:7ff.; 5:18), because the apostle is subject to the Kyrios Christ (2 Cor 4:5) and is integrated in the dynamic of God's will of salvation as a preacher of the Gospels, as the founder and leader of the community.

Paul sees himself among the apostles (see 1 Cor 15:7ff.). He does not understand himself as a "single-combat fighter,"[13] but knows that there are apostles before him, collectively as the "last of all" to join. So, when he emphasizes that he owes his apostolate to the will and choice of God alone, he does not exclude the fact that there were others who were apostles before him (see Gal 1:17; 2:8; see also 1 Cor 9:5; 12:28; 2 Cor 11:13). The apostle draws on a term that was apparently already established in the Church before him and is no Pauline neologism. The early Church probably knew a "twofold concept of the Apostle"[14]: on the one hand, there was the "Christ-Apostle" whose appointment is based on a Christophany (see 1 Cor 15:5–8); on the other hand (probably using language coming from Antioch[15]), there were early Christian itinerant missionaries whose authority was also expressed with the word *apostle*. The triad of "apostles, prophets, and teachers" mentioned in 1 Cor 12:28 within a list of charisms, as well as the designation of the messengers of the individual communities as "apostles" (see 2 Cor 8:23; Phil 2:25; Rom 16:7) supports this distinction. However, it still needs to be noted that within the *Corpus Paulinum*, the abstraction "apostolate" is reserved for the clearly defined, specific understanding of it. In particular, the use of the term *apostle* clarified through the genitive *apostle Jesu Christi* is used by Paul only for the characterization of his own Ur-apostolic service (see 1 Thess 2:7; Gal 1:1; 1 Cor 1:1; 2 Cor 1:1; 11:13; similarly Rom 1:1), which he naturally assumes takes place in the fellowship of the "Ur-apostles."

With the two basic pillars of apostolic existence marked by Paul's vocation, founded in the will of God, and the mission to preach the Gospels that took place within it, the question then arises of the meaning and particular importance of the apostolic *diakonia*. The preaching of the apostles could not be reduced to the mere communication of information about God's work of salvation. Because God himself is heard and asserted in the words and deeds of the apostles in the power of the *Pneuma* (see Rom 15:18–19), Paul understands his apostolic *diakonia* as one of the dynamics involved in God's salvific will. Where the preaching of the apostles awakens its hearers' faith in Christ and reaches its goal, it manifests God's work of saving Jews and Gentiles. Likewise, the preaching of the apostles confronts humans with God and sets the decision before them: to be for or against God's offer of reconciliation in Christ (see *1 Cor* 1:18; *2 Cor* 5:14—6:2). In the background of this idea is the basic principle of apostolic theology of inner conformity to Christ who is sent and the apostle who was sent.

The preaching of the apostles was made with a universal orientation (see *Rom* 1:14; *1 Cor* 9:19ff.). Christ's love urges and motivates it to direct the word of reconciliation to all (see *2 Cor* 5:14ff.). Paul expresses the idea of the mediation between God's foundational salvific work based on Christ's crucifixion and resurrection, and the faithful acceptance of this message by humanity, which takes place through apostolic preaching, by describing his apostolic work as *diakonia*. By calling himself a *diakonos*, Paul presents his apostolic service as one that benefits others (see 1 Cor 3:5; 2 Cor 5:18). Through him, the Christians from the communities he founded came to faith. The character of service is inherent to the Pauline apostolate. However, the specificity of the apostolic *diakonia* lies in the idea of the representation of Christ. As a *diakonos*, the apostle is a servant and messenger of the Gospels and is hereby the authorized representative of God's reconciliation with humanity.

Despite all its servitude and subordination, the title of *diakonos* also carries a characteristic aspect of dignity and mandate. Therefore, the term particularly lends itself to demonstrating the expectation of the principle of relation to Christ and the resulting authority of the *diakonia* of the apostle. As his work is *diakonia*, an apostle must let himself be measured on the cross, vouching for the Kyrios, who was himself degraded by God but exalted. Paul is the *diakonos* of Jesus as an apostle; he represents him for those hearing the Gospels. The word of the Gospels that the apostle announces has salvific power because the crucified and resurrected Christ is expressed within it (Rom 10:17; see 2 Cor 5:20). The apostolate is a service because it deals with the soteriological salvation of humankind. At the same time, this service is endowed with the authority of the Kyrios Jesus Christ. The idea of the *repraesentatio Christi* therefore belongs largely to the apostolate. This *repraesentatio* is in turn founded on the theology of the cross and pneumatology. Paul can only be the authorized envoy of his Lord as one who allows himself to be identified with the lowliness of Jesus in the interests of the weak.

BUILDING ON THE FOUNDATION

The question of the relationship between the service of the apostle and the development of the offices of the Church in postapostolic times is theologically significant. What meaning does the apostolate have for the Church? Is there an apostolic succession? If so, how and where does it exist?

Historical-critical exegesis has, over the course of its history, elaborated the variety of the forms in which the first Christian communities organized the *Ekklesia* into ministries of preaching, teaching, and direction.[16] Whether, when, and in what sense "offices" could be spoken of in the New Testament texts was discussed.[17] The terminological result within the exegetical research was interpreted very differently: it is sometimes seen as an indication that there can be no mention of "offices" in the New Testament, and sometimes seen as a clue that, in the early Church, "office" was of a different quality from that of the pagans or the Jews.

Above all, in 1 Corinthians 3:5–17, the apostle describes himself as the founder and leader of the community. He thus distinguishes his apostolic *diakonia* from other pastoral duties. The distinction aims less at the emphasis of human differences, but at the different role that Paul should play as an apostle in the *Ekklesia* in accordance with God's will. The temporal and also objectively primary object of the apostle's "sowing" refers to the foundation of the community (see 1 Cor 4:15; 9:1–2), that Paul carries out with God's help. It is important to Paul to record this (see 1 Cor 3:5–6): any service of preaching—including particularly that of the apostle—can therefore only be fruitful, because God himself is at work in word and deed in the message of the Gospels. Only after Paul had developed the basic idea could he devote himself to the different tasks and duties in the *Ekklesia* of God.

The images used by Paul in 1 Corinthians 3:5–17 of the "building" or of "God's field" do not only indicate that God alone is the Lord of the *Ekklesia*. They also emphasize the need for a living and ever-growing Church. The appeal of the apostle not to seal oneself off from this dynamic (1 Cor 3:8–9) contrasts with the reminder to keep building responsibly. The image of the building is especially suitable for Paul in order to symbolically address and require this responsibility in view of the nature of the construction and structure of the building. This is the context in which the apostle discusses his own, specific role:

> The one who plants and the one who waters have a common purpose, and each will receive wages according to the labor of each. For we are God's servants, working together; you are God's field, God's building. According to the grace of God given to me, like a skilled master builder I laid a foundation, and someone else is building on it. Each builder must choose with care how to build on it. For no one can lay

> any foundation other than the one that has been laid; that foundation is Jesus Christ. (1 Cor 3:8–11)

Then, at the beginning of his remarks on apostolic service, Paul emphasizes the grace given to him through his call by God (1 Cor 3:10). This grace characterizes and determines the life of the apostle and lends him apostolic authority. With the image of a master builder directing the foundations, Paul sheds light on the meaning of the apostolic *diakonia*. The gospel proclaimed by him during the founding of the community represents a predetermined, immovable, and unchanged foundation of the *Ekklesia*. If the Christians believe in the wording and content of these Gospels, the promise of the apostle applies to them: to stand in the new covenant and receive their part in the eschatological salvific gift of God (see 1 Cor 15:1–2). In substance, the faithful are referred to the message of the cross, which Paul proclaimed to be the word of life (see 1 Cor 1:18; 2:7ff.). This message, identified as the "word of the Cross" (1 Cor 1:18), also defines the messenger. His (often criticized) personal inadequacy appears as strength in the light of the cross because the strength of God manifests itself powerfully in the weakness of the apostle (see 1 Cor 1:17–31). The difficulty owed to his humanity, which distinguishes him from the possibilities of God, of having to carry the treasure of his apostolic call in fragile vessels (see 2 Cor 4:7), is also proved to be a necessary condition for the possibility to preach the gospel. Paul obtains a new perspective by looking at Jesus, whose "weakness" is shown in the powerlessness of suffering for many. It preserves the apostle from the temptation of claiming the work of the *Pneuma* without a connection with the theology of the cross: he is not characterized by the dazzling splendor of an authorized representative, but rather by the—of course self-assured—humility of a servant of Jesus Christ, graced by God.

The normative foundation of faith laid down by the apostle for Christians needs further development in the future. This dynamic, described by Paul himself as "further construction," at the same time brings the work of the *Pneuma* into the *Ekklesia* and, on the other hand, considers the respective temporality of the preaching of the gospel. The *Ekklesia* is in the eschatological tension frame between the already and the not-yet of the *Basileia* of God as the community of salvation founded in Christ, always a being and a becoming at the same time. This results in the practical need for a proclamation of the gospel, committed both to its normative beginnings and the respective challenges of the present. This continuation, understood in the sense of a construction of the apostolic *diakonia*, must be able to be measured against the first proclamation of the apostle.

From its beginnings, the task of encouraging the continued construction of the respective local communities has been part of apostolic work—even before the time of the apostle. Paul, therefore, does not only look at the normative laying of ecclesial foundations, but also speaks of the construction and ongoing building according to groundwork forever linked with his apostolic service (see 1 Cor 3:10ff.). Provided that the service of the apostle also includes the missionary preaching of the gospel, binding doctrine, its clarifying interpretation, and the founding and leadership of communities, this task is foundational for the church, although not unique. Apostolic service must be ongoing. Indeed, it is obligatory for all the faithful to ensure the righteous construction of the *Ekklesia*. Nevertheless, it must be ensured that the services that are crucial to the Church are continually and actively carried out. This requires that there always be men who vouch for the proclamation of the Gospels and the generation of faith with their whole existence and thereby represent the presence of the Lord in the ecclesial communities.

THE APOSTLE IN THE COMMUNITY OF THE CHURCH

It is a foundational paradigm of the universality of the gospel that it has several apostles (see Gal 2:7ff.). Therefore, Paul is not the only apostle, but is instead together with others. He does not derive his apostolate from the consent and appointment of people, but—he stresses (see Gal 1:1–12; 1 Cor 15:10)—through the grace of God alone. This is why the Apostle Paul is in close communion with those who are apostles before and with him (see Gal 1:17; 2:9; 1 Cor 15:7–9). This *koinonia* does not aim at uniformity but is a visible expression of an equally justified and mediated participation of all apostles in communion with Jesus Christ and his gospel. In this, it also marks the roots of the apostles, who do carry out the service of the foundation of the Church not only for others, but also with others. This shared *diakonia* carried out by the apostles is an important characteristic of the *Ekklesia*.

However, there is not only the *koinonia* of the apostles, but also the communion of the apostles with those who believe in Jesus Christ. However foundational are the apostles for the proclamation of the Gospels and the founding of the *Ekklesia*, they remain simply a part of this Church (see 1 Cor 12:12–28). Those who believe in Christ with Paul are his brothers and sisters. They are all—not only the apostles—in communion with the risen Lord, remain committed to him, and experience the power of his grace. An apostle is not equipped with a greater amount of grace than any other Christian. But he knows about a particular service which he is called to.

The Apostle Paul was no single-combat fighter during his apostolic mission. Rather, he initiated a permanent network of male and female collaborators. This initiation considered the fact that Paul was permanently connected as an apostle with the communities founded by him (except for Rome), and that the life of the community should go on, both when the apostle was not present or was no longer in the area. They were valuable "collaborators" on the "construction site" of the *Ekklesia*, in whom he placed great trust, and from whom he also demanded enormous commitment and efficacy. They were pioneers on the threshold between apostolic and postapostolic time.

NOTES

1. For the theological conditions and implications of this transfer, see. J.R. Michaels, "1 Pet," in *Disciples' Literal New Testament (Dlnt)* (Beaverton, OR: Reyma, 1997), 914–23, 917.

2. For this, see Ch. Stenschke, "Das auserwählte Geschlecht, die königliche Priesterschaft, das heilige Volk" (1 Pet 2:9): Funktion und Bedeutung der Ehrenbezeichnungen Israels im 1. Jahrhundert," *Neotestamentica* 42 (2008): 119–46, 127.

3. For the discussion on the authorship of 1 Pet see K.H. Ostmeyer, *Die Briefe des Petrus und des Judas*, V&R; 1. Auflage (Göttingen: Brill, 2021), 17–20; for more detail see R. Feldmeier, *Die Christen als Fremde. Die Metapher der Fremde in der antiken Welt*, im Urchristentum und im 1. Petrusbrief (Tübingen: Mohr Siebeck, 1993), 193–98.

4. See C.G. Müller, "Auserwählte als Fremde. Theologische Standortbestimmung im Ersten Petrusbrief," in *Der Erste Petrusbrief. Frühchristliche Identität im Wandel*, ed. M. Ebner, G. Häfner, and K. Huber, QD 269 (Freiburg i.Br., 2015), 9–48, 41.

5. See A. Deissler, "Das Priestertum im Alten Testament. Ein Blick vom Alten zum Neuen Bund," in *Der priesterliche Dienst I: Ursprung und Frühgeschichte*, QD 46 (Freiburg im Breisgau: Herder, 1970), 67–68.

6. See J.H. Elliott, *The Elect and the Holy: An Exegetical Examination of 1 Pet 2, 4–10* (Leiden: Brill, 1966), 53.

7. S.A. Fagbemi, "The Identity of the 'Elect' in 1 Pt.: Its 'Present' Significance and Implications for Believers," in *The Catholic Epistles and the Tradition*, ed. J. Schlosser (Hrsg.), BEThL 176 (Leuven: Peeters, 2004), 367–80, 371.

8. H. Goldstein, *Das Gemeindeverständnis des ersten Petrusbriefes. Exegetische Untersuchungen zur Theologie der Gemeinde im 1Pet* (Münster, 1973), 76.

9. See N. Brox, *Der erste Petrusbrief*, EKK XXI (Neukirchen-Vluyn: Benziger, 1993), 105.

10. See. Th. Söding, "Ein Haus des Geistes in der Fremde. Die Berufung der Kirche nach *1 Pt*," in *Zukunft der Kirche—Kirche der Zukunft. Christen in der modernen Diaspora*, ed. Thomas Söding (Hildesheim: Verlagsgesellschaft Bernward-Morus, 1994), 52.

11. A. Puig i Tàrrech, "The Mission according to the New Testament: Choice or Need?" in *Einheit der Kirche im Neuen Testament*, ed. A. Alexeev, C. Karakolis, and U. Luz, WUNT 218 (Tübingen: Mohr Siebeck, 2008), 231–47, 237.

12. See Müller, "Auserwählte als Fremde," 47.

13. Here see Th. Schmeller, *Schmeller, Kollege Paulus. Die Jesusüberlieferung und das Selbstverständnis des Völkerapostels*, ZNW 88 (Technische Universität Dresde, 1997), 260–83.

14. A. Vögtle and L. Oberlinner, *Anpassung oder Widerspruch. Von der apostolischen zur nachapostolischen Kirche* (Freiburg: Herder, 1992), 18.

15. Also K. Kertelge, "Apostel," *LThK* I (1993), 851–54, 851.

16. An overview of the historical research was written by K. Kertelge, ed., *Das Amt im Neuen Testament*, WdF 439 (Darmstadt, 1977).

17. For this, see J. Ysebaert, *Die Amtstheologie im Neuen Testament und in der Alten Kirche. Eine lexikografische Untersuchung*, Breda 1994.

3

LIVING THE ORDAINED MINISTRY TODAY

CARDINAL LAZZARO YOU HEUNG-SIK

DEAR CARDINALS, BISHOPS, Priests, Deacons, Men and Women Religious, Seminarians, and Brothers and Sisters in Jesus Christ,

We enter the afternoon session of our symposium, on this first day of reflection and thought, particularly dedicated to the relationship between Tradition and new horizons. It is these two "focal points" that constitute the essential dimensions of our ecclesial and Christian thought and action: on the one hand, we are heirs to a long ecclesial tradition, generated by the first Christian community and unfolding throughout history through the thought and practices of the people of God and their pastors; on the other hand, we must be aware that the Church is a living organism, that Christian life is never static, but is rather confronted every day by the questions and challenges of the reality we live in. There is no proclamation of the gospel except within the culture and history where it is proclaimed. For this reason, Tradition is a dynamic path that is articulated in the stages of human history and, as Pope Francis has mentioned, it "must not become a historical relic, otherwise it is no longer '*tradition*'! Tradition is either alive or it is not."*

In this context, especially today, when we are surrounded by the emerging challenges of the new evangelization, and at the same

* POPE FRANCIS, *Address to Participants in the Meeting Promoted by the Pontifical Council for Promoting New Evangelization*, September 17, 2021.

time invited to rediscover the importance of synodality as the very form of the Church, it is important to begin a deep reflection on the ordained priesthood. The Tradition we come from, which has in many ways forged a precise image of the priest, needs to open itself up to the encounter with the diverse and complex situations of modernity, letting itself be provoked by the signs of the times and trying to imagine new visions and new horizons. Specifically, we need to rethink the relationship between ordained priesthood and baptismal priesthood in order to encourage new forms of ministry, open to the missionary dynamism of a Church that wishes to go out to encounter the world with a renewed evangelical proclamation.

Let us listen, then, to our illustrious speakers, whom we thank for their presence and for what they offer us, with competence and generosity.

Afternoon Introductory Session
Thursday, February 17, 2022

4

PRIESTHOOD ACCORDING TO THE FATHERS OF THE CHURCH

Father Jean-Robert Armogathe

No-one thinks that ordinations are an earthly matter, because the priesthood is something heavenly.

—Pope Siricius (320–399), *Letter* 6, 3, 5 (PL 13, 1166)

PRESENTING AN OVERALL picture of the priesthood according to the fathers of the Church raises the preliminary question of method. I am not going to set out a doxography of five centuries of patristics. This inquiry covers the Latin and Greek fathers from the end of the first century to the seventh century, from the Apostolic Fathers to Maximus the Confessor.[1] I will follow the main lines, the major points identifiable in the teachings of the fathers. The common denominator of this study is the purpose of the priesthood: it is about *serving the economy of salvation* (1 Cor 4:1—"stewards [*οἰκονόμοι*] of God's mysteries"). This sacramental approach seems the most relevant for a fundamental theology of the priesthood.[2]

Four observations need to be stated from the outset.

The first is that it is difficult to determine the precise meaning of the terminology and the nature of the functions of the ministries of the apostolic and subapostolic ages. Two things should be noted: first, recourse to the Letter to the Hebrews to affirm the one priesthood of Christ, and then the mention of functions in the context of conflicts in the churches, both at Corinth (Clement of Rome) and at Philadelphia (Ignatius of Antioch).

The second observation is the diversity of ministries: proclamation of the word (*διδάσκαλος*) predominates at Alexandria, while at Antioch what is stressed is the offering of sacrifice (*ἱερεύς*) and at Jerusalem, followed by Rome, it is government (*πρεσβύτερος*). This diversity finds its unity in the mediation of Christ.

The third observation is the awareness of a particular link with Christ the priest through baptism, reconciliation, and the Eucharist. This relationship presupposes a stable, permanent sacramental institution. It elicits a life of humility and service, in imitation of Christ (Cyprian).

The fourth observation is that the oneness of baptism unites laypeople and priests in the "hypostatic unity of the Church" (Maximus the Confessor), as sharing one single priesthood in diversity of functions (Augustine and Origen).

The early Christian communities were contemporary with religions that included priestly functions: either the priests of paganism, or the priests and Levites of Judaism, whose memory must have lasted beyond the destruction of the temple in AD 70. The term *ἱερεύς* could in no case have formed part of their vocabulary. In Acts 14:12 we find a pagan priest; otherwise, the word was habitually used to designate the Jewish priesthood. A small group of writings applies it to Christ, to the Christian people as a whole, or to the martyrs. Nevertheless, the exercise of worship brought with it a specialization of functions and the recognition of a particular connection with sacrifice. "The text of Romans 15:16 applies indisputably sacerdotal terminology (*λειτουργός*, *ἱερουργέω*, *προσφορά*) to the ministry of the Gospel."[3] It was in the context of worship, and in particular of the Eucharist, that a specific terminology of functions took shape.

This overview leads to the four observations set out above:

1. terminology that is hard to define
2. a great diversity of ministries
3. a particular relationship with Christ
4. the overall unity of the Church

TERMINOLOGY THAT IS HARD TO DEFINE

As stated above, the first point is the difficulty in determining the precise meaning of the terms and the nature of functions for ministries in the apostolic and subapostolic ages. The vexed question of origins resurfaces here, and in my view, it has no answer. Prudence should be used in moving forward. The original Palestinian community was grouped under the authority of the apostles. Until St. Paul's great missionary journeys, the journeys reported in the Acts of the Apostles were mainly made by road (mention is made of the chariot of Queen Candace's eunuch, or Saul's expedition to Damascus). The new religion spread by gathering its followers together; it was not an individual belief system, unlike other Mediterranean religions. On the model of the Jewish communities, the new communities came together each week, on the day after the Shabbat (or the evening of the Shabbat itself). This brought the need for someone to be in charge, and here too there was an existing model: outside Jerusalem, Jewish religious practice was ruled by a college of wise men, or "elders" (in Greek: *πρεσβύτεροι*), heads of households endowed with civic and religious authority (and even in Jerusalem, it seems that besides the priests and doctors/teachers [scribes], there were also "elders"—Matt 16:21 and parallels; Acts 4:5, etc.). At Luke 22:66, "the assembly of the elders of the people gathered together, both chief priests and scribes." The same word is found at the end of Acts 22:5, when Paul recalls the mission that he had been given by the high priest and *πᾶντὸ πρεσβυτέριον*.

In the oldest Latin translations, the Greek *πρεσβύτεροι* are called *seniores*. The difficulty is highlighted here by the fact that writers alternated between *seniores* (the rendering used for the Jewish elders) and the loan word *presbyteri*, which eventually prevailed.[4] Besides, the pagan world also had "elders" in charge of civic or religious associations. The attribution to Paul (and Barnabas) at Acts 14:23 of the appointment of "presbyters" or "elders" (not known from other sources in the Letters) seems to be a retrospective identification by Luke of an authority structure he may have known as existing at Jerusalem.

It is, then, natural for a similar authority structure to have been transposed to the Judeo-Christian communities in Palestine. But the organization of the first groups of faithful, as reflected in St. Paul's Letters and the Acts of the Apostles,[5] was modeled on the organization of the synagogues, at least among the converts from Judaism. As well as this, it is quite possible that the expansion of Christianity into pagan areas may have occasioned some borrowings from the organization of the great initiation cults such as those of Mithras and Isis.

In the First Letter to the Thessalonians 5:12, the oldest of Paul's Letters, the apostle exhorts his readers to "respect those who labor among you and are over you [*προισταμένους*] in the Lord and admonish you." The participle of *προίσταναι* ("to be at the head," "stand before," "take care of") relates to the functions of elders in the first Christian writings: 1 Tim 5:17, and *The Shepherd of Hermas* Vision 2, VIII, 3. It is also used of the overseer/bishop (*episkopos*) in 1 Timothy 3:5.

The Letter to the Philippians begins with a greeting to the bishops and deacons, two functions that do not appear in the other Pauline letters (while other communities know *πρεσβύτεροι*).

The text of the Didache was finalized at the beginning of the second century. This text came from the rural communities of western Syria; it does not belong to the Pauline tradition, and certain sections seem to predate the first written versions of the Gospels. At chapter XV, the Didache instructs,

> Choose for yourselves[6] bishops and deacons worthy of the Lord, men who are gentle, not money-loving, truthful and well-tried, because it is they who, for you, also fulfil the office of prophets and teachers [*didaskaloi*]. Do not spurn them, therefore, because among you they are honoured for the same reason as the prophets and teachers.

This passage seems to point to some resistance against the new position occupied by bishops and deacons: "the general development goes clearly in the direction of a rise in noncharismatic functions like bishops and deacons."[7]

Finally, in the Syriac version of the *Didascalia Apostolorum* (first half of the 3rd century), the Christian bishop is described with the features of the *mebaqqer*,[8] who was, at Qumran, the person in charge of the council of the community; the biblical quotations accompanying it are also found in the Qumran texts. The hypothesis has been put forward that some Essenes were converted to Christianity and imported a function that existed in their community. Moreover, the *Didascalia* is an Antiochian text, and it was at Antioch, apparently, that the monarchical episcopate made its appearance.

Two notes may conclude this terminological inventory:

First, the great variety in local situations. The Pauline communities seem to be the best known, but the addressees of the letters, the fact that their content is sometimes interpolated, and the status of the letters (Pauline, Deutero-Pauline, and "pastoral") show that things are not as simple as they seem. And above all it only has to do with communities around the eastern end of the Mediterranean. But from the second half of the first century onward (and especially after the fall of Jerusalem), the Way of Jesus spread outward in all directions—Syria and eastward, Egypt and North Africa, Gaul and throughout the West.[9] There were dozens of communities or "assemblies" (the word *churches*[10] came to be used), formed around weekly worship and a "liturgical" calendar centered on Easter and baptisms. These local communities naturally wove local and regional links among themselves.

Second, there is the variety of terms used to designate the people who gathered these groups together, which include prophet, guide, teacher (*didaskalos*), servant of the word and of the table (deacon), president (such as Phoebe at Cenchreae near Corinth, Rom 16:1–2), overseer/bishop (*episkopos*) or elder (*presbyteros*). Concern to maintain the deposit received, that is, the "kerygma" of Jesus, very soon seems to have brought about the consolidation of this structure (Phil 1:1 already mentions overseers/bishops and servants/deacons); the Didache puts people on their guard against itinerant prophets.

Taking these two observations into account, we must recognize:

a) that it is very difficult to arrive at a fixed, specific terminology for the functions of ministers before the end of the second century; and
b) nevertheless, very early on in the Christian communities there were certain men, under whatever name, called to celebrate the sacrifice of the Lord's Supper, and they were recognized and respected as such.

> In just two or three generations, in apostolic times, the gigantic achievement of this foundational unity was already largely assured. It was assured to the point where, over and above the shocks that would come upon them, future Christians would always be able to take it as a reference-point, and to express their thought or describe their actions in the mirror of apostolic times.[11]

And in Chrysostom's writings the word *ἱερεύς* designates essentially the man to whom "the sacred things," *τὰ ἱερά*, are entrusted, "which are only accomplished by those holy hands" (whether of a priest or a bishop).[12]

A GREAT DIVERSITY OF MINISTRIES

The profusion of ministries and charismas presented by the Pauline Letters was reduced quickly in the organization of communities. The role of prophets and that of widows diminished, while the priestly hierarchy assimilated and absorbed both prophets and teachers. As already stated, proclamation of the word (*διδάσκαλος*) predominated at Alexandria, while at Antioch what was stressed was offering sacrifice (*ἱερεύς*) and at Jerusalem, followed by Rome, it was government (*πρεσβύτερος*).

The Didache, witnessing to Eastern tradition, stresses teaching: "Allow the prophets to give thanks [*εὐχαριστεῖν*] as much as they wish" (Didache 10, 7).

The author is concerned to maintain good doctrine (6, 1), while Ignatius in his Letter to the Ephesians (9, 1) puts them on their guard against wandering teachers who pass on "false teaching."

In the second century, lay teachers still had the right to speak to the Church—though they no longer had that right at Alexandria. After the appearance of Gnostic teachers, Origin gave first place to announcing the word: "All his works converge more on the sacrament of Scripture than on the sacrament of worship" (J. Daniélou).[13]

> If anyone wants to be a high priest not just in name but in worthiness, let him imitate Moses; let him imitate Aaron.

> What is said about them? "They did not leave the Tent of the Lord." Moses was constantly in "the Tent of the Lord." What was his work? That he should either learn something from God or teach the people. These are the two works of the high priest: that he either learn from God by reading the divine Scriptures and by meditating often on them, or teach the people.[14]

In the letters of Ignatius of Antioch, the emphasis is, by contrast, on the Eucharist. These often-quoted letters pose a double problem: first, their dating is controverted, and second, they present a triple division of the clergy that, at the beginning of the second century, is not found in any church (in particular, not in the church at Rome); in fact, it is not to be found before the year 160. Ignatius's terminology is curiously innovative regarding the ecclesiastical situation of the second century.

Ignatius recommends the Christians of Philadelphia "to have only one Eucharist." In his Letter to the Smyrnaeans (8, 1) he still stresses the Eucharist: "Let only that be considered a valid Eucharist, which is celebrated either by the bishop, or by one to whom he has entrusted that charge."

Justin mentions the *προεστώς* [15] (which links up with Hermas, Vision 2, 4, 3: the *πρεσβύτεροι* who are put in charge [*προϊσταμένοι*] of the Church): this was the title of the Essenes' local presidents.[16] It would, I think, be unduly reductionist to see it only as the person who presided at the celebration; and indeed, this word, the second aorist active participle of *προΐστημι*, is used as a substantive here. An ongoing classical tradition in the Septuagint and the New Testament attests to this usage (equivalent to *ἄρχων*).[17]

Cyprian of Carthage stresses Christ's sacrifice (in his Letter to the Hebrews 7, 27; 9, 14) renewed by the priest (*sacerdos*):

> That priest truly officiates in the place of Christ who imitates what Christ did, and he offers a true and full sacrifice to God the Father, in the Church, if he offers it as he sees that Christ Himself offered it.[18]

Dating from the end of the first century, Clement of Rome's Letter to the Corinthians does not offer a clear picture of the organization of the churches; what it does show plainly is the power of the bishop of Rome with regard to the Christians at Corinth.

Toward 250 the *Letters of the Clergy of Rome* do not fail to recall that "the Church [of Rome] watches [*excubat*] with the greatest solicitude over all who invoke the name of the Lord,"[19] and "It is right for all of us to watch over [*excubare*] the body of the whole Church, whose members are scattered in the different provinces."[20] It certainly seems that "all of us," *omnes nos*, means the Church at Rome, invested with the *sollicitudo omnium ecclesiarum*.[21]

The letter from Pope Cornelius (251–253) to Fabius of Antioch, preserved for us by Eusebius,[22] gives a valuable account of the organization of the Roman clergy in the third century. But the present inquiry is confining itself to the exercise of the various ministries and will therefore refrain from dealing with the question of the monarchical episcopate.

In their diversity, the ministries cover the three *munera Christi*—priest, prophet, and king, sanctifying, teaching, and governing. Among the fathers, Augustine is perhaps the one who, without ever having written a book *De Sacerdotio*,[23] best expresses these tasks, especially in his *Sermones*. The influence he exercised was all the greater in that he was the main source for Gregory the Great's *Regulæ Pastoralis*;[24] the advice to the bishop refers to both his own salvation and that of the people entrusted to his care.

Teaching, sanctifying, governing: the diversity of ministries finds its unity in Christ's mediation.[25]

A PARTICULAR RELATIONSHIP WITH CHRIST

In the apostolic and subapostolic age, the first communities identified Christ as the One presiding; that is primordially true of the Eucharist, where the words of consecration are in the first person (1 Cor 11:23–26). The end of Matthew 28:19 contains the injunction (which may take up a liturgical formula),[26] "Go therefore, make disciples of all nations, baptizing them in the name of the Father and of the Son and of the Holy Spirit."

Finally, in the fourth Gospel (John 20:22–23) the risen One confers on the Eleven the power to forgive sins.

Eucharist, baptism, penance: the first Church communities, with their variety of origins, found themselves gathered around these three definite signs of belonging to the Way of Jesus. In each of these signs, it is Christ who acts since it is operative "in his name."

Conflicts within the communities led to a clarification of the origin of the priesthood by recourse to the Letter to the Hebrews. Although it was quoted by Clement, Hebrews was not included in the canon of Scripture until the fourth century. The rare commentaries on it include that of Origen, preserved in fragments, which seems to have been the first (though he quotes Hebrews in his Homilies on Leviticus).

Clement's Letter to the Corinthians is clear on this subject. In the conflict between the *δεδοκιμασμένοι* or *πρεσβύτεροι* of the community, Clement appeals to the priesthood of Christ and concludes his letter with a prayer addressed to "the all-seeing God, the Master of spirits," "through our High Priest and protector Jesus Christ."

A little later, divisions in the community at Philadelphia led Ignatius to recall,

> The priests are venerable, but the High Priest is far above them, since the Holy of Holies was entrusted to him, and he alone was allowed into the secrets of God. He is the gate to the Father, through which Abraham, Isaac, Jacob, the prophets, the Apostles and the Church entered.

Cyprian of Carthage (c. 200–258) reproved those priests who put only water in the chalice:

> If Christ Jesus our Lord and God is himself the high priest (*summus sacerdos*) of God his Father…, certainly that priest [*sacerdos*] truly officiates in the place of Christ [*vice Christi*] who imitates what Christ did.[27]

The document known as the *Apostolic Tradition* is at the heart of a huge debate, which there is no room to cover here. It apparently dates from the beginning of the third century. In the second and third chapters it mentions the institution of "heads" (*ἄρχοντες*) and priests (*ἱερεῖς*). In his *Commentary on Daniel*, Hippolytus states generally that all the kings and priests of the Old Law were called *χρίστοι* because they represented, prefigured, the Lord, "until there came from heaven the perfect priest and king in whom the two dignities were joined."[28] But we should pause over the prayer of consecration of priests, which follows that for bishops.

It will be noted that in certain liturgical documents originating from Egypt, the prayer for priests is the same as the one for bishops.[29]

Finally, the importance of the verb *πρεσβεύειν*[30] must be highlighted. This verb has a double sense: it can mean "to be aged, venerable, superior" and thus "to preside," but it can also mean "to be an ambassador, sent by someone else" (the meaning given it by Paul at 2 Cor 5:20 and Eph 6:20). *Πρεσβεία* means deputation. But as has been noted elsewhere, to Greek ears, *πρεσβεύειν* was close to *πρεσβύτερος*, a distinguished person who presides, but also a deputy (Acts 14:25) to whom God entrusts the care of his Church (Acts 20:28).

> We are ambassadors of Christ, as though God exhorted through us.…So see what it means: the Father sent his Son to exhort the human race in his name and to fulfil in their presence the function of ambassador [*πρεσβεύσασθαι*]. Men put him to death, he left this world, we have succeeded him in this embassy [*πρεσβείαν*] and we exhort you in his name and in the name of his Father.[31]

The following general conclusions can be drawn from the developments in the constitution of the Church from the fourth century (stressing, as recalled by Dom Botte in 1957, that "we do not have the right to minimize the importance of the incidental riches added over the centuries").[32]

a) Accessing ministries always means entering an order, a community: bishops, priests, deacons, consecrated virgins, widows, and so on. It is a collective act by the episcopal body that adds the newcomer to the *ordo episcoporum*, as the priest is added to the presbyterium. Bishop, priests, and deacons constitute the "framework that supports the local Church, just as the order of bishops constitutes the framework that supports the universal Church" (Botte).

b) Bishops, priests, and deacons are not only "ministers of worship." Recognition of the typology of the Old Testament never made the claim to apostolic succession disappear. On the one hand, they are not the delegates of the community, but are invested by Christ as his "ambassadors"; and on the other, they are "set apart," as the Eastern Syrian rite puts it.
c) Their functions are *charismatic*; in other words, the Holy Spirit, invoked upon them, must transform their soul, in a pressing call to personal holiness. "The grace of the Holy Spirit was not given to them exclusively to ensure the juridical or sacramental validity of certain actions, but also to enable them to achieve a holiness that will serve as a model for the Christian people" (Botte).
d) The celebration of the Eucharist is the ritualization of *agape* in the Church (Ignatius of Antioch on Rom 7:3: "the blood of Christ, which is incorruptible love"—*ἀγάπη ἄφθαρτος*). The "altar" (Irenaeus) or sacrifice is linked to the ministry. And just as there is no Church without the Eucharistic *ἀγάπη*, there is no Eucharist without the "ordained" minister.

THE OVERALL UNITY OF THE CHURCH

It is always necessary to come back to sacramental life, and first to baptism. It is Christ who baptizes, as recalled by the apocryphal Letter of the Apostles (c. 160/170). This baptism is not like John's. It introduces the subject into the life of the Blessed Trinity and incorporates him or her into the people of God. "For by one Spirit we were all baptized into one body" (1 Cor 12:13). The baptized are "a chosen race, a royal priesthood, a holy nation, God's own people, that you may declare the wonderful deeds of him who called you out of darkness into his marvelous light" (1 Pet 2:9).

In the *Apostolic Tradition*, the *σφραγίς* (sign) is common to the ordination of priests and baptism, during the second baptismal anointing, and is given by the bishop: "having signed him [*σφραγίζειν*] on the forehead, he gives him a kiss."

It is the sacramental identity of baptism and holy orders that has led to the respective (and relative) states of the baptized, ordained, or nonordained being specified.

> The theologians of the 5th century, caught up as they were in bitter Christological disputes, strongly underlined the assimilation of the priest to Christ through participation in his very being. But because their reflections were fixed almost exclusively on the ontological structure, they were unable to explain the specific modality of the minister's participation in Christ's priesthood.[33]

The Constitution *Lumen Gentium* affirms that the difference between the common priesthood of the baptized and the ordained priesthood of ministers is essential and not merely a difference of degree.[34] These words should be taken seriously, meaning related back to the source of the priesthood, Christ; that is, we should project onto the distinction between laity and clerics the distinction between the two natures of the Son.[35] Deep christological reflection produced, in the sixth to seventh centuries, a synthesis of the three elements of the theology of the priestly character: the functional element (the apostolic *πρεσβεία*), the ontological element (participation in Christ), and the liturgical element (the *σφραγίς* of ordination).

A groundbreaking article by Frs. Garrigues, Le Guillou, and Riou drew my attention to the *Mystagogia* of Maximus the Confessor (580–662).[36]

To defend the definitions of Chalcedon on the different natures of Christ, which do not entail either division or confusion, Maximus explains how the Church shows that differences do not harm unity, by referring to the arrangement of church buildings, the two testaments of Scripture, the letter and the spirit, and the unfolding of the action of the synaxis in which humans, angels, and God all play a part. The Holy Church, he writes, "is an image of God because it realizes the same union of the faithful with God. As different as they are by language, places and customs, they are made one by it through faith" (187–88).

He goes on to describe the church building: it is divided in two, comprising one place reserved for priests and minsters alone, the sanctuary (*ἱερατεῖον*), and another place accessible to all the believers (*πᾶσι τοῖς πιστοῖς λαοῖς*), the nave (*ναός*). Nevertheless, it is one according to its identity (*κατὰ τὴν ὑπόστασιν*). Just as Christ has two natures, "without confusion, without change, without division and without separation," in the same way the Church can be said to have two natures, the clergy and the laity, of whom it can be affirmed, as it is affirmed of Christ, that "the difference of natures is in no way cancelled out because of their union, the property of one and the other nature being instead safeguarded and coming together in one single person and one single hypostasis" (which is the definition of Chalcedon).

This "essential" difference does not in any way break the unity of the Church, which is one—as the Father and the Son are one (John 17:21–23).

Maximus continues:

> [The Church] is one in its basic reality without being divided into its parts by reason of the differences between them, but rather by their relationship to the unity [ἕν] it frees these parts from the difference arising from their names. It shows to each other that they are both the same thing, and reveals that one is to the other in turn what each one is for itself. Thus, the nave [= the laity] is the sanctuary in potency by being consecrated by the relationship of the sacrament toward its end, and in turn the sanctuary [= the clergy] is the nave in act by possessing the principle of its own sacrament, which remains one and the same in its two parts. (188)

It may be appropriate to transpose the christological model of the building to the assembly: the clergy and the laity constitute one single body, manifesting this same distinction without separation or confusion. This model avoids the dovetailing effect of an ordained priesthood superimposed on the baptismal priesthood; the humanity of Christ is as perfect in its order as his divinity, he is "consubstantial with the Father according to his divinity and consubstantial with us according to his humanity" (cf. 164).

The unity of the *ἐκκλησία* ("that they may all be One…"), then, leads us back explicitly, in the models developed by Maximus, to

Christ, whose Body is the Church. Applied to the laity and the clergy, this unity, while maintaining the distinction between the two, does not lead to any separation, any division. The sanctuary and the nave are brought together by the Church "for the mystery accomplished on the divine altar" (195). Thus, the church "made by human hands which is its symbolic copy because of the variety of divine things which are in it, has been given to us for our guidance toward the highest good" (195).

CONCLUSION

The foregoing investigation is not without current relevance. Ever since the Protestant reformation, the word *priest* and related terms have been accused of causing the "wound of the Church" that Rosmini spoke of: "the division between the people and the clergy in public worship," or the "clericalization" that is so often denounced today. In this view, such terms worked to deprive laypeople, as being "nonpriests," of all responsibility in the Church and to endow the clergy with a "sacred power" that was in fact arbitrary authority over the Christian people.[37]

The above inquiry into patristics seems to me to show that it is *the practice of worship as sacrifice* that instituted a ministerial order distinct from the baptismal priesthood; and that order, entry into which was marked by the imposition of hands, very soon reserved priestly terminology exclusively to itself. As for the word *sacerdos*, it was used generally to mean a bishop until the Middle Ages, when a semantic change moved its meaning to a priest "of the second order."

The overall unity of the Church unites laity and priests as Christ's humanity and divinity are united; thus, the difference is not merely accidental or functional; it is a constitutive mark of the very being of the Church, the Body of Christ. Each of the two elements "are both the same thing"; "one is to the other in turn what each one is for itself."

NOTES

1. M. Fiedrowicz, *Priestertum und Kirchenväter. Quellentexte zur Theologie und Spiritualität des priestlichen Amtes* (Fohren-Linden: Carthusianus Verlag, 2013); E. Cattaneo, *Les ministères dans l'Église ancienne. Textes patristiques du ier au iiie siècle,* French. tr. (Paris: Éditions du Cerf, 2017) [*I ministeri nella*

Chiesa antica. Testi patristici dei primi tre secoli, 1st ed. (Milano: Ed. Paoline, 1997)].

2. K.-H. MENKE, *Sakramentalität. Wesen und Wunde des Katholizismus* (Regensburg: Pustet, 2018).

3. CATTANEO, *Les ministères*, 126.

4. See the detailed study by M. POIRIER, "Évolution du vocabulaire chrétien latin du sacerdoce et du presbytérat des origines à saint Augustin," *Bulletin de la Société Nationale des Antiquaires de France* (1997, 2001), 230–45.

5. Of the twelve occurrences of *πρεσβύτερος* in the New Testament, eight refer to the community at Jerusalem.

6. The verb here is *χειροτονεῖν*, which afterward took the meaning of "ordain by imposition of hands."

7. E. NORELLI, *La nascita del cristianesimo* (Bologna: Il Mulino, 2014; French tr. Bayard, 2015; Gallimard, 2019), 197.

8. As found in a Nabataean inscription (J. CANTINEAU, *Le Nabatéen*, vol. 2 [Paris: Leroux, 1932], 73).

9. See the very clear exposition by C. PERROT, *Histoire Générale du Christianisme*, vol. 1 (Paris: PUF, 2010), 53–64.

10. The first groups must, like the Essenes, have called themselves *yahad* (*κοινωνία*). The term *ἐκκλησία* spread unevenly, and some Jewish Christians retained the word "synagogue" (Jas 2:2). 1 Thess 2:4 mentions the "Churches of God" in Judaea—and first in Jerusalem (PERROT, *Histoire Générale*, 36).

11. PERROT, *Histoire Générale*, 75.

12. CHRYSOSTOM, *On the Priesthood*, III, 6, l. 7–8.

13. J. DANIÉLOU, *Origène* (Paris : La Table Ronde, 1948), 58; English tr. W. Mitchell (Sheed & Ward, 1955), 45.

14. ORIGEN, *Homilies on Leviticus 1—16*, VI, 6, trans. G. W. Barkley (Washington, DC: Catholic University of America Press, 1990), 128.

15. JUSTIN, *First Apology*, 65, 5.

16. HIPPOLYTUS, *Refutatio omnium haeresium* 9, 20; PG 16, 3398A.

17. T. G. JALLAND, "Justin Martyr and the President of the Eucharist," in *Studia Patristica* 5 (1962), 84; L. W. BARNARD, *Justin Martyr: His Life and Thought* (Cambridge: Cambridge University Press, 1967), ch. X, pp. 126ff.

18. CYPRIAN, *Letter* 63, 14, 4 (CCL 3/BC p. 410), dated between 254 and 256.

19. *Lett.* 8, 3, 3 (CCL 3/B, p. 43).

20. *Lett.* 36, 4, 1 (CCL 3/B, p. 176).

21. See CATTANEO, *Les ministères...*, 468n3.

22. EUSEBIUS, *Historia Ecclesiastica*, VI, 43, 7-17 (SC 41, pp. 155–58).

23. The *De Doctrina Christiana* is a manual for preachers.

24. Gregory the Great, *Pastoral Rule* (*Regulæ pastoralis liber*, 591); C. Dagens, *Saint Grégoire le Grand. Culture et expérience chrétiennes* (Paris: Éditions du Cerf, 2014), 585.

25. J. Pintard, *Le Sacerdoce selon saint Augustin* (Tours, Mame, 1960); M. Pellegrino, *"Verus sacerdos." Il sacerdozio nell'esperienza e nel pensiero di sant'Agostino*, ed. S. Palese (Roma: Vivere In, 2010).

26. Because the announcement of baptism by Peter at Acts 2:38 says merely "in the name of Jesus Christ" with the gift of the Holy Spirit.

27. Cyprian of Carthage, Letter 63, 14.

28. J. Lécuyer, "Épiscopat et presbytérat dans les écrits d'Hippolyte de Rome," in *Recherches de sciences religieuses*, XLI (1953): 30–50.

29. Lécuyer, "Épiscopat et presbytérat," 41n9. This refers to the *Canons of Hippolytus* and the *Constitution of the Egyptian Church*. It seems that every priest received the fullness of the priesthood, but only one of them had jurisdiction (which would explain the usage of the Church of Alexandria regarding the election of the patriarch).

30. J.-M. Garrigues, M.-J. Le Guillou, and A. Riou, "Le caractère sacerdotal dans la tradition des Pères grecs," *Nouvelle Revue Théologique* 93, no. 8 (1971): 806.

31. John Chrysostom, *In Ep. II ad Cor.*, Hom. XI, PG 61, col. 477–78.

32. B. Botte, "Holy Orders in the Ordination Prayers," in *The Sacrament of Holy Orders: Some Papers and Discussions Concerning Holy Orders at a Session of the Centre de Pastorale Liturgique 1955* (Collegeville, MN: Liturgical Press, 1962).

33. Garrigues, Le Guillou, Riou, "Le caractère sacerdotal," 814.

34. *Lumen Gentium* 10: "Though they differ from one another in essence and not only in degree [*licet essentia et non gradu tantum differant*], the common priesthood of the faithful and the ministerial or hierarchical priesthood are nonetheless interrelated: each of them in its own special way is a participation in the one priesthood of Christ."

35. Here I am following the article by Garrigues, Le Guillou, and Riou quoted above, 813–20.

36. "The Church's Mystagogy," trans. G. C. Berthold, in *Maximus Confessor: Selected Writings*, Classics of Western Spirituality (New York: Paulist Press, 1985), 181–226.

37. Because of the paper being offered by Fr. Emilio José Justo Dominguez, the present paper has not dealt with the question of marriage, continence, and celibacy.

5

ST. THOMAS AQUINAS ON THE PRIESTHOOD AND THE HOLY TRINITY

Father Dominic Legge, OP

ACCORDING TO St. Thomas Aquinas, "the priesthood of Christ is the fountainhead of the entire priesthood."[1] And again: "Every rite of the Christian religion flows out from the priesthood of Christ."[2] Priesthood in the Church, therefore, is a participation in the priesthood of Christ, the incarnate Son of God and the mediator between God and humanity.[3]

From a Thomistic perspective, this christological starting point is crucial, and it bears rich fruit for a theology and spirituality of the priesthood today. When viewed in the wider context of Aquinas's theology, it also allows us to see how St. Thomas conceives of Christ's priestly mediation—and thus also the mediation of ministerial priests configured to Christ—within a beautiful trinitarian frame. Not only is Aquinas's Christology richly trinitarian, but his theology of the priesthood is, too.

This lecture has three parts. First, we will present Aquinas's account of Christ's priesthood, set within the wider trinitarian frame of how God the Father brings all things back to himself by sending the Son into the world, breathing forth the Holy Spirit upon the Church. We will then investigate why Christ instituted ministerial priests in the Church, according to St. Thomas. Finally, we will discuss Aquinas on the ministerial priesthood, paying special attention to the little-known trinitarian dimensions of Aquinas's teaching.

THE PRIESTHOOD OF CHRIST AND THE HOLY TRINITY

For St. Thomas, the entire pattern of the dispensation of salvation is trinitarian, and therefore so is Christology and the theology of the priesthood.[4] In the incarnation, the Father sends the Son into the world, breathing forth the Holy Spirit, who is Love and Gift in person. Jesus is the Father's Son who is filled with the Holy Spirit in his human nature. Impelled by the Spirit, Christ not only teaches and heals, but also offers up prayers and supplications to his Father. This culminates in his perfect self-offering in the sacrifice of the cross, his decisive victory over death in the resurrection, and his breathing forth of the Holy Spirit upon the Church, to bring to life all those who were dead because of sin. Aquinas sees all this as an exercise of Christ's priesthood.

More specifically, he holds that Christ does these things as the Son of the Father who has become man, filled with the Holy Spirit in his humanity. As man, he is therefore the perfect mediator between God and human beings. And it is this—that Christ is the supreme and perfect mediator—that provides the deepest account of Christ's priesthood, according to Aquinas.

This is a point of capital importance, because it allows us to see that Christ's priesthood is neither a role assigned to him nor only something that he does; rather, as Jean-Pierre Torrell has noted, the priesthood is a key constitutive or structural feature of Aquinas's Christology, a dimension of the mystery of the incarnation in itself.[5] Indeed, Aquinas is unique among medieval theologians in defining Christ's priesthood in terms of mediation—he "seems to be the only thinker among his contemporaries to have treated this question."[6] This may be related to Aquinas's unique effort to comment on all of the letters attributed to St. Paul: he was almost the only one among his contemporaries who commented on the Letter to the Hebrews, with its focus on Christ's mediation and his priesthood.[7]

When Aquinas takes up the question of Christ's priesthood in the *Summa Theologiae*, he uses Hebrews 5:1 to define the priesthood specifically in terms of mediation:

> The proper office of a priest is to be a mediator between God and the people, namely, insofar as he gives divine things to the people, offers the prayers of the people to God, and in some way makes satisfaction to God for their sins. Thus, the Apostle says (*Heb* 5:1): "every high priest chosen from among men is appointed to act on behalf of men in relation to God, to offer gifts and sacrifices for sins." And this is maximally befitting to Christ.[8]

Christ is a mediator not as God, but only as man,[9] and hence he is a priest not as God, but as man.[10] Indeed, Aquinas even suggests that this is a reason why God would become man: to serve as our perfect high priest, able to suffer and have compassion for us in his assumed nature.[11]

According to St. Thomas, Christ's life and ministry as our great high priest involves a twofold mediation: ascending and descending. In his ascending mediation, Jesus offers prayers and sacrifices to God the Father, culminating in his supreme sacrifice on the cross. In his descending mediation, he teaches and sanctifies the people, giving them the new law of the gospel, which is nothing other than the grace of the Holy Spirit[12]—indeed, he gives the very fount of grace, the Holy Spirit himself, to the Church.

There is therefore a robust trinitarian dimension to Christ's priesthood in Aquinas, although this is rarely noticed. To be sure, Christ is constituted as a mediator by the hypostatic union, which pertains to his personal being, and makes his human nature absolutely the highest of all creatures, because it is united to the divine Son in person. Likewise, as the incarnate Son, every action of Christ is characterized by a filial mode: it is from the Father and oriented toward the Father.[13] Yet when Aquinas speaks of Christ's priesthood, he does not typically place the emphasis on the hypostatic union; rather, he focuses on Christ's reception of the Holy Spirit, which for Aquinas is another way of speaking about Christ's habitual and capital grace.[14]

In a key text in his Hebrews commentary, Aquinas makes this link very explicit: Jesus is our great high priest, from whom every share in the priesthood flows, because he is anointed as man with the Holy Spirit. Indeed, it is the anointing of his sacred humanity by the Holy Spirit that makes him, as man, to be a priest, a prophet, and a king:

> *"Therefore God your God has anointed you with the oil of gladness*...(Heb 1:9 [quoting *Ps.* 44:8])" These words speak of a spiritual anointing, because Christ is filled with the Holy Spirit...in his very conception: "*[The Word became flesh and dwelt among us,] full of grace and truth* (*Jn* 1:16)."...It is as if to say, in order that you would have an eternal throne, a scepter of justice, etc., God has therefore anointed you with oil, namely, the oil of holiness,...with which...the priests, and also the kings...and prophets were anointed.[15]

Space does not permit us to quote the entire text of Aquinas, but it is very rich. It explains that Christ's holiness as man "was brought about through this anointing," so that he would be a priest, a prophet, and a king, in line with the Old Testament types.[16] Aquinas is clear that the anointing with the Holy Spirit pertains only to his humanity: "Christ was anointed not as God...but as man."[17]

This full possession of the Holy Spirit is a key dimension of his place as mediator in the dispensation of salvation. "God [the Father] has anointed you [Christ] with God Himself [the Holy Spirit], but we are anointed through you, the mediator between God and man, Christ the man."[18] Aquinas's logic is perfectly in line with what he teaches in many other places: Jesus receives the absolute fullness of the Holy Spirit as man, and therefore has full dominion over the economy of grace: from his Spirit-filled humanity, he distributes every grace to the faithful.[19] What is distinctive here, however, is that Aquinas identifies his typical pneumatological account of Christ's capital grace as *a dimension of Christ's priesthood*.[20] Because a priest is a mediator, he gives divine things to humans. Christ is a priest as man insofar as he is anointed by the Holy Spirit and then pours out the Spirit's gifts—and the Spirit himself—on humanity. Pouring out the Spirit is a central feature of Christ's priestly mediation.

Aquinas extends this analysis to the sacraments as well: Jesus institutes the sacraments and fills them with the Holy Spirit, "the oil of sanctification and rejoicing. The sacraments, which are vessels of grace, are from him."[21] Established by Christ as man, they bear within them the grace of the Holy Spirit, a holy oil flowing from Christ's anointing with the Spirit. St. Thomas makes a similar point regarding sacred teaching and divine revelation: the people seek the law from the mouth of the priest, and this is supremely true in the case of Christ, who gives us the new law of the gospel.[22]

In all of this, St. Thomas emphasizes that every grace radically depends on Christ's anointing and therefore comes to us as part of Christ's descending mediation, a gift given through Christ's priesthood:

> What comparison is there between the anointed Christ and anointed Christians? It is this, namely that he has this anointing principally and first, while we and others have it as poured out from him: "*It is like the anointing on the head,* [*running down upon the beard, upon the beard of Aaron, running down on the collar of his robes*] (Ps 132:2). "And it says "[*God has anointed you...*] *beyond your comrades*," for "*from his fullness we have all received* (John 1:16)." Hence others are called holy, but he is called the holy of holies, for he is the source of all holiness.[23]

As St. Thomas says later in the same work, Christ is therefore the most holy minister of the most holy things:

> [Christ] is a more excellent minister [of holy thing than the Old Testament priests], not insofar as he is God (for as God, he is the source of holy things), but as man....For the humanity of Christ is an instrument of the divinity. He is therefore "*a minister of holy things*" because he administers the sacraments of grace in the present life, and of glory in the life to come...Christ the man is a minister, because every good of glory is dispensed through him.[24]

For Aquinas, then, Christ's priesthood is a dimension of a trinitarian-christological account of the entire dispensation of grace, including the sacraments. "All spiritual understanding, all gifts—in short, whatever can exist in the Church—all of this is superabundantly in Christ, and flows from him into the Church's members."[25] Every grace given to the world is a gift of the Spirit from the Father and the Son, which we receive through the mediation of Christ's humanity, which is to say, through Christ's priesthood.

We must hasten to add that Christ's priesthood involves not only this descending mediation, but ascending mediation as well. Here again, Aquinas's perspective is impressively comprehensive. "Christ himself [is the one] in whom and through whom we offer our prayers."[26] This ascending mediation is a part of the finality of the incarnation itself. Thus, Jesus ascended into heaven…

> "…*in order to appear on our behalf before the face of God* (Heb 9:24)." Here the Apostle alludes to a rite of the Old Law, according to which the high priest who entered into the holy of holies and stood before the mercy seat in order to pray on behalf of the people. So also Christ entered heaven as man, that he might stand before God for our salvation.[27]

Jesus does this "by representing" our humanity before the Father, and "by interceding for us…by expressing the desire of his most holy soul for our salvation."[28] Indeed, by entering the heavenly sanctuary in our human nature, Christ prepares the way for us to ascend with him and to enter into the Father's presence.[29]

St. Thomas emphasizes that Jesus's prayer is directed specifically *to the Father* as a properly priestly act of his humanity:

> The act [of his priestly office] was that he offered "*prayers and supplications* (Heb 5:7)," which is the spiritual sacrifice that Christ offered.…To whom? "*To God*," namely, God the Father.…The priesthood of Christ is ordered to this spiritual sacrifice."[30]

Aquinas includes Christ's human desires in this priestly prayer: he prays to the Father "assiduously," with humility, "with fervent affection," and with "pain," "groans," and "tears." "He did not weep for himself, but for us."[31] Christ's tears in his earthly life are therefore both an expression of his charity, and a prayer to the Father to save us from death.

Here, too, we find the Holy Spirit, who is the personal principle of Christ's human charity, which Christ receives as the created effect of the Spirit's invisible mission to his humanity.[32] The Spirit thus has a central place in Christ's ascending mediation by way of prayer.[33] As

Thomas puts it in one text, the Holy Spirit moves Christ's soul to its supreme reverence for God.

> The fear of God was in Christ...insofar as the soul of Christ was moved unto God by a certain affection of reverence, from the action of the Holy Spirit. Hence Heb. 5 says that, in all things, "he was heard for his reverence."[34]

That the Holy Spirit moves Christ to pray does not change the distinctive filial mode of his human act of prayer, of course, but it does mean that, for Aquinas, the Holy Spirit plays a role of fundamental importance in Christ's priestly actions.

Aquinas speaks in a similar way about Christ's sacrifice on the wood of the cross. Here, we encounter the most profound dimension of the ascending mediation of Christ's priesthood, which is at the same time both trinitarian and christological. Christ offers this sacrifice as a priest—that is, he offers to the Father not as God, but as man. He is moved to this act by the Holy Spirit.

> The cause why Christ shed his blood...was the Holy Spirit, by whose motion and instinct—namely, by charity for God and for neighbor—he did this....And so [the Letter to the Hebrews] says "through the Holy Spirit he offered himself." "Christ loved us, and handed himself over for us as an oblation and sacrifice to God in an odor of sweetness (Eph 5:2)."[35]

In this text, St. Thomas offers two related reasons why the Holy Spirit causes the passion. First, since Christ acted by the Spirit's "motion and instinct," the Holy Spirit is a true principle of Christ's human act of self-oblation.[36] Second, as the Ephesians quotation suggests, it is precisely the effect of the Holy Spirit's personal presence—the perfect supernatural charity of Christ as man—that makes Christ's voluntary acceptance of suffering and death the perfect "oblation and sacrifice" that satisfies for our sins and merits our redemption. This is because (as St. Thomas develops elsewhere in much greater detail) it is essential that one's sacrifice be pleasing and acceptable to God—and it was specifically Christ's charity, and not his suffering and death as such, that was "maximally acceptable to God."[37] In sum, then, the Holy Spirit, sent by the Father (and by Christ as God) to Christ as man, is a true cause of Christ's priestly sacrifice on the cross.[38]

The offering on the cross is, first and above all, Christ's own sacrifice—the sacrifice of the person of the Son in his incarnate humanity. But we should not lose sight of the logic of this offering: as our mediator and priest, he offers this sacrifice precisely so that it could become our sacrifice as well, as we are configured to him and share in his priesthood. It is an ascending mediation not only as he offers something *for* the world, but as he also *gives the world the way to offer something pleasing to God.* Indeed, Christ's ultimate purpose, the end of his priestly sacrifice, is that we would be brought back to the Father through this offering.

> Every high priest is appointed to offer gifts and sacrifices.... But Christ is a high priest....Therefore...because it was necessary for him to have something to offer, he offered himself....This was fitting, because it was fitting that a man would make satisfaction for man....He united to God those for whom he offers it, "that they may all be one, even as you, Father, are in me, and I in you, that also they may be in us (John 17:21)."[39]

We can conclude our discussion of Christ's priesthood, then, with this summary: Christ is a true high priest, who as man offers prayers and sacrifices to God on behalf of his brethren and gives divine gifts to them. The grace of the Holy Spirit—and, in fact, the indwelling presence of the Holy Spirit himself—is the supreme gift given by Christ the priest. This divine gift configures the faithful back to Christ, giving them a share in his priesthood, and thus setting them on a trajectory of return to the Father, through the Son, and in the Holy Spirit. That is, the priesthood of Christ and his mediation is for the sake of raising up what is below and bringing it to God. He accomplishes this according to a trinitarian pattern—and, as we shall see, the ministerial priesthood instituted by Christ in the Church follows this same pattern. It is to the ministerial priesthood that we now turn.

AQUINAS ON THE REASON FOR THE MINISTERIAL PRIESTHOOD

Why does Christ institute the sacrament of Holy Orders? Let us start with a familiar point about the sacramental economy: Jesus institutes visible sacraments and appoints human ministers in the Church in order to extend through time the effects of his saving mission, perpetuating his work of teaching, sanctifying, and governing by communicating grace to the world. If space permitted, we could add a great deal here about the divine missions and the sacramentality of the Church.[40]

This is related to Aquinas's view about how the incarnation is a supremely fitting remedy for sin: God raises the fallen minds of human beings who have become trapped in lower things, by becoming flesh in order to free us from slavery to corporeal things.[41] The appointment of visible ministers in the Church who administer visible sacraments is thus a supremely fitting way to reorder human beings to the invisible and supernatural realities that are above us. Thus, at the Last Supper, "because Christ was about to remove his bodily presence from the Church, it was necessary that he would institute others as his ministers, who would dispense the sacraments to the faithful.... This was given 'for building up the Church,' as the Apostle says,...and so it was necessary for this [priestly] power to continue...after the death of the disciples of Christ and even unto the end of the world."[42]

Since these points are rather well-known, however, let us pass to a less-noted point about the priesthood, one that is also probably less appreciated in our democratic age than in Aquinas's day: the importance of *hierarchical mediation* and *ordered distinction* in God's supremely wise plan for salvation. The backdrop here is Aquinas's teaching that God created a vast diversity of creatures so that that the infinite divine goodness might be better communicated to the world and represented in it by them in their finite multiplicity.[43]

> God brought things into being for the sake of communicating his goodness to creatures, and of representing it through them, and because his goodness could not sufficiently be represented through one creature, he produced many and diverse creatures, that what is lacking to one in its representation of

> the divine goodness might be supplied by another. For the goodness which in God is simple and uniform, is multiplied and divided in creatures. Hence the whole universe more perfectly participates in the divine goodness and represents it than any single creature.[44]

Aquinas applies the same logic to holy orders: "God instituted a variety of orders in the Church....for the sake of commending the wisdom of God, which supremely shines forth in the ordered distinction of things, not only in natural things but also in spiritual things."[45] What is more, God desires to give creatures a manifold and ordered participation not only in *representing* his goodness but in his activity of *communicating it to others*—and so he gives humans the gift of being mediators of spiritual goods for the sake of the perfection of the Church.

> God willed to lead his works unto his own likeness as much as possible, so that they might be perfect, and through them he could be known. And hence, so that he would not only be represented in his works as he is in himself but also as he influences other things, he established a natural law in all things, that the last things should be perfected by the middle things, and the middle by the first, as Dionysius says. And hence, that this beauty would not be lacking to the Church, he established order in it, so that some would hand on the sacraments to others, being in its way assimilated to God in this, as if cooperating with God, just as in a natural body certain members influence others.[46]

For St. Thomas, just as creation better reflects the beauty and goodness of God because it is filled with a rich multiplicity of creatures, so the same is true for the Church with its diversity of ministers. That anyone be appointed as a minister of Christ, therefore, is not to exalt that person, but rather so that he would be a mediator in service of the body of Christ. In fact, Aquinas considers an objection to the existence of a hierarchy of orders in the Church—that such a hierarchy entails having rulers and subjects, which seems contrary to the calling of Christ—to which he responds by distinguishing a hierarchical service from what we might label a clericalist misuse of holy orders for the sake of personal power:

> Servitude exists when someone dominates by using those subjects to him for his own benefit. But such subjection is not called for in holy orders, in which those who preside should not seek their own benefit, but the salvation of those under them.[47]

As St. Thomas says elsewhere,

> A priest is only a minister. Hence, he does not act except in virtue of Christ: "*This is how one should regard us, as servants of Christ and stewards of the mysteries of God* (1 Cor 4:1)." He does not act on his own authority, but by the authority of Christ.[48]

To be sure, it is a wonderful feature of God's generosity that he selects certain men to cooperate as instruments in his activity of communicating grace and salvation to others, but this is ordered to the perfection of the whole Body of Christ. To put it another way, the ministerial priests indeed raised up and does indeed receive a spiritual power, but this power flows from Christ's passion, and calls for the priest to be more and more configured to Christ the priest, who laid down his life for the sake of the world.

Here again, it is crucial to underline St. Thomas's understanding of the priest as a mediator, because a mediator does not exist for his own sake, but for the sake of those to whom the ultimate gift is intended. Aquinas writes, "Holy orders is not given as a remedy for an individual person, but for the whole Church."[49]

AQUINAS ON THE MINISTERIAL PRIESTHOOD

A ministerial priest is a priest only as a sharer in Christ's priesthood. A careful look at Aquinas's texts on holy orders uncovers a trinitarian dimension here as well, with important consequences for a contemporary priestly spirituality.

Let us start with Aquinas's treatment of holy orders in the *Summa contra Gentiles*. Thomas's argument moves through several stages. It starts with Christ, of whom a priest is a minister and instrument. By a straightforward syllogism, Aquinas concludes that a priest must be conformed to Christ:

> A minister is compared to his lord as an instrument to its principal agent.... But an instrument must be proportioned to its agent. Hence, the ministers of Christ must also be conformed to him.[50]

Next, Aquinas explains the source of Christ's authority and power for salvation in terms of the hypostatic union of the divine and human natures:

> But Christ, as Lord, works our salvation by his own authority and power, insofar as he was God and man: that as man, he would suffer for our redemption, and as God, his passion would be saving for us.[51]

This brings St. Thomas to ministerial priests, who must in some way be configured to Christ in his humanity *and* in his divinity. But how?

> It is necessary, therefore, for the ministers of Christ to be men, and to share in some way in his divinity according to some spiritual power: for an instrument also shares in some way in the power of the principal agent.[52]

Although he doesn't use the word *character*, it seems that this is what Aquinas has in mind; he consistently defines priestly character (the *res et sacramentum* of holy orders) in precisely these terms, as an instrumental spiritual power configuring a man to Christ, ordered to the salvation of others.[53]

Reading this text carefully yields marvelous trinitarian insights, starting with the person of the Son. Aquinas says elsewhere that Jesus did *not* receive a spiritual mark of priestly character in his human soul.[54] This is because "Christ himself is the eternal character, as Heb. 1:3 says, 'who is the brightness of his glory and the figure,' or character, 'of his substance.'"[55] To refer to Christ's own "character" is simply to refer to his divine sonship itself. He is the image or "character" of the Father in the most proper sense of those terms.[56] This helps us to flesh out what Aquinas says in the *Summa contra Gentiles* text we have been considering: the sacramental character received by a ministerial priest is a participation in Christ's eternal character, which is to say, it is an assimilation to something *proper to the divine person of the Son*.[57] It gives the human priest a new spiritual sharing in the Son's proper filial mode of being: from the Father and oriented to the Father.[58] In the incarnation, the divine Son assumed a human nature such that his humanity was thenceforth marked by the filial mode of the Son's being and acting. In holy orders, then, a man receives something that is like this hypostatic union in a certain distant way: a priestly character assimilating him to what is proper to the Son, and thus giving him an instrumental spiritual power to perpetuate Christ's saving activity through time.

Priestly character is very important for Aquinas's theology of the priesthood; our brief treatment cannot do it justice. At the risk of losing the trinitarian thread of our argument, one further point deserves mention. While it is true that, for St. Thomas, sacramental character grants to the priest an instrumental power for the conferral of sacramental grace, we should not forget that this is part of the sacramental economy that depends on *sacramental signs*.[59] The priest's sacramental character is what makes him able to make, by his actions, valid sacramental signs in Christian worship—for example, speaking the words of institution at Mass. In making those signs, the priest becomes an instrumental cause of grace because of his character. Note, however, that the character itself is a sacramental reality that depends on signs. Here, we find a connection to the Church's teaching on reserving ordination to men. It has to do with the sign involved in priestly ministry: in the context of Christian worship, priestly character makes a man able to serve as *a sign of Christ*, the divine Son made man, who is the principal agent of each priestly act. We also see a reason for priests to live their lives in close imitation of Christ, who himself was chaste for the sake of the kingdom of God. From a Thomistic perspective, priestly celibacy is not only functional—to make priests more available for a ministry of service—but more importantly serves to configure them better and more deeply to Christ through a complete consecration of the man and his power of generativity.

Let us return to the trinitarian dimension, and specifically to the Father. If priestly character configures a man to the Son who is the Father's eternal character and Image, then the ministerial priest's actions likewise point to the Father, just as Christ's priesthood is entirely relative to and oriented to the Father. And this is precisely what we see in, for example, the priest's words in the Eucharistic Prayer of the Mass, which he speaks to the Father *in persona Christi*.

This brings us to the Holy Spirit. Here, we must speak of what Aquinas and other medieval theologians call the *res tantum* or ultimate fruit of holy orders, the grace of priestly holiness. Aquinas distinguishes this grace from priestly character, which is the *res et sacramentum* of the sacrament. Character is a permanent mark on the soul, and so it remains even if a priest falls into grave sin and is therefore deprived of sanctifying grace.[60] (Such a priest can still validly celebrate the sacraments, although Aquinas holds that, in most circumstances, he commits a further sin if he does so.)[61]

By contrast, the *res tantum* of the priesthood is a modality of sanctifying grace. In holy orders, sanctifying grace is deployed in a man's life in a new way, so that he is not only made apt to worship God as a member of Christ's Body (by the grace of baptism), but also to do so as a priestly mediator, as a holy instrument of Christ the high priest, sharing in Christ's headship.[62]

> To be fit to exercise holy orders, not just any amount of goodness is enough; rather, excelling goodness is needed, so that, as those who receive holy orders are established in a degree of order above the people, they may also be higher by the merit of their holiness. Hence...in the reception of holy orders itself, a greater gift of grace is given through which they are rendered fit for greater things.[63]

Just as a *habitus* is needed on the natural level for a man to use his natural powers virtuously and well, so also a new *habitus* of grace is needed for a priest to employ the sacred power of the priesthood (that is, his priestly character) virtuously and well.[64]

This parallels how Aquinas speaks of Christ's fullness of habitual grace, the necessary complement to the hypostatic union. Because that union did not change the human nature of Christ, his humanity needed to be elevated in a way proportioned to it (that is, by habitual grace), to dispose it as a human nature to act as an instrument of his divinity.[65] And St. Thomas is explicit that the fullness of grace in Christ is synonymous with Christ's full possession of the Holy Spirit as man.

This should also make us think of the texts quoted earlier, from Aquinas's commentary on Hebrews. Christ as man is the perfect high priest who is anointed by the Holy Spirit. As mediator between God and humanity, Christ thus pours out the Holy Spirit on the faithful. He does this in the sacramental economy by giving his priests a share in the Holy Spirit which he possesses in full. On this point, we can now add an evocative text from Aquinas's *Commentary on the Gospel of John*. Jesus breathes out the Spirit upon the apostles and commissions them to forgive sins, Aquinas says, "to designate the propagation of grace in the sacraments, whose ministers they were."[66] And Jesus "makes them fit for this office by giving them the Holy Spirit."[67] It is precisely the same phrase we have already seen: Christ gives priests a special habitual gift of the Spirit (a modality of sanctifying grace, the *res tantum* of holy orders) so that they become fit to use well their priestly character for the salvation of the faithful.

One final text is worthy of mention because it is beautifully evocative for a priestly spirituality. Commenting on Hebrews 5:1–2 (a high priest "offer[s] gifts and sacrifices for sins" and "deals gently with the ignorant and wayward"), Aquinas explains, "As through the devotion of prayer [a priestly mediator] should touch God as one extreme, thus through mercy and compassion he should touch the other extreme, namely, man."[68] In Aquinas's theology, devotion refers to the interior act of religion, which is prompted by charity, that is, love for God. Mercy and compassion are likewise prompted by love for one's neighbor. In both cases, the Holy Spirit, who is love in person, is rightly identified as the source for these priestly acts of ascending and descending mediation. They are acts made first by Christ, which ministerial priests are called to imitate as the Holy Spirit sets them on fire with love for God and neighbor.

NOTES

1. Thomas Aquinas, *Summa Theologiae [STh.]* III, q. 22, a. 4. Unless otherwise noted, all references to works of Aquinas are to the Leonine edition; where no Leonine text is available, I have indicated the edition used. All translations are mine.

2. *STh* III, q. 63, a. 3: "Totus autem ritus christianae religionis derivatur a sacerdotio Christi."

3. For a discussion of the spiritual priesthood of the faithful in Aquinas, see G. Emery, "Le sacerdoce spiritual des fidèles chez saint Thomas d'Aquin," *Revue Thomiste* 99 (1999): 211–43; M. Morard, "Sacerdoce du Christ et sacerdoce des chrétiens dans le Commentaire des Psaumes de saint Thomas d'Aquin," *Revue Thomiste* 99 (1999): 119–42; B.-D. de La Soujeole, "Les tria munera Christi: Contribution de saint Thomas à la recherche contemporaine," *Revue Thomiste* 99 (1999): 67–70.

4. See D. Legge, *The Trinitarian Christology of St Thomas Aquinas* (Oxford: Oxford University Press, 2017).

5. As Torrell explains, Aquinas places it among "the realities 'consequent' upon the hypostatic union (qq. 16–26)," which deal with "the mystery of the Incarnation in itself, by which God became man for our salvation." Thus, "Thomas here understands the priesthood as one of the consequences of the hypostatic union with regard to Christ considered in his relation to God the Father." J.-P. Torrell, *Christ and Spirituality in St. Thomas Aquinas*, trans. Bernhard Blankenhorn (Washington, DC: The Catholic University of America Press, 2011), 129–30. See also G. Remy, "Sacerdoce et médiation chez saint Thomas," *Revue Thomiste* 99 (1999): 101–17; S.-Th. Bonino, "Le sacerdoce comme institution naturelle selon saint Thomas d'Aquin," *Revue Thomiste* 99 (1999): 41–57.

6. Torrell, *Christ and Spirituality*, 127.

7. Torrell, *Christ and Spirituality*, 127.

8. *STh* III, q. 22, a. 1: "Proprium officium sacerdotis est esse mediatorem inter Deum et populum: inquantum scilicet divina populo tradit...et iterum inquantum preces populi Deo offert, et pro eorum peccatis Deo aliqualiter satisfacit; unde Apostolus dicit, *Heb.* 5: *Omnis pontifex ex hominibus assumptus, pro hominibus constituitur in his quae sunt ad Deum, ut offerat dona et sacrificia pro peccatis.* Hoc autem maxime convenit Christo."

9. *STh* III, q. 26, a. 2.

10. *STh* III, q. 22, a. 3 ad 1.

11. *In Epist. ad Hebr.* c. 5, lect. 2 (No. 259). [*Super Epistolam ad Hebraeos Lectura*, in *Super Epistolas S. Pauli Lectura*, vol. 2, ed. R. Cai (Torino e Roma: Marietti, 1953)].

12. La Soujeole, "Les tria munera Christii," 70–71.

13. Legge, *Trinitarian Christology*, 111–22.

14. See, e.g., *STh* I, q. 43, a. 7 ad 6; *In Epist. ad Rom.* c. 1, lect. 4 (No. 73) [*Super Epistolam ad Romanos Lectura* in *Super Epistolas S. Pauli Lectura*, vol. 1, ed. R. Cai (Torino-Roma: Marietti, 1953)]. See also Legge, *Trinitarian Christology*, 131–71.

15. *In Epist. ad Hebr.* c. 1, lect. 4 (No. 63): "*Propterea*, etc. In verbis istis agitur de spirituali unctione, quia Christus est repletus Spiritu sancto…in ipsa conceptione fuit plenus Spiritu sancto, Io. I, 14: *Plenum gratia et veritate*….Quasi dicat: Ad hoc quod illa haberes, scilicet thronum perpetuum, virgam aequitatis, etc., quae dicta sunt, propter ea unxit te Deus oleo, scilicet sanctificationis, quod Dominus mandavit fieri, Ex. XXX, 24 ss.: quo ungebantur vasa et sacerdotes, Lev. VIII, 2 et IX, v. 1 s., et reges, ut patet de David, I Reg. c. XVI, 13, et Salomone, III Reg. I, 39; item Prophetae, ut patet de Eliseo, III Reg. XIX, v. 16."

16. *In Epist. ad Hebr.* c. 1, lect. 4 (No. 64).

17. *In Epist. ad Hebr.* c. 1, lect. 4 (No. 66): "Christus non sit unctus secundum quod Deus,…tamen unctus est in quantum homo."

18. *In Epist. ad Hebr.* c. 1, lect. 4 (No. 66): "Unxit te Deus per se ipsum Deum, nos autem per te, mediatorem Dei et hominum, hominem Christum."

19. See, e.g., *STh* I-II, q. 108, a. 1; III, q. 8. aa. 1, 5; *Compendium Theologiae* I, c. 215; *In Ioan.* c. 1, lect. 10 (Nos. 201–2) [*Super Evangelium S. Ioannis Lectura*, ed. R. Cai (Torino-Roma: Marietti, 1952)]; *In Epist. ad Tit.*c.3, lect. 1 (No. 93) [*Super Epistolam ad Titum Lectura*, in *Super Epistolas S. Pauli Lectura*, vol. 2, ed. R. Cai (Torino-Roma: Marietti, 1953)]; *In Epist. ad Col.* c. 1, lect. 5 (No. 50) [*Super Epistolam ad Colossenses Lectura*, in *Super Epistolas S. Pauli Lectura*, vol. 2, ed. R. Cai (Torino-Roma: Marietti, 1953)].

20. This same element is also found at *In Psalm.* 44 (No. 5) [*In Psalmos Davidis Expositio*, in *Opera omnia*, vol. 14 (Parma: Typis Petri Fiaccadori, 1863)] and *In Epist. ad. II Cor.* c. 1, lect. 5 (No. 44) [*Super Secundam Epistolam ad Corinthios Lectura* in *Super Epistolas S. Pauli Lectura*, vol. 1, ed. R. Cai (Torino-Roma: Marietti, 1953)].

21. *In Epist. ad Hebr.* c. 1, lect. 4 (No. 64): "Et convenit sibi ungi oleo sanctificationis et exultationis. Ab ipso autem sunt sacramenta, quae sunt vasa gratiae."

22. *STh* III, q. 22, a. 1.

23. *In Epist. ad Hebr.* c. 1, lect. 4 (No. 65): "Sed quae comparatio est inter Christum unctum, et christianos unctos? Ista, scilicet quia ipse habet eam principaliter et primo, nos autem et alii ab ipso effusam. Ps. CXXVII: *Sicut unguentum in capite*, etc. Et dicit *prae participibus tuis*. Io. c. I, 16: *De plenitudine eius omnes accepimus*. Unde alii dicuntur sancti, ipse vero sanctus sanctorum. Ipse enim est radix omnis sanctitatis."

24. *In Epist. Ad Hebr.* c. 8, lect. 1 (No. 382): "Hoc autem excellentius habet Christus, qui est minister, non quidem inquantum Deus, quia sic est auctor, sed inquantum homo….Humanitas enim Christi est sicut organum divinitatis.

Est ergo *minister sanctorum*, quia ministrat sacramenta gratiae in praesenti, et gloriae in futuro....Homo autem Christus minister est, quia omnia bona gloriae per ipsum dispensantur."

25. *In Epist. ad Ephes.*c. 1, lect. 8 (No. 71): "Omnes sensus spirituales, et dona, et quid quid potest esse in ecclesia, quae omnia super abundanter sunt in Christo, ab ipso deriventur in membra ecclesiae." [*Super Epistolam ad Ephesios Lectura*, in *Super Epistolas S. Pauli Lectura*, vol. 2, ed. R. CAI (Torino-Roma: Marietti, 1953).]

26. *In Epist. ad Hebr.* c. 13, lect. 2 (No. 744): "Ipse Christus, in quo, et per quem preces nostras offerimus."

27. *In Epist. ad Hebr.* c. 9, lect. 5 (No. 466): "*Ut appareat pro nobis vultui Dei*. Et loquitur Apostolus alludendo ritui veteris legis, secundum quam pontifex qui intrabat sancta sanctorum, stabat coram propitiatorio ut oraret pro populo: ita et Christus intravit caelum, secundum quod homo, ut astaret Deo pro salute nostra."

28. *In Epist. ad Hebr.* c. 7, lect. 4 (No. 373): "Interpellat pro nobis... *apud Patrem*...sanctissimae animae suae desiderium, quod de salute nostra habuit exprimendo."

29. *In Epist. ad Hebr.* c. 7, lect. 4 (No. 373).

30. *In Epist. ad Hebr.* c. 5, lect. 1 (No. 255): "Actus autem eius fuit, quia obtulit *preceset supplicationes.* Hoc est spirituale sacrificium, quod Christus obtulit....Ad quem? *Ad Deum*, scilicet Deum Patrem....Ad istud sacrificium spirituale ordinatur sacerdotium Christi." See A. GUGGENHEIM, *Jésus Christ, Grand Prêtre de l'ancienne et de la nouvelle Alliance: Étude du Commentaire de saint Thomas d'Aquin sur l'Épître aux Hébreux* (Paris: Parole et Silence, 2004), 297–306.

31. *In Epist. ad Hebr.* c. 5, lect. 1 (No. 256): "Non tamen flevit pro se, sed pro nobis."

32. See, e.g., *STh* III, q. 7, a. 13. Though the Holy Spirit is present in Christ according to charity, the gift of charity is efficiently caused in his human nature by all three divine persons acting inseparably. Attributing Christ's prayer to the Holy Spirit as a matter of efficient causality, therefore, is done by appropriation. In terms of exemplar causality, however, the Holy Spirit is the proper (personal) cause of charity.

33. See, e.g., *In Ioan.* c. 17, lect. 1 (No. 2180) (Christ prays to the Father out of love); *In Epist. ad Rom.* c. 8, lect. 5 (No. 694) (the Holy Spirit prompts the saints to desire what God wills, citing Christ's prayer at Gethsemane as an example of this). Further, following Heb 9:14, Aquinas affirms that, in his passion, moved by charity, Jesus offers himself to the Father through the Spirit. *De Pot.*, q. 10, a. 4 [*Quaestiones Disputatae de Potentia*, in *Quaestiones Disputatae*, vol. 2, ed. P. BAZZI, M. CALCATERRA, T. S. CENTI, E. ODETTO, and P.M. PESSION (Torino-Roma: Marietti, 1949)]; *In Epist. ad Hebr.* c. 9, lect. 14 (No. 444); *STh* III, q. 47, a. 3.

34. *STh* III, q. 7, a. 6: "In Christo fuit timor Dei... prout scilicet anima Christi quodam affectu reverentiae movebatur in Deum, a Spiritu Sancto acta. Unde *Heb.* V dicitur quod in omnibus *exauditus est pro sua reverentia.*"

35. *In Epist. ad Hebr.* c. 9, lect. 14 (No. 444): "[C]ausam quare Christus sanguinem suum fudit, quia hoc fuit Spiritus sanctus, cuius motu et instinctu, scilicet charitate Dei, et proximi, hoc fecit. Is. LIX, 19: Cum venerit quasi fluvius violentus quem Spiritus Domini cogit. Spiritus autem mundat.... Et ideo dicit per spiritum sanctum obtulit semetipsum. Eph V, 2: Christus dilexit nos, et tradidit semetipsum pro nobis oblationem et hostiam Deo in odorem suavitatis."

36. St. Thomas mentions charity, in particular, but we might wonder whether the gifts of the Holy Spirit are not also implied, since they endow the soul with a special divine "instinct," according to Aquinas.

37. *STh* III, q. 48, a. 3: "Hoc ipsum opus, quod voluntarie passionem sustinuit, fuit Deo maxime acceptum, utpote ex caritate proveniens. Unde manifestum est quod passio Christi fuit verum sacrificium." See also *In Epist. ad Rom.* c. 12, lect. 1 (Nos. 959–63).

38. Much more could be said on this score—for example, about Christ's love of God and neighbor manifested on the cross, about the importance of Christ's human desire for our salvation (e.g., "I thirst"), about how the Holy Spirit moves Christ's prayer in the garden and on the cross, and about how, in all this, Christ abides in the Father's love.

39. *In Epist. ad Hebr.* c. 8, lect. 1. (No. 384): "*Omnis pontifex* ad hoc *constituitur, ut offerat munera et hostias*... Christus autem est pontifex.... Ergo... [q]uia vero necesse fuit Christum habere quod offerret, ipse seipsum obtulit.... Item fuit congrua, quia congruum est, quod homo pro homine satisfaciat.... Item unit Deo illos pro quibus offertur. Io. XVII, 21: *Ut omnes unum sint, sicut tu, Pater, in me, et ego in te, ut et ipsi in nobis unum sint.*"

40. See, e.g., B.-D. de La Soujeole, "De l'actualité des missions visibles du Fils et de l'Esprit," *Revue Thomiste* 113 (2013): 399–410.

41. *STh* III, q. 1, a. 3 ad 1.

42. *ScG* IV, c. 74: "Quia igitur Christus corporalem sui praesentiam erat Ecclesiae subtracturus, necessarium fuit ut alios institueret sibi ministros, qui sacramenta fidelibus dispensarent.... data est enim eis *ad Ecclesiae aedificationem*, secundum Apostoli dictum. Tandiu igitur oportet hanc potestatem perpetuari... post mortem discipulorum Christi usque ad saeculi finem." See J. Yocum, "Sacraments in Aquinas," in *Aquinas on Doctrine*, ed. Th. Weinandy, D. Keating, and J. Yocum (New York: T&T Clark, 2004), 165–68.

43. *STh* I, q. 47, a. 1.

44. *STh* I, q. 47, a. 1: "Produxit enim res in esse propter suam bonitatem communicandam creaturis, et per eas repraesentandam. Et quia per unam creaturam sufficienter repraesentari non potest, produxit multas creaturas et diversas, ut quod deestuni ad repraesentandam divinam bonitatem, suppleatur ex alia, nam

bonitas quae in Deo est simpliciter et uniformiter, in creaturis est multipliciter et divisim. Unde perfectius participat divinam bonitatem, et repraesentat eam, totum universum, quam alia quaecumque creatura."

45. IV *Sent.* d. 24, q. 2. a. 1, qla 1: "Ordinum multitudo inducta est in Ecclesia...propter sapientiam Dei commendandam, quae in distinctione ordinata rerum maxime relucet tam in naturalibus quam in spiritualibus." [*Opera omnia,* vol. 7/2 (Parma: Typis Petri Fiaccadori, 1858).]

46. IV *Sent.* d. 24, q. 1 a. 1 qla 1: "Deus sua opera in sui similitudinem perducere voluit, quantum possibile fuit, ut perfecta essent, et per ea cognosci posset; et ideo ut in suis operibus repraesentaretur non solum quod in se est, sed etiam secundum quod aliis influit, hanc legem naturalem posuit omnibus, ut ultima per media perficerentur, et media per prima, ut Dionysius dicit. Et ideo, ut ista pulchritudo Ecclesiae non deesset, posuit ordinem in ea, ut quidam aliis sacramenta traderent, suo modo Deo in hoc assimilati, quasi Deo cooperantes, sicut etiam in corpore naturali quaedam membra aliis influunt."

47. IV *Sent.* d. 24, q. 1 a. 1 qla 1 ad 1: "Servitus est quando aliquis dominatur ad sui utilitatem subjectis utens. Talis autem subjectio non requiritur in ordine, per quem qui praesunt salutem subditorum quaerere debent, non propriam utilitatem."

48. *In Epist. ad Hebr.* c. 7, lect. 2 (No. 343): "Sacerdos autem tantum est minister. Unde non agit nisi in virtute Christi. I Cor. c. IV, 1: *Sic nos existimet homo, ut ministros Christi, et dispensatores ministeriorum Dei....*Item non agit auctoritate propria, sed auctoritate Christi."

49. IV *Sent.* d. 24, q. 1, a. 2 qla 1 ad 1: "Ordo datur non in remedium unius personae, sed totius Ecclesiae."

50. *ScG* IV, c. 74: "Minister autem comparatur ad dominum sicut instrumentum ad principale agens....Oportet autem instrumentum esse proportionatum agenti. Unde et ministros Christi oportet esse ei conformes."

51. *ScG* IV, c. 74: "Christus autem, ut Dominus, auctoritate et virtute propria nostram salutem operatus est, in quantum fuit Deus et homo: ut secundum id quod homo est, ad redemptionem nostram pateretur; secundum autem quod Deus, passio eius nobis fieret salutaris."

52. *ScG* IV, c. 74: "Oportet igitur et ministros Christi homines esse, et aliquid divinitatis eius participare secundum aliquam spiritualem potestatem: nam et instrumentum aliquid participat de virtute principalis agentis."

53. On this point, see, e.g., Colman O'Neill, "The Instrumentality of the Sacramental Character: An Interpretation of *Summa Theologiae*, III, q. 63, a. 2," *Irish Theological Quarterly* 25 (1958): 262–68; C. O'Neill, "The Role of the Recipient and Sacramental Signification," *The Thomist* 21 (1958): 257–301; 508–40. See also G. Mansini, "A Contemporary Understanding of St. Thomas on Sacerdotal Character," *The Thomist* 71 (2007): 171–98.

54. IV *Sent.* d. 4, q. 1, a. 3 qla 5 ad 1: "Ipse fuit sacerdos, quasi sacerdotium instituens. Et ideo ejus non est habere characterem." [*Scriptum super libros Sententiarum*, ed. MARIA FABIANUS MOOS (Paris: Lethielleux, 1947).]

55. *STh* III, q. 63, a. 3 sc. Aquinas seems to be aware that, in Heb 1:3, the Greek word underlying the Latin *figura* is *χαρακτὴρ*.

56. *In Epist. ad Hebr.* c. 1, lect. 2 (Nos. 27–29). Aquinas identifies the term "figure" or "character" as a synonym for the Son's proper name of Image. See also Gilles Emery, *The Trinitarian Theology of St. Thomas Aquinas*, trans. Francesca Aran Murphy (Oxford: Oxford University Press, 2010), 209.

57. IV *Sent.* d. 4, q. 1, a. 4 qla 4. See also *STh* III, q. 63, a. 3. While q. 63, a. 3 does not expressly say that sacramental character assimilates its recipient to a personal property *of the Son* (for example, ad 3 says "the character of Christ"), it seems to be the sense of Aquinas's meaning, especially since this is the direct meaning of the *sed contra,* and of Aquinas's rejection of the objections (which argue that character can be attributed either to the whole Trinity or to the Holy Spirit). This conclusion is reinforced by the fact that *In Epist. ad Hebr.* c. 1, lect. 2 (Nos. 27–29) teaches clearly that "character" is akin to the personal name of Image, which belongs properly to the Son.

58. LEGGE, *Trinitarian Christology*, 111–12.

59. See C. O'NEILL, "The Role of the Recipient and Sacramental Signification," *The Thomist* 21 (1958): 257–301, 508–40.

60. See, e.g., IV *Sent.* d. 24, q. 1, a. 1 qla 1 ad 3.

61. See, e.g., *STh* III, q. 82, a. 5.

62. See, e.g., *STh* III, q. 62, a. 2 & ad 3.

63. IV *Sent.* d. 24, q. 1, a. 2 qla 1 ad 3: "Ad idoneam executionem ordinum non sufficit bonitas quantacumque, sed requiritur bonitas excellens: ut sic ut illi qui ordinem suscipiunt, super plebem constituuntur gradu ordinis, ita et superiores sint meritos anctitatis; et ideo praeexigitur gratia quae sufficiebat ad hoc quod digne connumerarentur in plebe Christi; sed confertur in ipsa susceptione ordinis amplius gratiae munus, per quod ad majora reddantur idonei."

64. *ScG* IV, c. 74. See also M.-J. NICOLAS, "La doctrine de s. Thomas sur le sacerdoce," in *San Tommaso e l'odierna problematica teologica* (Roma: Pontificia Accademia Romana di S. Tommaso d'Aquino, 1974), 319–21.

65. See, e.g., *STh* III, q. 7, a. 1. See also LEGGE, *Trinitarian Christology*, 133–35, 155–57.

66. *In Ioan.* c. 20, lect. 4 (No. 2539): "Ad designandam propagationem gratiae in sacramentis, cuius ipsi ministri errant."

67. *In Ioan.* c. 20, lect. 4 (No. 2538): "Datur eis idoneitas officii per dationem Spiritus sancti."

68. *In Epist. ad Hebr.* c. 5, lect. 1 (No. 246): "Per devotionem orationis debet tangere Deum tamquam unum extremum, sic per misericordiam et compassionem debet tangere alterum extremum, scilicet hominem."

6

THE SIGNIFICANCE OF THE SECOND VATICAN COUNCIL AND PRIESTLY RENEWAL

Father Gabriel Richi Alberti

THE SECOND VATICAN Council, described by St. John Paul II as "the great grace bestowed on the Church in the twentieth century" (*Novo Millennio Ineunte* [NMI] 57), was, in the words of Pope Francis in *Lumen Fidei*,

> a Council on faith, inasmuch as it asked us to restore the primacy of God in Christ to the center of our lives, both as a Church and as individuals. The Church never takes faith for granted, but knows that this gift of God needs to be nourished and reinforced so that it can continue to guide her pilgrim way. The Second Vatican Council enabled the light of faith to illumine our human experience from within, accompanying the men and women of our time on their journey. (*Lumen Fidei* 6)

The Second Vatican Council thus has essential significance when proposing renewed theological reflection on the mystery of the one priesthood of Christ and the double participation by the Church (the common priesthood and the ministerial priesthood) by virtue of the sacramental economy of the Spirit. In this respect it may be stated that the teaching on the mystery of the people of God on its missionary journey (cf. LG I, II, and VII) is the basic framework for priestly renewal in our time.

There are plenty of good studies, both classical and recent, on Vatican II's teaching on the ordained ministry and specifically on the priesthood.[1] Therefore the object of the current paper is not to review the history of the process of drafting the documents, nor the precise content of the Council texts on the priesthood of Christ, of the Christian people, and of ordained ministers, but instead, to identify the main points offered by Vatican II for proposing a priestly renewal in our time.

JESUS CHRIST, THE ONE PRIEST

"Contemplation of the Face of Christ inspired by the Spirit, is the primordial heartbeat, perhaps hidden but infinitely real and dynamic, of Vatican II."[2] In these words, the Dominican Marie-Joseph Le Guillou described what seemed to him the inmost nucleus of the teaching of the Council. His theo-christological view of the Council is noticeably different from the more common view of contemporary theology, which considers the Council to have been basically a Council "about the Church."[3] Le Guillou's view is at one with Pope Francis's invitation to recognize "the primacy of God in Christ," quoted above.

Taking this approach as a starting point seems to identify the true theological and salvation-history perspective proposed by Vatican II for considering the mystery of the Christian priesthood.

It refers specifically to contemplation of the one definitive sacrifice and priesthood of Jesus Christ. The Council teachings take as their starting point the centrality of the New Testament teaching: "The former priests were many in number, because they were prevented by death from continuing in office; but he holds his priesthood permanently, because he continues forever" (Heb 7:23–24); "by a single offering he has perfected for all time those who are sanctified" (Heb 10:14)—a teaching that the healthiest theology has not ceased to underline.[4] The proclamation of the one mediation of Christ needs to be maintained as the central focus of all reflection: "For there is one God, and there is one mediator between God and men, the man Christ Jesus, who gave himself as a ransom for all" (1 Tim 2:5–6).

What perspective is opened to priestly renewal by taking the oneness of Christ's mediation as a starting point?

The trinitarian and historical-salvific perspective implied by this starting point situates theological reflection on the priesthood within what is most specific to our Christian faith. In Christ's paschal gift, made constantly present by the Holy Spirit down through the centuries, God the Father has definitively overcome distance and given us access to his inner life. In the Christian dispensation, which "as the new and definitive covenant, will never pass away" (DV 4), the priesthood is not the expression of an ascending journey to God but is the pathway that God himself has established once and for all in Jesus Christ the Eternal High Priest, who comes out to meet humankind on its journey.[5]

Jesus Christ's mediation, therefore, is one and definitive.[6] That fact radically excludes any concept of the Christian priesthood, whether the common priesthood of God's holy people or the ordained priesthood of sacred ministers, that implies any kind of substitution or replacement of the mediation of Jesus Christ.[7] The importance of this for ecumenism is immediately obvious.[8] In this regard it is worth quoting some truly illuminating words by Benedict XVI:

> The priest, who acts *in persona Christi Capitis* and representing the Lord, never acts in the name of someone who is absent but, rather, in the very Person of the Risen Christ, who makes himself present with his truly effective action. He really acts today and brings about what the priest would be incapable of: the consecration of the wine and the bread so that they may really be the Lord's presence, and the absolution of sins. The Lord makes his own action present in the person who carries out these gestures.[9]

A fundamental theology of the priesthood must necessarily, therefore, take the affirmation of the one mediation of Christ as a constant checking and underpinning all its formulations and proposals.

The Council texts reflect this perspective through their insistence on the consecration and mission of Jesus Christ as coordinates of their teaching on the priesthood (cf. LG 28; PO 2).[10]

HISTORY AND MISSION

The second key that the Council teaching offers for proposing a fundamental theology of the priesthood involves what has been called the "pastoral character" of Vatican II.[11]

This expression refers to the salvation-history and missionary perspective that guided the work of the Council from its announcement by St. John XXIII onward. It needs to be recognized that the essential standpoint for thinking about the pilgrim Church, that is, the path in history that the people of God is called to follow from the Lord's ascension until the Parousia, necessarily entails mission. This is clearly stated by the Decree *Ad Gentes*: "The pilgrim Church is missionary by its very nature" (AG 2).

This perspective of mission is essential in thinking about the double participation in the one priesthood of Christ, because both modes of participation, which as we shall see spring from the sacramental economy, can be correctly understood based on the missionary perspective, which essentially characterizes the Church on her journey through history.[12]

Two significant quotations from the magisterium of the Council are particularly relevant here. In the first place, on setting out the foundations of the apostolic succession, the Constitution *Lumen Gentium* clearly states its historical dimension: "That divine mission, entrusted by Christ to the apostles, will last until the end of the world (Matt 28:20), since the Gospel they are to teach is for all time the source of all life for the Church" (LG 20).[13] Without history, without mission, there would be no apostolic participation in the one priesthood of Christ. Therefore—and this is the second quotation to be noted—the title chosen for the first chapter of the Decree on the Ministry and Life of Priests is very much to the point: "The Priesthood in the Ministry of the Church" (cf. PO 2–3).[14] It highlights the radical importance of the Decree's first chapter, and prevents it from being read as a mere preliminary note to all that the Decree teaches about priests' ministry and spirituality.[15]

THE EVER-PRESENT CHARACTER OF CHRIST'S MEDIATION

Taking together the two focal points identified so far—the one priesthood of Christ and the essential link or bond between history and mission—leads directly to the question, In the course of the centuries, until the Lord comes, how is the one, indefectible priestly mediation of Jesus Christ offered indefectibly to the freedom of humanity?

The Second Vatican Council answered this question through its teaching on the Church as the universal sacrament of salvation.[16] *Gaudium et Spes* is a paradigmatic text on this topic: "Every benefit which the People of God during its earthly pilgrimage can offer to the human family stems from the fact that the Church is 'the universal sacrament of salvation,' simultaneously manifesting and exercising the mystery of God's love" (45).

To be able to speak accurately of the contemporary, ever-present character of the one mediation of Christ through the ages, any account must include the essential characteristics of the one mediation of Christ; and at the same time must not involve replacing it with anything else. It is the Holy Spirit who makes this ongoing dynamic possible through the sacramental economy.

These conditions are fulfilled by the sacramental origin and nature of the double participation in Christ's priesthood.[17]

This is because the way the sacraments work is diametrically opposed to the notion of replacing one thing by another.[18] The sacramental representation exists insofar as the difference between the one represented and the person representing him remains; but the person representing him is not a mere reference to the one represented, but the effective mode of his presence at a given historical moment.[19]

By virtue of the sacraments of Christian initiation, Christians are con-corporated with Christ, that is, made members of the priestly people.[20] When we speak, therefore, of the common priesthood, we are always mindful of the fact that the subject of this participation in the one priesthood of Christ is properly the people of God.[21] In the context of the present reflection on a fundamental theology of the priesthood, it could be said that ultimately the fact of the common priesthood of all the faithful, or, to use the term I prefer, the priestly people, is the same as the fact that the Church "is in Christ like a sacrament or as a sign and instrument both of a very closely knit union with God and of the unity of the whole human race" (LG 1; see also LG 9 and 48). Thus, the permanent presence of Christ's mediation throughout history corresponds precisely with the existence of the Church as a priestly people.

And, to ensure this priestly existence of the people of God unfailingly, Christ himself endowed the Church with the sacrament of holy orders as a permanent guarantee of its priestly existence, and that's the origin of the apostolic ministry.[22] This sacramental ministry assures the personal action of the risen Christ in the Church.[23]

The sacramental origin and nature of the double participation in the priesthood of Christ clearly mean that only through the gift and work of the Holy Spirit, without whom there can be no sacramental economy,[24] can there be any participation in Christ's priesthood. This is always and only a participation granted by the Spirit and given indefectibly—this is why we speak of the "sacramental character" for Baptism, confirmation, and holy orders. At the same time, both participations make of the Church a priestly people with certain faithful among of this people[25] as ordained ministers at the service of their brethren.[26] The teachings on the sacramentality of the people of God, and on the apostolic ministry with its sacramental origin, show how effectively the anthropological and sacramental dimensions of the Christian economy come together.[27]

In this context the statements of the Constitution *Lumen Gentium* on the common priesthood and the ministerial priesthood shine out in all their authentic truth:

> Though they differ from one another in essence and not only in degree, the common priesthood of the faithful and the ministerial or hierarchical priesthood are nonetheless interrelated: each of them in its own special way is a participation in the one priesthood of Christ. The ministerial priest, by the sacred power he enjoys, teaches and rules the priestly people; acting in the person of Christ, he makes present the Eucharistic sacrifice, and offers it to God in the name of all the people. But the faithful, in virtue of their royal priesthood,

> join in the offering of the Eucharist. They likewise exercise that priesthood in receiving the sacraments, in prayer and thanksgiving, in the witness of a holy life, and by self-denial and active charity" (LG 10).[28] In fact, the common priesthood and the ministerial priesthood are two participations in the one priesthood of Christ that are essentially different, since their sacramental origins are different—Christian initiation (Baptism) in the one case, and Holy Orders in the other. The ministerial or hierarchical priesthood exists to serve the common priesthood.[29]

Thus, the starting point for a fundamental theology of the priesthood is the one priesthood of Christ, in which, in the perspective of mission—which is to say, understood through the key of salvation history—the people of God shares as a priestly people, guaranteed indefectibly to be such by virtue of the ministerial priesthood conferred by the sacrament of holy orders.[30]

In the light of what has been said so far, we can see that reflection on the priestly people—what is normally termed the "common or baptismal priesthood"—is in fact a deepening in the mystery of the Church as such, that is, the mystery of the people of God as the universal sacrament of salvation.[31] This ecclesial subject—the "who" of the church—possesses a characteristic form of its own deriving from its trinitarian origin: the form of *communio*. This form characterizes all ecclesial expressions by the very fact of being ecclesial.[32] The mystery of the Church as the people of God, universal sacrament of salvation (which includes the images of the Body of Christ and the temple of the Holy Spirit), lets us answer the question of "who" the Church is, and think the *communio* like his specific form. It thus resolves undue conflicts and takes up the most valuable aspects of postconciliar ecclesiological thought.[33]

THE MINISTERIAL PRIESTHOOD

Against the background of the priestly people and its mission, it is now opportune to consider in more detail the renewal that Council teaching offers to theology, to the exercise of the priestly ministry and to its spirituality, with reference to the ordained priesthood.

If we consider the development of Christian reflection on the ordained ministry, especially on the basis of medieval theological synthesizing, three different aspects have been progressively juxtaposed: cultural, sacral, and ministerial dimensions. These correspond to three separate interests: dogmatic theology, spirituality, and pastoral practice.[34] So that, while theology, from the standpoint of worship, stressed the connection between Eucharist and priesthood more and more, from the viewpoint of spirituality, thinkers developed a sacral view of the priest understood as "mediator"—obviously to nurture ministers' personal holiness[35]—while in the sphere of pastoral practice the view of the ordained ministry as *amoris officium* was making headway. Clearly, these three lines of reflection on the priestly ministry held plenty of valuable elements, but it should be underlined that in practice, they had developed in parallel or even in fundamental juxtaposition. It may be felt that only the great priests who were canonized saints were capable, at least to a certain degree, although not always explicitly, of restoring the unity between theology, spirituality, and ministry.

It seems, then, that the great contribution of Council teaching on the ordained ministry was precisely to restore the unity between theology, spirituality, and ministry, offering us a complete, harmonious figure of the ordained ministry in the mission of the Church.[36]

We can now look at the essential features of this unified figure.[37]

A first reference, which I consider fundamental, is found in the description of the sacraments offered in the Constitution *Lumen Gentium* on the people of God (11). It explains how the seven sacraments (which imply the use of human freedom, since the sacraments are always *sacramenta fidei* [cf. SC 59]) build up ecclesial communion and display it in history, and so originate the different vocations and states of life in the Church. Indeed, "it is through the sacraments and the exercise of the virtues that the sacred nature and organic structure of the priestly community is brought into operation" (LG 11). After describing what Christians are by reference to the sacraments of initiation and the dynamic of reconciliation that accompanies them on their way (sacraments of healing), the document goes on to consider what the Catechism of the Catholic Church calls "the sacraments at the service of communion."[38] We are then offered a brief theological description of the sacrament that is at the origin of ministry: "Those of the faithful who are consecrated by Holy Orders are appointed to feed the Church in Christ's name with the word and the grace of God" (LG 11).

The first element to highlight is the fact that Vatican II describes the ordained ministry as a part of the priestly community that is the Church, thereby recognizing that its origin does not lie in the sacraments of Christian initiation but specifically in the sacrament of holy orders. As can easily be understood, we are looking at a further expression of the teaching from *Lumen Gentium* 10 referred to above.

This sacramental perspective of Vatican II underlines, once again, the fact that that Council proposed that the ordained ministry should be considered *in missione Ecclesiae*.[39] Thus, while the fundamental reference-point of the priesthood is always Christology, in that it deals with a specific participation in the one priesthood of Christ,[40] its nature is at the same time intrinsically one of communion and mission.[41]

This double nature—of communion and of mission—translates into an understanding of the priesthood in terms of ministry or service, that is, in an essentially *diaconal* understanding.[42] The *sacra potestas* that is received in the sacrament bestows on the ordained subject the capacity to carry out the actions of his ministry, and its scope and reason for being lie in service of the people of God. Its scope corresponds exactly to the historical mode of the priesthood of Christ, who "did not come to be served but to serve, and to give his life as a ransom for many" (Mark 10:45). The very "being-for" of Jesus Christ, who understood and lived out his mission in the light of the songs of the Suffering Servant,[43] clearly shows the need to think of the priesthood in terms of ministry, service. "The ministerial priesthood is defined as a *service to the mission of Christ in the Church* and is only justified by service to the People of God."[44] Accordingly it can be stated that the priest, by virtue of the sacrament of holy orders, exercises a ministry of service with respect to his brothers and sisters, without that implying any superiority. In this regard, Ratzinger noted very discerningly, years ago, "In so far as [the priest] left his position as servant and acted as lord, he descended to the pre-Christian and anti-Christian level; he rejected what was specific to the New Testament. No, he can never become lord of others, he will always be a servant towards them."[45] Along the same lines, it can be stated that Mary is also the paradigm of the ordained ministry—as she is of every aspect of the Church (cf. LG 53)—since its configuration is that of pure obedience to the mission received, always fleeing from the temptation of assuming mastery over it.[46]

How is this service performed? What are its specific content and scope? One of the most significant contributions of the Council's teaching is a description of the priestly ministry that considers in a unified way (just as they are presented in the second chapter of the decree *Presbyterorum Ordinis*) its reference to what are called the *tria munera*; its "constitutive relationships" (with the bishop, between priests, and with all the other faithful); and its universal missionary scope. So, the teaching on the ministry is not a study of a priest's *tasks* but a reflection on his "communional" *identity*, without which it is not possible to study the ministry, and on his mission, which obviously has the same extension as the mission of the Church itself, that is, the whole world.

About the *munera* (cf. PO 4–6), Vatican II presents a chronological description of the tasks of announcing the gospel, sanctifying, and shepherding, just as the Constitution *Lumen Gentium* does with regard to the episcopal ministry (cf. LG 25–27), without thereby devaluing the centrality of the Eucharist as the traditional given of all theology of the priesthood.[47] On the contrary, the Council teaching restores to the Eucharist all its theological, ecclesiological, and missionary depth, never reducing it simply to the sphere of worship.[48] This beneficial restoration had already been underlined in *Presbyterorum Ordinis* (2) which after quoting Romans 15:16 speaks of priests as those who "perform the sacred duty of preaching the Gospel, so that the offering of the people can be made acceptable and sanctified by the Holy Spirit" (PO 2).[49]

With regard to what was earlier termed "constitutive relationships" (cf. PO 7–9), it is essential to underline that the Council teaching does not think of them as developments of a virtuous ministry—in other words, it is not a matter of some relationships that the priest has to foster in order to fulfill his ministry satisfactorily—but these relationships belong to the very identity of the ministry as such.[50] That is why Vatican II constantly describes the priest in terms of "cooperators with the bishops."[51] Indeed, their participation in Christ's priesthood by virtue of the sacrament of holy orders is a participation in being "cooperators with the bishops"; in other words, to use the traditional expression, the priesthood is a *secundi meriti munus*.[52] And this is part of their sacramental identity just as much as their participation in Christ's priesthood (cf. LG 28).[53]

Likewise the decree stresses the sacramental fraternity that unites priests with one another, as reflected in the marked preference for the use of the plural *presbyteri* and references to the communional reality of the order of priests or the presbyterium.[54] Finally, priests, who "live on earth with other men as brothers" (PO 3), "are brothers among brothers with all those who have been reborn at the baptismal font. They are all members of one and the same Body of Christ, the building up of which is required of everyone" (PO 9). This communional understanding of the ordained ministry is obviously a powerful antidote against the temptation to clericalism.

Because priests are by their very constitution "cooperators with the bishops" it is possible to understand that the scope of their mission, which includes the *missio ad gentes*, is inscribed on the heart of the ministry, since the bishops are responsible, together with the pope as head of the episcopal college, for the universal Church and its mission (cf. PO 10). Realizing that the universal responsibility for mission is rooted in the priest's identity as cooperator with the bishop helps to ensure a correctly balanced view of the relationship between the particular and universal dimensions of the Church and the way that the priestly ministry is rooted in the local Church (cf. LG 23).

The last element I underline in drawing up a fundamental theology of the priesthood on the basis of the Second Vatican Council is "pastoral charity" as the hinge on which priestly spirituality turns (cf. PO 14).[55] This element has strong connotations of St. Augustine's teaching.[56] The emphasis on pastoral charity, which would be further developed by the magisterium following the Council,[57] highlights how the ministry itself is the main source of the minister's holiness: "Priests who perform their duties sincerely and indefatigably in the Spirit of Christ arrive at holiness by this very fact" (PO 13).[58] Consequently, the universal call to holiness takes concrete shape in the "evangelical radicalism" that is part of the exercise of ministry.[59] Pastoral charity is thus the backbone of the call to ordained ministers to practice the evangelical counsels personally and in their ministry (cf. PO 15–17).[60]

FATHERS, SONS, AND BROTHERS

My intention was simply to present in broad terms the essential coordinates offered by the teachings of Vatican II for proposing a renewal of the priesthood in our time, as the fruit of a fundamental theology of the priesthood. Each of these coordinates merit an entire study dedicated to it, and thank God, there are many such works in contemporary theology.

As already stated, a fundamental theology of the priesthood begins with the doctrinal fact of the one mediation of Jesus Christ, and how that mediation is offered sacramentally by the Spirit down through history for the salvation of the world (the common priesthood and the ministerial priesthood). In this sacramental, communional, and missionary perspective, it is possible to propose a theology of the ordained priesthood in terms of ministry, developed according to the different offices (the *munera*) and the constitutive relationships in the context of the Church's mission in the world. That ministry is, moreover, the source of the ministers' holiness (pastoral charity) with evangelical radicalism as its key, which means the *forma vitae et ministerii* of Christ himself in obedience, celibacy, and poverty.

Both the specific identity of the ministry and the Church's mission in our time demand of priests a life as sons, brothers and fathers, in which all can discover the Church as God's family, since in the Church, as St. Augustine says, "all are to one another fathers, when they look after each other; sons, when they obey each other; and above all brothers, because one and the same Father calls them with his covenant to one and the same inheritance."[61]

NOTES

1. I will list some of the most outstanding ones here. Regarding the Constitution *Lumen Gentium*, in particular 10 and 28: E. J. de Smedt, "El sacerdocio de los fieles," in *La Iglesia del Vaticano II*, ed. G. Baraúna (Barcelona: Juan Flors, 1967), 467–78; J. Giblet, "Sacerdotes de segundo orden," 893–915; G. Philips, *L'Eglise et Son Mystere Au IIe Concile Du Vatican: Histoire, Texte et Commentaire de la Constitution Lumen Gentium* (Paris: Desclée, 1967); P. Hünermann, "Theologischer Kommentar zur dogmatischen Konstitution über die Kirche *Lumen gentium*," in *Herders Theologischer Kommentar zum Zweiten Vatikanischen Konzil* 2, ed. P. Hünermann and B. J. Hilberath (Freiburg: Herder, 2009), 374–79 and 450–56; D. Vitali, "Il popolo di Dio," in *Commentario ai documenti del Vaticano II. Lumen gentium* 2, ed. S. Noceti and R. Repole (Bologna: EDB, 2015), 160–68; S. Noceti, "La costituzione gerarchica della Chiesa e in particolare l'episcopato,"

295–305. Regarding the Decree *Presbyterorum Ordinis*: R. Spiazzi, *Decreto sul ministero e la vita sacerdotale* (Torino: Elledici, 1967); J. Galot, "Le sacerdoce dans la doctrine du Concile," *Nouvelle Revue Théologique* 88 (1966): 1044–61; Y. Congar and J. Frisque, eds., *Les Prêtres* (Paris: Éditions du Cerf, 1968); "Dekret über Dienst und Leben der Priester," in *Lexikon für Theologie und Kirche* 14. *Das Zweite Vatikanische Konzil.* Kommentare Vol. III (Freiburg: Herder, 1986), 127–239; R. Waselynck, *Les prêtres. Élaboration du décret Presbyterorum Ordinis de Vatican II. Histoire et genèse du texte conciliaire* (Paris: Desclée, 1968); P. Delhaye, "Le décret sur les prêtres," *L'Ami du Clergé* 78 (1968): 479–86, 643–48, 664–72; P. J. Cordes, *Sendung zum Dienst. Exegetisch-historische und systematische Studien zum Konzilsdekret "Von Dienst und Leben der Priester,"* Frankfurter Theologische Studien 9 (Frankfurt: Verlag Josef Knecht, 1972); M. Caprioli, *Il decreto conciliare "Presbyterorum Ordinis." Storia—analisi—dottrina* I-II (Rome: Teresianum, 1989–1990); O. Fuchs and P. Hünermann, "Theologischer Kommentar zum Dekret über den Dienst und das Leben der Presbyter *Presbyterorum Ordinis*," in Hünermann and Hilberath, *Herder Theologischer Kommentar zum Zweiten Vatikanischen Konzil* 4, 342–410; E. Castellucci, "Presbyterorum Ordinis. Introduzione e commento," in *Commentario ai documenti del Vaticano II vol. 4. Christus Dominus. Optatam Totius. Presbyterorum Ordinis*, ed. S. Noceti and R. Repole (Bologna: EDB, 2017), 295–474.

2. M.-J. Le Guillou, *El Rostro del Resucitado. Grandeza profética, espiritual y doctrinal, pastoral y misionera del Concilio Vaticano II* (Madrid: Encuentro, 2012); orig. *Le Visage du Ressuscité* (Paris, Éditions Ouvrières, 1968), 59.

3. "Vatican II has gone down in history as the 'council of the Church about the Church,' bearing the standard of renewal and reform within and openness towards the outside, in dialogue with the modern world." S. Madrigal, "El giro eclesiológico en la recepción del Vaticano II," in *Presencia Teológica* 253 (Santander: Sal Terrae, 2017), 29.

4. A single example is St Thomas Aquinas's statement: "Et ideo solus Christus est verus sacerdos, alii autem ministri eius" (And therefore only Christ is the true priest, the others being only his ministers), Thomas Aquinas, *Super Epistolam B. Pauli ad Hebraeos lectura* caput 7, lectio 4. Reportatio vulgata.

5. On the difference between a "ritual sacralisation" and the "sacramental sacredness" of the Christian faith, see S. del Cura Elena, "Novedad del sacerdocio de Jesucristo: radicación trinitaria e implicaciones presbiterales," in *El ministerio presbiteral. Retos y tareas*, ed. J. M. de Miguel González (Salamanca: Publicaciones Universidad Pontificia de Salamanca, 2008), 101–36; here 124–25.

6. "Il ministero apostolico è interamente iscritto nella partecipazione del ministero di Gesù Cristo. Nello stesso tempo, non vi si aggiunge, non vi succede, non lo sostituisce, non lo riproduce in proprio. Il ministero, per entrare subito in argomento, è tutto in questo legame. Il ministero ordinato attualizza precisamente il ministero di Gesù Cristo. [...] Se il Signore non rimanesse l'attore

proprio—unico, singolare, insostituibile—del ministero della chiamata alla fede, della formazione della comunità, dell'offerta della salvezza, nessun altro potrebbe sostituirlo. È il puro e semplice risvolto della fede nell'Unico mediatore e nel Signore risorto" (The apostolic ministry is entirely inscribed in the participation in the ministry of Jesus Christ. At the same time, it is not added to it, it does not succeed it, it does not replace it, it does not reproduce it in itself. The ministry, to get straight to the point, is all in this bond. The ordained ministry specifically actualizes the ministry of Jesus Christ. If the Lord were not always the real subject—one, singular, irreplaceable—of the ministry of the call to faith, the formation of the community, and the offer of salvation, no one else could replace him. All this is purely and simply implied by faith in the One Mediator and in the Risen Lord." P. Sequeri, "L'inserimento del ministero nella Chiesa: mistero, comunione, missione," *Seminarium* 50 (2010): 517–29, here 517. See also Castellucci, "Presbyterorum Ordinis. Introduzione e commento," 322–23.

7. "No man can prescind from Christ in order to reach God; with all the more reason, no man can aim to replace Christ in order to lead other men to God. As mediation is the most specific aspect of priesthood, it is easily understandable why the author [of the Letter to the Hebrews] did not give Christians the title of 'priests'. The only priest in the full sense of the word is Jesus Christ. This is the great novelty of Christianity." A. Vanhoye, *Old Testament Priests and the New Priest according to the New Testament* (St Bede's Publications, 1986 / Gracewing 2009); orig. *Prêtres anciens, prêtre nouveau selon le Nouveau Testament* (Paris: Le Seuil 1980); Spanish *Sacerdotes antiguos, sacerdote nuevo, según el Nuevo Testamento* (Sígueme: Salamanca 1984). 231.

8. Vatican II's Decree on Ecumenism, referring to the centrality of the confession of Christ in ecumenical dialogue, does not hesitate to stress that his mediation is unique: "Our thoughts turn first to those Christians who make open confession of Jesus Christ as God and Lord and as the sole Mediator between God and men, to the glory of the one God, Father, Son and Holy Spirit. We are aware indeed that there exist considerable divergences from the doctrine of the Catholic Church concerning Christ Himself, the Word of God made flesh, the work of redemption, and consequently, concerning the mystery and ministry of the Church, and the role of Mary in the plan of salvation. But we rejoice to see that our separated brethren look to Christ as the source and center of Church unity. Their longing for union with Christ inspires them to seek an ever closer unity, and also to bear witness to their faith among the peoples of the earth" (UR 20).

9. Benedict XVI, *Audience*, April 14, 2010.

10. See Castellucci, "Presbyterorum Ordinis," 347–48.

11. On the pastoral character of Vatican II see A. Scola, *Riforma della Chiesa e primato della fede: Per un'ermeneutica del concilio Vaticano II* (Bologna: EDB, 2014).

12. "The perspective of Vatican II is essentially missionary," S. Madrigal, "Ser sacerdote según el Vaticano II y su recepción postconciliar," in *El ser sacerdotal: fundamentos y dimensiones constitutivas*, ed. G. Uríbarri Bilbao (Madrid: Universidad Pontificia Comillas, 2010), 119–57, here 125. See also: H. Denis, "La Teología del presbiterado desde Trento al Vaticano II," in Congar and Frisque, *Los sacerdotes*, 217–68, here 233–36 (orig. "La théologie du presbytérat, de Trente à Vatican II" in *Les Prêtres: Décrets Presbyterorum ordinis et Optatam totius*, 193–232); Cordes, *Sendung zum Dienst*, 54–55; G. Routhier, "L'écho de l'enseignement de Vatican II sur le presbytérat dans la situation actuelle," *Revue Théologique de Louvain* 41 (2010): 86–112 and 161–79, here 90, 94 & 103; Castellucci, "Presbyterorum Ordinis," 317.

13. "It is notable that from the beginning of Chapter III it is stipulated that the underlying reason for this structure of a "ministerial or hierarchical priesthood" (to quote article 10) is the continuation of Christ's *mission*: the divine mission of announcing the gospel of salvation entrusted by Christ to the Apostles has to last until the end of the world (LG III, 20a)." Madrigal, "Ser sacerdote según el Vaticano II y su recepción postconciliar," 126.

14. See Frisque, "Decreto 'Presbyterorum Ordinis'. Historia y comentario," in Congar and Frisque, *Los sacerdotes*, 144.

15. I consider as insufficient the opinion of J. Ratzinger, in a passage dating from 1967–68, on the structure of *Presbyterorum Ordinis* and the relative importance of each of the three chapters: "The Decree is composed of three chapters: 'The priesthood in the ministry of the church'—'The ministry of priests'—'The life of priests.' The emphasis of the whole is clearly on the second chapter, that is, on the question of the true essence of the priesthood. The first chapter only aims to locate the theme within the setting of Christology and theology in general. Its basic message lies in the observation that that ministry originates in the Paschal Mystery and that it should be understood, in union with all Christian truths, from the heart of that Mystery. From those roots in the Paschal Mystery, from the Cross and the Resurrection, it is also, however, shaped by its orientation to eternal life" J. Ratzinger, "La cuestión del sentido del ministerio sacerdotal," in *Obras completas XII. Predicadores de la palabra y servidores de vuestra alegría* (Madrid: BAC, 2014), 324–61, here 340.

16. See L. Scheffczyk, *La Chiesa. Aspetti della crisi postconciliare e corretta interpretazione del Vaticano II* (Milano: Jaca Book, 1998), 29–42; S. Pié-Ninot, *Eclesiología. La sacramentalidad de la comunidad cristiana* (Salamanca: Sígueme, 2007), 175–210; G. Richi Alberti, *Una débil criatura lleva a Dios. Vademécum de eclesiología* (Madrid: Didaskalos, 2020), 73–86.

17. The Constitution *Sacrosanctum Concilium* recalls in this regard that "to accomplish so great a work, Christ is always present in His Church" (SC 7).

18. Karl Rahner put it very clearly in this significant passage: "Die Tat des menschlichen bevollmächtigten Sakramenten spenders gehört zwar in die Konsti-

tution des *Zeichens* der Gegenwart Christi hinein, der Sakramentenspender vertritt zwar in der Dimension des Zeichens, des wirksamen '*signum*' die Stelle Christi. Da er aber nicht die sakramentale Gnade, die '*res sacramenti*' selbst wirkursächlich im eigentlichen Sinne bewirkt, ersetzt er nicht die Gegenwart Christi selbst. Mit anderen Worten: Der menschliche Spender des Sakramentes vertritt nicht den abwesenden Christus, sondern repräsentiert in der Dimension des (wirksamen) Zeichens den gegenwärtigen Christus, der durch sich selbst in seinem Pneuma die Gnade bewirkt." K. Rahner, "Die Gegenwart des Herrn in der christlichen Kultgemeinde," in *Schriften zur Theologie* VIII (Einsiedeln: Benzinger Verlag, 1967), 395–408, here 403.

19. "*Sacramentalism* is, in all its manifestations and forms, the *identification* of the visible Church with the invisible, of the infallibility of the Pope with the infallibility of Christ, of the liturgy with the event of Jesus Christ. By contrast, *sacramentality* is based on the *distinction* between a signifying plane and another that is signified, between the invisible Church and the visible one, between the authority of Christ and that of the apostolic ministry, between the truth itself and the dogma that signifies that truth. Yet the signifying plane is more than a symbol agreed upon by men. Because where there is a sacrament, the signifying plane, though distinct from the plane that is signified, is nevertheless inseparable from it." K. H. Menke, *Sacramentalidad. Esencia y llaga del catolicismo* (Madrid: BAC 2014), XII–XIV (orig. *Sakramentalität: Wesen und Wunde des Katholizismus*, 4th ed. [Regensburg: Pustet, 2020]).

20. Cf. *Lumen Gentium* 31. It seems more appropriate to make reference to the whole of Christian initiation and not simply, as the Council texts usually do, to baptism. This is because, if the whole process of Christian initiation is considered, reference to the Eucharist, which is the summit of that process, leads directly to consider the common priesthood and the ministerial priesthood as being intrinsically conjoined.

21. Cf. Vanhoye, *Sacerdotes antiguos*, 271–72; G. Colombo, "Il 'Popolo di Dio' e il 'mistero della Chiesa' nell'ecclesiologia postconciliare," *Teologia* 10 (1985): 97–169.

22. Cf. Madrigal, "Ser sacerdote según el Vaticano II y su recepción postconciliar," 137–38 and 150.

23. "The priesthood is in the Church and for the world a sacrament of the personal action of Christ, the Head, Shepherd and Spouse of his Church," A. Chapelle, *Pour la vie du monde. Le sacrement de l'ordre* (Brussels: Institut d'Études Théologiques, 1978), 93. See also: International Theological Commission, *Catholic Teaching on Apostolic Succession* section V; Sequeri, "L'inserimento del ministero nella Chiesa: mistero, comunione, missione," 518.

24. Cf. *Catechism of the Catholic Church* 1076. On the Spirit as key to understanding the ordained ministry see G. Hernández Peludo, "Ministerio del Espíritu y ministros del Espíritu. La dimensión pneumatológica del ministerio

ordenado," in *Deus semper maior. Teología en el horizonte de su verdad siempre más grande. Miscelánea homenaje al Prof. Santiago del Cura Elena*, ed. G. Tejerina and J. Yusta (Salamanca: Secretariado Trinitario, 2021), 1077–1111.

25. There is a very beautiful passage in PO 3 that speaks of priests *in sinu Populi Dei*. In this context I make so bold as to refer to G. Richi Alberti, *In sinu Populi Dei. Espiritualidad presbiteral tras los pasos del Vaticano II*, Subsidia 44 (Madrid: Ediciones Universidad San Dámaso, 2015).

26. Cf. Denis, "La Teología del presbiterado desde Trento al Vaticano II," 246–48.

27. Cf. A. Scola, *Chi è la Chiesa? Una chiave antropologica e sacramentale per l'ecclesiologia* (Brescia: Queriniana, 2008).

28. On the translation "in essence and not only in degree," see: D. VITALI, *Lumen gentium. Storia / Commento / Recezione* (Rome: Studium, 2012), 61–64.

29. Cf. Galot, "Le sacerdoce dans la doctrine du Concile," 1047–49.

30. "Sacrament means: I give what I myself cannot give; I do something that is not my work; I am on a mission and have become the bearer of that which another has committed to my charge. Consequently, it is also impossible for anyone to declare himself a priest or for a community to make someone a priest by its own *fiat*. One can receive what is God's only from the sacrament." J. Ratzinger, "On the Essence of the Priesthood," in *Called to Communion: Understanding the Church Today* (San Francisco: Ignatius, 1996), 115. See also S. Del Cura Elena, "Sacerdocio común y sacerdocio ministerial. El sentido del ministerio ordenado en la Iglesia," in Bilbao, *El ser sacerdotal*, 159–97, especially 178–79; B.-D. de La Soujeole, *Prêtre du Seigneur dans son Église* (Paris: Parole et Silence, 2009), 60.

31. "By his whole life, his teaching, his Cross, and his Resurrection, which communicates the gift of the Spirit, Christ, the one and eternal Priest, has brought to existence a Church, all the members of which constitute a priestly people, the sacrament of salvation for the world." International Theological Commission, "The Priestly Ministry," in *Texts and Documents 1965–1985*, vol. 1 (San Francisco: Ignatius, 1996), 3–90, here 22. Along the same lines Congar says, "*Who* is the sacrament of salvation? The people of God. Where and how? Throughout its whole life, all its lived history in the history of the world. That is why God (the Lord Jesus) gave us his Holy Spirit." Y. Congar, *Un pueblo mesiánico* (Madrid: Cristiandad, 1976), 119 (orig. *Un peuple messianique. L'Église, sacrement du salut*, Salut et libération [Paris: Éditions du Cerf, 1975]).

32. Cf. Richi Alberti, *Una débil criatura lleva a Dios. Vademécum de eclesiología*, 73–100 and 117–31.

33. See Congregation for the Doctrine of the Faith, *Letter to the Bishops of the Catholic Church on some aspects of the Church understood as communion. Communionis notio* (May 28, 1992), No. 1.

34. See E. Castellucci, *Il ministero ordinato*, Nuovo Corso di Teologia Sistematica 10 (Brescia: Queriniana, 2010), 79–207.

35. On this topic, see: J.-F. CHIRON, "Le 'sacerdoce' dans le discours catholique avant Vatican II," *Recherches des Sciences Religieuses* 109 (2021): 239–65.

36. I totally agree with the statement of Cordovilla, "The decree *Presbyterorum ordinis*, read in the perspective of the whole of Vatican II's teaching, contexualised in the new historical situation we are living in, and given depth by the light flowing from studies of Sacred Scripture, continues to be a basic compass for the long-desired renewal of the life of priests and, consequent on that renewal, that of the whole Church." A. CORDOVILLA, *"Como el Padre me envió, así os envío yo." Teología y espiritualidad del ministerio apostólico presbiteral*, Nueva Alianza 247 (Salamanca: Sígueme, 2019), 13. On the deeply unifying concept proposed by the decree, see FRISQUE, "Decreto 'Presbyterorum Ordinis'. Historia y comentario," 178; ROUTHIER, "L'écho de l'enseignement de Vatican II sur le presbytérat dans la situation actuelle," 91; CASTELLUCCI, "Presbyterorum Ordinis," 307.

37. On undertaking this task an obligatory reference is no. 2 of the decree *Presbyterorum Ordinis*. After situating the priesthood in the mission of the Church, as indicated by the title of chapter 1, the five paragraphs of no. 2 set out the relationship between the priesthood of Christ and the Church as a priestly people, the institution and transmission of the ministerial priesthood, the sacramentality of the priesthood, the function of priests in the Church and the theological-anthropological purpose of the ministry and of the life of priests. On the teaching of PO 2, see: FRISQUE, "Decreto 'Presbyterorum Ordinis'. Historia y comentario," 145–51; CAPRIOLI, *Il decreto conciliare "Presbyterorum Ordinis"* I, 53–94; DELHAYE, "Le décret sur les prêtres," 482–86; FUCHS, "Kommentierung," in FUCHS and HÜNERMANN, "Theologischer Kommentar zum Dekret über den Dienst und das Leben der Presbyter. *Presbyterorum Ordinis*," 418–32; G. RAMBALDI, "Natura e missione del presbiterato nel decreto 'Presbyterorum Ordinis' No. 2," *Gregorianum* 50 (1969): 239–60; G. MOIOLI, "Sul ministero presbiterale come ideale di vita," in *Scritti sul prete* (Milano: Glossa, 1998), 148–61, especially 152; CHAPELLE, *Pour la vie du monde*, 271. See further the synthesis offered by St. John Paul II in *Pastores Dabo Vobis* 12–18.

38. Cf. *Catechism of the Catholic Church* 1533–35.

39. Cf. FRISQUE, "Decreto 'Presbyterorum Ordinis'. Historia y comentario," 142 and 149–50; DELHAYE, "Le décret sur les prêtres," 643–44; RAMBALDI, "Natura e missione del presbiterato nel decreto 'Presbyterorum Ordinis,' No. 2," 245.

40. "Reference to Christ is thus the absolutely necessary key for understanding the reality of priesthood." JOHN PAUL II, *Pastores Dabo Vobis* 12.

41. Cf. CASTELLUCCI, "Presbyterorum Ordinis. Introduzione e commento," 297.

42. Cf. CORDES, *Sendung zum Dienst*, 171–76; G. Moioli, "Dogmatica e storia nella 'definizione' del ministero presbiterale," in ID., *Scritti sul prete*, 179–86, especially 184; H. U. VON BALTHASAR, "Existencia sacerdotal," in *Sponsa Verbi*.

Ensayos de teología II (Madrid: Guadarrama, 1964), 449–501; Castellucci, "Presbyterorum Ordinis. Introduzione e commento," 327, 344, and 389; Castellucci, *Il ministero ordinato*, 298–303; Sequeri, "L'inserimento del ministero nella Chiesa: mistero, comunione, missione," 520.

43. Cordes says in this regard, "Following the example of Jesus, the holder of the priestly office has the obligation not merely to serve at table, but to lead a life of service (a diaconal life) that characterises every action. Mark 10:45 reveals the full extent of this ministry: following Is 53:10ff, Jesus lays down as the ultimate specific aspect of his ministry giving his life as a ransom for many." Cordes, *Sendung zum Dienst*, 79. A very accurate description of Jesus Christ's mission as the innocent one who incarnates the prophecies of the Suffering Servant and manifests the mystery of the God who is mercy can be found in M.-J. le Guillou, *Celui qui vient d'ailleurs: l'Innocent* (Paris: Éditions du Cerf, 1998).

44. Le Guillou, *El Rostro del Resucitado*, 336. On the ministry as service, see further: A. Toinet, *L'Ordre sacerdotal et l'avenir de l'homme* (Paris: FAC, 1981), 115.

45. Ratzinger, "La cuestión del sentido del ministerio sacerdotal," 338.

46. Cf. M. Ouellet, *Sacerdotes, amigos del Esposo. Para una visión renovada del celibato* (Madrid: Encuentro, 2019), 163–66 (orig. *Amis de l'Epoux: Pour une vision renouvelée du célibat sacerdotal* [Paris: Parole et Silence, 2019]).

47. Cf. Galot, "Le sacerdoce dans la doctrine du Concile," 1053.

48. It is worth noting the three sections of Benedict XVI's Exhortation *Sacramentum Caritatis*, which are entitled respectively *Eucharistia, Mysterium Credendum* (6–33), *Eucharistia, Mysterium Celebrandum* (34–69), and *Eucharistia, Mysterium Vivendum* (70–93), helping us to realize that after saying that Christian living cannot be reduced to the Eucharist, what is found in fact is a real reduction suffered by the eucharistic mystery in theology, spirituality, and Christian life for several centuries now, at least in the West.

49. Cf. Frisque, "Decreto 'Presbyterorum Ordinis'. Historia y comentario," 155; Castellucci, "Presbyterorum Ordinis," 320 and 373–74.

50. Cf. Frisque, "Decreto 'Presbyterorum Ordinis'. Historia y comentario," 137; Delhaye, "Le décret sur les prêtres," 482; Routhier, "L'écho de l'enseignement de Vatican II sur le presbytérat dans la situation actuelle," 161–65; G. Como, "Non è bene che il prete sia solo. Il decreto *Presbyterorum ordinis* e la condizione attuale dei presbiteri," *La Scuola Cattolica* 143 (2015): 273–98, especially 289–90; Castellucci, "Presbyterorum Ordinis," 321–22. On this subject, St. John Paul II would speak of the "essentially relational aspect of the identity of the priest," John Paul II, *Pastores Dabo Vobis* 12.

51. Cf. LG 28; PO 2, 4, and 12.

52. On the expression *secundi meriti munus* reference must be made to the classic work by Botte: B. Botte, "*Secundi meriti munus*," *Les Questions Liturgiques et Paroissiales* 21 (1936): 84–88.

53. Cf. G. Richi Alberti, *La Iglesia somos nosotros en Cristo. Cuestiones de eclesiología sistemática* (Madrid: Encuentro, 2016), 299–309.

54. Cf. Frisque, "Decreto 'Presbyterorum Ordinis'. Historia y comentario," 142.

55. Cf. Castellucci, "Presbyterorum Ordinis. Introduzione e commento," 325 and 438–439.

56. Cf. Augustine, *Commentary on St John's Gospel* 123. Thinking about pastoral charity takes St. Augustine's teaching on the ministry as *amoris officium* as one of its fundamental points of reference. On this topic cf. G. Moioli, "Sulla spiritualità sacerdotale ed episcopale in sant'Agostino," in *Scritti sul prete*, 13–24; and P. Curbelié, "L'*officium amoris* selon saint Augustin," *La charité pastorale. Colloque à Ars, 27–28–29 janvier 2014* (Paris: Parole et Silence, 2014), 55–79.

57. See especially John Paul II, *Pastores Dabo Vobis*, 21–23.

58. Cf. John Paul II, *Pastores Dabo Vobis*, 19–20; Chapelle, *Pour la vie du monde*, 101–2; Routhier, "L'écho de l'enseignement de Vatican II sur le presbytérat dans la situation actuelle," 172; De La Soujeole, *Prêtre du Seigneur dans son Église*, 176.

59. Cf. *Pastores Dabo Vobis*, 20, 27 and 72. No. 27 is the first passage about "Priestly life and evangelical radicalism." Greshake also connects the practice of the Evangelical Counsels in the life of the priest, with the radical following of Christ in the ministry: cf. G. Greshake, *Ser sacerdote hoy* (Salamanca: Sígueme, 20103), 369–70 and 413–`15. Dianich takes up the same theme when he says that pastoral ministry is a "charisma of totality," cf. S. Dianich, "Ministerio pastoral," in *Nuevo Diccionario de Espiritualidad*, ed. S. de Fiores and T. Goffi (Madrid: Ediciones Paulinas, 1991), 1236–53, especially 1240–49 where he describes the ministry in terms of a "charisma of totality" based on the exercise of the *tria munera*.

60. "The Council did not mean that the spirit of the evangelical counsels is simply the same thing as professing them [in the religious state]. The spirit of the counsels is open to all forms of Christian living, and all of them gain considerably in evangelical and Christlike quality in the measure in which they allow themselves to be moulded by that spirit." G. Uríbarri Bilbao, *Portar las marcas de Jesús. Teología y espiritualidad de la vida consagrada* (Madrid: Universidad Pontificia Comillas, 2002), 221. On the evangelical counsels in priestly life, cf.: P. Martinelli, *Seguir hoy a Cristo. Vida sacerdotal y consejos evangélicos* (Madrid: Encuentro, 2018).

61. "Et invicem sibi sunt, et patres cum sibi consulunt, et filii cum sibi obtemperant, et fratres maxime, quia eos unus Pater testamento suo ad unam haereditatem vocat," Augustine, *True Religion* (*Christian Belief*) 46, 89.

7

MINISTERIAL AND BAPTISMAL PRIESTHOOD

Theological Issues and Pastoral Challenges

Father Philippe Capelle-Dumont

As you sent me into the world, so I have sent them into the world.

—John 17:18

SINCE THE POSTCONCILIAR period the question of the priesthood has been the subject of strongly conflicting interpretations and a whole range of new theories. They differ on everything from the most ancient theological foundations to the most widely shared pastoral practices. The "ministerial priesthood," either reduced to a mere functional, added-on structure, or else, quite the opposite, liberated from all historical influences, becomes the focal point both of genuine missionary desires and of arguments—sometimes very radical ones—against classic doctrinal teachings. In every case, the question of the priesthood involves the future of Catholicism and its modes of presence in today's disorientated world.

The title of this contribution points to the two parts into which it is divided. The first part will highlight and analyze different views of the "ministerial" and the "baptismal" priesthood in recent times and in the present. The second will try, on that basis, to formulate the theological issues and pastoral challenges suggested by the situation as analyzed.

Bearing in mind the restricted framework of this presentation, I will leave aside any discussion of the various movements affecting our various cultures, but about which the question of the priesthood cannot fail to be concerned—whether the unprecedented anthropological crisis, the theological-political changes, the ambitions of transhumanists, the virtues and dead ends of interreligious dialogue, or what is known as the "abuse crisis."

RECENT AND CURRENT CONCEPTS OF THE PRIESTHOOD

There is a remarkable abundance of postconciliar literature dealing directly or indirectly with the relationship between the theology of the priesthood and its pastoral exercise. It includes works by outstanding and sometimes controversial theologians, from Henri de Lubac to Edward Schillebeeckx, from Yves Congar and Hans Urs von Balthasar to Hans Küng, from Karl Rahner to Joseph Moingt. At the magisterium level, there are the major contributions made, unforgettably, by Popes John Paul II, Benedict XVI, and Francis. The literature also includes a flood of pastoral considerations by "communities" of various kinds, rooted in the concerns of ordinary daily living and pointing to the need, in the face of sometimes unprecedented experiences, for new ways of combining the contributions of priests, deacons, and laypeople. This heterogeneous literature reflects points of view concerning both the meaning of Vatican II's documents and the debates, arguments, and controversies aroused by those documents.

Since it is obviously physically impossible to cover all those publications exhaustively, I will focus on three main types of "requests" that are significantly connected to them according to their theological-pastoral correlation: (1) a mainly *academic* request for a historic reconsideration of the institution of the ministerial priesthood; (2) a *vocational* request for clarification on the identity of the priest; and (3) a *militant* request for a "democratic" approach to pastoral work.

A Triple Request

The first request comes in the setting of a particularly intensive renewal of historical studies, initially fostered by the encyclical *Divino*

Afflante Spiritu (1943), not unrelated to the work of the "Fourvière School," and extensively developed in the postwar period. These studies inevitably involved a historicized approach to the ministries of the patristic period, giving rise to, and credibility to, the idea of a permanent tension in the early centuries of the Church between, on the one hand, the effort to fulfill Christ's will to found the Church as committed to the Gospels, and on the other, inventive, communitarian, institutional pragmatism. A huge number of studies of both kinds were produced in the period between 1960 and 1980, which attempted to uncover, by working back through the different stages of codification, the Church that Christ originally wanted.[1]

The basic effort in such studies was to take a "step backward" (*schritt zurück*) past the mass of Scholasticism in order to highlight—as against any ahistorical preconceived ideas—a normative principle inspired by the creative flexibility of the dispositions of the ancient Church. This aim undoubtedly inspired several generations of theologians, who gathered important items of knowledge about a period of apostolic effervescence, and raised many questions on the connections between the various rules on ministry of Catholic tradition. Thus, an emblematic passage in one book on fundamental theology runs,

> On consulting the accounts of the origins of Christianity, we see no apostle or anyone else being set apart from the community in virtue of a sacred character, nor acting as the minister of a new kind of worship, nor performing any specific rites; we do not find a trace of any distinction between consecrated persons and non-consecrated persons....The specifications for the institution of the priesthood are blank.[2]

This assessment was not in fact new; it was a prolongation of the re-reading offered previously by the nineteenth-century German theologian Franz Overbeck,[3] and handed on some years later by the German historian Adolph von Harnack[4]—both of them Protestants—according to whom the "institutionalization," "clericalization," "dogmatic codification," and "sacralization" of the Church had been operating from the early centuries onward, together with a progressive denaturing of the gospel message in its original purity. This is understandable when we consider that the task of penetrating the mass of ministerial institutions of the early centuries was not always free from theological preconceptions about history.

The second request, a corollary of the first, aimed to draw out all the theoretical and practical consequences of this historical-pragmatic view of early decisions of the Church. It concerned the priest's identity and a reconsideration of the priesthood's distinctive features as codified classically, liturgically, and canonically. The ancestry of this request, which is being made still more loudly today, may be traced through a long and complex period with its roots in the time immediately after the Second World War, when the Church was undergoing severe internal upheavals, marked by the "Worker-Priests" crisis in 1953–54, the effect of the goals and activities of Catholic Action, the decrease in vocations that accelerated catastrophically in the 1960s and 1970s, the birth of liberation theology and, in conscious contradistinction to it, a Theology of the people, the Lefebvre crisis, the institution of a binary representation of Catholics as *either* traditional *or* progressive, and the appearance of massive religious indifferentism. By contrast, in the 1970s and 1980s new lay charismatic movements emerged in North America and were rapidly exported to other continents; and from the 1980s onward in many places, diocesan synods were held that generalized debate based on the undefined term *coresponsibility of priests and laity*.

Correlative with all of this, numerous reapproaches were undertaken in systematic theology, claiming to represent the spirit of some of the documents of the Second Vatican Council (*Lumen Gentium*, *Ad Gentes*), characterized by the widely held aim of participation by all Christians in the mission of the Church. Categories that had been in second place up until then such as "the common priesthood of the baptized" or "the people of God" were enthusiastically mobilized, the second even taking precedence in pastoral terms[5] over "the Body of Christ" and "temples of the Holy Spirit." The idea of the priesthood then found its primary "ontological" location in baptism, since baptism conferred on the new Christian the titles of "priest, prophet, and king." Scriptural and theological support for this seemed unassailable, such as these two phrases by "Peter": "Be yourselves built into a spiritual house, to be a holy priesthood" (*ἱεράτευμα ἅγιον*; 1 Pet 2:5); "You are a chosen race [*γένος ἐκλεκτόν*], a royal priesthood [*βασίλειον ἱεράτευμα*], a holy nation [ἔθνος ἅγιον]" (1 Pet 2:9)—both inspired by the Old Testament for which Israel was (according to an ambiguous expression) "a kingdom of priests, and a holy nation" (Exod 19:6), leaving unresolved the question of the superimposition or differentiation of these two expressions. Another claimed source of support was St. Leo's sermon: "Just as we call 'Christian' all those who have received in baptism the mystical anointing, so we should call 'priest' all those who are the members of the One Priest."[6] This common priesthood was not and could not be understood as an inferior priesthood of the simple faithful; it meant, in the words of St. Thomas Aquinas approved by Henri de Lubac, a "mystical priesthood."[7]

Thus, what was at stake was to discover how the ministerial priesthood was *specifically* identified in view of the various New Testament and theological statements. With the Council's decree, *Presbyterorum Ordinis,* the ministry of the priest was then principally understood as essentially ordered to proclaiming the gospel,[8] following the words of the Apostle Paul: "Faith comes from what is heard, and what is heard comes by the preaching of Christ" (Rom 10:17). This directly raised the question of the theoretical and practical connection and interaction between the priestly/episcopal mission and the baptismal mission. Admittedly, the sacramental origin of the priesthood was stated by the same decree in the very next paragraph, referring to the participation "in a special way" (*speciali ratione effecti*) of the ministries of the bishop and the priest "in the priesthood of Christ," rooting their exercise in the sacrament of the Eucharist (§5). But the critical re-reading given notable currency by Hans Küng in a well-known book[9] found medieval forms of ceremonial investiture in priestly ordination and its rites. A similar direction was taken by Joseph Moingt, who diagnosed in the sacral configuration of the priest a strategy inspired by the *Apostolic Tradition of Hippolytus of Rome,* itself taking up "the model of the Old Testament priesthood."[10]

Correlating with the idea of shared mission, the role of the priest was then widely seen in terms of "function," the parameters of his action being found in the needs of ecclesial communities; thus, to quote another relatively recent emblematic statement, "The functionality of the priesthood is confided to the hermeneutic of the Church, which defines it according to [the Church's] needs."[11] The word *priesthood* fell progressively into abeyance, giving place to the singularly indeterminate terms *pastoral ministry* (E. Schillebeeckx) and *ecclesial ministry* (H. Küng).

The third request, which I called "democratic," cannot be dissociated either from the changes in sociopolitical connections developed over the past two centuries in the West and beyond or from the more recent "critical" re-reading of the hierarchical systems that had previously prevailed in the religious sphere. The departure point for this approach was found, as Edward Schillebeeckx wrote, in broadening the concept of apostolicity to embrace faith communities: "Apostolicity is, at the New Testament level and in the first place, a qualifying denomination of the community *itself*, founded on the Gospel of Jesus the Christ."[12] Introducing the notion of "spontaneous managers" of the nascent communities, Schillebeeckx erased the difference between them and the apostles: "The co-workers had to carry on with building up these foundations, but consequently they shared in the powers and rights of the Apostles."[13]

The distinction or even separation between the notions of "power" and "service" that was the subject of pastoral debates for a time was not in reality a basic theological position. Hans Küng himself brought the two terms into solidarity with one another: no service without power. "The special authority of the person in charge of the community came from the special service for which he had received the vocation and sovereign power."[14] Note taken. The request here centrally formulated was therefore different: "In the current situation it is in *democratic structures* that the authority of this service will discern precisely possibilities and chances to perform the reciprocal service of everyone demanded by the New Testament."[15]

This democratic request, claiming to be directly inspired by the New Testament, found new expression in the following organizational proposal:

> The bishop will let these communities manage and organize themselves in democratic mode; he will check up on them discreetly, while respecting their autonomy and the decisions taken by their managers and people in charge. Since there is no Christian community without the sacramental and eucharistic life, he will enable their managers to provide

> it. To sum up, he will provide them with all the help they need, whether for their religious needs, or for their doctrinal formation, putting his priests at their disposal![16]

We shall pass over the small consideration accorded to the poor priests consigned to satisfy "religious needs" while others are required for the noble tasks of formation. What is to be noted above all is the destiny of priests in a Church that is unilaterally and consequentially democratic.

Questions and Objections

Each of these requests, which characterize a change of era, is supported by several lesser requests not altogether devoid of legitimacy.

Thus, the first of them reflects the perennial demand for a discourse of truth that is enriched with historical data. But—an old debate that crystallized in the "modernist crisis"—the type of knowledge that is offered by historical science and that undoubtedly enables plenty of useful indications to be compiled, nevertheless does not include all the criteria that would enable us to appreciate theological and pastoral decisions, which belong to another order of reality, namely the effect of tradition. The philosophers Maurice Blondel in past times, and then more recently, Hans Georg Gadamer[17] were able to restore to it a strong, unshakeable epistemological status. In fact, the apostolic tradition under whose auspices the ministries were deployed in history rightly calls for its own hermeneutical lights to be respected. On the one hand, it is certainly not reduced, as Edward Schillebeeckx believed, to mere "continuity in history"; furthermore, it refuses to exclude institutional creativity from its own requirements, which are spiritually rooted in the message of the Christ of the Gospels. The evidence is fundamental: the conservation of the primitive "deposit" of the faith and the need to explore it in a circumstantial way obliged the Apostolic Fathers of successive generations to endow themselves with institutions that were necessarily marked by the changing features of the cultures around them. Because the covenant is co-extensive with the mission, the first apostles sought to honor no less than a mission *entrusted* in the Spirit, and on that account, humanly co-*initiated*: "He who believes in me will also do the works that I do; and greater works than these will he do!" (John 14:12).

The second request, which concerns the constitutive features of the identity of the priest, undoubtedly has to do with the contingent instability of the way the priesthood is expressed in theology, but carries with it the permanent risk of passing over its original characteristics, namely its plural, liturgical, institutional, and spiritual rootedness not only in the apostles' vocation, but also, correlatively, in the zeal of their lives, to the point of a sacrificial death that conferred on their ministry the full meaning of their christological mediation. Nor can we forget here the link that unites the priest not only with the bishop but also with the "presbyterium," other priests—"priests," in the plural, Vatican II repeats; in other words a shared Christological mediation.

The third request, the democratic one, is likewise not to be rejected out of hand, unless the etymology of the word confines it unilaterally to the political sphere and intrudes politics into the field of religion. In fact, from the exodus onward, the people of God were endowed, through the "seventy" men from among them, with the gifts of the Spirit; on the day of Pentecost, the members of the nascent Church were affected both physically and spiritually by the Messiah's universal intent. But the important aspect, in both cases, was not so much a request to be allowed to speak as a free gift enabling them to hear God's word, respond to it, and spread it. The introduction of the democratic coefficient into the ecclesial sphere, then, is pertinent only in so far as it is a genuine welcoming of God's initiative. In other words, what becomes of the relationship between hierarchy and apostolic succession in a democratic context?

INCARNATION, REVELATION, REDEMPTION

The foregoing survey points toward *three types of theological issues with pastoral effects*: (a) the reason and method of Christ's incarnation; (b) the memory of the Father's act of revelation; and (c) the historical effectiveness of redemption through the Spirit. These issues are thus none other than that of the absolute in history; that of divine-human revelation; and that of eschatology. As such they are directed toward the action of the Son, the love of the Father, and salvation in the Spirit. All three point to the central question of sacramental mediation.

Priesthood, Incarnation, and Creation

The first issue at stake concerns the inaugural placing of the priesthood within the mystery of the founding of the Church. Now the priesthood cannot *not* be received and thought of in the first place as that of Christ the "great High Priest" (Heb 4:14) who both subverts and fulfills the Old Testament meaning of priesthood. From that radical standpoint the priesthood cannot be either first or only conceived from within the reality of the Church: it is not a functional aspect of the Church, but a constitutive vector of it; not an element of the whole, but the beginning of a new temporality. This initiating, incarnated temporality is signified by the representation in a person of flesh and blood of the work properly accomplished by Jesus Christ to the point of sacrifice. The divine mission can only be actualized as the expression of the will of the Father who "sends," which is accomplished by the Son, who is at the same time both "sent" and "sender," in the strength of the Spirit, to the whole world to sanctify it. Consequently, without the concrete ministerial incarnation of this foundational memory of the apostolic mission, without the continued mediation of the spirit of Christ-Servant, the priesthood of the baptized itself loses its substance: it forgets the divine-human temporality in which it is *received*, and it loses the specific understanding of the act through which the participation of all the baptized in the gifts of Christ comes about, and which constitutes the *source of their own missionary zeal.*

From this there follow two correlated statements in the Council decree *Presbyterorum Ordinis*: first, "there is no member who does not have a part in the mission of the whole Body"; and second, "having sent the apostles just as he himself had been sent by the Father, Christ, through the apostles themselves, made their successors, the bishops, sharers in his consecration and mission. The office of their ministry (*quorum munus ministerii*) has been handed down, in a lesser degree indeed, to the priests."[18]

St. John's Gospel offers a wonderful prayer with regard to this: "Consecrate them in the truth; your word is truth. As you sent [ἀπέστειλας] me into the world, so I have sent [ἀπέστειλα] them into the world. And for their sake I consecrate myself, that they also may be consecrated in truth" (John 17:17–19). Exegetes unanimously highlight the lexical and thematic interplay between the words "consecrate" (here in the sense of "devote to," "set apart") and the inaugural "sending" (which constitutes the apostles' identity) on the mission of salvation. Thus the trajectory that leads from the sending by the Father to the reception by human beings of all Christ's gifts does not make the apostles and their successors simply into superintendents of the Church. To put it differently, bishops and priests are not ordained for the exclusive service of the ecclesial community that is proclaimed to be a missionary community; they are themselves *missionaries who are constituted as such* by Christ to proclaim the message of salvation to all men in the mediation of the Church which they institute with the baptized, in accordance with the responsibility entrusted to Peter.

Thus the ministerial priesthood is not merely a function of the institutional Church but participates, in memory of Christ sent, incarnate, crucified, and risen, in the ceaseless founding of the ecclesial and universal mission.

It is by this yardstick that the controversial but often truncated phrase should be understood: *In persona Christi capitis* ("in the person of Christ the head"). Prepared for by Pope Pius XII in 1943 (*Mystici Corporis*) and especially in 1947 (*Mediator Dei*), it was used by the Second Vatican Council (Constitution *Lumen Gentium*, 1964; Decree *Presbyterorum Ordinis*, 1965). As was later stated in the declaration *Inter Insigniores*,[19] the aim of this phrase was to complete the previous imprecise phrase *in persona Christi* that implied the identification of the priest with the whole Christ. Widely quoted and commented on by the Popes John Paul II and Benedict XVI, it should be understood in consequence of what has just been recalled of the mission of the Son: not according to a psycho-personal projection but according to the sacramental alliance that confers on the ordained minister, under the title of service, the charge of representing the person of Christ as sent by the Father and head of the Church...the Church to whom he gives all his gifts: the Body of Christ. The patristic image of the Church as *mysterium lunae* can help us greatly here to avoid any appropriation by the Church or the priest of the light that comes from Christ and, through him and secondarily, from the Church.

Consequently, the ministry of the priest is *essentially* inscribed within what Christ was, did, said, and aimed for through the Holy Spirit: he is hallowed by belonging to Christ. This is why the question of "priestly celibacy"[20] cannot be foreign either to this foundational economy in which Christ is totally given to "the things of [his] Father" (Luke 2:49) and has "nowhere to lay his head" (Matt 8:20); or to the type of spiritual demand that that economy inspires. Thus the attempts, on the basis of greater or not-so-great erudition, to reduce this question to the formal conditions of its canonical obligation in the twelfth century (First Lateran Council, 1123), in other words to associate it with a contingent, accidental institutional decision, can only arouse perplexity. Because Christ was celibate for the sake of exclusive dedication to his mission, the first century of Christianity would hear recommendations to match his state from St. Paul and Clement of Rome, and then in the fourth and fifth centuries from the Councils of Elvira and Carthage. It was this foundational spiritual choice which produced the missionary flourishing of Catholicism to which we are indebted.

From the pastoral point of view, the strong pressure to which priests, including younger ones, have been subjected in this regard for several years, leading them to relativize something that in fact determines their absolute commitment, cannot be dissociated from the question of the structural attractiveness of the vocation to the priesthood.

Priesthood and Revelation

The priesthood of Christ can only be understood as subverting the Old Testament priesthood, and so as a central, constitutive part of revelation itself. This subversion is inscribed in the temporality of the incarnation, as explained above, but includes a specific temporality. To understand the outlines of its range, there is an analogy in the slow but decisive adoption over the course of the early centuries of Christianity of the terms *philosophy* and even *theology* and *religion*; this could only be done by subverting their previous semantic layers, not deleting them. The first use of "Christian philosophy" is attested in St. John Chrysostom's homily *In Kalendas* (386–387). But from the second century, it was taken for granted that the message of Christianity should be called a "philosophy," "our philosophy" (Tatian, 2nd century), "true philosophy" (Clement of Alexandria, 2nd–3rd century), the "philosophy of God" (Eusebius, 4th century) and even the "philosophy of the

Bible" (Tatian; Gregory of Nyssa, 4th century) or the "Gospel philosophy" (Theodoret, 4th century).

The analogy is also maintained by the word *theology*, initially coined by Plato (*Republic* II, 379c) and which, because of its pagan connotation, took several centuries to be integrated into the discourse of the *intellectus fidei*—also via a series of semantic subversions—as in the "mystical theology" of Pseudo-Dionysius or, later, the "systematic theology" inspired by Abelard.

Astonishingly, the word *religion*, though taken up by St. Augustine (*De vera religione*) and the whole of Catholic tradition, would become the object of dislike at the beginning of the twentieth century, notably on the part of Karl Barth and Max Weber, who saw it as, if not the opposite, at the very least a vector of pollution of the faith of the gospel. To understand this, it should be realized that they saw "religion" as made up of magical elements drawn from ancient human sources, of which the "faith," rooted in the gospel alone, needed to free itself. This separation, connected with the troubling binomial "impure/pure," also shares the request for the ministerial priesthood to be laid aside; marked by the patriarchal world of male power, the ministerial priesthood ought to disappear before the ethical-spiritual demand implied in the idea, stripped of all magical verticality, of the common priesthood.

Now the appropriation by Christianity of the word *religion* can be seen analogically to that of the very idea of priesthood. The New Testament takes up the concept of priesthood afresh since it is part of the working of the covenant, both old and new. That the priesthood of the new covenant fulfills that of the old covenant was clearly understood with regard to the condemnation in 144 of Marcion, who had urged the abandonment of the Old Testament as obsolete; and also with reference to the notion of fulfilling. Fulfilling the Old Testament law brings about an insoluble tension between rupture and continuity. Thus the newness of the priesthood of Christ *neither abrogates the Old Testament priesthood, nor acts as a linear development of it.* Its newness brings rupture, and *it is this rupture that constitutes the fulfillment.* It is by this very tension that the priesthood of Christ is a "revelation." The Old Testament priesthood is revealed in the revelation of the priesthood of Christ. And it is in that revelation, where the rupture participates in the fulfillment and summing-up, that the ministerial priesthood is located.

Priesthood and Redemption

The question was raised recently of whether the sacred, whose lexical form is present in the word *sacrament*, should not be relativized or even abandoned, in view of the ethical demand implied in the word *holy*: sacred versus sanctity. Admittedly, the assignation of the sacred to "paganism" and the holy to the "biblical," a type of division that owes much to the ideas of Emmanuel Levinas (*Du sacré au saint*, 1977), warns us: use of the sacred cannot be sanctioned from the outset because in many of its ancient expressions it justified the most savage, dire, genocidal actions. Still, assuming the distinction, it still does not suffice for an understanding of the status accorded to the dimension of the sacred by Catholicism and Orthodoxy. The presence, apparently disconcerting, of pagan or even wicked figures on the roofs of churches and cathedrals recalls their profound originality, inspired by the gospel principle: everything should and can be saved, including evil—not the "process" of evil but the evil that has been committed—in accordance with the double affirmation of 2 Corinthians 5:21, "For our sake he made him to be sin" (*ὑπὲρ ἡμῶν ἁμαρτίαν ἐποίησεν*) and of the Nicene-Constantinopolitan Creed that Christ "descended into hell." As the philosopher Schelling (19th century) maintained, Christianity really does love the pagan.

Besides the constantly and rightly highlighted fact that the word *sacred* belongs in human terms to the domain of what is most intimate, most deserving of reverence, and most valued, its etymology provides plentiful legitimacy to the integration of the sacred into the sphere of sanctity. For one thing, coming from the Sanscrit *Sacer*, it marks both a distance regarding the profane, and the respect inspired by its own mysterious domain. For another, the biblical semantics of the Hebrew word for holiness, coming from the Semitic notion of *qôdèš*, which meant what is separated, what cannot be touched but can be approached on certain conditions, significantly modified the understanding of the term, placing it at the heart of God himself: his holiness is inaccessible to human efforts, but it can fill us because of God's gracious, infinite generosity, of which the kenosis of Christ is the supreme expression. Sanctity therefore does not imply here a unilateral and eternal separation, but the communion of what is human with the very essence of God. "As he who called you is holy, be holy yourselves," wrote St. Peter

(1 Pet 1:15), echoing the reiterated command in the Book of Leviticus (twice in 11:44–45: "Consecrate yourselves therefore, and be holy, for I am holy...you shall therefore be holy, for I am holy"; and at 19:2, "You shall be holy; for I the Lord your God am holy"). All that humanity is, with what its being holds of good and bad, is thus called to share in God's holiness. In Catholicism, then, one does not go from the sacred to the holy, but each person is called to sanctify all that is sacred and confer upon it its true breadth.

It is by this singular paradigm that Christianity—indebted to Judaism in this respect too—is distinguished from many religious traditions. The fact that the Constitution *Sacrosanctum Concilium* (Vatican II) gives such weight to the "sacred" (sixty-four occurrences) and harmonizes it with "holy," "holiness" (about twenty occurrences) is highly instructive.

What is centrally at stake concerns the yoking of the idea of sacramental mediation to priestly ordination...which in the Eucharist celebrates the whole history of the redemption of humankind willed by the Father, realized by way of restoration in Christ, and achieved through the power of the Spirit. This connecting-up of the sacramental mediation of the ministerial priesthood could not be contained, enveloped, set out, enclosed, totalized in the mediation of the Church alone; it falls to it to take up the trinitarian figures of paternity, fraternity, and inspirer.

That is why Fr. de Lubac said,

> This priesthood of the Christian people is not concerned with the liturgical life of the Church, and it has no direct connection with the production of the Eucharist. Within the "holy nation," and for the purpose of making it holy, certain men are therefore "set aside" by a new consecration that is of a different order. They receive the imposition of hands, which has been handed down uninterruptedly from the first Apostles of our Lord, and hear in their turn the words that those Apostles heard: "Do this for a commemoration of me." It is the "hierarchical" Church that produces the Eucharist.[21]

Two additional remarks may be made here. First, Henri de Lubac recommended understanding the word *hierarchy* in the original sense given it by Pseudo-Dionysius: "Celestial Hierarchy," that is, the precedence of the divine disposition. Second, the eucharistic "commemoration" also finds its expression in the determined spreading of the message of Christ; it cannot be dissociated either from the kerygma or from the process of sanctifying the world.

CONCLUSION

It belongs to those who have the authority to do so to promote a pastoral approach differentiated from the *call* to the priestly ministry; one that is at the same time joined to the common priesthood and deployed in accordance with its own aim. Against the hierarchical verticalization of the priestly ministry and, equally clearly, against its "horizontalization" in the undifferentiated practice of the "pastoral ministry," there should be traced more appropriately the path of a call to follow Christ in his continuing and demanding mission, which is self-sacrificing and therefore joyful.

NOTES

1. For further details, see Jean-Robert Armogathe's contribution to this collection.

2. J. Moingt, *Dieu qui vient à l'homme*, vol. 2/2 (Paris: Éditions du Cerf, 2007), 842.

3. F. Overbeck, *Studien zur Geschichte der alten Kirche* (Schloss-Chemnitz: E. Schmeitzner, 1875); *Über die Anfänge der Kirchengeschichtsschreibung*, Unveränderter reprografischer Nachdruck der Ausgabe (Basel, 1892).

4. A. von Harnack, *Das Wesen des Christentums* (Leipzig: J. C. Hinrichs, 1901).

5. The notion of the "people" at the heart of Latin American theology was the target of several strategies for appropriation at the crossroads of political and ecclesiastical combat but was also the subject of several doctrinal clarifications from associates of Cardinal Jorge Bergoglio, Archbishop of Buenos Aires and future Pope Francis. See M. Costantini, "Parler du peuple—Note lexicale," *Communio* XLVI 6, no. 278 (Nov–Dec 2021): 29–37; and see, in the same issue, C. Hoevel, "Théologie du peuple—Histoire, idées et interprétations," 13–27.

6. St. Leo, *Sermo* 4, C. I, *Patrologie latine*, 54, 148.

7. "Omnis bonus homo dicitur esse sacerdos mystice, quia scilicet mysticum sacrificium Deo offert seipsum, scilicet hostiam viventem Deo: *Rom* XII.," Thomas Aquinas, 4, *Sent.* S. I, ad. 2m. See Henri de Lubac, *The Splendor of the Church* (San Francisco: Ignatius Press, 1999), 93 (orig. *Méditation sur l'Eglise* (1953) [Desclée de Brouwer, 1985], 114).

8. "Priests, as co-workers with their bishops, have the primary duty (*primum habet officium*) of proclaiming the Gospel of God to all" (PO 4).

9. H. Küng, *Prêtre pour quoi faire?* (Paris: Éditions du Cerf, 1971).

10. J. Moingt, *Dieu qui vient*, 843.

11. J. Moingt, *Dieu qui vient*, 843.

12. E. Schillebeeckx, *Le ministère dans l'Église* (1980), French trans. M. Kesteman (Paris: Éditions du Cerf, 1982), 21. Emphasis in the original.

13. E. Schillebeeckx, *Le ministère dans l'Église*, 23. On this point see the criticism by P. Grelot, *Eglise et ministères* (Paris: Éditions du Cerf, 1983), 70–74.

14. Küng, *Prêtre, pour quoi faire?*, 98.

15. Küng, *Prêtre, pour quoi faire?*, 99. Emphasis in original.

16. J. Moingt, Conference on September 24, 2010, published in *Faire Bouger l'Église catholique* (Desclée de Brouwer, 2012), 50–51.

17. M. Blondel, *Histoire et dogme* (1905); H.G. Gadamer, *Wahrheit und Methode* (Tübingen, 1960).

18. Decree *Presbyterorum Ordinis* 2.

19. Congregation for the Doctrine of the Faith, Declaration *Inter Insigniores*, V, in *AAS* 69 (1977) 112–13.

20. See the contribution by Emilio Justo to this collection.

21. H. de Lubac, *The Splendor of the Church*, 96. See also Y.-M. Congar, "La hiérarchie comme service, selon le Nouveau Testament et les documents de la Tradition," in *L'épiscopat et l'Église universelle*, ed. B. D. Dupuy, Collection Unam sanctam No. 39 (Paris: Éditions du Cerf, 1962), 67–99. It is perhaps permissible for me to refer to my conference paper "Le statut théologique de la hiérarchie. Catholicisme et Orthodoxie," Stretensky Orthodox Academy of Moscow, November 11, 2021.

DAY TWO

TRINITY, MISSION, AND SACRAMENTALITY

February 18, 2022

8

A TRINITARIAN UNDERSTANDING OF PRIESTHOOD

Introductory Address

CARDINAL ARTHUR ROCHE

HAVING REACHED THE second day of this symposium, I suggest that, when we consider the themes of Trinity, mission, and sacramentality, we are not only arriving at the central point, but at the true theological fulcrum of this symposium. The recovery and renewed appreciation of the role of the Trinity in the life of the Church has profound implications for how we think about mission, sacramentality, and vocation.

A trinitarian understanding of priesthood brings us to an ever-deeper appreciation of the fundamental connection between the priesthood of baptism shared by all the faithful, and the specific character of the ministerial priesthood. Last Monday, we celebrated the feast of Ss. Cyril and Methodius. The great bishop Cyril, who was first called Constantine, wanted to become a monk. The liturgical texts say that, after taking the holy monastic habit, he took the name of Cyril, thus adding light to light—*lucem luci addens*. In a certain sense, we can say that the light we have received in our baptism shines brighter when we take up our mission along the pilgrimage of life. When we respond to the call to mission, we add light to light, thus giving vitality to the Church.

A trinitarian understanding that enriches the christological dimension of the sacramentality of the Church prompts us to consider the real meaning of a full, conscious, and active participation in the liturgy. What we start to understand is that true liturgical participation takes place when we enter into the very mystery of the life of God that reveals itself to us in the paschal mystery. This dynamic of *divinae consortium naturae*—"partakers of the divine nature"*—allows us to make our lives a living sacrifice of praise, and this sacrificial love is at the center of the mystery of the Most Holy Trinity.

This morning, we are therefore very lucky to have with us as speakers His Eminence Cardinal Marc Ouellet, Professor Piero Coda, and His Eminence Cardinal Kurt Koch, who will participate in our reflections.

* Paul VI, Apostolic Constitution, *Divinae Consortium Naturae,* August 15, 1971.

9

THE HOLY SPIRIT AND THE PRIESTHOOD OF CHRIST IN THE CHURCH

CARDINAL MARC OUELLET

IT WOULD BE hard to exaggerate the importance and significance, for the missionary transformation of the Church in our times, of the Second Vatican Ecumenical Council, whose masterpieces include a renewed theology of the priesthood.[1] The inclusion of a much-needed reflection on the sacramentality of the episcopate enables us to reframe and resituate the Catholic vision of the priesthood, while the ecumenical opening-up and the experience of multiple dialogues provides for mutual enriching through complementary perspectives. Certain formal agreements show this clearly and offer hopes of new progress.[2]

For example, the restoration of the common priesthood of the baptized (LG 10) offers a path toward a new closeness with our Protestant brethren, while the quite remarkable progress in the theology of the Holy Spirit and of the Blessed Trinity builds bridges toward Eastern Orthodox and other traditions. The necessary response to Vatican II's ecumenical commitment is a patient search for ways to reconcile still-divergent points of view, to fulfill the Lord's prayer for the unity of his disciples, and to meet the missionary challenges faced by Christianity regarding the phenomena of secularization and the scientific reprogramming of *Homo technicus*. My contribution to this search explores the connection between the Holy Spirit, Christ, and the exercise of the priesthood in the Church. It is a systematic approach that aims to consider more deeply the gift of communion with the Trinity given to the world through the conjoined missions of Christ and the Spirit, which configure ecclesial communion.

What is the place of the Holy Spirit in the Church's participation in the priesthood of Christ? What is his role regarding the sacramentality of the Church? How should we give an adequate foundation to the essential difference, which is not just a difference of degree, between the participation of the baptized and that of ordained ministers in the one priesthood of Christ, within the people of God?

These are the questions that will guide our attempt to integrate pneumatology into research on a fundamental theology of the priesthood. Dealing with these questions requires certain preliminary considerations to be made on the person of the Holy Spirit in the life of the Blessed Trinity, on his role in the incarnation of the word and Christ's paschal mystery, as well as his relationship with the Church; such considerations will necessarily be very brief, in order to concentrate attention on the proper role of the Holy Spirit in making the priesthood of Christ accessible to the Church.

Pope Francis's pontificate has restored primacy of place to the Church's missionary conversion, now broadened to include a synodal conversion, both implying a reassessment of the place of the Holy Spirit in the ecclesiology of the people of God as it journeys toward the kingdom. Indeed, both directions set by the pope require a taking stock of our accumulated awareness of the presence and action of the Holy Spirit in the Church in terms of communion, participation, and mission. This conviction also forms the basis for the search for a fundamental theology of the priesthood, which I outline from a trinitarian perspective, beginning with the notion of the Church as sacrament, which the Council made the basis of its study of ecclesiology.

More specifically, I will focus on the Council statement on the different participations by the baptized and by ordained ministers in the one priesthood of Christ. This statement needs the light of pneumatology shone on it, to justify the difference of nature, not just of degree, between the two kinds of participation. The structure of the study will therefore be, first, some preliminary remarks on the Holy

Spirit and the priesthood of Christ; second, the Holy Spirit and the Church as sacrament of communion with the Trinity; and finally, the pneumatological and trinitarian integration of the two kinds of participation in the priesthood of Christ in the Church.

THE HOLY SPIRIT AND THE PRIESTHOOD OF CHRIST

We need to begin this enquiry with some reflections on the Holy Spirit and Christ that reveal God to us as trinitarian love.[3] The Book of Genesis evokes the Spirit as the creative breath, then in the prophets, the Spirit is the inspirer of their mission. He is associated in other places with wisdom and word. In the fullness of time, he accompanies the whole mission of the Word incarnate from his conception to his confirmation as Son of God by his resurrection from the dead (Rom 1:4). In John, the Holy Spirit is designated as the "Spirit of Truth" who proceeds from the Father (John 15:26), whose function in the economy of salvation is to be the interpreter of Christ, as Christ is the interpreter of the Father.[4]

In the life of the Blessed Trinity, the Holy Spirit appears as the third gift, the *donum doni*, who proceeds from the Father but also from the response of the Son (*Filioque*) in trinitarian love. His ineffable personality escapes our grasp and cannot be enclosed in any category; and therefore, Scripture speaks of him by means of symbols such as wind, fire, water, dove. Theologians try to understand his true nature within the divinity through different analogies, none of which is totally satisfying. In the love that is God, he is seen as the joint personal pronoun "we" of the Father and the Son, and yet this pronoun still does not express him fully since he is also "another" of the same nature as themselves. "He is the love between Father and Son by being simultaneously their fruit and hence their witness."[5] Von Balthasar later adds more precisely, "The Spirit is both the expression of what is most 'subjective' in the divine love and, at the same time, the 'objective' witness of this 'subjective' love between Father and Son."[6]

We will shortly take a more detailed look at the trinitarian structure of the priesthood as discoverable in the figure of Christ the high priest of the new covenant, which can be summed up in three fundamental aspects: offering, mediation, and communion. The Holy Spirit appears very explicitly in the aspect of communion, in accordance with his hypostasis in the Trinity and his own mission in the economy of salvation in company with the Word incarnate. Indeed, we should not forget that the Spirit participates in Christ's priesthood from the first moment of his incarnation, since the Son of God was conceived by the Holy Spirit, and took flesh of the Virgin Mary under the action of the Holy Spirit, which lasted for the entirety of his mission on this earth. Thus the Spirit configured the priesthood of Christ by imprinting on his human life the features of the Son of God, making his human existence filial, not only as an example to those men and women who would believe in him, but with the power to grant them a share in his own filiation. This was initiated by the life and preaching of Jesus, but finally accomplished by the gift of his Spirit, the Spirit of the Son, as the fruit of his death and resurrection. And this gift was decisive for the disciples' participation in his priesthood, as is clear from the solemn proclamation in the temple: "If anyone thirsts, let him come to me and drink. He who believes in me, as the scripture has said 'Out of his heart shall flow rivers of living water'" (John 7:37–38). John explains that Jesus said this about the Spirit, whom those who believed in him were to receive, "for as yet the Spirit had not been given, because Jesus was not yet glorified" (John 7:39).

Christ's priesthood is therefore constituted and configured by the Holy Spirit who participates intimately in his incarnation of the trinitarian love in history. This participation involves first the hypostatic union, where the Holy Spirit joins together the divine and human natures, without confusion or separation, in the person of the incarnate Word.[7] It is continued by the existential unfolding in time of that union (anointing or unction, as Irenaeus calls it) in the mission of the Redeemer, which is fulfilled under the sign of obedience unto death;[8] and it culminates in the paschal event when the Father, recognizing the work of his divine Son, raises him from the dead by the power of his Spirit (Rom 1:4). The Body of Christ is then filled with the plenitude of the Spirit of the Father, becoming radiant with the Holy Spirit, the life-giving Spirit of the high priest who can even introduce reconciled humankind into the trinitarian communion.

For our present purpose, what should be retained here is the fact that Christ's priesthood as mediation necessarily involves the participation of the Spirit not only as its fruit but also as the condition for it to be possible, because the Redeemer's obedience in love is made possible by the grace of the Holy Spirit who mediates for him the will of the Father even unto death. This redemptive obedience expresses in the economy of salvation his eternal procession as Son of the Father, and the glorification of Christ by the Holy Spirit confirms the divinity of the incarnate Son and the perfect unity of Father and Son in the common work of reconciling the world with God. In short, Christ's paschal mystery manifests the trinitarian economy of salvation, where the Holy Spirit confirms the fruitfulness of the new covenant by being poured out himself, effecting humankind's participation in the communion of the Trinity. The Church is the concrete manifestation of this under its social form as people of God, a form that acquires a sacramental meaning through the work that is properly that of the Holy Spirit but is always accomplished jointly with the risen Christ, the one mediator of the new covenant.[9]

Speaking of Christ's priesthood, then, essentially includes three basic aspects that emanate from him as incarnate: offering, mediation and communion. Jesus Christ is the Father's envoy to humankind to incarnate his love and offer in return a sacrifice of expiation for sins, that re-establishes our communion with God through the paschal gift of the Holy Spirit. These three aspects make up the trinitarian structure of the priesthood: the offering is, first, that of the Father, who gives his Son to the world (John 3:16), then that of the Son, whose mediation consists of taking on our sinful flesh to offer it to the Father, redeemed, in response to his love. The incarnate Son thus obtains from the Father the outpouring of the Holy Spirit, who raises him from the dead, absolves the sin of the world, and gives believers access to the eternal life of the Father and the Son in the communion of the Spirit.

This trinitarian structure of the priesthood is effected through the mystery of the incarnation and of the Church, where the Holy Spirit pays his own role, which we still need to examine more closely and appreciate more fully. The next stage will set out in detail the very close connection between the Holy Spirit and the Church, in a way that highlights both the continuity with the economy of the incarnation, and the difference deriving from the Spirit's own personhood as mystery of communion.

THE HOLY SPIRIT AND THE PRIESTHOOD IN THE CHURCH

Here we draw inspiration from the opening theme of the Dogmatic Constitution *Lumen Gentium*, the Church as sacrament, in other words "a sign and instrument both of a very closely-knit union with God and of the unity of the whole human race" (LG 1). This notion of a sacrament in the broad sense implies that the Church, as institution and communion, exercises a certain mediation in humankind's relationship with God by virtue of its participation in the one priesthood of Christ. The Council lays aside the ecclesiological concept of *societas perfecta* in favor of a mystical, trinitarian view found in the first chapter of the Constitution, and also in the introductory sections of most of the Council documents. This sacramental turn in ecclesiology is then developed in the chapter on the people of God: it enables the priesthood to be understood fundamentally based on its purpose, which is communion with the Holy Spirit and communicating the Holy Spirit to the world (LG 12).[10] The Oriental churches express this purpose in terms of *theosis*, while the Latins speak of it in terms that are more juridical but no less profound, of the *theandric* character of the Church.

The fundamental relationship of the Spirit with the Church is described eloquently in *Lumen Gentium* (4): "The Spirit dwells in the Church and in the hearts of the faithful, as in a temple (cf. 1 Cor 3:16; 6:19). In them He prays on their behalf and bears witness to the fact that they are adopted sons (cf. Gal 4:6; Rom 8:10–11)." This is the basic aspect that precedes in dignity and importance all the other manifestations of the Spirit: it is his witness to filial adoption that is at the base of the mission of the Church—the Church that the Spirit animates, sanctifies, renews, builds up, and guides "with hierarchical and charismatic gifts," embellishing it and leading it "to perfect union with its Spouse" (LG 4). Thus, this remarkable passage concludes, the universal Church is seen as "a people made one with the unity of the Father, the Son and the Holy Spirit" (LG 4).

Based on this fundamental pneumatology, which underlines our adoption as children, the trinitarian unity of the people of God, and the nuptial dimension of the Church, Christians are equipped to awaken their missionary dynamism, highlighting the responsibilities shared by the common priesthood of the faithful and the hierarchical priesthood of ordained ministers in a way that stimulates cooperation instead of exacerbating tensions. This is a concern and a conviction of current research in ecclesiology, which aims, with the help of pneumatology, to overcome not only clericalism but also the type of church organization that is too exclusively centered on the ordained ministry. In this sense, the synodal practice is a call to develop the missionary awareness of the baptized, but also to develop genuine, charismatically diverse ministries, duly recognized and integrated into the pastoral and missionary dynamics of ecclesial communities. Hence, the urgency and importance of going deeper into pneumatology.

Despite its notable progress in the theology of the episcopate and the practice of collegiality, the Council's ecclesiological turn has not yet been adequately transposed into a synodal and missionary style in the Church. Among the many reasons for this are the legacy of past controversies, the ecclesiological "Christo-monism" denounced by Yves Congar OP,[11] acquired pastoral habits, and the notable shrinking of numbers, all of which hamper efforts at reform and missionary initiatives. What is more, under the pressure of powerful contemporary cultural movements, it is not rare to find sterile rivalries prevailing between clergy, religious and laity, and the organization and missionary outreach of Christian communities being harmed by power struggles.[12]

Theological and pastoral development, while moving at different rates depending on cultures and geographical location, is a response to the impulse of the Spirit throughout the Church. It needs to include an all-out effort to promote vocations, so that the missionary conversion being undertaken is based not just on generous ideas springing from improved Church organization, but on people who are conscious that they have been called and sent by God with the grace of the Holy Spirit. Likewise, the current synodal enquiry should not end up in "ecclesio-centrism" by developing a new ecclesial model that, although more participative and inculturated, is less centered on announcing and communicating salvation to the world. The fundamental study of the priesthood keeps this primordial aim and this raison d'être of the Church in first place.

Returning to Scripture, we note that the institution of the priesthood in the old covenant involves major figures—Aaron, Melchizedek, the Levites—in Israel's worship. This worship is closely connected to the holiness of the chosen people and includes the immolation of animals as victims the priest offers to God on the Day of Atonement.[13] This institution was not taken up in historical continuity by the New Testament, whose language emphasizes instead a discontinuity with the Old Testament priesthood and external worship. This is why there are relatively few passages in the New Testament about the priesthood. The early witnesses of faith in Jesus gave primary importance to the figures Messiah, Lord, and Savior in explaining the meaning of his life, and not that of high priest.

However, the Letter to the Hebrews takes up the subject of the priesthood forcefully, exalting the one priesthood of Christ and emphasizing the difference between that priesthood and the external, ritual priesthood of the old covenant. The priesthood of Christ, the high priest of the new covenant, gives access to God by virtue of his own sacrificial offering to the Father in the Spirit (Heb 9:14).[14] There is a vast difference between the two priesthoods, but it should not be seen as a total difference regarding the figure of the priest. St. Thomas Aquinas wrote, "Christ is the source of all priesthood, for the priest of the ancient Law was the figure of Christ, and the priest of the new Law acts in the person of Christ."[15] Furthermore, the First Letter of St. Peter applies the idea of the priesthood to the people of the new covenant, and St. Paul takes up the idea of the priesthood of the faithful in his Letter to the Romans (12:1). These are important but relatively exceptional passages in the New Testament writings.

Ought we to deduce from this that the Catholic interpretation of the priesthood lacks scriptural support and should therefore be rethought in a different way, not in current terms of a distinction between the common priesthood of all the baptized and the hierarchical or ministerial priesthood? Indeed, some think so, but the existence of these two participations in the one priesthood of Christ was solemnly reaffirmed at the Second Vatican Council (LG 10). It is opportune, then, to stress its true value, and it is urgent to do so in view of the low numbers of vocations and the excessive sacralization of the ordained ministry, to which, moreover, are attributed the misdeeds of those ministers who abuse their "sacred power" to obtain gains that are dubious or even, in the case of sex abuse, criminal. These painful events are front-page news for the media, but they should not prevent us from looking more deeply at the hierarchical priesthood, whose true image should be made clear in its sacramental specificity in relation to the common priesthood of the faithful whom the ordained minister is called to serve.

From this viewpoint, theological research should bring about a healthy relativization of the "sacral" way of identifying the ordained minister with Christ, so that the traditional stress laid on the fact that the minister as *in persona Christi* is balanced by a contribution from pneumatology that includes the ministerial agency of the Church.[16]

After this brief look at the biblical and pastoral questions raised by the priesthood in the Church, we need to point out the presuppositions of the Church's participation in the priesthood of Christ understood as a sacramental mediation of the Holy Spirit in the world. These presuppositions can be grouped around the following topics. First, the theandric nature of the Church, founded on its participation in the trinitarian communion in Christ and the Holy Spirit, pursuing the question to the point of asking, Who is the Church? And what is the nature of her subjectivity?[17] Second, the sociological identity of the Church, both universal and particular, in view of its trinitarian identity founded on the missions of the Word and the Holy Spirit and actualized in the Eucharist. Third, the nuptial dimension of the Church, starting from Mary, who assumes and accompanies the incarnation of the Word from the initial *fiat* in the Holy Spirit to the ultimate sacrificial and sacramental expression. Fourth, the personhood of the Holy Spirit as gift-communion, fruit of the priesthood of Christ that guarantees the divine and human, sacramental and missionary identity of the Church. Finally, all of these are joined together in a trinitarian, eucharistic, and nuptial ecclesiology in which considerations of hierarchical and synodal structures take second place without losing any of their importance, since they are opportunities for the service of the spread of the divine and human communion of the Church with humankind.

We can now briefly explore these presuppositions which show how Christ's priesthood, with all its forms and degrees of participation, is in the Church the great nexus of the Blessed Trinity's loving plan. Christ being the one mediator of creation and salvation, his mediation embraces the creation of the universe, the incarnation of the Word,

Christ's paschal mystery, the outpouring of the Holy Spirit, the birth of the Church and its growth through its sacramental mysteries, and the journey of the priestly people toward the eschatological fulfillment of all things in "God, all in all."

The hymn to Christ as head of the universe in the Letter to the Colossians (Col 1:12–23) is the perfect summing-up of this priestly aspect:

> He is the image of the invisible God, the first-born of all creation; for in him all things were created...all things were created through him and for him....He is the head of the body, the church; he is the beginning, the first-born from the dead, that in everything he might be pre-eminent. For in him all the fullness of God was pleased to dwell, and through him to reconcile to himself all things, whether on earth or in heaven, making peace by the blood of his cross. (Col 1:15–20)

Here the apostle directly draws out the consequences of this mystery for the faith of the members of the Church by a testimony about his own share in the mystery (Col 1:24), and appeals to them to make their way of life conform to the image of God's Son; while in the Letter to the Ephesians, at the end of his solemn evocation of God's plan, St. Paul explores the pneumatological dimension of Christ's priesthood: "In him you also, who...have believed in him, were sealed with the promised Holy Spirit, which is the guarantee of our inheritance until we acquire possession of it, to the praise of his glory" (Eph 1:13–14).

The priesthood of Christ culminates in this communicating of the Holy Spirit that brings the trinitarian plan of salvation to fulfillment. Humankind attains the end for which it was created by sharing in this priesthood of Christ to the point of full possession of the Holy Spirit, the Spirit of glory who consummates the fertile communion of the new covenant. That is the setting for our study of the relationship between the common priesthood of the baptized and the hierarchical priesthood of the Church's ministers. We start with baptism, to lay a firm base for it, and to escape from the habitual way of dealing with the question that begins with the ministerial priesthood, and often ends up by undervaluing the priestly dimension of baptism. However, that dimension is not limited to the aspect of self-offering as described in Romans 12:1, but also includes the aspect of mediation, although certain well-known authors, including Albert Vanhoye, reserve the notion of mediation to the ministerial priesthood, too exclusively in my opinion.[18] Indeed, baptism consecrates the person as a member of Christ's Body, bringing about an ontological and ecclesial identification that associates him or her to the whole of Christ's priesthood, in that his body is the instrument of his filial offering and his redeeming sacrifice. By becoming sons and daughters of God through baptism, Christians are associated with Christ's filial priesthood with their whole being, as members of his Body, becoming by that same fact temples of the Holy Spirit and "fellow workers" with the gift of the Holy Spirit to the world. This is because the incarnate Son of God participates by his obedience in the outpouring of the Holy Spirit in the economy of salvation, as he participates by his divine filiation in the co-spiration of the Holy Spirit within the immanence of the Blessed Trinity. Analogously, the priesthood of the baptized not only has an ascending dimension of filiation insofar as it is an offering that is pleasing to God the Father, or intercession on behalf of humankind; it also has a specifically descending dimension, a living communication of the Holy Spirit who comes down from God the Father through Christ and passes through the corporality of the servants of God, whose active charity penetrates humankind, helps it, serves it, and sanctifies it. The Council texts on the mission of the laity speak of the Holy Spirit who vivifies them and sanctifies them through their participation in worship (LG 34), in the prophetic office (LG 35), and in royal service (LG 36), spreading abundant spiritual fruits throughout the world in the Spirit of the beatitudes proclaimed by the gospel.

What specific shape does this prophetic, royal, and worshiping form of priesthood of the baptized take? First, that of a community of faith, hope, and love, because the Holy Spirit is the source of communion and solidarity in mission. The Holy Spirit who gives life to the baptized is incarnate, in some sense, in a people belonging to God, a people unified and structured together in living, missionary communities in which the divine persons in circumincession give themselves to human beings in communion and participation. In this sense the universal priesthood of the Church, founded on the presence of Christ and the indwelling of the Holy Spirit, brings with it an exchange of gifts that involves the interaction of the divine persons with human beings for the sake of prolonged communication with the world to be evangelized. The world is then invited and above all attracted and inspired by the Spirit to put its faith in Christ and the Blessed Trinity, communion with whom offers a foretaste of the joy of salvation in the experience of ecclesial communion. So that the priesthood in the Church is not just one charism among many, a special function of certain people within the Church, but a life of communion which involves its whole being, all its activities, all its relationships *ad intra et ad extra*, having as its content and supreme goal, holiness in love through the action of the Holy Spirit, poured out and possessed as a pledge even before being tasted in fullness. For, at the bottom of the multiple exchanges of gifts that take place in the Church, there is a reflection and even a share of the life of the Blessed Trinity, an exchange of intratrinitarian love that is mediated *ad extra* through the incarnation of the Son in Jesus Christ and, analogously, through the incarnation of the Spirit in the Church. These two specific, complementary manifestations of the gift of God to the world are deployed in one another and with one another, in historical and eschatological continuity, in what is recognized as the sacramental nature of the Church.

Adopting this pneumatological-sacramental view of the priesthood of Christ and the Church casts a light on the divine but also sacramental vocation of every human being, called to participate in the mystery of divine filiation and in its personal fruitfulness that defines that priesthood. The essence of the priesthood, in fact, consists in a mediation between God and humankind, between humankind and God. All religions, or almost all of them, have positive and sometimes deformed (magical) expressions of this necessary mediation. Christianity brings to fulfillment the shadowy attempts at mediation found in the religions of the world, because Christ, through his sacrificial filial offering (his priesthood) brings about the reconciliation of the world with God, whose fruit is the remission of sins and the sanctification of humankind thanks to the universal, sacramental outpouring of the Holy Spirit. This outpouring of the Spirit constitutes the priestly fruitfulness of Christ as the historical and eschatological goal of his mission, a fruitfulness already inherent in God's intention to create, redeem, and glorify all things in himself.

The interest of the pneumatological dimension of the priesthood is that it enables us to envisage this mystery from its conclusion—the eschatological participation of created beings in the trinitarian communion: "God all in all." That presupposes seeing God's revelation as the deployment *ad intra* of the divine fruitfulness of love in three consubstantial persons, then contemplating the procession "through Christ and toward Christ," to arrive at the full possession of the Holy Spirit, that is, the perfect indwelling of the Trinity not only in the souls of the faithful but also in their mutual relations and in their missionary activity in the world. To speak of the priesthood in this way means contemplating the mystery of Love at its source and understanding its deployment *ad intra et ad extra*, the priesthood signifying the connecting of the passage of the infinite to the finite and the finite to the infinite, that passage being fundamentally the person of the Word incarnate who attracts everything to himself by his paschal sacrifice and who baptizes in the Holy Spirit everyone who is called to eternal glory.

In daily human living, this priesthood, whose horizons are so vast, means serving God's glory by the humble, persevering practice of faith, hope, and above all, charity. Indeed, every act of love of God and neighbor, even the most hidden and invisible, is *theophorous*—it bears God. It is borne by God as a created reality, but it also bears God in his act of total gift to his creatures in the Holy Spirit. This is because in the fullness of time the Holy Spirit, poured out generously, does not merely add a few aesthetical touches to the work of the Father and the Son; he universalizes the sacramentality of the crucified and risen Christ through his Body, which is the Church, prolonging the incarnation of trinitarian love according to the modality of his own hypostasis of communion, progressively bringing about the *connubium* of the Trinity and humankind in a symphony of gifts exchanged and reciprocal glorifications. Already here below this symphony anticipates the glory of the kingdom in the humble face of Mary-Church,[19] the Bride without spot or wrinkle, consecrated to serve the glory of God who is all in all, today and throughout all ages. Who will deny that the service of this eminent member of the Church, Bride and Mother, is a fruitful mediation of the fullness of Christ's priesthood?

Having thus sketched out the christological and ecclesiological presuppositions that support the fact of participation by the Church in the gift of the Holy Spirit to the world, we now come to deal directly with the relationship between the two participations in the one priesthood of Christ in the Church. We can reply in advance to the spontaneous objection that considers the oneness of Christ's priesthood as excluding a priori all participation properly so called on the part of the Church. Such an objection illustrates the deficient pneumatology referred to earlier, because the special role of the Holy Spirit within the immanence of the Blessed Trinity, as in the economy of salvation, is to exalt fruitfulness and to seal unity in diversity. The oneness of Christ's priesthood does indeed logically exclude all other priestly mediation that does not come from himself, but not a participation given by the Spirit of Christ by virtue of his nuptial union with the Church. This participation is not founded on the nuptial symbolism as such but on the nuptial bond which is the Holy Spirit. It is, in fact, he who joins Christ the Spouse and the Church-Bride in indissoluble and fruitful union. He associates the Bride, who is a servant and poor, with all the priestly fruitfulness of her Spouse. The supreme image of this truth is obviously the Virgin Mary, Mother of God and Mother of the Church, in virtue of her fullness of grace and the eschatological wedding of the Church with the Lamb, slain and victorious, of which she is the protagonist at the cross and at Pentecost.[20]

Because of its goal and its fruit that is the gift of the Holy Spirit, the one priesthood of Christ confers on all its recipients a participation in his pneumatological fruitfulness in terms precisely of participation in his mediation. The oneness of Christ's priesthood does not exclude but includes the mediation of the Church-sacrament as believing community, thanks to the two specific forms of the priesthood within it, whose dependence on the priesthood of Christ is ensured by the Holy Spirit who guarantees its proper use by his person-communion. Speaking of the Church's participation in the priesthood does not, therefore, mean affirming an autonomous mediation distinct from the one mediation of Christ, but rather affirming a fructifying of his one mediation through the Holy Spirit, who is the fruit of it and who communicates its virtue and fruitfulness in his own person united to the Church.

THE PNEUMATOLOGICAL AND TRINITARIAN INTEGRATION

All the foregoing developments lead us to the previously promised deepening, which will show that participation in Christ's priesthood in the Church derives from a pneumatology underpinning a trinitarian and nuptial ecclesiology that foregrounds the communion of the divine persons with human beings, set against the background of the historical and eschatological reality of the Church. God chose to incarnate his love and grace in the sacramental structure of the Church because the incarnation of the Word in Christ is his definitive, irreversible choice, a choice that is prolonged in history in a more universal mode by the sending of the Holy Spirit. It falls to the Holy Spirit to continue Christ's mission by taking it up and spreading it throughout humankind, through the sacramental mediation of the Church. That mediation brings a real participation in the trinitarian communion because of the paschal sacrifice of the incarnate Word, through means of baptism and the other sacraments. The Holy Spirit accomplishes this sacramental universalization of Christ's mission by letting himself be poured out freely by the Father and the Son, and by giving himself to the Church in a way that is beyond the power of speech to describe, and beyond all analogy. The nuptial analogy, for example, fits Christ's relationship with the Church, but not the Holy Spirit's, because the Spirit is not so much the partner of the Church as the actual nuptial link with Christ. He himself is the "we" that roots the subjectivity of the Church in the trinitarian communion.

This indescribable presence of the Holy Spirit is the foundation for the Church's participation in the trinitarian communion, and the principal agent of the differentiation of the sacramental gifts and the multiple interactions between the divine persons and human beings in the service of communion and mission. The Church's sacramental structure, whose aim is to bring about the divine-human communion of the new covenant, presupposes that the divine persons should be represented by human beings in order to make the invisible God's communion with his partners in the covenant sacramentally visible.

In the case of baptism, what is effected is no representation but rather the identification of each baptized person, and the community of the baptized, with the Son, and through him with the Father in the Spirit. For it is the Spirit who always brings about communion, without confusion or separation, between the divine persons and the ecclesial community; who configures the grace of divine sonship in the souls of the baptized in an indelible way that is expressed by the concept of sacramental character. This character (*sphragis*) prints the seal of filiation as an irreversible gift, signifying the irrevocability of God's gifts, even when the human person betrays and rejects the gift received. Just as Christ's pasch leads necessarily to the gift of the Holy Spirit, so too the baptism that prolongs it marks the subject with an unbreakable seal of the Spirit. Hence, the permanent possibility possessed by each baptized person, whether in a state of grace or of sin, to offer him or herself to the Father with Christ, in the power of the Spirit who is always available to make the filial priesthood of the baptized bear fruit.

In the case of the sacrament of holy orders, it is not purely and simply identification of the priest with Christ that is brought about, because that has already been accomplished in baptism. Instead, holy orders effects a sacramental representation of the paternal dimension of Christ's mission, because in the economy of salvation Christ manifests himself as the Son who is obedient to his Father and subject to his parents, but also is revealed as the apostle of God the Father, the Father's minister or servant: "He who has seen me has seen the Father." It is this that, in my humble opinion, lies at the base of the distinction between the two participations by the Church in the one priesthood of Christ.[21] It is important to grasp thoroughly this capital aspect, which situates us at the heart of the mystery of the incarnation and its sacramental continuity in the Church through the power of the Holy Spirit. If the Word of God was conceived by the Holy Spirit and accompanied by him for the whole of his incarnate life on earth, it was so that he would live integrally his human condition and his mission as Son of the Father assisted by his filial Spirit, to fulfill his redemptive mission to the end, which included carrying the sins of the world in the offering of love he made on the cross; and to obtain the Father's absolution in response to his sacrifice. Now, that absolution by the Father is signified and given to him in the very act of his resurrection from the dead by the power of the Holy Spirit. It is then that the fullness of the Holy Spirit is communicated to him as Spirit of the Father, sovereign Spirit who absolves from sin, raises the dead, and "pneumatizes" Christ's humanity to make it a life-giving Spirit, able to be prolonged throughout history under a new corporal, *sacramental* modality in the Church, the Body and Bride of the risen Christ. The essential distinction between the two participations in the one priesthood of Christ is based, therefore, on the pneumatology that distinguishes the Spirit of the Son at the source of the filial priesthood of all the faithful, and the Spirit of the Father at the source of the paternal priesthood of ordained ministers. In the light of this, it is obvious that both participations are ordered to one another, the more fundamental one being the eternal filial priesthood, in the service of which the hierarchical sacramental priesthood is deployed for the time of the economy of salvation.[22]

The sacrament of holy orders is clearly instituted by God in Christ's two commands at the Last Supper and on the evening of his resurrection: "Do this in remembrance of me," and "Receive the Holy Spirit. If you forgive the sins of any, they are forgiven; if you retain the sins of any, they are retained." The *exousia* (*potestas*) of the ordained minister proceeds from the Spirit of the Father raising Christ from the dead and conferring on him from then onward a power that radiates from his transfigured humanity. He can communicate that power by his physical breath, which the Church will later express by the imposition of hands enabling ministers to announce the word with authority, and to administer the sacraments for the building up of the Church. This is how the ecclesial Body of Christ is structured and joined together, a "pneumatized" Body really configured and personalized by the Spirit to the point of assuming the social figure of a people, but also the mystical figure of the Bride of Christ. Hence the nuptial meaning of the sacrament of holy orders, to ensure the representation of the Spouse and be able, *in persona Christi capitis*, to make his eucharistic wedding present throughout time.

It follows that this sacrament also brings about a stable "pneumatized" character that configures the subject and makes him capable of representing Christ the head precisely as apostle of God the Father, sacramentally signifying the Father's sovereign initiative in the whole of God's plan and at the same time guaranteeing the apostolicity of the Church's mission. The Church thus lives from day to day on the Eucharist, the mystery of the new covenant, the nuptial mystery, the theandric mystery configured by the trinitarian bond of the Spirit of the Father and the Son communicated in fullness by the risen Christ!

The deep meaning of the sacrament of holy orders is then undoubtedly to signify to the community that it does not hold Christ's one mediation as its own property, but that it should always receive it as a gift. However, beyond that basic meaning, it could also be seen as a reminder to the whole Church that the one priesthood of Christ makes radical reference to the Father from whom the Church receives on a permanent basis its participation in that priesthood, both by the fundamental grace of divine sonship, and by the hierarchical and charismatic gifts that proceed from the generosity of the Father, through the Son, in the Spirit.

In this way, understanding of the priesthood is developed in a trinitarian direction, in the sense of a participation in the Spirit of the Father and the Son; the same Spirit of communion who manifests his filial side in the common priesthood of the baptized, and his paternal side in the ordained ministry of ministers. The two sacramental manifestations thus converge toward a building-up of ecclesial communion where the peaceful, joyous complementarity between faithful and ministers is founded on and nourished at the spring of the communion of the divine persons. This participation in the loving relationship between the Father and the Son sanctifies human relationships, heals those that are sometimes subject to conflict, places questions of power and authority in their correct setting, and above all, opens a space of freedom for the creativity of the Holy Spirit.

The relationship between authority and community is thus decentered from the over-human dimension, so often a locus of conflict, and recentered on grace, namely the communion of the divine persons given participatively in the filial identity of the baptized and the paternal identity of ordained ministers, both being inhabited and sanctified by the Spirit of the Father and the Son. This grace is not a dream, an ideal, or a symbol; it is the ontology of the divine persons and human beings in the exercise of communion in the Spirit. It is he who gives access to his own personal pronoun "we" referring to himself and the Father and to himself and the Son, by allowing himself to be poured out into souls and into the ecclesial relationships founded on baptism and holy orders. But his gift of himself is not limited to these two services that he renders to the Father and to the Son by radiating their presence in the relationships between the baptized and hierarchical ministers. He also expresses himself in an "overflowing" that corresponds to his own identity in the life of the Blessed Trinity.

Indeed, while the fruitfulness of this trinitarian approach first appears in the communion between pastors and faithful, it truly blossoms and flourishes in the flowering of an ecclesial community rich in charisms. For ecclesial communion strengthened by harmonious participation in the relationships of filiation and paternity liberates the sphere of action of the Holy Spirit, which is then expressed in an abundance of charisms and vocations of all sorts, lay, matrimonial, religious, and priestly, in the service of the sacramental mission of the Church. The presence of consecrated life, in particular, in all its forms, as *sequela Christi*, is a witness to the freedom and gratuity of the Holy Spirit who builds unity in love on the basis of respect for diversity. Just as in the Trinity, the love that is the Spirit flows back upon the love of the Father and the Son giving them an inexpressible increase, so too in the economy of the Church, the witness of consecrated life flows back on the spirituality of ministers and faithful, stimulating them to gratuity and the perfection of charity, for a more fruitful witness to communion and the ecclesial mission.

The "sacramental" ordained minister leads straight back to God the Father, who is represented by Christ and by his ministers after him, through a specific gift of the Spirit of the Father, though without hardening that identification in a "sacral" or "idolatrous" way. All excessive sacralization in this domain leads to abuses of power and phenomena of rejection. The key to understanding the "sacramental" nature of this "ministerial" identification is the mediation proper to the Holy Spirit, whose personal characteristic is to unite while distinguishing, to unite without confusing together. Therefore it is he who unites the minister to the one he represents in a real way, but in this "sacramental-pneumatological" order, in which distinction remains in the union, with a margin that respects the freedom of the subject and his possible or real failure, but nevertheless guarantees to the minister's mediation an effectiveness that is partly independent of his own moral value. This is the *ex opere operato* dimension of the ordained ministry that applies to acts that are actually sacramental, but not in the same way to the totality of the priest's life.

It is clear from this pneumatological study that the ordained ministry should be understood as an ontological reality that configures the person lastingly, and not as a simple social function with no permanent character. That configuring is not at the level of the personal sanctification of the subject, but an objective charism for the service of the ecclesial community.[23] In fact, the whole sacramental order is ontological because it is "pneumatological!" The Holy Spirit fills the Church with the presence of the divine persons; he enriches human beings by connecting them to and actually including them in the trinitarian relationships. Indeed, the Spirit molds with his grace personal and ecclesial relations, conferring on them consistency and outreach. The action that is proper to him in terms of communion refers baptized and ministers to each other on the basis of the sacramental gifts that bring into play the ontology of the trinitarian relationships and the sociology of human relationships.

To sum up, everything is effected by the person of the Holy Spirit, who is, so to speak, the trinitarian hypostasis of the Church.[24] He conjoins the Trinity and humankind in a nuptial mystery that is beyond analogy, uniting and distinguishing them in love, safeguarding the difference between Creator and creature, while bridging the gulf between the thrice-holy God and the mass of sinners, not by penal exclusion but by the kenotic sacrificial inclusion of the trinitarian Love manifested in Christ, crucified and risen "to the praise of his glorious grace" (Eph 1:6).

CONCLUSION

The formula that can sum up the overall view offered here is the pneumatological view of *Ecclesia, sacramentum trinitatis.* The Church is, in fact, constituted by the divine missions of the Word and the Spirit, who base and build its participation in the trinitarian communion on its faith in the priesthood of Christ, the one and only mediator of salvation. This faith grants it, through baptism, the gift of being his Body and his Bride in the Spirit, the people of God journeying to the kingdom, a priestly people, a royal priesthood, a holy nation....This priestly people, the sign and instrument of the trinitarian communion in the service of the unity of humankind, is, as such, introduced into two specific participations, according to the Spirit of the Father and the Spirit of the Son, with a view to the total gift of the trinitarian life to its covenant partner in history and through him to the whole of humankind that awaits salvation. The mutual reference of the two participations, far from shutting them off within this communion, propels them, under the apostolic impetus of the ministers, to evangelize the world together.

The Church is the dawning of the kingdom insofar as it already incarnates "sacramentally" the eschatological communion promised to all humankind. Its ecclesial relationships of communion and mission, based among other things on the sacraments of baptism, the Eucharist, and holy orders, express the involvement of the divine persons in the communion of human beings indwelt by the Holy Spirit with all the riches of his trinitarian identity: the Spirit of the Father in the gift of the hierarchical ministry, Spirit of the Son in the personal and existential offering of the community of the baptized, Spirit of communion and freedom in the abundance and flourishing of charisms in the service of communion and mission.

This trinitarian view of ecclesiology and this pneumatological integration of the twofold participation by the Church in the one priesthood of Christ enable us not only to frame the Church's missionary pastoral activity better, but also to resolve centuries-old disagreements and recurrent conflicts. This view of the priesthood, radically centered around participation in the trinitarian communion, could have a major impact on all vocations, sowing enthusiasm for a true ecclesial communion that is missionary by its attractiveness, welcome, and solidarity with the coming of the kingdom of God starting in this present life.

NOTES

1. Cf. J. Esquerda Bifet, *Teologia de la espiritualidad sacerdotal* (Madrid: BAC, 1976), with an ample annotated international bibliography in chapter XIV, 314–68; Report of the International Theological Commission, *Le ministère sacerdotal* (Paris: Éditions du Cerf, 1971; G. Martelet, *Théologie du sacerdoce. Deux mille ans d'Église en question*, 3 vols. (Paris: Éditions du Cerf, 1984–1990); G. Greshake, *Priester sein* (Freiburg: Herder Verlag, 1991); J. Ratzinger, *Kunder des Wortes und Diener eurer Freude,* Gesammelte Schriften vol. 12 (Freiburg: Herder

Verlag, 2010); M. Nicolau, "El Episcopado en la constitución 'Lumen Gentium,'" *Salmanticensis* 12 (1965): 451–507; G. Rambaldi, "Natura e missione del Presbiterato nel decreto 'Presbyterorum Ordinis,'" *Gregorianum* 50 (1969): 239–61; J. Coppens, ed., *Sacerdocio y Celibato* (Madrid: BAC, 1971); G. L. Müller, *Priestertum und Diakonat* (Einsiedeln: Johannes Verlag, 2000); M. Ouellet, *Amis de l'Époux* (Paris: Parole et Silence, 2019), 250, published in seven languages; M. Troupeau, *L'unité du sacrement de l'ordre dans la réforme des ordinations de 1968*, LQF (Aschendorff Verlag, 2022), 737; R. Penna, *Un solo corpo. Laicità e sacerdozio nel cristianesimo delle origini* (Rome: Carocci, 2020).

2. Cf. W. Kasper, *Harvesting the Fruits: Basic Aspects of Christian Faith in Ecumenical Dialogue* (New York: Continuum, 2009); N. Lossky et al., eds. *Dictionary of the Ecumenical Movement* (Geneva: World Council of Churches Publications); J. Gros, FSC, H. Meyer, and W. G. Rusch, eds., *Growth in Agreement II: Reports and Agreed Statements of Ecumenical Conversations on a World Level, 1982–1998* (WCC Publications, 2000); C. L. Rossetti, *Uniti nel nome del Padre. Una chiave per la comunione tra cattolici e ortodossi sullo Spirito Santo e il primato del Papa* (Siena: Cantagalli, 2021).

3. Cf. H. Muhlen, *Una mistica persona. La Chiesa come il mistero dello Spirito Santo in Cristo e nei cristiani: una persona in molte persone* (Rome: Corti, 1968); H. U. von Balthasar, *Spiritus Creator. Skizzen zur Theologie III* (Einsiedeln: Johannes Verlag, 1967); *Sponsa Verbi. Skizzen zur Theologie II* (Einsiedeln: Johannes Verlag, 1961) (*Explorations in Theology II: Spouse of the Word* [San Francisco: Ignatius Press, 1991]); *Pneuma und Institution. Skizzen zur Theologie, IV* (Einsiedeln: Johannes Verlag, 1974); F. Bourassa, "L'Esprit Saint, 'communion' du Père et du Fils," *Science et Esprit* 29, no. 3 (1977): 251–81; Y.- Congar, *Je crois en l'Esprit Saint* (Paris: Éditions du Cerf, 1979–1980); Evdokimov, *Lo Spirito Santo nella tradizione ortodossa* (Rome: San Paolo Edizioni, 1971); L. F. Ladaria, *Jesus y el Espiritu: la uncion* (Burgos: Monte Carmelo, 2013); J. Zizioulas, *L'Être ecclésial* (Geneva: Labor et Fides, 1981); for a critical analysis of a certain lack of pneumatology in the Latin tradition, see A. M. Putti, *Il difficile recupero dello Spirito. Percorsi e luoghi teologici della Pneumatologia nella tradizione latina del secondo millennio* (Rome: PUG, 2016).

4. "The Spirit's entire role is to guide us into the truth and to declare it: all the other, manifold utterances concerning the Spirit that we find in John and in the Scriptures of the Old and New Covenants come back to this fundamental role. As we have seen, the Son, become incarnate, was the adequate declaration of the Father, but this declaration remained closed to men so long as the Spirit had 'not been given' (John 7:35)." H. U. von Balthasar, *Theo-Logic III: The Spirit of Truth* (San Francisco: Ignatius, 2005), 17.

5. H. U. von Balthasar, *Theo-Logic III*, 18.

6. H. U. von Balthasar, *Theo-Logic III*, 141.

7. This same aspect can be expressed by the theme of "anointing," as Irenaeus does so eloquently: "In the name 'Christ' are included He who anointed, he who was anointed, and the Unction itself by which he was anointed. He who anointed is the Father, he who was anointed is the Son, and he was anointed in the Spirit, who is the Unction" (Irenaeus, *Adv. Haer. III*, 18, 3).

8. Thomas Aquinas, *Super Epistolam B. Pauli ad Hebraeos* lectura, cap. IX, 3, 10: "(The Apostle shows) the reason why Christ shed His blood, because this was done by the Holy Spirit, through Whose movement and instinct, namely, by the love of God and neighbor, He did this," quoted by A. Guggenheim, *Jésus-Christ, Grand Prêtre de l'Ancienne et de la Nouvelle Alliance. Étude du commentaire de Saint-Thomas d'Aquin sur l'Épître aux Hébreux* (Paris: Parole et Silence, 2004), 297–99.

9. H. U. von Balthasar constructs the third part of his pneumatology in *Théologique III: L'Esprit de Verité* by taking inspiration from Irenaeus of Lyons's vision of the relationship between the Son and the Spirit as "the Father's two hands" (165–217); this vision well explains the common work of the Son and the Spirit, each according to his own hypostasis: "Furthermore, the 'Father's two hands' are those with whose assistance he carries out the entire world project—from creation, via the redemption, to its final consummation in God" (167).

10. Vatican II, Dogmatic Constitution *Lumen Gentium* 12: "It is not only through the sacraments and the ministries of the Church that the Holy Spirit sanctifies and leads the people of God and enriches it with virtues, but 'allotting his gifts to everyone according as He wills,' (1 Cor 12:11) He distributes special graces among the faithful of every rank. By these gifts He makes them fit and ready to undertake the various tasks and offices which contribute toward the renewal and building up of the Church."

11. Cf. Y. Congar, "Pneumatologie ou 'christo-monisme' dans la tradition latine?," *Ephemerides Theologicae Lovanienses* 45 (1969): 394–416. For a review of Congar's contribution, cf. A. Nisus, *L'Église comme communion et comme institution. Une lecture de l'ecclésiologie du cardinal Congar à partir de la tradition des Églises des professants* (Paris: Éditions du Cerf, 2012).

12. The lively conflicts accompanying the "synodal way" of the Church in Germany illustrate the difficulty of constructing a synthesis between critical cultural elements and the reform of the Church in our time.

13. Cf. Y. Simoens, "Sacerdoce," *Dictionnaire Critique de théologie* (Paris: PUF, 2007), 1246: "He who offers and ordinarily immolates a victim gives it to the priest to present to God according to the sacrificial rites. This essential function attains its apogee when the High Priest, who receives, after the Exile, a royal type of anointing (cf. *Ps* 110:4; *Da* 9:25ff.; *2 Mac* 1:10), celebrates the rite of the 'Day of Atonement.'"

14. The difference between the two should not be absolutized, because the institutions of the old covenant—prophecy, priesthood, kingship—are positive

things, figures that await their fulfillment in Christ. The high priest, in particular, surpasses the Levitical priesthood and is a prefiguring of the high priest of the new covenant. Cf. A. GUGGENHEIM, *Jésus-Christ, Grand Prêtre de l'Ancienne et de la Nouvelle Alliance,* chap. 5.

15. THOMAS AQUINAS, *STh*, IIIa, q. 22, a. 4, c.

16. Cf. "Nuovi cammini per la ministerialità ecclesiale," in *PATH*, vol. 20, 2021&1, IF Press. In particular the articles by Ignazio Sanna, Dario Vitali, Serena Noceti, and Cardinal Marcello Semeraro. Along the same lines, Martin Troupeau explores the liturgical resources that offer a deeper understanding of the differentiated unity of the sacrament of Holy Orders: "According to the prayers of consecration, the central and unifying element of the sacrament of Holy Orders is found in a specific outpouring of the Spirit according to the order in question," in *L'unité du sacrement de l'ordre*, 115. See also chap. III, "In Persona Christi Capitis," 93–114.

17. On this topic, an important one that is relatively neglected in current theological work, see the reflections of BALTHASAR, "Who Is the Church?" in *Spouse of the Word*, 148–202.

18. Cf. A. VANHOYE, *Il sacerdozio della nuova alleanza* (Bologna: EDB, 1992), 49ff. The distinction between the natures of the two participations in the one priesthood of Christ can be safeguarded in other ways, that do not involve amputating an essential part of it, as will be seen later.

19. Cf. G. GRESHAKE, *Maria è la Chiesa. Un tema antico, una sfida per il presente* (Brescia: Queriniana, 2020); *MariaEcclesia. Perspektiven einer marianisch grundierten Theologie und Kirchenpraxis* (Regensburg: Verlag Friedrich Pustet, 2014); J. RATZINGER and H. U. VON BALTHASAR, *Maria-Kirche im Ursprung* (Einsiedeln: Johannes Verlag, 2005).

20. Cf. M. OUELLET, "*L'Esprit Saint et le sacerdoce de la femme*," Journées d'étude de l'Institut Catholique de Toulouse, *La femme au cœur de l'Église*, January 18–19, 2022 (Paris: Éditions du Cerf, 2022).

21. This distinction can also be expressed as the subjective filial priesthood of Christ and his objective priesthood of representation of the Father. This second aspect is secondary because it is linked to the temporal economy of the incarnation and does not last into eternal life. That is true both of Christ and of his ministers, who represent him by virtue of an objective gift deposited in them for the time of the economy of the Church. In heaven the functions disappear and there remains the filial priesthood, the shared possession and enjoyment of the full reality of the divine persons and human beings. Cf. M. DE LA TRINITÉ, *Filiation et sacerdoce des chrétiens* (Paris: Lethielleux, 1986).

22. D. VITALI, "Nuovi cammini per la ministerialità ecclesiale," in *PATH*, 48: "The 'Copernican revolution' of the Council finds here its structural principle: in fact, the centuries-old pyramidal scaffolding of the Church is demolished the moment it is stated that the two different modes of participation in Christ's

priesthood are ordered to one another." Cf. Vitali, "Sacerdozio comune e sacerdozio ministeriale o gerarchico: rilettura di una questione controversa," *Rassegna di Teologia* 52 (2011): 39–60.

23. The very well-argued study of liturgical sources of the renewed theology of the priesthood by Martin Troupeau offers in conclusion an overall confirmation of the pneumatological considerations that I have attempted to explore more deeply from a dogmatic standpoint: "In addition to this service to the community which is common to the three degrees, we propose to think of the unity of the sacrament by way of pneumatology: the Spirit is poured out on the ministers of the different orders so that they may build up the Church as a holy people, by guiding it, sanctifying it and teaching it." Troupeau, *L'unité du sacrement de l'ordre*, 407.

24. Balthasar, "Who Is the Church?": "But this inchoate subject, the Church, is fulfilled only in the mystery of the Holy Spirit, who is embedded in her as her inmost ground, and who can therefore constitute it in its perfected state because he is a Divine Person precisely as testifying to the eternal opposition of the Persons" (149).

10

THE CHRISTOLOGICAL FOUNDATION OF THE PRIESTHOOD

Father Piero Coda

IN THE *KAIROS* OF THE MISSION OF THE CHURCH TODAY

ALLOW ME TO start with two statements by Pope Francis that will help us position ourselves relevantly within the *kairòs* of God that challenges the Church today, along with a suggestion put forward years ago by the notable biblical scholar and later Cardinal Albert Vanhoye, who urges us to face the subject of our study courageously.

In the speech given on the fiftieth anniversary (2015) of the institution of the Synod of Bishops—in which the inspirational lines of the ongoing synodal process can be traced—Pope Francis, following in the footsteps of the Second Vatican Council, said,

> *Synodality*, as a constitutive element of the Church, offers us the most appropriate interpretive framework for understanding the hierarchical ministry itself. If we understand, as Saint John Chrysostom says, that "Church and Synod are synonymous," (*Explicatio in Ps. 149*) inasmuch as the Church is nothing other than the "journeying together" of

> God's flock along the paths of history toward the encounter with Christ the Lord, then we understand too that, within the Church, no one can be "raised up" higher than others. On the contrary, in the Church, it is necessary that each person "lower" himself or herself, so as to serve our brothers and sisters along the way [...Consequently, those who exercise authority are called "ministers"...]. For the disciples of Jesus, yesterday, today and always, the only authority is the authority of service, the only power is the power of the cross. As the Master tells us: "You know that the rulers of the Gentiles lord it over them, and their great men exercise authority over them. It shall not be so among you; but whoever would be great among you must be your servant, and whoever would be first among you must be your slave" (*Mt* 20:25–27). *It shall not be so among you*: in this expression we touch the heart of the mystery of the Church, and we receive the enlightenment necessary to understand our hierarchical service.[1]

Five years later (in 2020), in the postsynodal exhortation *Beloved Amazon*, the same Pope Francis extended an invitation to "broaden our vision, lest we restrict our understanding of the Church to her functional structures," and emphasized,

> Jesus Christ appears as the Spouse of the community that celebrates the Eucharist through the figure of a man who presides as a sign of the one Priest. This dialogue between the Spouse and his Bride, which arises in adoration and sanctifies the community, should not trap us in partial conceptions of power in the Church. The Lord chose to reveal his power and his love through two human faces: the face of his divine Son made man and the face of a creature, a woman, Mary. Women make their contribution to the Church in a way that is properly theirs, by making present the tender strength of Mary, the Mother. As a result, we do not limit ourselves to a functional approach, but enter instead into the inmost structure of the Church.[2]

There are those who have seen a tension between these last statements and the previous ones relating to the synodal Church: but is this really true? Or do we rather find ourselves in front of an invitation to turn our gaze, to make it even more similar to the gaze of Christ (the *νοῦς Χριστοῦ* of the Apostle Paul in 1 Cor 2:16; cf. *Veritatis Gaudium*, foreword, 4d) and thus openly welcome the breath of the Holy Spirit, as we embark on a new phase of the pilgrimage of the people of God, who now calls on us and asks for a faithful and creative attention to the written and transmitted word of God and for patient, respectful, and courageous discernment of the signs of the times?

Over forty years ago (in 1980), Albert Vanhoye concluded his essay *Prêtres anciens, prêtre nouveau selon le Nouveau Testament*, dedicated to "contributing to the discussion starting from the data of the New Testaments and in connection with the living tradition of the Church" with the following words:

> The use of hieratic categories involves a manifest danger, that of an unconscious return to the ritual concept of the cult of the Old Testament. Thus we come to create *un nouveau "prêtre ancien"* (a new "old priest:). In the past, this danger of regression has not always been avoided. In our days, however, it seems to be the inverse tendency that has become dominant—the one that leads us to reject priestly expression in Christian reality. Is this not another kind of regression? Some do not take the trouble to assimilate the new concept of priesthood as elaborated in the New Testament, and we are left with old ideas of the priestly cult to debate this question, as if nothing else existed. An effort is constantly necessary to maintain an authentic Christian orientation, which consists of never building walls of division between concrete existence and the relationship with God, or between the relationship with God and real existence, but in uniting them in the most intimate way possible in such a way to transform the entirety of human life thanks to the meditation of Christ who communicates the fire of the Spirit, and in making them a continual offering of filial obedience to God and fraternal dedication to men.[3]

Keeping these priceless indications in mind, with the objective of a synthetic and organic articulation of what I consider essential in the *doctrina fidei* with regard to our theme, I divide the discussion in three segments to shine a light on the christological foundation of the priesthood of the Church and in the Church: the paschal mystery, the Eucharist, and the eschaton, finally turning our gaze toward—almost to contemplate their living icons—the presence of Mary in the mystery of Christ and of the Church.

PASCHAL MYSTERY: *DE LATERE CHRISTI IN CRUCE DORMIENTIS ORTUM EST TOTIUS ECCLESIAE MIRABILE SACRAMENTUM*[4]

First, to discern what is asked of us today as disciples of Jesus so that the Lord Jesus can make himself actively present in history through the Church, which—as *Lumen Gentium* 1 teaches—is in him "like a sacrament or as a sign and instrument both of a very closely knit union with God and of the unity of the whole human race," one must contemplate and penetrate the inexhaustible novelty of the paschal event, the center of the mystery of Christ and salvation history, with the eye of faith. This applies specifically when we wish to understand the foundation of the priesthood of Christ, participated by him in the Holy Spirit to the Church. The magisterium of the Second Vatican Council has offered us a rich synthesis, firmly rooted in the attestation of Sacred Scripture and in Tradition: syntheses that are not exhaustive and definitive, marked by some oscillations on a linguistic and theological level, but doctrinally authoritative and orienting, so as to propitiate a generous and robust leap in quality today, on the level of self-awareness and self-configuration, listening to "what the Spirit is saying to the churches" (cf. Rev 2:7).[5]

Since the Dogmatic Constitution on the divine liturgy, *Sacrosanctum Concilium*, Vatican II in fact invites us to turn and even immerse our gaze into the paschal mystery of Christ. It proposes the concise formula, derived from the fathers, which summarizes the deepest content of the *lex orandi* and of the *lex credendi* of the Church: "*from the side of the sleeping Christ on the cross the wondrous sacrament of all the Church sprung forth.*"[6] In this formula, the paschal event is proposed in its double and indissoluble meaning *propter nos et propter nostram salutem*: so far as it presents the new and eternal priesthood of Christ, which expresses his mission, in the act of generating with the gift of his life in the Holy Spirit of the Church—"the seed and beginning of the Kingdom of God in the earth"—which is his Bride. The priestly metaphor and the spousal metaphor are thus closely linked as they express the performative meaning of the event from which the Church springs and after which the Church is molded. The New Testament records them together and intertwines them distinctly and forcefully, and the Tradition of the Church preserves them, valorizes them, and deepens them. Let us briefly see how.

The "Other" Priesthood of Christ

Jesus Christ, Word and Son of God and God himself made flesh (cf. John 1:1,14, 21), "through the eternal Spirit offered himself without blemish to God" (Heb 9:14): for this reason, he is "the mediator of a new covenant" (Heb 9:15) as he is *ἱερεὺς ἕτερος...κατὰ δύναμιν ζωῆ ςἀκαταλύτου* ("*another* priest...through the power of an indestructible life," Heb 7:15–16). The mission of Christ—an expression of his identity, hypostatically both divine and human, "without separation and without confusion" (Chalcedon)—can and should therefore be interpreted and summarized, according to revelation, in terms of the true and definitive priesthood, which is "other" compared to all its other previous forms, because it is singular and eternal on its own. The priesthood of Christ, in fact, while declaring the temporary nature of the priesthood that preceded it, reveals and realizes its secret intention: to gracefully offer the mediation necessary to humanity to live a full and endless communion with God, closing the creatural distance, in itself uncrossable, which separates one from the other and is exacerbated by the reality of sin. Jesus is the unique and universal Mediator (cf. 1 Tim 2:5) through the offer of his life "to the end" (cf. John 13:1) on the wood of the cross, in obedience to the will of the Father and in dedication to his brothers. With this, the sacerdotal language in its general religious sense and its specifically Old Testament sense is forever "transubstantiated": it becomes something other than what it had been before, and just like that it reaches the truth which it had always tried inchoately to reach, always failing. With his usual striking brevity, St. Thomas Aquinas states—on the basis of the teaching found in the Letter to the Hebrews and more generally in the New Testament and in the fathers of the Church—that "it is greatly suitable for Christ to be a priest,"[7] precisely because his priesthood differs from the priesthood of the old covenant as "what is true from what is a symbol of it,"[8] so that he, in the fullness of time—looking forward and looking back—is fully *fons totius sacerdotii*.[9]

The Church, a Priestly People

This transformation—of reality first, and of intelligence, languages, ethos, and practices—leads to a fundamental consequence: the novelty and configuration of the Church as a people of the new covenant and a priestly people, in virtue of the priesthood of Christ and as his Bride. "Omnes sacerdotes quoniam membra sunt unius sacerdotis," writes St. Augustine.[10] We are looking at two faces of the same coin: the Church is the Bride of Christ as he, the only and supreme priest of the new covenant, loved her and loves her as himself—this is the *μυστήριον μέγα* (great mystery) of the Letter to the Ephesians (cf. 5:29–32)—that is, he loves her even with that love with which the Father loves the Son (cf. John 17:23), thus constituting the Church his Bride (as it is described in *Lumen Gentium,* repeating the affirmations in the Book of Revelation and in the First letter of Peter):

> "A kingdom and priests to God the Father." (Cf. *Rev.* 6:1; cf. 5:9–10) The baptized, by regeneration and the anointing of the Holy Spirit, are consecrated as a spiritual house and a holy priesthood, in order that through all those works which are those of the Christian man they may offer spiritual sacrifices and proclaim the power of him who has called them out of darkness into his marvelous light (Cf. *1 Pt.*2:4–10). (LG 10).[11]

The Church has thus been rightly described by Vatican II as a *communitas sacerdotalis* (LG 11), as Christ has not only "forever associated her with him as his most beloved Bride" in the celebration of the divine liturgy as "the exercise of [his] priestly ministry" (cf. SC 7); but this is also how he forms her mission in history as a sacrament, in himself, "of the intimate union with God and of the unity of all the human race" (cf. LG 1), through the Church introducing in society the light and the strength that spread from the Holy Spirit, pouring out from his Passover into our hearts (cf. Gal 4:6), which are activated through faith, hope, and charity (GS 42).

This fundamental point can never be emphasized enough: the novelty shown in the paschal event, as a singular and eschatological priestly and spousal act in which the mission of Christ in relation to the Church, and therefore the principle and form of the priesthood of the entire people of God, was carried out. Jesus brought an end to a prefigurative and provisory form of the priesthood and eschatologically disclosed another, definitive in itself as it rang in the "new creation" (cf. 2 Cor 5:17; Gal 6:15): it was no longer the priesthood that declared the separation between God and humanity, between what is sacred and what is profane, between a priestly caste and the rest of the people, but the priesthood of Christ who is truly a "mediator," who effectively serves as a bridge between the two, which are made one in him.

A priesthood that is so new and exceeding that the apostolic Church—whose self-awareness is attested to in the pages of the New Testament—distinguished it from the preceding forms and, guided by the Holy Spirit, deemed it was not possible to use traditional language to express it without forming a radically new understanding of its meaning in reference to the following: (a) the singularity of the paschal event of Jesus (as the Letter to the Hebrews does in a broad and theologically argued manner); and (b) the universality of those who, through faith and baptism, are made participants in and as the Church (this is the priestly people of God, which we find thus formulated in the Book of Revelation and in the First Letter of Peter).

It follows from this that the use of priestly language in reference to what the Church—in loyalty to the event of Christ and his uninterrupted *παράδοσις* (cf. *Dei Verbum* 8)—defines in time as "ordained ministry" in relation to those who, in the Church, are authorized to carry out the service of a guide in the faith and of unity in the celebration of the sacraments in the heart of the priestly people, is only subsequent and derived: because, when it is not contextualized with christological and eschatological pertinence, such language risks neutralizing the novelty of the event of Christ, the principle and the form of the universal priesthood of the people of God that is peculiar to the new covenant.

The Priesthood Exercised by the Ordained Ministry

Therefore, as testified to by the New Testament and the uninterrupted transmission of the *Traditio vivens Ecclesiae*, in the context of the participation of the Church *communitas sacerdotalis* in the priesthood as Christ, we find the theological space for the exercise of the specific ministry in service of the priesthood of Christ, which the exercise of that specific ministry that finds its theological place at the service of the priesthood of the people of God, granted by Christ in the Holy Spirit for the Church his Bride. The theological reason, and consequently, the form of exercise of such a ministry derives from the sacramental nature of the Church.

This, in fact, continues and transmits the mission of Christ as his living sign and his effective instrument: one Body with him, being distinct from him as the Bride is from the Bridegroom, in a relationship of unity in the distinction that finds no adequate analogy except the relationship of unity in the distinction between the persons of the Most Holy Trinity. In fact, the unity and sanctity of the Church, professed in the Symbol of faith, are guaranteed and expressed by Christ in the Holy Spirit through catholicity and apostolicity: that is, in the fact that only the link with the whole (*καθ' ὅλον*)—which is catholicity—and the link with the origin—which is apostolicity—certify and promote the permanence and authenticity of the mission of the Church as a sacramental extension of the mission of Christ in time and space.[12] But this requires that there be an instance in the Church that guarantees its apostolicity and catholicity in the transmission of the word of God and in the sacraments of faith: an instance intrinsic to and at the service of the sacramental nature of the Church. "In this way," the International Theological Commission (ITC) emphasizes, the ordained ministry "is the sacrament of the operative presence of Christ and of the Holy Spirit in the heart of the people of God,"[13] representing "Christ at the head of the community and as if in front of it."[14]

Starting here, we can understand why we are dealing with a ministry rooted in a specific sacrament, ordination, in virtue of which a specific grace is conferred: that of sacramentally representing Christ as the Head and Bridegroom of his Church. This is a grace formally distinct from the grace conferred by the sacrament of baptism and confirmation—in virtue of which we are conformed to Christ as his Body and Bride in the participation in his same filial life—made fully available through the celebration of the Eucharist for the salvation of the world. It follows—I again quote the ITC—that the episcopal and presbyteral ministry, in continuity with that of the apostles, "is sacerdotal in the sense that it makes present the service of Christ in the effective proclamation of the Gospel message, in the gathering and guide of the Christian community, in the remission of sins and in the Eucharistic celebration where the unique sacrifice of Christ is made real in a singular way."[15] And this is without minimizing the immediate action of the grace of Christ and the Holy Spirit in every baptized person, which is indeed guaranteed and promoted by the exercise of the ordained ministry in the performance of the action that is proper to it.

The Ministerial Priesthood in the Service of the Priestly People

As the ITC specifies, "The New Testament makes use of a specific term to express the power of communicating salvation that Jesus has received from the Father and which, in the strength (*δύναμις*) of the Holy Spirit, he exercises on all creatures: *ἐξουσία* (in Latin *potestas*, in Italian *autorità*)."[16] This consists—we read in the prologue to the Gospel of John—of the grace that makes us "children of God" in Christ (John 1:12) who the entire people of God is made a participant in, in virtue of baptism. "The *ἐξουσία* of the risen Lord," the ITC continues, "is expressed in the Church through the plurality of the spiritual gifts (*τὰ πνευματικά*) or charisms (*τὰ χαρίσματα*) that the Spirit bestows in the bosom of the People of God for the edification of the only Body of Christ."[17] Among these is that gift of the Holy Spirit put at the service of all the others to guide the Church, in Christ, along the journey of unity and sanctity in fidelity to its apostolicity and catholicity. It is endowed with a specific *ἐξουσία* (*potestas*) to this end, expressed in a specific ministry, which, precisely because of its nature and its purpose, is not separated from the living context of the people of God; nor does it relativize the equal dignity of all the baptized of the Church. On the contrary: it is totally and only and always put at the service of the mission of the people of God as a *communitas sacerdotalis*, exercised in it according to the synodal dynamic in which the *modus vivendi et operandi* expresses that "the whole Church is a subject and that everyone in the Church is a subject."[18]

In this evangelical logic, the letter *Iuvenescit Ecclesia* of the Congregation for the Doctrine of the Faith (2016), which records the experience of the Church from its origins in the light of the magisterium of Vatican II and of the popes in continuity with it, emphasizes that not only "the hierarchical gifts" but also "The authentic charisms…come to be considered as gifts of indispensable importance for the life and mission of the Church" (9). It specifies, "even if the historical forms of the latter are not guaranteed to remain always the same, nonetheless the charismatic *dimension* will never be lacking in the life and mission of the Church" (13). And, taking up the affirmation of John Paul II, it reiterates "the *coessentiality* of these hierarchical and charismatic gifts," as

> they have the same origin and the same purpose. They are gifts of God, of the Holy Spirit, of Christ, given to contribute, in diverse ways, to the edification of the Church. he who has received the gift to lead in the Church has also the responsibility of keeping watch over the good exercise of the other charisms, in such a manner that all contribute to the good of the Church and to its evangelizing mission, knowing well that the Holy Spirit distributes the charismatic gifts to whomever he desires (cf. 1 Cor 12:11). The same Spirit gives to the hierarchy of the Church the capacity to discern the authenticity of the charisms, to welcome them with joy and gratitude, to promote them generously, and to accompany them with vigilant paternity. (8)

In this context, the well-known theological affirmation of *Lumen Gentium* 10 is fully illuminated:

> The common priesthood of the faithful and the ministerial or hierarchical priesthood, although they differ in essence

> and not only in degree, are nevertheless ordered to each other; for they participate, each in its own particular way, in the one priesthood of Christ.[19]

This is a clarification added onto the original edition of the text inserted into chapter 2 of *Lumen Gentium*, dedicated to the people of God, to avoid possible misunderstandings. Three things are specified: (a) the *ordinatio ad invicem*, one with respect to another, of the two forms of the priesthood, that (b) both emanate and take form from the priesthood of Christ, (c) being distinct from each other "not in degree but in essence." The intentionality of the affirmation is completely clear, taking account of the precise ecclesiological context within which it is located. In fact, it reaffirms, on the one hand, that the two forms of priesthood refer to each other reciprocally, as the universal priesthood is the only purpose of the ministerial priesthood, and is therefore put at the complete service of the first, which, in turn, cannot exist if it is not being generated and nourished by the only priesthood of Christ, represented sacramentally by the ordained ministry. On the other hand, it also emphasizes that, precisely because of the peculiar and unrenounceable quality of this ministry, the difference between the two is not of degree (that is, it does not involve a relationship of superiority and inferiority) but of essence (as it expresses two realities that are formally differentiated, which cannot and should not come into competition, or worse, in conflict) but rather are "ordered" one to another.

We can say—to clarify this rigorous distinction and at the same time this intrinsic correlation—that both priesthoods have their source and take their form from the priesthood of Jesus, as he, in the paschal event, eschatologically became the one and only Mediator between God and humankind, and between people in God, in the exercise of the gift of self in the Holy Spirit "unto the end" for our brothers and sisters in obedience to *Abba*. Thus, it opens the space in which all are now called to live self-giving, one to another, in him, realizing in him the grace of unity: "As you, Father, are in me and I am in you, may they also be one in us" (cf. John 17:21–22). In this sense, the universal priesthood of the disciples is the participation as subject and thus in an existentially performative way in the new life that springs forth in the Spirit of the paschal Christ; while the ordained ministry (which can only be called priesthood in a derived sense with reference to the one priesthood of Christ) is deputed to the objective and sacramental representation of the priesthood of Christ, who is the principle and the originating, configuring form of the priesthood of all the people of God.

As a result, the ordained ministry is indeed *ministerium*, service (*διακονία*),[20] and this implies two directions: (a) in the service of the objective representation of the paschal event of Christ; and (b) in service to the subjective appropriation of this very event on the part of all the people of God. By virtue of its sacramentality, this effectively attests to "the way in which the love [of God in Christ] is reached up to the extremity of offering, which means sacrificing, himself…thus proving that his love was truly love and nothing but love."[21] The love lived by Christ in the *kenosis* of the incarnation and of the paschal event in fact reaches the extremity of handing over the *ἐξουσία* expressed in this eschatological gesture ("For this reason the Father loves me, because I lay down my life in order to take it up again. No one takes it from me, but I lay it down of my own accord. I have *ἐξουσία* to lay it down, and I have *ἐξουσία* to take it up again." John 10:17–18) to those who, though always unworthily, represent him and sacramentally represent the eschatological gesture; and they, in correspondence to this grace, are thus called to live the ministry they have received, in humble and generous service as baptized disciples, for Christ and for the people of God in the gift of their entire lives.[22]

EUCHARIST: *HOC EST SACRIFICIUM CHRISTIANORUM: MULTI UNUM CORPUS IN CHRISTO*[23]

From what has been said so far, the ordained ministry is clearly constitutional of the Church, being founded upon the priesthood of Christ and being conferred in the Holy Spirit in the service of the universal priesthood of the *communitas fidelium* as a *communitas sacerdotalis,* called to witness and communicate the salvific efficacy of the priesthood of Christ for the salvation of the world. Salvation, in the redemption from the slavery of sin and death, is realized along the paths of time, making the journey of union with God and the unity of all the human race accessible and feasible, always more and always better (cf.

LG 1). Now, in the context of the mission of the Church, the specificity of the ordained ministry appears in a more evident and efficacious way "in its own task of presiding over the Eucharist," through which the priesthood of the people of God is achieved and promoted. This is the deep experience and faith of the Church, rooted in its apostolicity and expressed in the exercise of its catholicity. Here a few essential comments are sufficient.

At the Heart of the Local Church

If the paschal mystery of Christ is the living center of salvation history, the Eucharist is its effective memorial and its celebration, "the summit toward which the activity of the Church is directed; at the same time it is the font from which all her power flows" (SC 10); in fact, thanks to this, "the faithful, united with their bishop, have access to God the Father through the Son, the Word made flesh, Who suffered and has been glorified, and so, in the outpouring of the Holy Spirit, they enter into communion with the most holy Trinity, being made 'sharers of the divine nature' (*2 Pt* 1:4)" (UR 15). This is an affirmation of fundamental importance for the intelligence of the doctrine in regard to the priesthood of Christ, of the people of God, and of the ordained ministers, which is taught by Vatican II.

In fact, to state—as in LG 26—that "in any community of the altar, under the sacred ministry of the bishop, there is exhibited a symbol of that charity and 'unity of the mystical Body, without which there can be no salvation,'" because "in these communities, though frequently small and poor, or living in the Diaspora, Christ is present, and in virtue of his presence there is brought together one, holy, catholic and apostolic Church," means stating that the ministry of the bishop—and, in communion with him and under his leadership, that of the priests his collaborators and of the deacons (cf. LG 20)—makes Christ present through the eucharistic celebration, in the local Christian community, as expression of the one, holy, catholic, and apostolic Church. In this sense, according to the magisterium of Vatican II, there is an organic connection: in regard to the episcopate, between its sacramental nature (cf. LG 21) and its intrinsic collegiality in relationship with the ministry of unity carried out by the Bishop of Rome (cf. LG 22); and in regard to the presbyterate and the diaconate, between their intrinsic relationship with the ministry of the bishop in service of the local Church and their essentially communitarian nature and mission (cf. LG 28, PO 7 and 8), in the peculiar form of the presbyterate one belongs to.[24]

But let us return to the celebration of the Eucharist. Here, the efficacy of the paschal mystery of Christ is manifested and expressed in the fullest possible way for the building of every local Church in the communion of the one and catholic Church for the *diakonia* of mission: because, in and for this, "Christ indeed always associates the Church—his beloved Bride—with himself" in the exercise of his *munus sacerdotale* that he realizes through his mystical Body, head and members (as SC 7 specifies). In fact, to "accomplish so great a work, Christ is always present in his Church, especially in her liturgical celebrations" (SC 7). *Sacrosanctum Concilium* illustrates this, contextualizing the specific presence of Christ that is realized in the liturgy thanks to the exercise of the ordained ministry in the convergent concert of the many ways Christ makes himself present to the Church:

> [Christ] is present in the sacrifice of the Mass, not only in the person of his minister, "the same now offering, through the ministry of priests, who formerly offered himself on the cross," but especially under the Eucharistic species. By his power he is present in the sacraments, so that when a man baptizes it is really Christ himself who baptizes. he is present in his word, since it is he himself who speaks when the holy scriptures are read in the Church. he is present, lastly, when the Church prays and sings, for he promised: "Where two or three are gathered together in my name, there am I in the midst of them" (Matt 18:20). (7)

The presence of Christ in the person of the minister—for whom the formula describing his action in a sacramental context as *agere in persona Christi capitis* is theologically pertinent—refers, on one hand, to how Christ is both head and bridegroom to the Church, his Body and his Bride; and, on the other hand, to the intentionality of his presence and his actions here being ordered in conformation to him, as his

Body and his Bride, through the Eucharist in service of the witness and communication of salvation to all the human family.

For Mission, the Sign of Reciprocal Charity to All

What does this entail concretely? St. Augustine illustrates this in book X of *De Civitate Dei*, a theme St. Thomas takes up again and deepens in the *Summa Theologiae*, while also referring to book IV of *De Trinitate:* where the one Mediator, Jesus Christ, is described as "reconciling us with God by means of his sacrifice of peace, he remaining one being with God to whom he offered himself, making all those to whom he offered himself one in him, he who offered being one with what he offered."[25] The Church—St. Augustine emphasizes—in the celebration of the Eucharist, "being a single Body with its Head, learns to offer itself through him."[26] Thus, in and through the sacrifice on the altar, it offers what it has received—the sacrifice of Christ—offering itself in this. Indeed, here the Church is constituted in its deep reality as *Corpus ipsius Capitis*. The Eucharist is therefore the inexhaustible spring of the divine energy that gives life to the Church—being the historical presence of the *populus Dei* as a *communio sanctorum* to which, as a *communio sanctorum*, God the Trinity, the angels and the faithful (both those still on their pilgrimage and those who have already arrived home) are bound together in *sancta societate*—which becomes a sign and efficacious instrument among humans of the eschatological advent of the *civitas Dei* in which God, at the end, will be "all in all" (1 Cor 15:28).

Through the mediation exercised by Christ and realized eschatologically in the sacrifice on the cross, the true and definitive worship is established in the Eucharist, wherein the Church is always newly offering itself in sacrifice for the salvation of the world, in the fire of charity sparked in hearts by the effusion of the Holy Spirit.[27] The "new commandment" of Christ (cf. John 13:34) is thus exercised in the double commandment of love in which the Law and the Prophets are summarized. It is, therefore, the form of the reciprocal charity received in the Holy Spirit by God the Trinity through the sacrifice of the one Mediator, Christ Jesus, the form of life of the Church in which his mission is realized: "By this everyone will know that you are my disciples, if you have love for one another" (John 13:35).

So much so that, with a striking formula, St. Augustine can conclude, "This is the sacrifice of the Christians: *Many, a single body in Christ.*"[28] This is an affirmation echoed, in the varied context and rapid change of the contemporary age, in Vatican II in *Gaudium et Spes*:

> While helping the world and receiving many benefits from it, the Church has a single intention: that God's kingdom may come, and that the salvation of the whole human race may come to pass. For every benefit which the People of God during its earthly pilgrimage can offer to the human family stems from the fact that the Church is "the universal sacrament of salvation," simultaneously manifesting and exercising the mystery of God's love. (GS 45)

In fact, Christ

> revealed to us that "God is love" (*1 Jn* 4:8) and at the same time taught us that the new command of love was the basic law of human perfection and hence of the world's transformation. To those, therefore, who believe in divine love, he gives assurance that the way of love lies open to men and that the effort to establish a universal brotherhood is not a hopeless one. (GS 38a)

ESCHATON: *VITA ECCLESIAE ABSCONDITA EST CUM CHRISTO IN DEO*[29]

The singular and eschatological quality of the priesthood of Christ has already emerged, as described above. This is expressed in the fact that, in his paschal event, he—as the Letter to the Hebrews puts it—offered himself ἐφάπαξ,[30] one time for all, made forever perfect as the priest of the new and eternal alliance (cf. Heb 7:26–27), is seated "at the right hand of the throne of the Majesty in the heavens" (Heb 8:1), whence he is able "for all time to save those who approach God through him, since he always lives to make intercession for them" (Heb 7:25). And thus, the Church, *communitas sacerdotalis*, in the celebration of the

Eucharist, professes its faith, acclaiming with gratitude, joy, and hope: "We announce your death, O Lord, and proclaim your resurrection, until you come again!"

The Eschatological "Seal" of the Priesthood of Christ

The eschatological quality of the paschal event of Christ is in fact participated in through grace by all the people of God: "you are dead,"—we read in the Letter to the Colossians—"and your life is hidden with Christ in God" (Col 3:1). It is in the light of this datum of faith that *Lumen Gentium* describes the Church as a Bride who invokes the final coming of her Bridegroom (cf. Rev 22:17), emphasizing that that the Church, "while on earth it journeys in a foreign land away from the Lord, is like in exile. It seeks and experiences those things which are above, where Christ is seated at the right-hand of God, where *vita Ecclesiae abscondita est cum Christo in Deo* (the life of the Church is hidden with Christ in God) until it appears in glory with its Spouse (cf. Col 3:1–4)" (LG 6).

The intrinsic eschatological quality of the paschal mystery of Christ, who invests and forms the mission of the Church as *communitas sacerdotalis*, being continually made present and nourished in the Eucharist, is imprinted as a seal (*σφραγίς*, cf. John 6:27) not only on the baptismal priesthood but also on the ministerial priesthood. And it is guaranteed through this. The very fact that—we find in the Letter to the Hebrews—through the priesthood of Christ "there is...the introduction of a better hope, through which we approach God" (Heb 7:19), implies that the exercise of the ministerial priesthood springs from the permanent grace conferred by the sacrament of orders as it is tied to the faithfulness of God and to the definitive gift made by Christ in his Passover: and not simply to the ever-fragile and fleeting correspondence of those who receive it. This experience of faith is the foundation for the traditional doctrine of faith according to which "the sacrament of Holy Orders confers an *indelible spiritual character* and cannot be repeated or conferred for a limited time."[31]

Thanks to this as well, the pilgrim Church on earth now experiences communion, in Christ, with the heavenly Church: and well-aware of the fact that it "in her sacraments and institutions, which pertain to this present time, has the appearance of this world which is passing" (LG 48), it, "embracing in its bosom sinners, at the same time holy and always in need of being purified, always follows the way of penance and renewal" (LG 8).

The Transformation of the World and the Prophecy of the Consecrated Life

In this eschatological context, we find the duty of all the people of God to transform the world, because—as *Gaudium et Spes* illustrates—"the expectation of a new earth must not weaken but rather stimulate our concern for cultivating this one. For here grows the body of a new human family, a body which even now is able to give some kind of foreshadowing of the new age" (39). Thus is realized, in service of the promotion of the universal brotherhood in justice and peace, the sacerdotal, prophetic, and regal *munus* of the people of God, in the certain hope in "the values of human dignity, brotherhood and freedom, and indeed all the good fruits of our nature and enterprise, we will find them again, but freed of stain, burnished and transfigured, when Christ hands over to the Father: 'A kingdom eternal and universal, a kingdom of truth and life, of holiness and grace, of justice, love and peace'" (39).

The kingdom of God, in fact, "is already present in mystery" (39): it is of this, in particular, that the specific state of life that, in the Church, is defined as "consecrated life" is called to bear witness to: following the path of the evangelical counsels of poverty, chastity, and obedience in the exercise of *vita communis*, through the dynamic equilibrium of contemplation and service to humanity in one's brothers and sisters who are in some way in need of spiritual and material care.[32] In consecrated life, the profundity of the eternal and infinite love of God witnessed to by the paschal mystery of Christ and communicated in the Eucharist is in fact made luminous and almost transparent: because it touches "the very roots of being" human (cf. *Vita Consecrata* 18) and transfigures it, in the chiaroscuro of "already" and "not yet," through the free and freely given involvement through Christ in the life of trinitarian love, the guarantee of "a new heaven and a new earth" (cf. Rev 21:1; 2 Pet 3:13).

The Historical Direction: "Let Us Then Go to Him Outside the Camp"

The eschatological quality of the paschal mystery, which the Church participates in through the Eucharist, finally traces a precise direction and imprints a specific style to the pilgrimage and to the *diakonia* of the Church, always extending an ever-renewed invitation to conversion, purification, and reform (cf. *Evangelii Gaudium* 30). It is not by chance that the Letter to the Hebrews, pointing to the paschal Christ as the chief priest of the new and eternal alliance, invites to "run with perseverance the race that is set before us, looking to Jesus, the pioneer and perfecter of faith" (Heb 12:1–2). This means—the Letter to the Hebrews expresses it with extraordinarily plastic vigor—to model one's own existence and animate one's own mission on the pro-existence of Jesus: who "suffered outside the city gate in order to sanctify the people by his own blood." Hence the invitation extended to the people of God: "Let us then go to him outside the camp, bearing the disgrace that he bore" (Heb 13:12–13).

With these pressing exhortations, we come to the coherent consequence of the novelty of the priesthood of Christ in which the Church participates. Going out, following Christ "outside the camp,"[33] means recognizing that the priesthood of Christ has destroyed, ἐφάπαξ, the "dividing wall of enmity" (cf. Eph 2:14) between who is "inside" the "camp" and who is "outside." In the sacrifice consummated on the cross "the curtain of the temple was torn in two, from top to bottom" (Mark 15:38). The priesthood of Christ is carried out on the Golgotha of the world, "outside" the camp, among the least, the discarded, the outcasts. No more is anyone a stranger or a foreigner: "whatever you did for one of the least of these brothers and sisters of mine, you did for me" (Matt 25:40).

It is not my task here to illustrate the consequences and the existential and pastoral implications for the exercise of the priesthood of the faithful and the ministerial priesthood in the mission of the Church, which derive from this intrinsic quality and intentionality of the priesthood of Christ. It is enough to say that it is in this very direction that we are invited to look, with παρρησία and ὑπομονή (parrhesia and perseverance)—to repeat two terms dear to the text of the Letter to the Hebrews—by the magisterium of gestures and words of Pope Francis.

MARIA: *MARIAE MATERNUM MUNUS ERGA HOMINES UNICAM MEDIATIONEM CHRISTI VIRTUTEM OSTENDIT* (CF. LG 60)

A last thing—certainly not of small or accessory importance—remains for me to say, reminding me of what was mentioned at the beginning: Pope Francis's invitation to look at Christ and be able to "enter" along with Mary "into the intimate structure of the Church," with the penetrating, loving look of faith. Yes, one cannot look at Christ, and at his priesthood, without also looking at Mary, the Mother of God, as the Council of Ephesus proclaimed her—the Mother of the Church, as St. Paul VI proclaimed her in his speech at the conclusion of the third period of the Council on November 21, 1964, to seal, as he himself states, the promulgation of the Constitution of the Church "Mary Most Holy Mother of the Church, of all the People of God, both of the faithful and the pastors."

The fact that *Lumen Gentium* is crowned by the illustration in chapter VIII of the *munus maternum* of the Blessed Virgin in the mystery of the Word incarnate and his Mystic Body (cf. 54) is pregnant with meaning, as she—to quote St. Augustine—"is truly the mother of the members (of Christ)...because she cooperated with charity in the birth of the faithful in the Church, who are the members of that Head" (53).[34] Hans Urs von Balthasar left us as a valuable legacy a profound theological reflection that invites us to examine, in the logic of faith, this specific *munus* of Mary in relation to the *communitas sacerdotalis* and also, in this and in service to this, to priestly ministry.[35]

If, as St. Thomas Aquinas notes in the tradition of the fathers of the Church, the annunciation of the angel to Mary was the manifestation of the event of a "certain spiritual marriage between the Son of God and human nature," so that "through the annunciation the consent of the Virgin was awaited *locus totius humanae naturae*, in the place of all human nature";[36] and if Mary's consent, expressed in the fiat of the annunciation, is replicated and consummated in the silent fiat expressed at the foot of the cross, the scope of her specific and "generative" *munus maternum* is not only christological but also ecclesiological. After all, the New Testament attests to it, respectively in the Gospel of Luke: "The angel said to her, 'The Holy Spirit will come upon you, and the power of the Most High will overshadow you; therefore the child to be born will be holy; he will be called Son of God'" (Luke 1:35) (Mary and the mystery of Christ); and in the Gospel of John: "When Jesus saw his mother and the disciple whom he loved standing beside her, he said to his mother, 'Woman, here is your son.' Then he said to the disciple, 'Here is your mother.' And from that hour the disciple took her into his own home" (John 19:26–27) (Mary and the Church, Body, and Bride of Christ).

In truth, Mary's fiat opens its virginal womb to welcome the incarnation of the Son of God in the Holy Spirit and the generation in the Holy Spirit of all as sons in the Son, "the firstborn among many brothers" (cf. Rom 8:29), through the divine *δύναμις* of the Holy Spirit thus made *Θείας κοινωνοὶφύσεως*, participants in the divine nature (2 Pet 1:4). Mary is almost "as though fashioned by the Holy Spirit and formed as a new creature," writes the Council (cf. LG 56): so that, in her—von Balthasar notes "the Church that springs from Christ finds its personal center and the full realization of its ecclesial idea"[37]—keenly representing, in the light and the strength of the Holy Spirit, "the pneumatic environment, the sole and exclusive place in which the events of the ministry can be verified…an environment formed by laypeople in the same way as by priests."[38] Mary in Christ is therefore the "super-ministerial foundation of the Church."[39]

Hence the Marian profile of the Church which envelops its apostolic-Petrine profile, specific to the ordained ministry constituted in it in service of the growth and journey of the people of God.[40] Hence the Marian form, which, depending on and deriving from the priesthood of Christ, both the universal priesthood and the ministerial priesthood receive through grace and are called to assume in the mission of the Church: the first, only by living the fiat of Mary does it participate synergically, in virtue of the sacrament of baptism, confirmation, and marriage, in the salvific action of Christ in the Holy Spirit; the second, also only by living the fiat of Mary in adhesion to the specific grace conferred by the sacrament of orders does it become a cooperator, not only in the efficacious transmission of the gift of God but also in its transparent and incisive fruition.

As Antonio Rosmini loved to say, living in Christ is the "short formula" of existence of all Christians, such that every disciple of Christ should come to say with Christ, "I have been crucified with Christ; and it is no longer I who live, but it is Christ who lives in me" (Gal 2:19–20), and as he lives in me he must live among us (cf. Matt 18:20) because Jesus has prayed to the Father "so that all will be one, like you and I"; through the ordained minister the specific grace conferred with ordination brings with it the intrinsic requirement, or rather the "postulate"—von Balthasar writes—"of the assimilation to the existing priesthood of Christ. Every voluntary misuse of this is not simply against 'professional morality'...but is a violation of the structure of love of the Trinity itself."[41]

But we can take yet another step. The reference to the ideal Marian form of the Church illuminates and stimulates us in the interpretation and living-out of the relationships between those who incarnate the states of life in which Christian existence is determined—in its vibrant and creative pluriformity, operated and harmonized by the Holy Spirit—from the call of grace and from the correspondence in faith, hope, and love. In the pneumatic space opened up by Mary's fiat, "the gift and duty to implement the 'reciprocal inhabitation (*circumincessio*)' of these states of life are 'in simply being one for the other' is unfolded."[42] The gift of the life of God the Trinity, of which the Church is a sacrament, flows from the Father and through the crucified and risen Son, and is shared by the Holy Spirit in a total and ever-new way, through the Eucharist, to all the people of God. The Eucharist is given to the Church through the ministerial priesthood, which makes present the priesthood of Christ in the communication of the life of God—who is the life of trinitarian love—to the brothers and sisters who thus exercise it on their own, each in their own state of life in the relationships of love that one lives for another in service of the human society and family: anticipating, in the persevering and generous tension toward the evangelical perfection of charity (cf. LG 39), the certain promise of the heavenly Jerusalem. This is the *res*, and therefore reality realized and promoted in the "already" and "not yet" of history from, in, and as Church: as it is, in Christ, for the world, "a sacrament or as a sign and instrument both of a very closely knit union with God and of the unity of the whole human race" (LG 1). For this reason, as Card. Marc Ouellet writes, today we need

> a deep trinitarian examination of the common belonging of the ecclesial states of life in which the state of the evangelical counsels can assume a role of mediation between the priesthood and the laity. In the ordered trinitarian representation of the ecclesial states of life, a mutual exchange and interpenetration is realized in which the nuptial mystery of the one God is reflected and given in Christ to his creation, in service, in his being an end in himself, in the altruism and free-ness of love. It belongs to the *kairós* of consecrated life in the world to provide and enrich with the freedom of the Holy Spirit this reciprocal fertile influx of the ecclesial states of life in a discreet, kenotic way.[43]

To accept and carry the incommensurable and inexhaustible gift of God in their fragile "earthen vessels" (cf. 2 Cor 4:7), each makes their own contribution, as do, in reciprocity, the different states of life lived by the people of God in making themselves freely and joyously be shaped by the Spirit of Christ *in the womb of Mary, Mater misericordiae* and *Mater unitatis*. The gaze of faith, hope, and love that the disciples—all of them!—are called to learn at her school, in order to live the synodal Church and build a truly just and fraternal planetwide society, in dialogue with their brothers and sisters of every faith and conviction (I am pleased to conclude with these words by Pope Francis) that is in fact

> this inclusive way of seeing things, which transcends tensions by "keeping" and "pondering," is the way of mothers, who, in moments of tension, do not divide, they *keep*, and in this way enable life to grow. It is the way so many mothers embrace the problems of their children. Their maternal "gaze" does not yield to stress; it is not paralyzed before those problems, but sees them in a wider perspective.... Theirs is a gaze that is conscious and realistic, but at the same time

offering, beyond the pain and the problems, *a bigger picture, one of care and love that gives birth to new hope.*[44]

NOTES

1. Pope Francis, *Speech on the Occasion of the 50th Anniversary of the Institution of the Synod of Bishops*, Paul VI Audience Hall, October 17, 2015.

2. Pope Francis, postsynodal apostolic exhortation *Querida Amazonia*, February 2, 2020, 101.

3. A. Vanhoye, *Prêtres anciens, prêtre nouveau selon le Nouveau Testament* (Paris: Éditions du Seuil, 1980), 348–49, our translation.

4. SC 5.

5. As the bibliography regarding our theme available in the theological literature is immense, I will limit myself to pointing at E. Castellucci's balanced and fortunate essay, *Il ministero ordinato*, Nuovo Corso di Teologia sistematica, 10 (Brescia: Queriniana, 2002), which has the merit of offering an updated panoramic on the state of the art in relation to Sacred Scripture, dogmatic and theological Tradition, the magisterium of Vatican II, with a recognition of the debate and the postconciliar study (specified by the reference to the works and proposals of, among others, H. U. von Balthasar, J. Ratzinger, L. Scheffczyk, Y. Congar, K. Rahner, E. Schillebeeckx, S. Dianich, G. Greshake, G. Martelet) and a coherent and forward-looking systematic treatment, all enriched by a vast bibliography (351–81) and by the timely "themes of study" annotated at the end of the individual chapters.

6. *Sacrosanctum Concilium* 5: "Nam de latere Christi in cruce dormientis ortum est totius Ecclesiae mirabile sacramentum."†

7. Thomas Aquinas, *S.Th.*, III, q. 22, a. 1 *corpus*: "Unde Christo maxime convenit esse sacerdotem."

8. Thomas Aquinas, *S.Th.*, III, q. 22, a. 2*um*: "Quia igitur sacerdotium veteris legis erat figura sacerdotii Christi, noluit Christus nasci de stirpe figuralium sacerdotum, ut ostendetur non esse omnino idem sacerdotium, sed differre sicut verum a figurali."

9. Thomas Aquinas, *S.Th.*, III, q. 22, a. 4 *corpus*: "Christus autem est fons totius sacerdotii: nam sacerdos legalis erat figura ipsius; sacerdos autem novae legis in persona ipsius operator."

10. Augustine, *De Civitate Dei*, XX,10.

11. The Decree *Presbyterorum Ordinis,* in an even more explicit and articulate form, states, "The Lord Jesus, 'whom the Father has sent into the world' (*Jn* 10:36) has made his whole Mystical Body a sharer in the anointing of the Spirit with which he himself is anointed. In him all the faithful are made a holy and royal priesthood; they offer spiritual sacrifices to God through Jesus Christ, and

they proclaim the perfections of him who has called them out of darkness into his marvelous light. Therefore, there is no member who does not have a part in the mission of the whole Body; but each one ought to hallow Jesus in his heart, and in the spirit of prophecy bear witness to Jesus. The same Lord, however, has established ministers among his faithful to unite them together in one body in which, 'not all the members have the same function' (*Rm* 12:4). These ministers in the society of the faithful are able by the sacred power of orders to offer sacrifice and to forgive sins, and they perform their priestly office publicly for men in the name of Christ" (2).

12. Cf. CTI, *L'apostolicità della Chiesa e la successione apostolica* (1973), n. 5; in Commissione Teologica Internazionale, *Documenti 1969–2004*, 2nd ed., revised and expanded (Bologna: Edizioni Studio Domenicano, 2010), pp. 48-64, in particular nos. 5 and 6, pp. 57–62.

13. CTI, *L'apostolicità della Chiesa e la successione apostolica* (1973), n. 5, in Commissione Teologica Internazionale, p. 61.

14. CTI, *Il sacerdozio cattolico* (1970), n. 4; in Commissione Teologica Internazionale, pp. 42–43.

15. CTI, *Il sacerdozio cattolico*, n. 3. J. M. Tillard also emphasizes that the "sacerdotalization" of the ministries seems to be a typical case of the creativity of the community that goes beyond the reading of Scripture without actually betraying the spirit of Christ" ("La 'qualité sacerdotale' du ministère chrétien," *Nouvelle Revue Théologique*, 95 [1973]: 481–514, here 513). It should also be noted that the BEM as well (*Baptism, Eucharist and Ministry*, of the World Council of Churches, Lima 1982) states that the bearers of the ministry, "as they strengthen and build the priesthood" of the faithful, can "appropriately be called priests" (cf. 17). In truth—as LG 28 states, following in the footprints of the Council of Trent— "the divinely established ecclesiastical ministry is exercised on different levels by those who from antiquity have been called bishops, priests and deacons," but the deacons are—LG 29 clarifies—"at a lower level of the hierarchy," "upon whom hands are imposed 'not unto the priesthood, but unto a ministry of service.'"

16. ITC, *Synodality in the Life and Mission of the Church*, March 2, 2018, no. 17. Cf. also see this entry in GLNT ([II, 558–69] 629–57), edited by W. Foerster, who emphasizes both "the position of Jesus as the head of the community that has received every power and transmits it to others" and "that freedom that marks the Christian community's way of being" ([II, 563] 643).

17. ITC, *Synodality in the Life and Mission of the Church*, no. 18.

18. For this concept of synodality, see the already-quoted document of the ITC, *Synodality in the Life and Mission of the Church*, cf. here, in particular, nos. 55 and 70.

19. *Lumen Gentium* 10: "Sacerdotium commune fidelium et sacerdotium ministeriale seu hierarchicum, licet essentia et non gradu tantum differant, ad

invicem tamen ordinantur; unum enim et alterum suo peculiari modo de uno Christi sacerdotio participant."

20. LG 24 clearly notes this: "And that duty (*munus*) which the Lord committed to the shepherds of his people, is a true service (*servitium*), which in sacred literature is significantly called 'diakonia' or ministry (*ministerium*). (cf. Acts 1:17,25; 21:19; Rom 11:13; 1 Tim 1:12)." Pertinent things here are also written by Castellucci, *Il ministero ordinato*, 297–303.

21. H.U. von Balthasar, *Gli stati di vita del cristiano* (Milan: Jaca Book, 1996), 221 (Eng. ed. *Christian State of Life* [San Francisco: Ignatius Press, 1977]).

22. This is what was sublimely understood and lived by, for example, St. Julian Eymard, the great saint of the Eucharist, who out of the contemplation of it developed the requirement for his priestly life to make a gift of his own personality with a vow to Christ, because he could fully take its place: "You will live for me, because I will live in you—says Christ to the saint. I will fill your soul with my desires and my life which will consume or annihilation everything that is your own…I will be the person of your personality and your personality will be the life of mine in you" (quoted by L. Saint-Pierre, *L'heure du cénacle dans la vie et les ouevres de P.-J. Eymard* [Lyon, 1968], 293).

23. Augustine, *De Civ. Dei*, X.

24. We should not ignore or undervalue the theological and specifically ecclesiological significance of the clear affirmation of the sacramentality of the episcopate with the meaning implied in reference to the one priesthood of Christ, which, in such a way, is recognized as being conferred ministerially to the individual bishops in conformity to the *indoles et ratio collegialis* (cf. LG 22), which is proper to it as it emanates from the sacrament itself that, as such, expresses its intentionality, derived from its relationship with the one priesthood of Christ, only in the *communio hierarchica* of the episcopal college: which—on its own level—is reproposed for the priest in the *communio* of the presbyterate, under the presidency of the bishop, to whom per se it belongs. The relationship with the priesthood of Christ that expresses itself in the independently communional nature and reason of its meaning and its exercise in service of the people of God is therefore rooted in the sacramental nature of the ordained ministry.

25. Augustine, *De Trinitate*, IV, 14, 19: "Quattuor considerantur in omni sacrificio: cui offeratur, a quo offeratur, quid offeratur, pro quibus offeratur; idem ipse unus verusque Mediator, per sacrificium pacis reconcilians nos Deo, unum cum illo maneret cui offerebat, unum in se faceret pro quibus offerebat, unus ipse esset qui offerebat et quod offerebat" cf. *S.Th.*, III, q. 22, a. 3, ad 1*um* e ad 2*um*.

26. Augustine, *De Civ. Dei*, X, 20: "Cuius rei sacramentum cotidianum esse voluit Ecclesiae sacrificium, quaecum ipsius capitis corpus sit, se ipsam per ipsum discit offerre."

27. Benedict XVI writes in *Sacramentum Caritatis*, "The Eucharist reveals the loving plan that guides all of salvation history (cf. Eph 1:10; 3:8–11). There

the *Deus Trinitas*, who is essentially love (cf. 1 John 4:7–8), becomes fully a part of our human condition. In the bread and wine under whose appearances Christ gives himself to us in the paschal meal (cf. Luke 22:14–20; 1 Cor 11:23–26), God's whole life encounters us and is sacramentally shared with us" (8). "Jesus left us the task of entering into his 'hour.' 'The Eucharist draws us into Jesus' act of self-oblation'" (11), and therefore the "mysticism" of the Eucharist does not only have an "ecclesial character" (15), but also has a "social character" (89).

28. Augustine, *De Civ. Dei*, X, 6: "Hoc est sacrificium Christianorum: Multi unum corpus in Christo."

29. LG 6, cf. Col 3:1–4.

30. As Gustav Stählin states, "In the NT it is a technical term to indicate the unique and therefore definitive character of the death of Christ and the redemption that follows from it," as is clear from Rom 6:10 and Heb 7:27; 9:12; 10:10 (in GLNT [I,380–383] 1019–28).

31. Cf. *Catechism of the Catholic Church*, 1582. It is worth noting how J. Zizioulas emphasizes that in the ordained ministry we are dealing not with "something of *temporal* but of *eschatological* value," so that "the sacramental character of the priestly ministry in its consequences for ordination cannot be defined either through ontologism or through functionalism, but only through the concept of *koinonía*, which is participation and love, and through its *eschatological* definitivity" ("Priesteramt und Priesterweihe Im Licht der östlich-orthodoxen Theologie," in *Der Priesterliche Dienst. Amt und Ordination in ökumenischer Sicht*, ed. H. Vorglimler [Freiburg: Herder Verlag, 1973], 72–113, here respectively 99 and 101, no. 83; English language version in *Being as Communion: Studies in Personhood and the Church* [Crestwood, NY: St. Vladimir's Seminary Press, 1997], 209–46; cf. B. Petrà, "Il ministero ordinato nella teologia ortodossa del XX secolo. Percorsi storici e prospettive," in ATI, *Il ministero ordinato. Nodi teologici e prassi ecclesiali*, a cura di M. Qualizza, [San Paolo: Cinisello Balsamo, 2004], 205–41).

32. To discern the relevant theological meaning of the concept of consecrated life and as a consequence the specific role of this state of life in concert with the people of God, one must bear in mind that in the ecclesial lexicon, *consecration* means being freely drawn, through grace, into the sphere of irradiation of the sanctity of God, three times holy, which happens in the discipleship of Jesus Christ in virtue of the Holy Spirit. This takes place for us in baptism, from which the progressive conformation to the sanctity of God blossoms until he becomes all in all, corresponding to the freedom in the action of grace: "Be perfect, therefore, as your heavenly Father is perfect" (Matt 5:48). On this foundation, the consecration referred to when one speaks of "consecrated life," through the initiative of God and within the space of the universal vocation to sanctity (cf. LG chap. V), *proprio quodam modo* (cf. LG 39), calls and enables this particular union with God, in Christ and in the participation in a charism of the Holy Spirit, which is

intended to appear "as a sign which can and ought to attract all the members of the Church to an effective and prompt fulfillment of the duties of their Christian vocation" (LG 44). In this sense, as St. John Paul II emphasizes in *Vita Consecrata,* "the consecrated life is at the very heart of the Church as a decisive element for her mission, since it 'manifests the inner nature of the Christian calling and the striving of the whole Church as Bride toward union with her one Spouse'" (3). The nature of the "sign," therefore, which characterizes consecrated life in the historical journey of the people of God, gives it a privileged position in the dimension of evangelical prophecy, as testimonial visibility and realistic anticipation, in the journey of the people of God along the paths of history, of the eschatological goal to which the Christian vocation is itself directed *qua talis* in faithful and creative response to the election of grace and mercy of God the Trinity.

33. In fact, according to the Letter to the Hebrews, "While the preceding exhortations invited to enter (4:11) in imitation of Christ who entered into the true sanctuary, or to draw closer to the high priest seated on the right hand of God, the present invitation pushes us toward a movement in the opposite direction. All the same, the goal of the movement is the same, toward him. The change of direction in movement required is similar to the significant changes in the antitheses of the discourse of the central section, where the essential element of the 'heavenly' sacrifice did not result from a passage through the planetary spheres or the halls of a celestial temple, but from entering into the world (10:5). In the same way, here it is stated that the approach to Christ is reached not by entering a particular sacral sphere but, in imitation of the 'inaugurator of the faith,' requires a movement 'outside the camp.'" (H. W. Attridge, *La Lettera agli Ebrei. Commento storico esegetico* [Città del Vaticano: Libreria Editrice Vaticana, 1999], 653).

34. Augustine, *De S. Virginitate*, 6; PL 40, 399.

35. cf. M. Ouellet, "Identità del sacerdote e dignità dei laici. Piste di riflessione a partire da H. U. von Balthasar, " in *La sfida dell'unità. I carismi e la Trinità,* Le Cattedre di Sophia, 2 (Rome: Città Nuova, 2011), 49–88.

36. Thomas Aquinas, *S.Th.*, III, q. 30, a. 1: "Ut ostenderetur esse quoddam spirituale matrimonium inter filium Dei et humanam naturam. Et ideo per Annuntiationem expetebatur consensus virginis loco totius humanae naturae."

37. H. U. von Balthasar, "Chi è la Chiesa?," in *Sponsa Verbi. Saggi Teologici*, II (Rome: Jaca Book, 19722), 157. "Who Is the Church?" in *Spouse of the Word.*

38. Id., *Il laico nella Chiesa*, 317.

39. Id., *Il laico nella Chiesa*, 312.

40. On this theme in reference to the lesson of von Balthasar, see B. Leahy, *Il principio mariano nella Chiesa* (Rome: Città Nuova, 1999).

41. H. U. von Balthasar, "Sacerdoti della nuova alleanza," in *Lo Spirito e l'istituzione* (Brescia: Morcelliana, 1979), 312–13 (even if it would perhaps be correct to deepen the conversation, asking if it might be possible to speak of a created

trinitarian structure intended for divinization as "trinitization" in the temporal realities Balthasar indicates).

42. H. U. von Balthasar, *Gli stati di vita del cristiano,* 333.

43. M. Ouellet, *La sfida dell'unità*, 86–87.

44. Pope Francis, *Holy Mass on the Solemnity of Mary, Mother of God. 54th World Day of Peace*, January 1, 2022.

11

THE ECUMENICAL CHALLENGES OF THE PRIESTHOOD

Cardinal Kurt Koch

MINISTRY AS THE REAL ISSUE OF ECUMENISM

DURING THE PAST sixty years, in the different ecumenical dialogues that the Catholic Church has carried out and continues to carry out with various Churches and ecclesial communities, broad agreements or at the very least promising rapprochements have been reached. A theme that still proves itself to be a great ecumenical stumbling-block is the question of ministry. As the Catholic theologian Wolfgang Beinert observes, it is "perhaps the only ecumenical problem that is still truly far from a universally acceptable solution."[1] The difficulty is evident from the fact that the lack of eucharistic communion between the Churches is due not only to the differences in the doctrine of the Eucharist or the Supper of the Lord, but chiefly to the doctrine of ministry, because from a Catholic perspective, celebration of the Eucharist essentially requires the presence of a priest. The difficulty becomes even more fundamental when it comes to defining and evaluating the ecclesial nature of the non-Catholic ecclesial communities from a Catholic perspective.

This difficulty had already emerged during the Second Vatican Council. When it came to the Orthodox and Eastern Orthodox churches, there was no particular problem in defining them as Churches because they involve the episcopal ministry in the apostolic succession and all the valid sacraments, the Eucharist in particular, and therefore present the essential ecclesial elements that make them individual Churches.[2]

However, when it comes to the Western communities born of the Reformation, a problem is posed of whether or not it is possible to use the term *Church* in a theologically full sense, even for the communities where there is not, or at least there is no certainty of being, an episcopal ministry in the apostolic succession, and where only some of the sacraments are recognized. As Johannes Feiner reports in his commentary on the Decree on Ecumenism, *Unitatis Redintegratio*,[3] there was great dissent between the Council fathers who wanted to call the non-Catholic Western communities "Churches," although only analogously, and the other fathers who objected that a community where an episcopal ministry in the apostolic succession did not exist could not be defined as a "Church." Given this serious dissent, Cardinal Franz König of Vienna proposed[4] in the conciliar debate that these communities could and should be called *communitates ecclesiales*. In the end, this proposal won out. The intention of this term was to express the presence, on one hand, of an ecclesial nature, and on the other hand, the absence of the structural elements necessary to be fully a Church. The Decree on Ecumenism, *Unitatis Redintegratio*, mentions here that the chief deficit is the *sacramenti ordinis defectus* and consequently the lack of the preservation of the "genuine and whole substance of the Eucharistic mystery."[5]

The episcopal ministry in the apostolic succession and the validity of the Eucharist are therefore the decisive criteria for the Second Vatican Council when it comes to the use of the term *Church* for the ecclesial communities that are separate from the Catholic Church. The Congregation for the Doctrine of the Faith has recorded this fundamental ecclesiological theme during the Jubilee in 2000 with its "Declaration on the Unicity and Salvific Universality of Jesus Christ and the Church" entitled *Dominus Iesus*.[6] In this document, the Eastern Churches are defined as "true particular Churches," while the ecclesial communities that "have not preserved the valid episcopate and the genuine and integral substance of the Eucharistic mystery" are not considered "Churches in the proper sense."[7] This difference of definition between the Churches of the East and the ecclesial communities in the West has also made it clear that the ecumenical discussion on the question of ministry must be conducted in a distinct and different way in the various ecumenical dialogues.

MINISTRY IN CATHOLIC-ORTHODOX DIALOGUE

During the first decade, from 1980 to 1990, the Joint International Commission for Theological Dialogue between the Catholic Church and the Orthodox Church as a whole was concerned with the fundamental questions of faith and the important theological themes on which it was possible to reach full convergence.[8] After addressing questions related to the theological understanding of the concept of Church and of the relationship between faith, sacraments, and the unity of the Church, in 1988 the Plenary Assembly at Uusi Valamo in Finland reflected on the theological meaning and the mission of the consecrated ministry in the Church and published the important document entitled "The Sacrament of Order in the Sacramental Structure of the Church, with Particular Reference to the Importance of Apostolic Succession for the Sanctification and Unity of the People of God."[9] As the title hints, convictions of faith offer a broad common foundation and, in particular, a significant convergence with regard to the consecrated ministry between the ecclesial communities.

The Connection between Ministry and Eucharist

The decisive reason for this resides in the fact that both communities preserve the basic ecclesiological structures that developed from the second century onward, which means the basic sacramental-eucharistic and episcopal structures of the Church, in the sense that in both the Churches, unity in the Eucharist, and the episcopate in the apostolic succession as a service of unity, are considered foundational to being a Church. Pope Benedict XVI spoke of this broad common ground with precision: "Among Christian Churches and communities, it is undoubtedly the Orthodox who are theologically closest to us; Catholics and Orthodox have maintained the same basic structure inherited from the ancient Church; in this sense we are all the early Church that is still present and new."[10]

So it is not surprising that at the center of the Catholic-Orthodox document are the episcopal ministry and the sacrament of the Eucharist, with their intrinsic connection. In fact, according to Orthodox ecclesiology, which is strictly eucharistic, ministry in the Church is understood chiefly starting from the Eucharist. Above all, this applies to the episcopal ministry, whose fulcrum is the eucharistic celebration: "The role of the bishop is fulfilled by presiding over the Eucharistic assembly" (41). The strong emphasis put on the bishop in the Orthodox theology of ministry is based on the fact that the "fullness of priesthood" (28) is conferred on the bishop, in the consecration that takes place through the gift of the Holy Spirit. And so the other ministries derive from the bishop, in particular the ministry of the priest, who, "consecrated by the bishop and dependent on him" is also understood starting with the Eucharist, as the very first Catholic-Orthodox document affirms: "One of the essential tasks of the priest is to gather the community of the faithful to the Eucharistic celebration of the bishop and nourish them with the apostolic faith of which the bishop is witness and guarantor."[11] Lastly, the deacon is at the service of the bishop and the priest and "acts as a link between them and the assembly of the faithful" (41).

The close connection between ministry and Eucharist becomes fully understandable when we realize that the statements on the consecrated ministry of the Church in Catholic-Orthodox dialogue are based on the presentation of the mystery of the Church as a community of faith and sacrament, a community that manifests itself and is supremely realized in the eucharistic celebration. Because the Church has a sacramental character, clearly the ecclesial ministry as well is of a "sacramental nature." This vision of the sacramentality of the consecrated ministry is built on the fact that Jesus Christ is made present in the Church by means of the Holy Spirit; which implies that "the minister is a member of the community of the faithful to whom the Holy Spirit confers special functions and powers to gather the community and preside, in the name of Christ, over the acts with which the community celebrates the mysteries of salvation" (11).

Therefore, it becomes clear as well that the consecrated ministry is at the service of the whole Church. As there can be no Church without ministries derived from the Holy Spirit, so there is "no ministry without the Church; in other words, without or above the community." The ministries only find "their meaning and their reason for being" in the Church (5). The ecclesial dimension also includes the common baptismal priesthood, regarding which the ecumenical document states that all the members of the Church, as members of the Body of Christ, participate in his priesthood. This in turn becomes particularly clear and effective in the celebration of the Eucharist, where the whole assembly, each in their own place, is the "liturgy of the koinonia." This is where the bishop assumes the "ministry of presiding over the assembly of the faithful in unity" (24–25). And because it is essential for the Church, in virtue of the Eucharist, to be in communion with the other communities, the unity of the local Church is inseparable from the universal communion of the Churches, and this communion is manifested and realized in the college of the bishops.

The Unity of Sacrament and Jurisdiction

These few references demonstrate that there are almost no differences between the Catholic Church and the Orthodox Churches regarding the consecrated ministry, but rather a full convergence that reaches as far as the exclusion of the consecration of women: "Our Churches remain faithful to the historical and theological tradition wherein only men are consecrated to the priesthood" (32). The greatest problem, yesterday and today, continues to be the different understanding of the ministry of the Bishop of Rome, an understanding that still has an impact on the interpretation of ministry in general. But even here, it has been possible to take steps closer to the Orthodox Church. In fact, Pope Benedict XVI went so far as to state that the Eastern Churches are "true particular Churches," even if they are not in communion with the pope, and in this sense unity with the pope "is not foundational to the particular Church." Nonetheless, this lack of unity is also "an internal lack of the particular Church" and, therefore, a lack of communion with the pope is "an insufficiency of this vital cell." In short, the pope claims, "A cell remains, it can call itself a Church, but an element is lacking in the cell, which is the connection with the entire organism."[12]

The truly controversial point in ecumenical dialogue lies therefore in the fact that, even if Orthodoxy recognizes the Bishop of Rome as first (*protos*) in the order of the bishoprics, as the Council of Nicaea already established, from a Catholic perspective the idea that "the Pope is first and also has specific functions and tasks" is fundamental.[13] On the basis of this difference, there is a much deeper problem, which is of great importance for the question of ministry from an ecumenical perspective. The reason that Orthodoxy sees in the primacy of the Bishop of Rome, especially in the historical development that took place in the second millennium, an upheaval or, in fact, a "destruction of the ecclesial structure as such," "in the wake of which something new and different took the place of the old form of the Church,"[14] is because Orthodox theology considers the inseparable unity between sacrament and jurisdiction to be fundamental, a unity that is violated in the papacy, as the papacy is not sacramental, but "only" a juridical position, which is still imposed on the sacramental order. A renewed reflection on the relationship between sacramentality and jurisdiction is necessary not just for the Catholic-Orthodox dialogue but could also be useful for the ecumenical discussion on the consecrated ministry between the Churches and the ecclesial communities born of the Reformation.

MINISTRY IN CATHOLIC-PROTESTANT DIALOGUE

In the ecumenical dialogue with the ecclesial communities of the West, different documents have been produced that address the topic of ecclesial ministry. This is especially true of Catholic-Lutheran dialogue, which has allowed for the publication of numerous documents of consensus and convergence: the so-called Malta Report, "The Gospel and the Church" in 1972, "Spiritual Ministry in the Church" in 1981, "The Apostolicity of the Church" in 2009, and "From Conflict to Communion" in 2013. To these we can add documents that were born from dialogues with various Protestant communities, in particular the in-depth studies of the Ecumenical Working Group of Protestant and Catholic theologians in Germany, like the text "Doctrinal Condemnations—a Cause of Division in the Church?" on justification, the sacraments, and the ministry, and "The Ecclesial Ministry in the

Apostolic Succession" (2004–2008). Of course, we cannot yet speak of a sustainable consensus capable of paving the way to a mutual recognition of the respective ministries, because there are still open questions that need to be addressed.

The Sacerdotal and Episcopal Ministries

Starting with the question of the episcopal ministry, the most obvious thing is that, during the Reformation, while fundamentally recognizing this ministry, the behavior of the bishops was largely spoken of in a critical or hostile way, something that is also reflected in the Augsburg Confession. Although this includes positive affirmations of the episcopal ministry, the extensive article 28 consists of the clear distinction between the true spiritual tasks of the bishop *iuredivino* and his secular political powers *iurehumano*, and more precisely in the "difference between the power of the Church and the power of the sword." With regard to the clear need to not mix ecclesial and political powers, there can be no difference in confession, and in fact, there could not be any difference, even at the time, as the statement of St. Bernard of Clairvaux, appealing to the conscience of Pope Eugene, demonstrates: "Do not believe that you are the successor of Constantine; you are not the successor of Constantine, but of Peter. For you the authoritative book is not the Code of Justinian, but Sacred Scripture."[15] Today, however, this topic has lost its relevance.

In the historical context of the Reformation, one must first consider the question of the structure of the ecclesial ministry, that is, the question of its division into three levels, according to the understanding of the time. It is well-known that the Reformers were convinced that the episcopal ministry was of equal importance to spiritual ministry in general, but one occupying a different ecclesial level. With this conviction, they also defended the practice of ordinations performed by pastors, invoking Hieronymus, for whom the distinction between bishop and priest was a difference only as it pertained to human jurisdiction. This conviction was still present in the Middle Ages, especially for Pietro Lombardo, who recognized the true power conferred at the moment of ordination in the power of consecration, in regard to which he still did not believe that there was a difference between a bishop and a priest. As a consequence, the difference was not on a sacramental level but a juridical one, with the consequence that the episcopal consecration was not seen as a sacrament, but only sacramental. The Second Vatican Council marked a significant turning point, teaching that "the fullness of the sacrament of Holy Orders is conferred by episcopal consecration," "with the office of sanctifying, also the offices of teaching and ruling"[16] being conferred. Since from a Catholic perspective, the episcopal ministry is seen as the complete form of the consecrated ministry and therefore as the starting point for the theological interpretation of ecclesial ministry in general,[17] the episcopal ministry must have a special place among the themes dealt with in ecumenical dialogues.

The Baptismal Priesthood of All the Faithful and the Ecclesial Ministry

To address the question adequately, it is, of course, necessary to go deeper. In the dialogue between the Churches and the ecclesial communities born of the Reformation, we should start with the common priesthood of all baptized believers, which has its biblical foundation in the second chapter of the First Letter of Peter, in which an ancient baptismal catechesis is preserved. Regarding the baptismal priesthood, there is a consensus on the fact that all the baptized participate in the priesthood of Christ and are called to proclaim the gospel. The differences emerge when trying to understand the precise relationship that exists between the baptismal priesthood common to all believers and the specifically ministerial priesthood. To this end, the Second Vatican Council locates the difference between the two forms of priesthood not on the subjective-personal level of vocation, but on the objective-theological level of mission: "Though they differ from one another in essence and not only in degree, the common priesthood of the faithful and the ministerial or hierarchical priesthood are nonetheless interrelated. Each of them in its own special way is a participation in the one priesthood of Christ."[18]

The unanswered question that needs further discussion in the dialogue with the ecclesial communities born of the Reformation is to understand whether the ecclesial ministry is composed of a specific reality with an "ontological" nature, based on a sacramental consecration, such that a sacramental identity is proper to the ministerial priesthood, according to the Catholic vision, or if the ecclesial ministry derives directly from the baptismal priesthood common to all the faithful, conferred by the community of the faithful and for this reason called "ordination."

This last perspective is outlined more pronouncedly with the ordination of women in the Churches of the Reformation, as in these Churches, because of the close connection between the common baptismal priesthood and the ministry bound by ordination, the ordination of women is seen as an element so essential that when other Churches refuse to practice it, they are criticized as having a *defectus ordinis*. All the same, even setting aside this question, which has become crucial in ecumenical dialogues, the Protestant theology of ministry generally maintains the derivation of the ordained ministry from the common baptismal priesthood, while the specificity of the ordained ministry is defined by its public character, or more precisely in the public task of the "proclamation of the Gospel through word and sacrament within the community."[19]

A Divine Institution or a Delegation of the Community of the Faithful?

An important ecumenical question is therefore posed—whether ministry is foundational to being Church and appertains to its essence, to the *esse ecclesiae*, or whether it appertains simply to the *bene esse* and is therefore at the discretion of the Church. If we consider the Augsburg Confession, the basic Lutheran Confessional document, the facts are clear. The article on ecclesial ministry directly follows the article on justification and emphasizes that the ministry "that proclaims the Gospel and administers the sacraments" is instituted so that we can acquire faith in justification: "The word and the sacraments are in fact the means through which the Holy Spirit is bestowed. He bestows faith when and where God wants."[20]

In article 7 of the Augsburg Confession, which is fundamental for ecclesiology, the Church is defined as a "congregation of saints" "in which the Gospel is rightly (*pure*) taught and the sacraments are rightly (*recte*) administered"; it is then added that it is "enough" (*satisest*) for the true unity of the Church "to agree concerning the doctrine of the Gospel and the administration of the Sacraments." In ecumenical terms, the way that this *satisest* is interpreted is important. On the one hand, it is stressed that *satisest* in no way suggests that the ministry and its responsibility to order are irrelevant to the unity of the church, but it should also be noted that the ecclesial ministry is not explicitly mentioned in article 7 on ecclesiology, because it has already been covered in the fifth article as ministry of preaching that passes on the justifying faith. In this sense, Vinzenz Pfnür points out, as an object of ecumenical consensus, the fact that ministry "should hardly be classified among the 'ceremonies instituted by men'" and concludes: "The AC, like Lutheran Confessional writings in general, maintains that the ecclesial ministry does not derive from the universal priesthood, but from the mission and the appointment of God."[21] The question then arises of how the Leuenberg Concord, which was also signed by the Lutheran Church, can be reconciled with the Augsburg Confession, when the second article of the Concord reads, "The Church is founded solely on Jesus Christ, who brings her together and invites her to mission, extending His salvation to her in preaching and the sacraments. According to the vision of the Reformation, a consensus on the correct teaching of the Gospels and on the correct administration of the sacraments is therefore necessary and sufficient for the true unity of the Church." But here, is the *satisest* of the Augsburg Confession not perhaps interpreted as "necessary and sufficient" so that ministry is no longer considered an element essential to the Church?[22]

This raises the even more fundamental question of understanding whether an ecumenical consensus exists on the fact that the ecclesial ministry was instituted by God. Again, we can affirm that the situation was clear for the theologians of the Wittenberg Reformation. Martin Luther spoke of the "status of the parish instituted by God, that should govern a community with sermons and sacraments."[23] He has emphatically pointed out that the ministry was instituted with the death of Jesus Christ: "He has truly bought it at a dear price so that this ministry could be in all the world."[24] This is why Philipp Melanchthon could actually define ordination as a sacrament: "But if ordination is understood starting from the ministry of the Word, we would not be reluctant to call ordination a sacrament. The minister of the Word indeed has the mandate of God and bears great promises."[25] Despite these clear affirmations, within Lutheran theology, especially from the nineteenth century to today, the question of whether ordained ministry is founded on a divine institution or on the authorization of the community of the faithful is undecided. It is possible to find a response when the Lutheran Churches today are asked about their way of interpreting ordination.

Ordination as a Theological Necessity or an Adiaphoron?

There are a great variety of positions on this subject, ranging from the definition of ordination as a theological necessity for the understanding of ministry, to the inclusion of ordination among the so-called adiaphora, or those realities that are neither required nor forbidden by the Gospels.[26] To cite just two examples: in 1990, the Swedish Lutheran bishops published a letter on ministry in the Church entitled "Bishop, Priest, and Deacon in the Church of Sweden." In this letter, ecclesial ministry is called "the gift and the dowry of God" that forms a "part of the basic structure of the Church," which is "tripartite" and transmitted "through prayer and the imposition of hands in ordination" and cannot be lost. Ordination is understood as a "prayerful action of the Church," "in which the divine vocation to life-long ministry finds its expression and its validation."

In strict contrast with this, in the Evangelical Church in Germany, the bishops or the presiders of Churches are seen as parish priests with supraregional leadership tasks entrusted to them for a certain period of time and are therefore not ordained but introduced into their new ministry. An even clearer difference can be found in the United Evangelical Lutheran Church of Germany (VELKD), which published the document "Ordnungsgemäss berufen" in 2006, which starts with the assumption that there is an objective correspondence between the ordination of theologians, generally from an academic background, and the duties entrusted to equally qualified preachers. Because the impression that derives from this is that ordination is a particular type of duty, a sacramental interpretation of ordination is excluded, which is anticipated by the Augsburg Confession 14, the reason for which the VELKD document expressly observes, "Any interpretation of the transmission of the ministry in the sense of consecration should be rejected."[27] Together with Stefan Scholz, we see in this the "clear confession of a functional interpretation of ordination" and therefore a "particular path of Protestantism."[28]

The examples mentioned provide evidence of the fact that in Lutheranism, there is no full and clear consensus on how to understand ordination. Because in the apology of the Augsburg Confession XIII:11 ordination is defined in a fuller sense as a sacramental reality, and because Luther himself used both the terms *ordination* and *consecration* synonymously, it is especially surprising that even the most confessional of the Lutheran churches, or those most faithful to the Book of Concord, actually characterize ordination as an "adiaphoron." In fact, C. F. W. Walther, the founder of the Missouri Synod, wrote, "Ordination is an adiaphoron, a middle way, it does not create vocation or ministry but only confirms it, as ecclesial copulation does not create marriage, but only confirms a marriage that has already been carried out."[29]

These few references make it clear that, starting with an examination of the interpretation and the practice of ordination, an attempt should be made to clarify the way the ecclesial ministry is understood in the Churches of the Reformation and in the ecumenical dialogues, as Augustinus Sander rightly emphasizes: "Final theological decisions are made in the divine service of the Church. In the presence of the living God, our words and our actions should be true. All ecclesial liturgies should respond to this need, including the forms of ordination in Lutheranism."[30] This premise is particularly pregnant when it comes to a possible recognition of the ministries in the Churches of the Reformation by the Roman Catholic Church. In this sense, the Protestant ecumenist Wolfhart Pannenberg believes recognition is possible only on the condition that

> the Protestant Churches understand their practice of ordination in the sense of the Lutheran confessional writings, as an expression of an emergency law that does not trace back to the universal priesthood of the faithful as a source of a ministerial power established by delegation; otherwise, they would develop an alternative concept of ministry and ordination, incompatible with the tradition followed by the Roman Catholic Church.[31]

ECUMENICAL DIALOGUES AND ECCLESIAL COMMITMENT

As a result of the above, one can say that it is necessary to make a distinction between the ecumenical documents that today largely state or postulate a complete consensus on the question of ministry and the ecclesial reality of the Churches of the Reformation that often point in a different direction, as a current example demonstrates: the Ecumenical Working Group of Protestants and Catholics in Germany recently presented a statement that postulates the "reciprocal participation in the respective celebrations of the Supper of the Lord/Eucharist in respect to each liturgical tradition, to be considered as existing on a theological foundation." This *votum* also included the recognition of ministries of ecclesial guidance, "as foreseen in the celebrating communities who, in the name of Jesus Christ, invite the baptized of other confessions to participate in the celebration."[32] This *votum* was based on the conviction that, as regards the question of ministry, a large-scale consensus has been reached, considering "ordained ministry in its various confessional manifestations to have an apostolic foundation."

Nevertheless, the Evangelical Church in Germany (EKD), which welcomed and approved the statement, has a completely different vision of ecclesial ministry. In fact, it emphasizes that the Reformation has brought "a completely new order of the Church," consisting in the fact that every Christian "can as a matter of principle administer the sacraments; that is, administer baptism and distribute the Supper of the Lord" and that only "for questions of organization" are there men and women pastors who "exercise the tasks assigned to every Christian in a special way, or rather are qualified and publicly called to do so. The community of the faithful assigns their ministry to them, which should assure the adequacy and the continuity of the preaching of the Gospel and the administration of the sacraments. The pastors do not have a special spiritual quality, but they have a special vocation."[33] It is not clear how this question can be reconciled with the consensus postulated in the *votum* on the question of ministry.

From these observations, one can only draw the conclusion that the documents of the ecumenical commissions, however praiseworthy, are not enough to reach a binding declaration of ecumenical consensus, especially on the question of ministry. Rather, only those documents that have been received by the respective Churches and accepted authoritatively by their ecclesial leaders can mark important turning points for the future. From this, we can understand the special importance covered by the "Joint Declaration On the Doctrine of Justification," agreed on between the Lutheran World Federation and the Pontifical Council for Promoting Christian Liberty in the name of the Catholic Church on October 31, 1999 in Augsburg, which surely represents a milestone in ecumenical relationships between the Catholic Church and Lutheranism.[34]

The phrase used by the Joint Declaration, "consensus on the fundamental truth of the doctrine of justification" indicates honestly that a consensus has not yet been reached, especially on the consequences of this doctrine for the understanding of the concept of the Church and for the question of ministry.[35] Since the still-unanswered questions are connected to a more precise understanding of the concept of the Church and the mission of the ecclesial ministry, at this time the implications presented by the consensus achieved from a perspective of ecclesiology and theology of ministry should figure in the agenda of ecumenical dialogues. Discussion on such themes could be a further step on the road of ecumenical understanding, which could lead to the elaboration of a future joint declaration on the Church, Eucharist, and ministry, in their intrinsic connection,[36] analogous to the "Joint Declaration on the Doctrine of Justification."

It should be noted with gratitude that this subject has been confronted by various national dialogues: the Lutheran-Catholic dialogue in the United States has already produced the "Declaration on the Way: Church, Ministry, and Eucharist,"[37] and the national dialogue in Finland has also published the extensive declaration "Growing Communion."[38] From an ecumenical perspective, it will be important to make progress on the basis of useful preliminary works. In fact, a similar Joint Declaration on Church, Ministry, and Eucharist would undoubtedly allow for a decisive step forward toward the clarification of the question of ministry from an ecumenical perspective, and that could represent an important step on the road to visible ecclesial and eucharistic communion, the final objective of all these ecumenical efforts.

NOTES

1. W. Beinert / U. Kühn, *Ökumenische Dogmatik* (Leipzig: Evangelische Verlagsanstalt, 2013), 557.

2. This also applies when there is not a binding relationship with the person who exercises the Petrine ministry as a hierarchical foundation of the unity between the individual Churches and the universal Church, and the unity between the individual Churches.

3. J. Feiner, "KommentarzumDekretüber den Ökumenismus," in *Lexikon für Theologie und Kirche*, vol. 13 (Freiburg i. Br., 1967) 40–126, here 50–58 and 92–93.

4. Relatio König vom November 19, 1963, in Acta Synodalia Sacrosancti Concilii Oecumenici Vaticani II / 5, 552–54.

5. *Unitatis Redintegratio* 22.

6. The Declaration *Dominus Iesus* on the unity and salvific universality of Jesus Christ and of the Church.

7. *Dominus Iesus* 17. To avoid this definition, which has become the source of harsh criticisms in the Protestant communities as well as in ecumenical environments, Cardinal Walter Kasper has suggested speaking about a different type of Church. Cf. "Situation und Zukunft der Ökumene," *Theologische Quartalschrift* 181 (2001), 175–90, 185. Pope Benedict XVI has also used the same terminology, when he emphasized that the ecclesial communities born of the Reformation are Churches "in a different way": "they are not, as they themselves claim, Churches inscribed in the great ancient tradition." Cf. Benedetto XVI, *Luce del mondo. Il Papa, la Chiesa e i segni dei tempi. Una conversazione con Peter Seewald* (Vatican City: Libreria Editrice Vaticana, 2010), 140.

8. Cf. K. Koch, "Auf dem WegzurWiederherstellung der einenKirche in Ost und West," in *Dialog 2.0—Braucht der orthodox-katholische Dialog neue Impulse? = Schriften des Ostkircheninstituts der Diözese Regensburg*, ed. D. Schon (Regensburg:Verlag Friedrich Pustet, 2017), 19–41.

9. Documented in H. Meyer, D. Papandreou, H. J. Urban, and L. Vischer, eds., *Dokumentewachsender Übereinstimmung*, vol. 2, 1982–1990 (Paderborn: Bonifatius Verlag, 1992), 556–65. The numbers in the text refer to this document.

10. Benedict XVI, *Meeting with Representatives of the Orthodox Churches in the Seminary Hörsaal* (Freiburg im Breisgau, September 24, 2011).

11. *Das Geheimnis der Kirche und der Eucharistieim Licht des Geheimnisses der Heiligen Dreifaltigkeit*, in Meyer et al., *Dokumentewachsender Übereinstimmung*, 2:531–39.

12. Benedict XVI, *Luce del mondo*, 133.

13. Benedict XVI, *Luce del mondo*, 132.

14. J. Ratzinger, "Die ökumenische Situation—Orthodoxie, Katholizismus und Reformation," 204, in *Theologische Prinzipienlehre* (Munich: St. Ulrich, 1982), 203–14, here 204.

15. Bernardo di Chiaravalle, *De consideratione ad Eugeniumpapam* IV 3, 6.

16. *Lumen Gentium* 21.

17. Cf. K. Koch, "Der Bischof als Bindeglied der Katholizität. Die episkopale Dimension der katholischen Ekklesiologie," in *Gottes Freude und Freude an Gott. Perspektiven heutiger Glaubensverantwortung* (Freiburg i. Br.: Verlag Herder, 2020), 296–338.

18. *Lumen Gentium* 10.2.

19. *Die Apostolizität der Kirche. Studiendokument der Lutherisch / Römisch-katholischen Kommission für die Einheit* (Paderborn: Bonifatius Verlag, 2009), no. 200.

20. *Augsburg Confession*, article 5.

21. V. Pfnür, *Einig in der Rechtfertigungslehre? Die Rechtfertigungslehre in der Confessio Augustana (1530) und die Stellungnahme der katholischen Kontroverstheologie zwischen 1530 und 1535* (Wiesbaden: Ph. von Zabern verlag, 1970), 378–79.

22. In the document "The Church of Jesus Christ," however, it is underlined that the Churches that signed the Concordia of Leuenberg or which adhered to it agree "that the ordained minister belongs to the nature of the Church" (2.5.1.1). It is also affirmed that "the ministry of public preaching is conferred with ordination" (2.5.1.2). See *Die Kirche Jesu Christi. Der reformatorische Beitrag zum ökumenischen Dialog über die kirchliche Einheit.* Im Auftrag des Exekutivausschusses für die Leuenberger Kirchengemeinschaft hrsg. von W. Hüffmeier = Leuenberger Texte 1 (Frankfurt a. M., 1994). Since this is a text that was edited and published after the conclusion of the communion of the Churches, one cannot conclude from it that the affirmations it contains about ministry were carried out in all the member Churches of the Concordia of Leuenberg, especially since it also firmly states that "no form of ecclesial leadership and historically developed structure of ministry can and should be applied as a precondition for communion and for mutual recognition" (2.5.1.1).

23. M. Luther, *An den christlichen Adel deutscher Nation*, 1520, in WA 6; 441, 24–25.

24. M. Luther, *Eine Predigt, das man Kinder zur Schulen halten solle*, 1530, in WA 30/II; 526, 34.

25. Ph. Melanchthon, *Apologia Confessionis Augustanae XIII*, in *Die Bekenntnisschriften der evangelisch-lutherischen Kirche* (Göttingen 1976, 7. Auflage), 139–404, here 293, 42: "Si autem ordo de ministerio verbi intelligatur, non gravatimvocaverimusordinemsacramentum."

26. Cf. A. Sander, OSB, "Die Ordination imLuthertum. Bedenkenswertes undBedenkliches," *Heiliger Dienst* 61 (2007): 249–61.

27. Bischofskonferenzder VELKD, "Ordnungsgemäss berufen" Eine Empfehlung der Bischofskonferenz der VELKD zur Berufung zu Wortverkündigung und Sakramentsverwaltung nach evangelischem Verständnis (Hannover, 2006), 17.

28. S. Scholz, "Vielesind berufen, aber nur wenige auserwählt? Ein Vorschlagzur Abschaffung der Ordination," *Deutsches Pfarrerblatt* 106 (2006): 246–48.

29. C. F. W. Walther, *Americanisch-Lutherische Pastoraltheologie* (St. Louis 1875, Zweite Auflage 1875), 65.

30. Sander, "Die Ordination im Luthertum," 249–61, here 261.

31. W. Pannenberg, *SystematischeTheologie*, vol. 3 (Göttingen: Vandenhoeck & Ruprecht, 1993), 440.

32. *Gemeinsam am Tisch des Herrn. Ein Votum des ökumenischen Arbeitskreisesevangelischer und katholischer Theologen*, ed. D. Sattler und V. Leppin (Freiburg i. Br., 2020) nos. 8.1 and 8.3.

33. *Rechtfertigung und Freiheit. 500 Jahre Reformation 2017. Ein Grundlagentext des Rates der Evangelischen Kirche in Deutschland*, EKD (Gütersloh, 2014), 90–91.

34. Cf. K. Koch, "Ein Meilenstein auf dem Weg zur Einheit der Kirche. Die Gemeinsame Erklärung zur Rechtfertigungslehre als ökumenische Errungenschaft und als bleibende Herausforderung," in *Wachsende Zustimmung und offene Fragen. Die Gemeinsame Erklärungzur Rechtfertigungslehreim Licht ihrer*, ed. B. Oberdorfer, Th. Söding (Freiburg: Verlag Herder, 2019), 371–402.

35. The Declaration itself mentions the questions that require further clarification: "These include, among other topics, the relationship between the Word of God and church doctrine, as well as ecclesiology, ecclesial authority, church unity, ministry, the sacraments, and the relation between justification and social ethics." Joint Declaration on The Doctrine of Justification, no. 43.

36. Cf. K. Koch, "Auf dem Wegzur Kirchengemeinschaft. Welche Chance hateinegemeinsame Erklärungzu Kirche, Eucharistie und Amt?" *Catholica* 69 (2015): 77–94.

37. Bishop's Committee for Ecumenical and Interreligious Affairs–United States Conference of Catholic Bishops and Evangelical, Lutheran Church in America, *Declaration on the Way: Church, Ministry and Eucharist* (2015).

38. Evangelical Lutheran Church of Finland, Catholic Church in Finland, eds., Communion in Growth: *Declaration on the Church, Eucharist, and Ministry. A Report from the Lutheran-Catholic Dialogue Commission for Finland* (Helsinki 2017).

12

DEEPENING THE THEOLOGICAL MEANING OF THE PRIESTHOOD

Cardinal Giuseppe Versaldi

UNDER THE SAME heading as the contributions given this morning—"Trinity, Mission, and Sacramentality"—this symposium's reflection on the priesthood continues with a rich series of contributions that I will present, gladly noting that it is, for the most part, women who guide us in the deepening of the theme.

Allow me to highlight the importance of this symposium and to thank Cardinal Ouellet (and his collaborators) for their initiative in a period that, while difficult, can also certainly be influential over time and throughout the Church.

Deepening the theological meaning of the priesthood is a challenge that, in a time of synodality, particularly invites theologians, and not only theologians, to rediscover the essential foundations of the common priesthood arising from baptism and the ministerial priesthood, to avoid a solely functional vision of the role of the sacred ministers in the Church. The coexistence and complementarity of diverse vocations must connect to the trinitarian mystery. It must also be substantiated in the common meaning of the call to witness to the love that flows from the Trinity and is modeled upon it.

These are, of course, not new themes. Looking at them in the context of recent historical developments, which, as Pope Francis states, signal a change in era, acquires a great value, and challenges all of us to deepen the incarnation of revelation within the changing circumstances of the life of the Church, and overcome the risk of applying old schemes to new realities.

The contribution of our speakers is invaluable when looking at the other theme, the presence and vocation of women in the Church, not as a sterile claim to equality, but as a precious gift that Christ gives to his Church. Our comprehension starts with the example that he himself has given, according to developments in understanding that have become concrete over time, and it aims to receive the essence and distinguish it from the historical incrustations that may have retarded or distorted its genuineness and richness.

I confidently hope that the reflections and contributions to come will realize the aim of this important symposium, which, as Cardinal Ouellet said in his presentation, is not intended to offer practical solutions to the pastoral and missionary problems of the Church, but rather "help to deepen the foundation of the mission of the Church," which is centered on the priesthood of Christ, in which the Church participates. This priesthood is shared by all the baptized, and is also given as ordained ministry in the triple form of the episcopate, the priesthood, and the diaconate. Deepening the relationship between these two forms of participation in the priesthood of Christ in times of change and the presence of new problems (such as the problem of the scarcity of the ordained ministry) is fundamental for the Church in its synodal road of missionary and pastoral conversion according to the indications of Pope Francis.

I now present the individual speakers, whom I thank and whom we will certainly listen to with interest.

Afternoon Introductory Session
Friday, February 18, 2022

13

THE SACRAMENTALITY OF THE EPISCOPATE

Father Benoît-Dominique de la Soujeole, OP

BISHOP, PRIEST, AND deacon represent the three degrees of the one sacrament of holy orders, not three different sacraments. In other words, there is a common reason for these three dignities, which enables them to share the same name: "holy orders." But the dignity is not effected in an identical way in each of the three. Hence, the interest in showing how this sacrament is effected in each. The object of this paper is to show the "architecture" of the sacrament of holy orders and how it reaches its perfection in the episcopate. On that basis, it will be possible to understand the lower degrees, and it could even throw light on the much-debated question of why ordination to the priesthood and the diaconate is reserved to the bishop.

IS THE EPISCOPATE A SACRAMENT?

The arguments and discussions of the past about the sacramentality of the episcopate may seem surprising today, since it is now so clear to church thinking that the episcopate is a sacrament. Careful study has shown that it was the appearance of the distinction between *ordo* and *iurisdictio* in late medieval Latin that gave rise to the question. According to this distinction, which was juridical in origin, at the level of sacramental capacity (*ordo*) there was no difference between the bishop and the priest, since both had the capacity to celebrate the Eucharist and forgive sins; the difference between the two dignities had to be located at the level of government alone (jurisdiction).[1] This approach contains some notable risks in embryonic form, including, precisely, that of losing awareness of the sacramentality of the episcopate, as well as no longer knowing where to set the ministry of preaching—holy orders or jurisdiction? The great medieval theologians received this view of things docilely; it seemed to be confirmed by plenty of church practices, but they were careful to underline the link between holy orders and jurisdiction, particularly by the distinction and relationship between the capacity (holy orders) and the effective use of the capacity (jurisdiction).[2] Without that link, jurisdiction could be understood as a merely sociological phenomenon.

FROM *ORDO-IURISDICTIO* TO THE *TRIA MUNERA CHRISTI*

It is not hard to see that Vatican II never took up the *ordo/iurisdictio* distinction, and although the word *iurisdictio* does appear, though rarely, in the Council texts, it is never connected with *ordo*.[3] Furthermore, and this has not often been emphasized, the repetition by Vatican II of the dogma of Vatican I on the primacy of the Bishop of Rome follows the terms of the dogmatic definition very closely—but omits any mention of a primacy of *jurisdiction*.[4]

The main reason for this reserve on the part of Vatican II is, in my opinion, that the *ordo/iurisdictio* distinction evolved in order to espouse the distinction between what is specifically spiritual and proper to the mystery of the Church (orders) and what belongs to the sociological realm in the Christian community (jurisdiction); that could come dangerously close to the distinction, fast becoming separation, between the visible Church and the invisible Church.[5] Furthermore, it still raised the question of where to locate the ministry of preaching.[6]

For this reason, the Council made two very clear choices. First, it based the whole of the bishop's ministerial capacity on the sacramental episcopal ordination; which capacity requires *hierarchical communion* in order to be exercised effectively.[7] As presented by the *Nota praevia* to chapter 3 of *Lumen Gentium*, this communion that belongs properly to ministers is the condition for genuine use of this ministry, in other words for it to build up and not tear down (cf. 2 Cor 13:10). Second, the ministerial capacity is presented by the doctrine of the *triamunera Christi,* namely, the charges of teaching, sanctifying, and ruling. There could be no better way of resolving all the unanswerable questions raised by the *ordo/iurisdictio* distinction.

At that point, another question arose: What is the underlying connection, the inner link between these three charges? Vatican II did not tackle this question directly, but the terms in which its statements were expressed show the underlying structure very clearly. Presenting the episcopal ministry in the Constitution *Lumen Gentium*, Vatican II expounds, first, the function of preaching (LG 25), then that of sanctifying (LG 26), and finally, that of ruling (LG 27). This order is repeated regarding priests (PO 4 for preaching, 5 for sanctifying, 6 for ruling).[8] The vocabulary, here, that enables this consistency to be understood are the terms that distinguish the first from the second and the principal from the subordinate. The first *munus* is always that of preaching, because its end is faith, either to be brought to birth or to be nourished.[9] In this context, the charge of sanctifying comes second, because it will only be fruitful for those who receive it in faith. What distinguishes the first from the second is, accordingly, efficient causality: the ministry of preaching leads to the sacraments. Here, sanctifying is designated as the main charge, which subordinates the other two to itself, very especially when it is accomplished in the eucharistic celebration.[10] The sacrament of the Eucharist, indeed, "contains the entire spiritual good of the Church" (PO 5), being at once the source (Christ present) and summit (building up the "whole Christ") of all ministry (LG 11 §1 and PO 5 §2). Here the principal is distinguished from the subordinate by reason of the final cause.[11]

The Council thus showed the close connection between the sacrament of holy orders received in the *episcopal* degree and received in the *presbyteral* degree; it is the same sacrament with an internal "architecture," made up of the three charges, that is identical. However, it remains to be shown in what respect the episcopate is the fullness of the sacrament of holy orders, while the priest only participates in it. To do this, it seems appropriate to proceed in two stages; first, to situate the importance of the episcopal college as such, and second, to see what that implies for each of its members.

THE EPISCOPAL COLLEGE IS THE CHURCH IN ITS QUALITATIVE CATHOLICITY

We find here a passage in *Lumen Gentium* (23 §1) that did not pose any particular problem during the Council debates, but proved to be hard to grasp after the Council, to the point where the Congregation for the Doctrine of the Faith was compelled to intervene. It is the following: "The individual bishops, however, are the visible principle and foundation of unity in their particular churches, fashioned after the model of the universal Church, in and from which churches comes into being the one and only Catholic Church."[12]

The Council statement involves an apparent contradiction: How can the universal Church be at the same time, and under the same aspect, both anterior to (i.e., the image on which the particular churches are modeled) and posterior to the particular churches (i.e., it comes into being from the particular churches)? How can this dilemma be resolved? Several proposals can be made about this, which can be grouped into three main ones.

The first is the simplest: it takes the phrase "universal Church" to have the same meaning in both its occurrences in the passage. So, to get rid of the contradiction, it is necessary, and sufficient, to remove one of these two occurrences. There is no universal Church anterior to the particular Churches, there is only a universal Church as the totality of particular churches in communion. Besides the fact that this proposal does not take account of the literal meaning of the Council statement, it reduces the universal Church to being merely a sociological-type quantitative entity, as a country is formed by the totality of its provinces.[13] It is clearly not just insufficient, but directly opposed to the actual letter of Vatican II. Presented in these terms, this proposal has not been found in the Catholic or Orthodox world; it may represent a tendency among some Protestant communities.

The second proposal is "Platonic."[14] It holds that the universal Church that gives birth to the particular churches is the divine intention that is realized in each particular church, and thus exists in the collectivity of all of them. That, I think, does not express the reality here below of the universal Church in its real anteriority in relation to the particular churches, but one single simultaneity.

The third proposal invokes a notion taken from trinitarian theology, the circumincession or *perichoresis*, according to which by virtue of the consubstantiality of the divine persons, each is spoken in the other two. The relationship between the universal Church and the particular churches is, according to this model, a relationship of existing in mutual interiority, simultaneously, without any anteriority or posteriority of one over the other.[15] Here too, it is the real, "foundational" anteriority of the universal Church that is disregarded.

John Paul II, in a significant speech to the Roman curia, had the following to say on this subject: "The universal Church finds its concrete existence in each particular church, in which she is present and active, and from another angle, the particular Church does not exhaust the totality of the mystery of the Church, given that some of its constitutive elements cannot be deduced merely from an analysis of the particular church itself. These elements are the office of the successor of Peter and the episcopal college itself."[16] The Congregation for the Doctrine of the Faith explained in its turn, "[The universal Church] is not the result of the communion of the [particular] Churches, but, in its essential mystery, it is a reality ontologically and temporally prior to every individual particular Church."[17]

It is clear from the foregoing that the universal Church, from which the particular churches come forth with regard to their foundation and life, is the body of the bishops whose head is the Bishop of Rome. It is to this college, after Pentecost, that the gospel and sacraments were entrusted, which engender and maintain in existence each particular church. It is what can be called the "qualitative catholicity" that designates the presence of the whole collection of means of salvation given by Christ in the Holy Spirit by means of the apostolic succession. The word *Catholic* is, indeed, first a qualitative term—a person is Catholic—for someone who receives the fullness of sanctifying gifts, a fullness that is only found in the Church that for that reason is called "Catholic."[18] In this sense, the Church has been Catholic from its origin at Pentecost and lives out this "ongoing Pentecost" by reason of the continuity of the apostolic succession.

As for the second kind of catholicity, the kind that is the result of the particular churches, which one could call "quantitative catholicity," it grows in the measure that missionary work is done. Consequently, the Church becomes more and more catholic in time and space. It cannot be reduced to a mere sociological, federal-type pattern, because it is the fruitfulness in time and space of the qualitative catholicity.

It should be noted that the adjective *catholic* evokes the idea of a "whole" and is hence linked to the idea of unity: a whole is a collection of parts united together and forming a single unit. In the expression *Catholic Church*, then, two things are expressed. One, which is perceived more directly, is the *quantitative* assembly of the particular churches; the other is the principle that unifies this whole, giving birth to the parts and, inseparably, uniting them closely together: the *qualitative* catholicity.

For our present purpose, it is helpful to underline the position, which is "source" and even "cause" for the Church, of the episcopal college, united thanks to the service done by the Bishop of Rome. It is the episcopate that effectively, constantly, and indefectibly brings the gospel in its truth and, because of that, the authentic sacraments that form the Church in different places. It is the single ministerial source of the Church. This decisive quality and role of the episcopal college as such reposes in the perfection of the sacrament of holy orders received by each of its members and in the ministry of unity of the Bishop of Rome. It is this which will now be expounded briefly.

THE ONTOLOGICAL FOUNDATION IN EACH BISHOP OF THE EPISCOPAL COLLEGE

"In his consecration a person is given an ontological participation in the sacred functions [*munera*]."[19] The sacrament of holy orders confers in the most perfect degree a character and a grace that are proper to it. The "ontological participation" in question here, in other words episcopal consecration, is what makes the bishop capable of exercising the three functions or charges in the "first" place regarding everyone, priests, deacons, and faithful. An ancient tradition expressed this by saying that the bishop is the *perfector*, the active cause of perfection, for the faithful.[20] This is not about moral perfection, which, like every baptized person, the bishop should aim for throughout his life, but an operative perfection. For the three charges or functions, he operates by right in the name of Christ and as his vicar, and it is this that makes him into the "principle and foundation of the unity" of the particular church that is entrusted to him (LG 23 §1).

For the exercise of the *munus docendi*, the bishop receives what Tradition calls a "certain charism of truth."[21] This expression comes from St. Irenaeus who, in the face of the diversity of interpretations of Scripture, leading to heresies, sees in the bishops the decisive criterion of judgment: "(They have) the sure charism of truth with the succession in the episcopate."[22] Other expressions, not so strong but meaning the same, are also found in Vatican II: "authentic teachers...witnesses to divine and Catholic truth" (LG 25 §2). While the subject of a charism is an individual, its exercise here is closely linked to belonging to the entirety of the episcopal college, because it must be exercised in "hierarchical communion." The most solemn expression of this charism is the universal council, but it is also present in the bishops' many forms of daily preaching. Priests, the bishop's privileged cooperators, do not have this charism even in a lesser form.

In the case of the *munus sanctificandi*, the episcopal character is no different from the presbyteral character regarding their instrumental capacity to confer the sacraments. Here, the episcopal character differs from that of priests in another way. The bishop celebrating a sacrament has a significant value that is all his own. This can easily be seen in the liturgy, which reserves presiding over the Eucharist to the bishop, and the celebration of the sacrament of confirmation, which, as the completion of baptism, incorporates the subject fully into the Church. Generally, it is appropriate to say of the celebration of all the sacraments what *Lumen Gentium* says of the eucharistic celebration: "Every legitimate celebration of the Eucharist is regulated by the bishop, to whom is committed the office of offering the worship of Christian religion to the Divine Majesty and of administering it in accordance with the Lord's commandments and the Church's laws" (LG 26 §2). It is in connection with the bishop, communion with him and his own membership of the episcopal college, that every sacramental celebration owes its legitimacy. That is why the bishop of the diocese is always named in the Eucharistic Prayer.

As for the *munus regendi*, it is too often reduced to an administrative-type function, which is totally insufficient.[23] It is much more: this function is exercised upon the community that is born of preaching and the sacraments to enable it to bear the fruits of the grace received. The grace having been bestowed by the two first *munera* as described above, the community thus formed must be led to its goal, which is the place where its members' holiness should flourish. In other words, the purpose of ecclesial government is to lead the faithful to "spring into action," to live by charity, that is, the whole field of "works" (Jas 2:14–24). Vatican II states this as follows: "Bishops, as vicars and ambassadors of Christ, govern the particular churches entrusted to them by their…authority and sacred power, which indeed they use only for the edification of their flock in truth and holiness" (LG 27 §1). There is a virtue that is specific to those who govern: prudence in ruling.[24] Its objective here, in its supernatural state, is to serve the common good of the Church which is charity. Thus, the bishop within the episcopal college has, for his particular church but also for the universal Church, responsibility for the community's being a propitious place for the flourishing of grace in its members. That requires the first shepherd to take a series of measures, from those most closely connected with the sociological conditions of his diocese, to those which are most highly moral. But as this concerns the common good of all the faithful, it is prudent for the bishop to associate the diocesan faithful in the entire work of discernment leading up to his decisions of prudence, in the same way as the execution of the decision will involve prudence on the part of the faithful.

CONCLUSION

It remains to situate the other two degrees of the sacrament of holy orders in their relationship to the bishop: the degrees of ordination to the priesthood and to the diaconate. Despite what many of the baptized spontaneously imagine, it is not a question of a downgraded participation in the same line that renders the priest inferior to the bishop and the deacon inferior to the priest. It is, in the two cases of the priest and the deacon, a differentiated participation in the episcopal perfection. These two participations set the subjects in a position of their own, one that is of itself permanent, in the ecclesial hierarchy.

The priest participates in the three episcopal functions, even if he does not necessarily exercise them all (we may think more particularly of the charge of ruling, which may not be entrusted to a priest, as in the case of many religious priests who do not have the responsibility of leading a portion of the people of God). To exercise these functions, the minister must be in communion with the bishop if he wishes to build up and not tear down or destroy. That is the quality of the first shepherd of the diocese who authenticates the priestly ministry. That link, it should be emphasized, is not simply a moral one. It is part of the specific character and grace of the sacrament received by the priest, which makes him a sharer in the episcopal perfection. This can be clearly seen, for example, in the fact that the *charisma veritatis certum* (DV 8 §1) only resides in the bishop, and that the priest benefits from it like all the baptized to the measure in which he follows the bishop's preaching.

For the deacon, things are less clear, because the Latin tradition has tended to narrow the distance between deacon and priest, by giving the deacon the faculty of preaching and of celebrating the sacraments of baptism and matrimony as ordinary minister. If we look at the tradition of the first millennium that we share not only with Eastern Rite Catholics but also with the Orthodox Churches, we see that the deacon is in direct relationship with the bishop.[25] It is certain that this refers to the service of charity. Proclaiming the gospel at Mass, assisting the bishop at the altar, and taking holy communion to the faithful, the deacon draws out from the source of charity to bring it to the faithful. Here, we do not have the doctrine of the *triamunera* but a specific participation in episcopal government as outlined above, with the works of charity as its goal. This is what might be called the "great diaconal tradition."

In the Book of Numbers, we find the reference to Moses, who associates seventy elders to himself in the work of caring for the people of Israel. God says, "I will take some of the spirit which is upon you and put it upon them; and they shall bear the burden of the people with you" (Num 11:17, repeated at v. 25). Here, there is the idea of a fullness, a plenitude in Moses, which is partially communicated to others. This passage is quoted by the *Apostolic Tradition of Hippolytus* (8) and features in the current rite of ordination to the priesthood.[26] There is only one sacrament of holy orders because it is the same Spirit who is given to each, but in a different way. The notion of a potential whole expresses it well: a perfection resides in each of the degrees, but only one possesses it perfectly. For example, the reality called "life" is present in plants, animals, and humans, but only humanity possesses it fully (rational life).

It is, consequently, at the dogmatic level, even before setting things at the moral and disciplinary levels, that the sacrament of holy orders should be understood in its ontological and operative perfection fully realized in the bishop and participated in, each along their own lines, by the priest and the deacon. It is indeed at the first level of being that one can grasp the dependence of the subordinate degrees and hence the need for strict unity in which all ministers should act "for the glory of God and the salvation of the world."

NOTES

1. Cf. L. Villemin, *Pouvoir d'ordre et pouvoir de juridiction. Histoire théologique de leur distinction* (Paris: Éditions du Cerf, 2003); A. Carrasco Rouco, *Le primat de l'évêque de Rome.Étude sur la cohérence ecclésiologique et canonique du primat de juridiction* (Fribourg: Éditions Universitaires Fribourg Suisse, 1990).

2. Cf. S.-T. Bonino, "La place du pape dans l'Église selon saint Thomas d'Aquin," *Revue thomiste* 86 (1986), 393–404. The phrase "effective use" of the capacity is used to designate the *moral* rectitude in the exercise of the capacity that conditions the fruitfulness of its exercise; this is not the canonical distinction between licitness and validity of the act performed. On this important point, see the study by J. Lécuyer, *Etudes sur la collégialité épiscopale* (Le Puy-Lyon, Éditions Mappus, 1964), 96–98.

3. The word *iurisdictio* appears nine times in Vatican II, as follows: *Sacrosanctum Concilium* 130: pontificals are reserved to bishops and those who have "*some particular jurisdiction*"; *Lumen Gentium* 23: bishops have solicitude for the universal Church even "*though it is not exercised by an act of jurisdiction*"; *Lumen Gentium* 45: the Supreme Pontiff can, for the good of the Church, remove a religious institute "*from the jurisdiction of the local Ordinaries*"; *Nota praevia* to chapter III of *Lumen Gentium* 2: the interpretation of documents of recent pontiffs "*regarding the jurisdiction of bishops…*"; *Orientalium Ecclesiarum* 4: hierarchs who

have "*jurisdiction within one and the same territory...*"; *Orientalium Ecclesiarum* 7: an Eastern patriarch has "*jurisdiction over all bishop...of his own territory or rite*"; *Christus Dominus* 35: exempted religious who are "*withdrawn from the jurisdiction of bishops...*" for the internal order of their communities (two instances), are not, however, excluded "*from the jurisdiction of bishops*" regarding pastoral work.

4. Cf. *Lumen Gentium* 18 §2; 22 §2; 23 §1.

5. On this point Vatican II responded by reaffirming the inseparable oneness of the single, complex reality that is the Church; cf. *Lumen Gentium* 8 §1.

6. By way of example, if the charge of preaching is set within the scope of jurisdiction, see the reflection by M.-J. Nicolas, who stresses that "teaching is a fundamentally different thing from commanding," in his review of *L'Église du Verbe incarné* by C. Journet, in *Revue Thomiste* 46 (1946): 391.

7. The most complete study of this point remains that by G. Ghirlanda, "Hierarchica communio. Significato della formula nella *Lumen gentium*," *Analecta Gregoriana* 216 (1980).

8. The *Catechism of the Catholic Church* follows the same order; cf. nos. 888–92 (teaching), 893 (sanctification) and 894–96 (ruling); and no. 1592.

9. Cf., for example, *Lumen Gentium* 25: "Inter praecipua Episcoporum munera eminet praedicatio Evangelii..."; *Presbyterorum ordinis* 4: "Presbyteri, utpote episcoporum cooperatores, primum habent officium Evangelium Dei omnibus evangelizandi...."

10. Cf., especially LG 26 §1: "Episcopus...est 'oeconomus gratiae supremi sacerdotii' praesertim in Eucharistia quam ipse offert..."; PO 13: "In mysterio Sacrificii Eucharistici, in quo munus suum praecipuum sacerdotes adimplent..."

11. For more details see two studies: B.-D. de La Soujeole, "Les *tria munera Christi*; contribution de s. Thomas à la recherche actuelle," *RT* 99 (1999): 59–74; and D. Logue, "Le premier et le principal du sacrement de l'ordre," *Revue Thomiste* (2002): 431–53.

12. The Decree *Christus Dominus* takes up this teaching more briefly (11 §1): "A diocese...constitutes a particular church in which the one, holy, catholic, and apostolic Church of Christ is truly present and operative." The *Catechism of the Catholic Church* quotes *Lumen Gentium* 23 in its no. 833. On this point, see the careful study by J. Hamer, "L'Église particulière, présence locale de l'Égliseuniverselle," in *Innecessariis unitas, Mélanges offerts à J.-L. Leuba* (Paris: Éditions du Cerf, 1984), 209–20.

13. Cf. Paul VI, encyclical *Evangelii Nuntiandi*, December 8, 1975, 62: "Let us be very careful not to conceive of the universal Church as the sum or... federation of...individual Churches....The Church is universal by vocation and mission, but...puts down her roots in a variety of cultural, social and human terrains."

14. For example, J.-M. R. Tillard writes, "The Spirit makes the Church (one and unique) which God has had in his design from all eternity: in the par-

ticular churches and from each of them, he brings the *catholica* into existence. He does not make it exist by adding together all these particular churches.... He makes it present in each of them, in accordance with its true, *catholic* nature." J.-M. R. Tillard, "Église catholique ou Eglise universelle?" in *Cristianesimo nella storia* 16, no. 2 (1995): 356–57.

15. By way of example: "There is no priority, either historical or ontological, of the universal Church with regard to the local Church, or the other way round. The universal and the local are necessarily simultaneous, and both necessarily have concrete existence." Comitémixte catholique-orthodoxe, *La primauté romaine dans la communion des Églises* (Paris: Éditions du Cerf, 1991), 115.

16. John Paul II, Speech to the Roman curia, December 20, 1990, *AAS* 83 (1991): 746.

17. Congregation for the Doctrine of the Faith, Letter *Communionis notio* dated May 28, 1992, *AAS* 85 (1993): 843.

18. Cf. *Lumen Gentium* 8 §2; *Unitatis Redintegratio* 3 §5.

19. *Nota praevia* to chapter III of *Lumen Gentium* 2.

20. This is what Vatican II refers to in LG 41 §2: "Those chosen for the fullness of the priesthood are granted the ability of exercising the perfect duty of pastoral charity by the grace of the sacrament of Orders." The Council here is quoting Thomas Aquinas, *STh* IIa-IIae, q. 184, a. 5 et 6.

21. Constitution *Dei Verbum* 8 §2, on the *sensus fidei* of the whole people of God: "Qui cum episcopatus successione charisma veritatis certum acceperunt."

22. Irenaeus of Lyons, *Adversus haereses* IV, 26, 2. For a study of Irenaeus on this point, see A. Faivre, "Irénée, premier théologien 'systématique'?," *Revue des sciences religieuses* 65 (1991): 11–32.

23. The bishop's role does, however, take on this aspect in that it administers the human and material resources of the Church necessary to provide for preaching and the celebration of the sacraments.

24. Cf., for example, Thomas Aquinas, *STh* IIa-IIae, q. 50, a. 1 et 2.

25. Even today, in the rite of ordination to the diaconate, it is the bishop alone who imposes his hands on the candidate. In fact, when *Lumen Gentium* says that deacons are ordained "not unto the priesthood, but unto a ministry of service," the words "...*to the Bishop*" should be understood, as is stated in the *Apostolic Tradition of Hippolytus*, 9, from which this expression is derived.

26. Cf. Roman Ritual, *Prayer of Consecration* (no.22).

14

THE COMPLEMENTARITY OF STATES OF LIFE

Sister Alexandra Diriart, CSJ

BY INVITING THE whole Church to a synodal process, Pope Francis hopes to recenter the question of the complementarity and the reciprocity of states of life in the Church-as-communion. The object is to understand how all—laity, clerics and consecrated persons—are called to "walk together" to meet Christ,[1] each in accordance with the richness of her own state of life, participating harmoniously in building up the Church, and thus showing its nature as communion and people of God.[2] This call to undertake a synodal journey is therefore an opportunity to recognize the diversity of vocations that, through their relation with each other, make up the Church.

Therefore, I will deal with the states of life from the specific angle of complementarity and reciprocity. It is important to add the term *reciprocity* to that of *complementarity*. Indeed, *reciprocity* refers us more clearly to a dynamic of exchanges according to mutual synergy, circularity, and ordering, where one cannot exist without the other.[3] On its own, the term *complementarity* could lead to laity and consecrated persons being seen as complementary to the ministerial priesthood, as though they were the "*longa manus* of the clergy."[4] The term *reciprocity* gives preponderance to the notion of co-responsibility.

Reflecting on this theme is still more important in the current ecclesial context, marked as it is by the consequences of clericalism[5] and abuse cases. It must be admitted that a wrong understanding of the relationship between the various states of life, or even quite simply ignorance or setting some aside while emphasizing others, have led to many imbalances.[6] The context invites us, then, to discern the right place for each person as an active subject in the Church. But to do that, we need to move our attention from the question of the distribution of powers in the Church, to the question of God's call, the primacy of his grace,[7] and his loving plan for the good of all.

But what should be understood by the expression "state of life"? While there is no clearly fixed concept of a state of life,[8] it is nevertheless possible to try and sketch the outlines of a definition. A state of life indicates a stable position within the Church that is the fruit of a free commitment in response to a call from Christ. It implies a total, definitive gift of self,[9] expressed by a public commitment in the Church. Thus baptism, the profession of the evangelical counsels, holy orders, and the sacrament of matrimony are forms of public commitment in the Church that mean the person belongs to a state of life, and hence has a specific place and mission in the Church.

The typology of states of life has been consolidated around the triad of laity, consecrated persons, and clerics.[10] All the same, when speaking of states of life in the Church, care must be taken not to fix or compartmentalize these categories too rigidly, since they describe the richness and dynamism of the many forms of Christian existence raised up by the Spirit in the Church.[11] Also, the number of three states of life can be increased if marriage is taken into account, and if the laity are distinguished from the category of *Christifideles*, "faithful of Christ," the identity given at baptism that is common to all states of life.[12] Moreover, certain theologians, such as Olivier Bonnewijn, propose that the state of nonvoluntary celibacy should be recognized as a state of life in its own right in the Church.[13]

The subject of the theology of the states of life is both traditional and recent. Traditional because it was already present in the patristic and medieval periods. Recent, because after a long period of oblivion it owes its restoration to the Council's renewal of ecclesiology, particularly due to major theological contributions. The two groundbreaking monographs by Hans Urs von Balthasar[14] and Paolo Martinelli[15] proposed a trinitarian approach to the states of life starting from the unity of God's plan. They showed that a theology of vocation is the indispensable background to any reflection on this subject. The article by Lorenzo Rossetti,[16] following Balthasar's intuition, presented the trinitarian reading as the key to understanding the states of life, illustrating their reciprocity by the concept of *perichoresis*. And finally, the study by Giancarlo Ghirlanda is fundamental in resituating reflection on the states of life within the framework of the Church-as-communion, based on recent contributions from the magisterium.[17] These works form the basis of the present study.[18] However, I have decided not to give a summary of them, so as not to repeat what has already been expressed so well. I would simply like to propose some questions and reflections around the topic.

First, I begin by looking at the providence of God, who wills the diversity of his gifts as a fortunate source of charity and the foundation of the coresponsibility of the states of life with each other.

Second, I show that it is important to abandon the binomial "clergy/laity" and promote the consecrated life to accord more weight to the pneumatological dimension of the Church.

Finally, I consider the need not to overshadow the state of life of marriage; it is sometimes hidden behind the category of laity, but it is essential for a healthy understanding of the relationship between the states of life.

FORTUNATE DIVERSITY, A SOURCE OF CHARITY AND CORESPONSIBILITY

For several centuries, discourse on the states of life has been associated with the question of the state of perfection, establishing a scale of values from the most perfect to the least perfect. New emphasis on the universal call to holiness offers a different interpretational key to the relationships between the states of life: that of charity.[19] Defined by charity, the vocation to holiness joins up with humanity's fundamental vocation to love.[20] There is only one vocation, the vocation to love, to total self-giving, revealed in its fullness by the mystery of the incarnate Word[21] offering his life to reconcile humankind with the Father in the Spirit, and gathering us in communion with his Body that is the Church. Thus, the vocation to love is rooted in our predestination in Christ: the call to be sons and daughters in the Son and to live in the Spirit of his offering to the Father.[22] This one vocation to charity is fulfilled in the diversity, reciprocity, and communion of the states of life,[23] each of which expresses a different aspect of the one mystery of Christ.[24]

Looking at love as the key to the order among the states of life enables us to turn from a pyramidal view to a circular view according to a mutual ordering[25] that can be expressed in terms of *perichoresis* or circumincession (reciprocal indwelling) that refers us straight to the model of the Blessed Trinity, in which are found order and communion, differentiation and compenetration.[26]

God does not think of each person's particular vocation in isolation,[27] but with reference to the whole, to his Body that is the Church, an organic body, differentiated and one, in which each has his or her own place and is called to holiness according to the singularity of his or her own specific grace (Rom 12:45; Eph 4:11–12; 1 Cor 12:12–30).[28] God, in his providential plan, has chosen to endow men and women with different, unequal gifts, so that no one can satisfy himself or herself, but each has need of the services of others, in order to constrain us, so to speak, to practice charity. This is what God the Father explained to St. Catherine of Siena in the *Dialogue* (and I permit myself this reference to Catherine because she is not only a mystic but also a theologian).[29]

> I could easily have created men possessed of all that they should need both for body and soul, but I wish that one should have need of the other, and that they should be My ministers; to administer the graces and the gifts that they have received from Me. Whether man will or no, he cannot help making an act of love. It is true, however, that that act, unless made through love of Me, profits him nothing so far as grace is concerned. See then, that I have made men My ministers, and placed them in diverse stations and various ranks, in order that they may make use of the virtue of love. Wherefore, I show you that in My house are many mansions, and that I wish for no other thing than love.[30]

Here, St. Catherine of Siena underlines the fact that all of us, whatever our state, are ministers of the distribution of the Father's graces. It is an important point. The different states are willed by providence not to produce envy and rivalry but charity. Recognizing that we need God and the other states of life through the experience of our insufficiency, opens us to welcoming the other, to gratitude, and mutual service. That implies a certain conversion of outlook in a culture such as ours, marked by autonomy and individualism.[31] From the perspective of God's plan, diversity becomes a source of charity and communion, because each person possesses what they have for the sake of others and the benefit of others.[32] This gives rise to mutual responsibility and ordering of each of the states of life with regard to the others.[33] All the vocations are thus linked to one another and none of them can be expressed without the others.

In this connection *Lumen Gentium* (10) states that the common priesthood of the faithful and the ministerial priesthood are ordered to each other (*ad invicem tamen ordinateur*). Postconciliar reflection has emphasized the fact that the ministerial priesthood is ordered to the service of the baptismal priesthood and the divine filiation of the faithful, particularly by celebrating the sacraments and preaching the word. However, as François Daguet points out, little study has yet been done on the question of the ways in which the faithful, both laity and consecrated persons, are at the service of the ministerial priesthood.[34] *Lumen Gentium* (10) states that the faithful serve the ordained priesthood through their participation in the eucharistic offering, their prayer, and their charity. Admittedly, we should call it an asymmetrical reciprocity,[35] but the question deserves further research and study.

The shock caused by the abuse crisis and the decline of authority have provided an opportunity to highlight another specific way for the laity to serve the ministerial priesthood. Many laypeople, led by their love for the Church and their missionary concern, have offered priests (but also consecrated persons) their skills in governance, in pastoral leadership, in the exercise of pastoral relations and healthier communities,[36] and in accompanying and listening to abuse victims.[37] Married couples have opened networks of friendly family-style houses for priests suffering from exhaustion or burnout, or afflicted by doubt, offering them a place of human and spiritual renewal.[38] The laity have thus put their skills at the service of improved pastoral ministry. In this mutual welcoming of the different states of life, charity has been spread around, enriching all of them.

PROMOTING CONSECRATED LIFE TO FAVOR THE CHARISMATIC DIMENSION OF THE CHURCH

Abandoning a Binary View of the Church

The Second Vatican Council emphasized the importance of the baptismal vocation and highlighted the place and mission of laypeople in the Church. By doing so, it offered a counterbalance to the view of the Church centered on its hierarchical structure that placed the accent on the role of the clergy. Despite this major rebalancing, we need to realize that we remain locked in a binary view of the Church, one that is ultimately reductionist, still setting clergy and laity in contradistinction and not taking sufficient account of the richness of the Church-as-communion expressed in the different states of life. Now, to think about the communion of the states of life, we need to step outside this reductive kind of dualism.[39]

A binary system of relationships always includes the risk of rivalries and exclusion, where one side predominates over the other. To avoid undue dualism and open up to a real relationship, psychotherapists know that the presence of a third party is needed. This is the concept of the primary triangle used in psychodynamics and systemic family theory: this triangulation allows for dynamism and interaction in relational exchanges between the two parents and the child, and not just between the child and only one of the parents.[40]

Similarly, in ecclesiology the clergy/laity binomial is an emblematic example of these reductive dualisms that call for the presence of a third party—here, the consecrated life. I subscribe to the view put forward by Agnès Desmazières that "the Church's identity crisis is partly linked to forgetting the tripartite structure of clergy—laity—religious, replaced by a dialectical opposition between clergy and laity."[41] The consecrated life as such (and religious life in particular) is then subsumed into the category either of clergy or of laity, and thus risks losing its own specific identity. The clericalization or secularization of the consecrated life then becomes a real danger.

Today, given the crisis that the ordained ministry is going through, caught up in clericalism and the sex abuse crisis, there is the danger of falling into the extreme opposite: devaluation of the ministerial priesthood, and lay supremacy. At the risk of repeating myself, I would say that without the presence of a third party the clergy-laity binomial is still subject to the danger of swinging between the clericalization and secularization of the Church. Hence, the importance of making room for the third party, which is consecrated life, so as to enter into a virtuous relational circle of communion where each one can be oneself, bring to the other one's unique richness, and receive from the other what the other has to give of oneself.

Promoting Consecrated Life to Integrate the Church's Charismatic and Hierarchical Dimensions

Giving due place to the third party, consecrated life, enables the charismatic dimension of the Church—in particular, its pneumatological dimension[42]—to appear clearly, while integrating its hierarchical dimension into the whole. As Giancarlo Ghirlanda loves to recall,

> The mystery of the Church is not fully expressed by the dialectical relationship laity-sacred ministry which determines the hierarchical structure. The emerging fundamental structure of the Church is a sacramental-charismatic structure, which assumes an institutional form, including within itself the hierarchical structure.[43]

An opposition has too often been drawn between hierarchical powers and charisms, as though they were two different orders that did not match up, as though there were "a 'Church of the Spirit', distinct and separate from the hierarchical-institutional Church."[44] Nevertheless, as John Paul II said, they are two coessential[45] gifts that mutually imply one another.[46] The institutional hierarchical structure originates in the gift of the Holy Spirit. By focusing on the institutional hierarchical position of the priest, some have forgotten the charismatic origin of his ministry which gives it its deepest meaning and ultimate purpose.

A look at the vocabulary used in *Lumen Gentium* shows how difficult it is to integrate the charismatic and hierarchical dimensions. The fluctuating character of the texts, when speaking of the place of consecrated life (referred to as "religious"[47]) is symptomatic.

Thus, *Lumen Gentium* 43 §2 states that the Church is divided into clergy and laity and that the condition of consecrated persons should not be seen as an intermediate state between the condition of cleric and that of layperson (*non est intermedius inter clericalem et laicalem conditionem*). Indeed, the religious belong either to the category of clergy (this is most frequently the case for members of male institutes) or to the category of laity if they do not belong to Holy Orders (this is therefore the case of consecrated women and members of institutes of nonordained religious brothers).[48]

However, earlier, *Lumen Gentium* (31 §1) defined the laity by explicitly excluding from the definition those in Holy Orders *and* the religious: "The term laity is here understood to mean all the faithful except those in holy orders and those in the state of religious life specially approved by the Church."

The question arises: Are religious who are not in Holy Orders really laypeople? According to *Lumen Gentium* 43 §2, yes they are, because they are not an intermediate category between clergy and laity. According to *Lumen Gentium* 31 §1, no, they are not, because the religious state is excluded from the category of laity. Which is right? It is true that the two paragraphs speak from two different angles. Looking at the Church in its hierarchical dimension, there exist only laity and clergy (LG 43 §2); while looking at it in its charismatic dimension, the category of consecrated life can, with *Lumen Gentium* 31 §1, be accorded its place alongside holy orders and laypeople.

This point of view is not totally satisfactory because it fails to resolve the uncertainty as to the place of consecrated persons in the ecclesial structure, or to combine in any unified way the hierarchical and charismatic dimensions of the Church. Admittedly, the place of the consecrated state of life in the Church has always been "uncomfortable," as Hans Urs von Balthasar recalled—anticipating eschatology, but still part of the world:

> In the parish and in the diocese, [the consecrated person] is an element of Christian unrest; when all tasks have been neatly assigned, he is there as the uncomfortable "seamless robe," the disturber of the peace, the disrupter of all plans. By his state of life, he shares in a special way in Christ's expulsion and abandonment "outside" the camp, which he, too, experiences; within the Church, his position is analogous to that of the Church as a whole within the world: the position of a stranger who can never be completely at home there. The lay person and the secular priest have this in common, that they are both somehow rooted by their vocation in the order of creation; the religious state, on the contrary, has no foundation in this order. Even from the perspective of the "ecclesial world," it is suspended in mid-air—as the Lord was suspended on the Cross between heaven and earth with no place to call his own.[49]

Indeed, we should not be too quick to enclose consecrated life within the single framework of the eschatology it announces, as though it no longer had its place in the heart of the world. That would be to risk making the presence of these consecrated persons, and especially consecrated women, into something that belonged more to eschatology than to the here and now. It would also make it more difficult to give them their rightful place in the Church and hear their voice within it. Unquestionably, this difficulty concerns consecrated women in active apostolic life more than contemplative life. And yet, does not their prophetic and eschatological voice offer to the other states of life a different view of temporal reality, a vision drawn from their intimate connection with Christ that opens to the discernment of the Holy Spirit?

If the consecrated life is merely distributed between the laity and the clergy, that would make it something marginal to the Church's structure. However, by dedicating an entire chapter to the religious in a document about the constitution of the Church, Vatican II became the first Council to integrate consecrated life in the perspective of its relation to the actual constitution of the Church.[50] Following the line of *Lumen Gentium* (44), the apostolic exhortation *Vita Consecrata* specifies that the consecrated life expresses the nature of the Church because it is a constitutive part of it.[51] Thus consecrated life is an element that the Church cannot dispense with because it expresses the Church's spousal nature[52] and its charismatic dimension as the temple of the Holy Spirit. Consecrated life exists precisely to recall that all the members of the people of God are invited to the wedding feast of the Lord. It shows—particularly to the laity and the clergy—the primacy of the Holy Spirit in the Church. That constitutes the prophetic dimension of the consecrated life, which makes visible the essential thing, the purpose that is the same for everyone, namely God's primacy and the new life in the Spirit that models all relationships by charity.

Through this primacy of God, consecrated life reminds pastors that their ministry, "Feed my sheep," is a service of charity, brought about by the personal call of Jesus, "Do you love me?" and finding its fruitfulness in that personal relationship of love: "You, follow me."[53] It is this primacy that gives the origin and the meaning of the hierarchy, and also shows it the modality for its exercise—charity—in relation to the other states of life.

I recall here a contribution that is specific to the consecrated woman. She is an important sign for the priest by reason of the apparent uselessness or poverty of her life. She renounces conjugality, but also what constitutes the true beauty of women: motherhood. She dispossesses herself of it at the risk of being mistrusted, reviled, or even despised as deprived of her womanly dignity, and she receives nothing in exchange—at least apparently.

The priest also renounces conjugality and biological fatherhood, but "in exchange" he receives the immense gift of the priesthood. The risk will still exist that a priest may consider his priesthood as a function, a power, or ministry that he possesses and that demands effective activity if he is to build it up. The consecrated woman reminds him that God's fruitfulness is held in this chaste apparent emptiness that is, in fact, receptivity to the love of Christ the spouse, availability and welcome to God's gift, and therefore fruitfulness of the Spirit. By doing this she reveals to him the true face of the fruitfulness of his priestly fatherhood, and undoubtedly the deep meaning of his priestly celibacy. Mary is mother precisely because she is virgin. Hans Urs von Balthasar even specifies that "she is a virgin so that she may become mother."[54]

Mary, and consecrated persons following her, are thus witnesses in the Church to the fruitfulness and freely given gift of the Holy Spirit.[55]

This primacy of God is also what consecrated life reveals to married people, reminding them that his primacy is not in competition with family relationships, that he does not reject them, but, under the breath of the Holy Spirit, orientates and sustains them on the basis of the love of charity of Christ.[56] Abandoning the laity-clergy binomial has not only enabled the place of consecrated life to be reconsidered, but also invites the question of the place of marriage. Is it a state of life that has been forgotten, hidden in the category of laity?

MARRIAGE, A FORGOTTEN STATE OF LIFE?

For the apostolic exhortation *Vita Consecrata*, "The vocations to the lay life, to the ordained ministry and to the consecrated life can be considered paradigmatic, inasmuch as all particular vocations, considered separately or as a whole, in one way or another are derived from them or lead back to them."[57] It is regrettable, nevertheless, that the trilogy—clergy-laity-consecrated persons—leaves marriage in the shadow, by including it in the laity, where it appears as a "'state' within the 'state.'"[58] Admittedly, marriage belongs to the laity,[59] and yet, does not marriage as such also say something more about the mystery of the Church than "mere" laity does? Is it not also a constitutive element of the essence of the Church whose mystery is expressed in terms of a wedding?[60] The theologian Carlo Rocchetta states forcefully, moreover, that "without spouses there is no Church."[61]

Like Lorenzo Rossetti,[62] I wonder whether it might not be a good idea to restore the traditional ancient trilogy of "orders" (clergy, continent people, and married people).[63] Cardinal Velasio de Paolis remarks, moreover, that the 1983 Code of Canon Law never refers to the laity explicitly as a "state," whereas it calls marriage a "state of life" in Can. 226 §1.[64] *Lumen Gentium* twice calls the sacrament of marriage a state of life, in 11 and 35 (more than the laity, to whom that title is explicitly applied only once, in 30).

The sacrament of marriage is a proper state of life involving a permanent, public commitment in the Church made according to a set form. *Gaudium et Spes* (48) presents it as a sacramental consecration.[65] By virtue of the sacrament, spouses occupy a special place in the Church and receive a specific mission of building up the Church, by generating children and handing on the faith.

It is not without significance that the *Catechism of the Catholic Church* presents in the same section both the sacrament of holy orders and the sacrament of marriage as two special consecrations, founded on the consecration of baptism, which confer on ordained ministers and on spouses a new mode of exercising Christ's priesthood orientated toward communion, whence their title as "sacraments at the service of communion":[66]

> Through these sacraments those already *consecrated* by Baptism and Confirmation (cf. LG 10) for the common priesthood of all the faithful can receive **particular** *consecrations*. Those who receive the sacrament of Holy Orders are *consecrated* in Christ's name "to feed the Church by the word and grace of God" (LG 11 §2). On their part, "Christian spouses are fortified and, **as it were**, consecrated for the duties and dignity of their state by a special sacrament" (GS 48 §2).[67]

With Paul de Clerck, it is important to note that the *Catechism* (no. 1535) uses the word "consecrated/consecrations" four times, emphasizing it by putting it in italics each time,[68] testifying to the stress laid on the notion of consecration.[69] We can also note the emphatic repetition of the word "for" (or "to") throughout the passage, underlining the fact that all consecration is given *in view of* an ecclesial mission. The *Catechism of the Catholic Church* seems to be going in the direction of an analogical interpretation of consecration that brings together baptism, confirmation, the sacrament of holy orders, and the sacrament of matrimony. In the case of matrimony alone the statement appears to be "tempered" by the phrase "as it were," following the term (*veluti consecrantur*) used in *Gaudium et Spes* 48 §4.

As a baptized person, the member of the faithful is *already* consecrated, that is, already belongs *fully* to God as member of the Body of Christ called to priestly worship. Now the consecration of the sacrament of matrimony introduces the spouses into a *new mode of incorporation into Christ* as *unacaro*.[70] The idea that is found in Augustine's writings also resounds in those of Bonaventure, who proclaims an even more complete incorporation of the spouses in Christ by virtue of the grace of the sacrament of matrimony.[71] This new belonging to God as *unacaro*—this new way of being a member of the Body of Christ—enlarges the perspective of baptismal priesthood into a conjugal priesthood: from now on, it is as forming *one flesh*, and not individually, that the spouses offer themselves to God and receive the mission of transmitting life and participating in the growth of the Body of Christ. Neither is it now only a matter of offering oneself to God, but also of offering oneself *with the other* and, further, offering one's spouse to God while allowing oneself to be offered to the Lord by him or her. The spouses become in some way priests to one another and to their family.[72]

Side by side with the ordained ministers, they receive the mission of building up the communion of the Church.[73] It should not be forgotten that the Christians of the first three centuries celebrated the Eucharist, prayed together and learned about the faith by listening to the word in the family homes that formed the heart of the first Church communities.[74] With the growth of the Church and the birth of the first places of public worship, the family community was invited not to lose its ecclesial dimension, a sign that the Church of the early centuries lived by this interconnecting of the different states of life. Thus, John Chrysostom exhorted spouses to make their home into a little Church.[75] While awareness of the ecclesial nature of the family became progressively diluted through centuries, the twentieth century highlighted this dimension once again, especially in *Lumen Gentium* (11), which speaks of the family as a domestic Church.

The mention of the family as a "domestic Church" is stimulating for ecclesiology and pastoral work. It opens the possibility of perceiving in depth the nature and mission of the family by contemplating them in the light of the nature and mission of the Church. In this perspective the family is seen as a true ecclesial subject called to cooperate in the Church's mission together with the other states of life.[76]

Restoring Marriage as a State of Life

For the theology of the states of life, I see several major elements for restoring the category of marriage.

1) Marriage highlights the *fruitfulness of the communion of masculine and feminine* at the origin of God's plan of creation as a place where God's image would shine forth. Moreover, as St. Paul says in the Letter to the Ephesians 5:2, communion of man and woman in one flesh is expressed in reference to the great mystery of the union of Christ and the Church. Thus, to quote François Daguet, "the duality of masculine and feminine is...present at the very heart of the understanding of the Church and its mystery."[77] Furthermore, it should not be forgotten that the work of redemption is marked by this duality of feminine and masculine as indicated in chapter 8 of *Lumen Gentium*, which underlines the Blessed Virgin Mary's association with the work of redemption.[78] The eclipse of the reciprocity of sexual difference in our culture represents an additional challenge to the theology of the states of life. But God reveals himself through this language of the nuptial covenant which assumes sexual difference. Marriage is precisely the place of this fruitful polarization, and it reminds the Church that, to be completely fruitful, the communion of the states of life requires the differentiation of masculine and feminine.
2) Marriage, with the gift of the body, underlines the *spousal meaning of the body made for gift*. Consecration to God in celibacy or virginity for the kingdom, far from ignoring the body in its masculinity or femininity, needs to be lived out, John Paul II said, on the basis of "a full awareness of this spousal meaning that masculinity and femininity contain in themselves."[79] Continence for the kingdom does not remove consecrated persons or celibate priests from the life of the body: it is a *new way of living out, in the body*, the spousal vocation of every human being, in the light of the spousal union of Christ and the Church (Eph 5:25–33).[80] This realization enables consecrated persons and priests to enter into the reality of their offering, as men or as women, without disincarnated spirituality, and without despising the flesh. To consecrated persons and

celibate priests, spouses bear witness that the gift of self to the Lord is not only "spiritual" but also involves the truth of the language of the body. Against the risk of defining the consecrated life or priestly celibacy by contrast with the life of the body and affectivity, against the risk of spiritualizing or dissociating what is spiritual from what is corporal, which could lead in the end to dehumanizing the celibate person (or even to the worst perversions), and against the temptation to individualism that can grow up within "solitude for God," spouses remind consecrated persons and priests of the concrete incarnation of their vocation: a call to the gift of self and to communion that integrates the body (male or female), feelings, emotions, vulnerability and the narrative dimension of the person. This is fidelity in the flesh that travels by way of concrete daily reality.

3) Through the fruitfulness of the relationships that construct their family communion, spouses show the *fruitfulness of all spousal love*. This fruitfulness is made visible in the children who are born, but it goes far beyond biological and physical generation, and is fulfilled in a fatherhood and motherhood according to the Spirit. Through their motherhood and fatherhood, spouses recall to consecrated persons and priests that they were made to give life, and that their spousal gift to Christ, if it is total, cannot *but* give life, in faith, perhaps invisibly but nevertheless very truly. The fatherhood and motherhood of spouses remind them of the humility of this fruitfulness: it is first and foremost a gift, a grace that is received. They teach consecrated persons and priests that having children demands time, fatigue, but also "labor-pains" that go far beyond the pain of giving birth: pains that accompany their children's growth in time.[81] By their renunciation of physical motherhood or fatherhood, priests and consecrated persons show parents that biological generation, in order to receive its ultimate meaning, should be fulfilled in generation according to the Spirit. It is not

only a matter of giving life to children for this earth but, in faith in Christ, of giving life to children of God for eternal life.

The Spousal Form of the States of Life

Finally, the state of life of marriage offers the "grammar" for understanding the whole economy of salvation, which is given under the form of a nuptial covenant between God and his people, culminating in the spousal offering of Christ for his Bride the Church (Eph 5:32).

The category of the union of Christ with his Church-Bride is additionally a hermeneutical key to express the different vocations. Each of them expresses the same nuptial love in accordance with its own tonality.[82]

- Thus, baptism was presented by the early Church fathers as a mystical wedding between Christ and the faithful.[83]
- The grace proper to the sacrament of matrimony gives spouses the gift of being able to "signify and partake of the mystery of that unity and fruitful love which exists between Christ and His Church" (*Lumen Gentium* 11).
- Consecrated persons are called to express the face of the Church-Bride indissolubly united to Christ her Spouse.[84]
- Finally, "the priest is called to be the living image of Jesus Christ, the spouse of the Church,"[85] giving up his life for love of her.

Thus, each state of life, by representing one facet of Christ's and the Church's spousal self-giving, takes on its own paschal form.

United by the same spousal and paschal form of love, the vocations of baptism, marriage, ministerial priesthood, and consecrated life are closely interlinked. They stimulate each other and refer to one another. It is not possible to love one and belittle another. Promoting one means promoting all of them. As will be readily understood, a symposium on the priesthood therefore directly concerns all the states of life.

CONCLUSION

Reflecting on the complementarity and reciprocity of the states of life had led us to contemplate the Church as at once charismatic and hierarchical. Indeed, it would be impossible to describe the Church in its true nature without connecting it in the first place to the action of the Holy Spirit, who unites the members of the Body of Christ by charity. This is unquestionably what consecrated life says. Trying to think together, in unity, about the charismatic and hierarchical dimensions of the Church enables us to realize not only the diversity of the states of life but also their being-in-relation, as coresponsible ecclesial subjects called to carry the Church's life and mission together.

The circular process of blessing (in the sense of the literal etymology of the Latin verb *benedicere*, to "speak well") the different states of life of the Church is more necessary than ever for building up the Church-as-communion. Being open to the riches of the states of life to journey together in the Church implies cultivating mutual esteem and gratitude. And to cultivate mutual esteem, we need to go by way of listening and getting to know the different states of life. Getting to know one another nurtures esteem and does away with mistrust and any temptation to presumption. The theology of the states of life should also be included effectively in the training and studies of priests and consecrated persons,[86] but equally in those of laypeople and spouses.

Opening up to the riches of other states of life also implies loving and getting to know the riches of one's own vocation in order to be more at the service of the Church in accordance with the specific nature of one's own calling. Being oneself helps the others to be themselves, and stimulates reciprocity between the different vocations. This is one of the great intuitions of St. Francis of Sales, who was an ardent promoter of the theology of the states of life. I end with the words he wrote to Madame Brûlart: "Do not wish not to be what you are, but wish to be well and truly what you are."[87]

NOTES

1. See especially Pope Francis, *Speech for the Commemoration of the 50th Anniversary of the Institution of the Synod of Bishops*, October 17, 2015; 16th

Ordinary General Assembly of the Synod of Bishops, "For a Synodal Church, Communion, Participation and Mission," preparatory document, September 7, 2021.

2. See 16th Ordinary General Assembly of the Synod of Bishops, "For a Synodal Church," no. 1.

3. See C. Rocchetta, *Senza Sposi, non c'è Chiesa* (Assisi: Porziuncola, 2018), 10. See also 106; G. Ghirlanda, "Sviluppo dell'ecclesiologia alla luce delle tre Esortazioni apostoliche post-sinodali *Christifideles laici—Pastores dabo vobis—Vita Consecrata* e rapporto tra gli stati di vita," in C.E.I., *La vita consacrata alle soglie del terzo millennio alla luce dell'Esortazione apostolica post-sinodale*, Atti del Convegno, Rome, Domus Mariae, 14–17 April 1997, Centro studi USMI, Roma 1997, 36.

4. Rocchetta, *Senza Sposi, non c'è Chiesa*, 10. See also 106.

5. See especially Pope Francis, *Letter to Card. Marc Ouellet, President of the Pontifical Commission for Latin America*, March 19, 2016.

6. Cf. A. Desmazières, *L'Heure des laïcs. Proximité et coresponsabilité* (Paris: Salvator, 2021), 17.

7. Cf. A. Desmazières, *L'Heure des laïcs. Proximité et coresponsabilité*, 84.

8. J. Fornés in his historical-doctrinal study *La noción de "status" en Derecho Canónico* (Pamplona: EUNSA, Ed. Universidad de Navarra, 1975), showed that no homogenous concept of a *status* exists. The term is a fluid one, with no rigor of application nor any single meaning.

9. Thomas Aquinas defines the Christian state of life as a stable position, requiring some degree of immobility. *Summa Theologiae*, Ia IIae, q. 183, art. 1, c., ad 2, 3.

10. Fixed in the 1917 Code of Canon Law, then by Pius XII in the apostolic constitution *Provida Mater Ecclesia* (1947), the triad was consolidated by the Second Vatican Council and subsequent magisterium, especially the 1983 Code and the three postsynodal apostolic exhortations *Christifideles Laici* (1988), *Pastores Dabo Vobis* (1992), and *Vita Consecrata* (1994).

11. See D. Wiederkehr, "La Chiesa come luogo di una multiforme esistenza cristiana," in *Mysterium Salutis*, IV/2, *L'evento salvifico nella comunità di Gesù Cristo*, ed. J. Feiner and M. Löhrer (Brescia: Queriniana, 1975), 416–83.

12. See V. De Paolis, "Stati di vita delle persone nella Chiesa secondo il CIC," in *Episcopato, Presbiterato, Diaconato*, ed. E. Cappellini (Cinisello Balsamo, Ed. Paoline, 1988), 105–6 who distinguishes the state of faithful (common to all states of life) from that of layperson.

13. O.Bonnewijn, *"J'existe !" Un autre regard sur les célibataires* (Paris: Ed. Emmanuel, 2020). I will also refer to Alexandra Diriart, "Les célibataires dans l'Église: un état de vie à part entière ? Dialogue avec Olivier Bonnewijn," *Nova et Vetera* 96 (2021/3): 323–38.

14. H. U. von Balthasar, *The Christian State of Life* (San Francisco: Ignatius Press, 2002).

15. Martinelli, *Vocazione e stati di vita del cristiano. Riflessioni sistematiche in dialogo con H.U. von Balthasar* (Rome: Edizioni Collegio S. Lorenzo da Brindisi-Laurentianum, 2001). The author published an updated version of this work, changing the title slightly from *stati di vita* ("states of life") to *formedella vita* ("forms of life"): *Vocazione e formedella vita cristiana. Riflessioni sistematiche* (Bologna: EDB, 2018). The 2018 edition is the one I have used for the present study.

16. C. L. Rossetti, "La 'pericoresi' tra le forme e stati di vita nella Chiesa. Tesi di ecclesiologia trinitaria," *Gregorianum* 85 2 (2005): 312–44.

17. Ghirlanda, "Sviluppo dell'ecclesiologia," 9–36.

18. The study by Trianni, *Stati di vita* (Assisi: Cittadella, 2021), should also be noted.

19. See John Paul II, apostolic exhortation *Christifideles Laici* (Dec. 30, 1988) [henceforth CFL] 55.

20. See especially *Gaudium et Spes* 12 & 24. See also John Paul II, encyclical *Redemptor Hominis* (March 4, 1979), 10; apostolic exhortation *Familiaris Consortio* (November 22, 1981), 11. See also C. Anderson & J. Granados, *Chiamati all'amore* (Milan: Piemme, 2010).

21. *Gaudium et Spes* 22 and 24.

22. See *Lumen Gentium* 4; Martinelli, *Vocazione e forme della vita cristiana*, 174–80.

23. See CFL 20; John Paul II, apostolic exhortation *Vita Consecrata* (March 25, 1996), [henceforth VC] 31; Ghirlanda, "Sviluppo dell'ecclesiologia," 15.

24. See VC 32.

25. See *Lumen Gentium* 10; CFL 55.

26. See Rossetti, "La 'pericoresi' tra le forme e stati di vita," 312–44. See also Balthasar, *The Christian State of Life*, 362; Martinelli, *Vocazione e forme della vita cristiana*, 21.

27. See *Lumen Gentium* 9.

28. *Lumen Gentium* 32.

29. See Ch. Journet, "Sainte Catherine de Sienne," conference given to the Little Brothers of Jesus, Annemasse, April 30, 1966, in *Bulletin des Amis du cardinal Journet* 8, December 1985, 7–16.

30. Chapter 7, *The Dialogue of the Seraphic Virgin, Catherine of Siena*, trans. A. Thorold (London: K. Paul, Trench, Trübner & Co., 1896), 34.

31. See Ch. Taylor, *A Secular Age* (Cambridge, MA: Harvard University Press, 2007).

32. *Lumen Gentium* 13 §3 and 18 §1.

33. See Desmazières, *L'Heure des laïcs*, 99.

34. See F. Daguet, "La relation des deux sacerdoces dans une Église synodale," in *La Femme au cœur de l'Église*, ed. F. Daguet (Paris: Éditions du Cerf, 2022).

35. This expression was used by Gabriel Richi Alberti during the symposium: "For a fundamental theology of the priesthood," Aula Paul VI, February 17–19, 2022.

36. Regarding France, see for example the Talentheo institute (https://www.talentheo.org/) or the association Chemins d'humanité (http://www.chemins-humanite.org/).

37. Regarding France, see for example the association offering help to victims of physical, psychological, or spiritual abuse C'est-à-dire (https://cestadireweb.org/).

38. In France, see for example the Réseau Melchisédech.

39. Rossetti, "La 'pericoresi' tra le forme e stati di vita," 316–17.

40. Cf. E. Fivaz-Depeursinge and A. Corboz-Warnéry, *The Primary Triangle: A Developmental Systems View of Fathers, Mothers, and Infants* (New York: Basic Books, 1999), 1–30. I am grateful to Roberto Giorgis, OP, for drawing my attention to this work.

41. Desmazières, *L'Heure des laïcs*, 17. See also 59.

42. Saying this, one should bear in mind that the Church's pneumatological dimension is always coextensive with its christological dimension. See Congregation for the Doctrine of the Faith, Letter *Iuvenescit Ecclesia* to the bishops of the Catholic Church regarding the relationship between hierarchical and charismatic gifts in the life and the mission of the Church, March 14, 2016, 11. Allow me also to refer to A. Diriart, *Sesfrontièressont la charité. L'Eglise Corps du Christ et* "Lumen Gentium," coll. Études Charles Journet (Paris: Lethielleux-DDB, 2011), 431–541.

43. Ghirlanda, "Sviluppodell'ecclesiologia," 34: "Il mistero della Chiesa non appare pienamente espresso dal rapporto dialettico laicato-ministero sacro, che determina la struttura gerarchica. La struttura fondamentale della Chiesa che emerge è una struttura sacramentale-carismatica, che assume una forma istituzionale, comprende in sé quella gerarchica." SeealsoId., "Les différents sens du terme 'consécration' dans le CIC de 1983," in CIVCSVA, *Consecratio et consecratio per evangelicaconsilia*, Actes du Séminaire International, Université pontificale antonienne, Rome, March 1–3, 2018 (Vatican City: Libreria Editrice Vaticana, 2019), 41.

44. CDF, Letter *Iuvenescit Ecclesia* 11.

45. John Paul II, *Message to Participants in the World Congress of Ecclesial Movements and New Communities*, May 17, 1998, 5; *Speech to the International Colloquium of Ecclesial Movements*, March 2, 1987.

46. Ghirlanda, "Sviluppodell'ecclesiologia," 33 & 35. See also Y. Congar, *Jalons pour une théologie du laïcat* (Paris: Éditions du Cerf, 1954), 478; Desmazières, *L'Heure des laïcs*, 119.

47. On the ambiguity of the terminology "religious" adopted by Vatican II to denote consecrated life as a whole, see V. DE PAOLIS, "Ecclesialitàdella Vita consacrata," in *Punti Fondamentali Sulla Vita Consacrata*, ed. G. GHIRLANDA (Rome: PUG, 1994), 581–85; GHIRLANDA, "Les différents sens du terme 'consécration'," 19–20.

48. Moreover, the Code of Canon Law follows this distinction (Can. 207.2). From this viewpoint, then, the vocation of "faithful of Christ" is subdivided into two: clergy and laity, with consecrated life being distributed between one and the other categories.

49. H. U. VON BALTHASAR, *The Christian State of Life* (San Francisco: Ignatius Press, 2002), part II, section III, subsection 5.

50. See DE PAOLIS, "Ecclesialitàdella Vita consacrata," 568. See also J. DANIÉLOU, "La place des religieux dans la structure de l'Église," in *L'Église de Vatican II*, ed. G. BARAÚNA, trans. Y. CONGAR, vol. III (Paris: Éditions du Cerf, 1966), 1173–80.

51. VC 29: "The profession of the evangelical counsels *indisputably belongs to the life and holiness of the Church*. This means that the consecrated life, present in the Church from the beginning, can never fail to be one of her essential and characteristic elements, for it expresses her very nature."

52. See VC 105.

53. Cf. John 21:15–22. See J. PÉREZ SOBA, "La vocazione all'amore come fondamento di tutti gli stati di vita," in *Liberi par amare. È possibile vivere i consigli evangelici nel mondo?*, ed. M. J. CHAVEZ and V. FERNANDEZ, Ateneo Pontificio Regina Apostolorum (Rome: If. Press, 2022), 11–30.

54. BALTHASAR, *The Christian State of Life*, 67.

55. See M. OUELLET, "Rencontre avec Noëlle Hausman," *Vies Consacrées* 93, no. 4 (2021): 3–8.

56. Cf. PÉREZ-SOBA, "La vocazioneall'amore come fondamento di tutti glistati di vita."

57. VC 31.

58. G. CANOBBIO, F. DALLA VECCHIA, and G. MONTINI, "Introduzione," in *Gli Stati di vitadelcristiano*, in QuaderniTeologici del Seminario di Brescia (Brescia: Morcelliana, 1995), 11.

59. DE PAOLIS even calls it the "ideal model of the lay state," in "Stati di vita delle persone nella Chiesa secondo il CIC," 116.

60. See E. CORECCO, "Il sacramento del matrimonio: cardine della costituzione della Chiesa," in *Ius et communio. Scritti di Diritto Canonico,* ed. DE PAOLIS, vol. II, Facoltà Teologica di Lugano–Casale Monferrato (Piemme, 1997), 564–91.

61. ROCCHETTA, *Senza Sposi, non c'è Chiesa.*

62. ROSSETTI, "La 'pericoresi' tra le forme e stati di vita," 316.

63. See Y. Congar, "Les laïcs et l'ecclésiologie des *ordines* chez les théologiens du XIe et XIIe siècles," in *I laici nella "societas christiana" dei secoli XI e XII. Atti della Settimana internazionale di studio Mendola*, August 21–27, 1965, ed. G. Lazzati and C. D. Fonseca (Milan: Vita e Pensiero, 1968), 83–117.

64. Cf. De Paolis, "Stati di vita delle persone nella Chiesa secondo il CIC," 115.

65. *Gaudium et Spes* 48 §2: Christian spouses have a special sacrament by which they are fortified and receive a kind of consecration (*veluti consecrantur*) in the duties and dignity of their state.

66. "The Sacraments at the Service of Communion" is the title of the third chapter of part II, "The Celebration of the Christian Mystery," of the *Catechism of the Catholic Church* (Geoffrey Chapman, 1997), 343.

67. Italics: emphasis in the original. Bold or underlined: emphasis added.

68. de Clerck, "Ressources du nouveau rituel de 1991: une théologie en voie de développement," in *Le Sacrement de mariage entre hier et demain*, ed. L.-M. Chauvet (Paris: Éditions de l'Atelier, 2001), 143.

69. On the topic of consecration, see M. Homedes-Palau, *La consécration chrétienne. Ses fondements, expressions et caractéristiques* (Paris: Éditions du Cerf, 2019).

70. See J. Granados, "La relation entre l'Eucharistie et le mariage," *Nova et Vetera* 92 (2017): 165–81.

71. See J. Granados, *Una sola carne e un solo spirito. Teologiadelmatrimonio* (Siena: Cantagalli, 2014), 323–25, which refers to Augustine, *De bonoviduitatis* 3, 4 (CSEL 41, 308) and Bonaventure, in *IV Sent.*, d. 26, a. 2, q. 2, c. 1.

72. Cf. H. Caffarel, "Mariage et Eucharistie," in *L'Anneau d'or* 118 (1964): 250. See also J. Elliott, *What God Has Joined* (New York: Alba House, 1990), 151–52.

73. See R. Bonetti and S.Bucolo, *Una missione da condividere. Sacerdoti e sposi: insieme per testimoniare il Vangelo* (Assisi: Edizioni Porziuncola, 2020).

74. Cf. 1 Cor 16:19; Rom 16:5; Col 4:15; Phlm 2. See R. Fabris and E. Castellucci, eds., *La Chiesa domestica* (Sao Paolo: Cinisello Balsamo, 2009); M.-F.Baslez, *L'Église à la maison. Histoire des premières communautés chrétiennes, ier-iiie siècle* (Paris: Salvator, 2021). M.-F. Baslez points out (14) that "households in antiquity were not restricted to the nuclear family, but contained a larger group, including spouses, children, servants, and all the people living under the same roof."

75. Cf. J. Chrysostom, *Homily 20 on the Letter to the Ephesians*, 6 (PG 62, 143); F. Quéré-Jaulmes, *Le mariage dans l'Égliseancienne* (Paris: Centurion, 1969), 93. See also Chrysostom, *Sermons on Genesis*, 6, 2, *SCh* 433 (Paris: Éditions du Cerf, 1998), 295–96; *Homily on the Letter to the Romans* 24, 3 (PG 60, 626); *Homily on the Gospel of St Matthew*, 32, 7 (PG 57, 385), 48, 7 (PG 58, 495).

76. Cf. K. Wojtyła, *Sources of Renewal: The Implementation of Vatican II* (London: HarperCollins, 1980).

77. Daguet, "La relation des deux sacerdoces."

78. See Daguet, "La relation des deux sacerdoces."

79. John Paul II, *Wednesday Audience*, April 28, 1982.

80. See John Paul II, *Wednesday Audience*, April 21, 1982.

81. Parents who live the grace of adoption witness especially to the pains involved in having children, which took the form, first, of the suffering of renouncing the joy of having children of their own flesh.

82. In her book *Il n'y a qu'un amour*, Le livre ouvert (Lagord, 2013), 146–52, N. Hausman studies Vatican II's references relating to the nuptial analogy of Ephesians 5, bringing into its scope not only marriage and religious life but also the priesthood, particularly with reference to *Presbyterorum Ordinis* 16, which itself refers to *Lumen Gentium* 42 and 44. See also N. Hausman, "La vie religieuse apostolique selon Vatican II," *NRT* 107 (1985): 658–74, 668–69.

83. See A. Diriart, "La dimension nuptiale des catéchèses baptismales. Entresimilitude, circularité et dissymétrie," *Nova et Vetera* 93, no. 1 (2018): 25–45.

84. *Lumen Gentium* 44 speaks of the consecration to God in consecrated life, saying that it "will be the more perfect, in as much as the indissoluble bond of the union of Christ and His bride, the Church, is represented by firm and more stable bonds." See VC nos. 19 and 34.

85. John Paul II, apostolic exhortation *Pastores Dabo Vobis*, March 25, 1992, 22.

86. See the recommendations of Pope John Paul II in *Familiaris Consortio* 70 and VC no. 50, and those of Pope Francis in the apostolic exhortation *Amoris Laetitia* 202–3. See also D. Waymel, "Les instituts de vie consacrée dans les Églisesparticulières: appel à un discernement synodal" *NRT* 143 (2021): 231–32; see also A. Krohn, *Priestly Formation for Celibacy: Nuptial and Trinitarian*, in *God and Eros*, ed. C. Patterson and C. Sweeney (Eugene, OR: Cascade Books, 2015), 191–211.

87. Francis of Sales, *Letter 400, to Madame la Présidente Brûlart*, Annecy, June 1607.

15

CHRISTIAN INITIATION AND FORMING FOR SPECIFIC VOCATIONS

Father Édouard Adé

THE SITUATION OF vocational crisis or vocational flourishing being experienced by certain Church communities seems to be linked to the vitality of their catechetical pastoral work. At least, this is what initial sociological observation seems to show. In particular churches where there are many catechumens and Easter baptisms, the seminaries and novitiates receive many candidates for the priesthood and the religious life. This correlation is logical, since the attraction exercised by these two states of life has more chance of being fruitful where religious practice in society is strong. But would increasing the number of baptisms be sufficient to produce a vocational reawakening? Have not the Christian communities that are facing a crisis of vocations today, also experienced their own time of "fat cows" in the past? Paradoxically, is not the growth in numbers of vocations in the new churches, for example, in Africa, a warning of a future collapse in vocations, signs of which are already apparent in certain circles, especially those of intellectuals who are on the way to secularization, where Eloi Messi Metogo's provocative question, "Can God die in Africa?"[1] is beginning to be answered in the affirmative?

These sociological considerations, however pertinent they are, do not in fact enable the underlying question to be articulated at its true level, the level of theology and pastoral practice. The point at issue revolves around the intrinsic connection between Christian initiation and the flowering of specific vocations. Is the flourishing of vocations linked to the catechetical teaching given during the journey of young people as they grow into the Catholic faith?

The hypothesis to be verified is the following: the more the catechetical approach employed aims for in-depth evangelization, the more it leads to vocational flourishing. It is not simply a question, as Pope Paul VI said in *Evangelii Nuntiandi*, "of preaching the Gospel in ever wider geographic areas or to ever greater numbers of people, but… of affecting and as it were upsetting, through the power of the Gospel, mankind's criteria of judgment, determining values, points of interest, lines of thought, sources of inspiration and models of life, which are in contrast with the Word of God and the plan of salvation" (EN 19). Basically, it is not so much about increasing the numbers of the baptized in the hope of having numerous vocations, as of evangelizing in depth those whom the Holy Spirit leads to the person who is Christ.

To help reflection on this theme, which is of concern to every ecclesial community, the present contribution will first outline the ecclesiological framework of relevance for this whole question in Africa. It will then identify within the Church's tradition an institution capable of serving as a blueprint for a long-term vocational culture: the catechumenal initiation of the Church fathers. This institution can be analyzed with special reference to its characteristic pedagogical method, namely the kerygma, and updated in accord with experience; this, if it is taken seriously in pastoral practice, will bring to maturity many solid vocations that complement one another in a totally missionary Church.

THE ECCLESIOLOGICAL FRAMEWORK

Although the Christian communities in Africa show signs of great vitality, and candidates for the priesthood and consecrated life are crowding at the doors of centers of formation,[2] the documents of the magisterium on the life of the Church in Africa constantly return to the question of vocations.

In his postsynodal apostolic exhortation *Ecclesia in Africa* (1995), Pope John Paul II pointed out that "a major challenge emphasized almost unanimously by the Episcopal Conferences of Africa in their replies to the *Lineamenta* concerned Christian marriage and family life. What is at stake is extremely serious: truly 'the future of the world and of the Church passes through the family'" (EA 50). To this challenge concerning the state of marriage, another challenge is immediately added: vocations to the priesthood and the consecrated life. And it is presented as follows: "to discern them wisely, to provide competent directors and to oversee the quality of the formation offered" (EA 50). This challenge concerns the future of the Church, of Africa, and of the world: "The fulfillment of the hope for a flowering of African missionary vocations depends on the attention given to the solution of this problem, a flowering that is required if the Gospel is to be proclaimed in every part of the Continent and beyond" (EA 50). These precise indications summarize in a single paragraph the great vocational problems raised for the Church today:

- A better grasp of the interdependence of vocations, the intervivification of vocations (where marriage and the family are in crisis, the vocation to the priesthood and the vocation to the religious life are also in crisis; where they are healthy, the other vocations are also holding up);
- Better discernment and better accompaniment of vocations, which demands foresight in forming the formators (today's crisis within the ranks of the clergy should lead us to ask ourselves: "Whom did we send into the centers of formation?");
- Keeping our sights on the mission *ad gentes* (no Church flourishes if it is only concerned with itself; only a missionary outlook keeps the Church healthy and holy); hence the Synod's insistence on encouraging vocations of missionaries (EA 56).

The same document brings to light a new dimension of the complementarity of vocations (cf. 94). In Africa, where there is so much still to be done in terms of social projects and development, there is a great risk that religious will seem to be mere social workers or developmental NGO agents. The vocational culture must, therefore, lay stress not only on the apostolicity of the active religious life, but also the contemplative forms, as an expression of that "pure oblation," that "pure gratuitousness" that gives the things of the earth their ultimate value. For this purpose, it is important to provide for "an integral human formation, as well as one which is solid in its spiritual and doctrinal, apostolic and missionary, biblical and theological dimensions...faithfully and regularly updated down through the years" (EA 94).

Furthermore, the fact that large numbers of young people are knocking at the doors should not lead to a multiplication of religious foundations. Without saddening the Holy Spirit, the only Master of charisms, prudence and attentive discernment are needed. Along the same lines, "Religious Institutes that do not have houses in Africa" may not go there "seeking new vocations without prior dialogue with the local Ordinary" (EA 94). The importance of this dialogue is connected to the necessary cultural dimension of formation.

What the document says about the formation of future priests also applies to future religious; they need to be formed "in the true cultural values of their country, in a sense of honesty, responsibility and integrity" (EA 95).

The other major magisterial document for Africa is Benedict XVI's postsynodal apostolic exhortation *Africae Munus* (2011).

It underlines the need to recognize that Africa is "called to contribute to the new evangelization in secularized countries which once provided numerous missionaries but are today sadly lacking in vocations to the priesthood and to the consecrated life" (AM 167). Africa could respond all the more fully to this call because a great number of her sons and daughters have welcomed the invitation from the Lord of the harvest (cf. Matt 9:37–38) to work in his vineyard (cf. Matt 20:1–6), so that, "gathered in various associations, movements and communities," they "devote their lives to the spread of the Gospel of Jesus Christ" (AM 168). On this subject, however, the document recalls the exhortation of the apostle to the Gentiles: "Do not quench the Spirit, do not despise prophesying, but test everything; hold fast to what is good, abstain from every form of evil" (1 Thess 5:19–22).

Echoing *Ecclesia in Africa*, *Africae Munus* underlines the contemplative life as one of the outstanding gifts that the Holy Spirit has made to the Church in Africa from the earliest centuries:

> Africa is the cradle of the Christian contemplative life. Present from earliest times in North Africa, especially in Egypt and Ethiopia, it took root in sub-Saharan Africa during the last century...Their hidden life is like leaven in the dough. Their constant prayer will sustain the apostolic efforts of the bishops, priests, other consecrated persons, catechists and of the entire Church. (AM 119)

The document returns insistently to the question of the formation of seminarians. Together with the "obviously primary" theological and spiritual formation, the Synod fathers "emphasized the importance of the psychological and human growth of each candidate" (AM 121). This open concern is a sign that fifteen years of putting the recommendations of *Ecclesia in Africa* into practice had not sufficed to fill the gaps that were observed in the formation of future priests, which had impelled many national Bishops' Conferences to set up junior seminaries, and religious institutes to set up prepostulancies.

In the formation of the "human material" something important still needed to be done. Yet Africa had not failed to emphasize the importance of inculturation during those years. But this emphasis seemed to take another direction, which was the cause of the document's warning: "Future priests must develop a correct understanding of their own culture while not being locked within their own ethnic and cultural limits" (AM 121). The reminder of the need for them to be "rooted in Gospel values so as to strengthen their commitment in faithfulness and devotion to Christ" (AM 121) shows that the crisis is at the interface of human and spiritual values: the human material that has been found to be fragile is the family fabric from which vocations to the priesthood and to consecrated life spring; whence the need to put in place a new framework of vocational culture.

Such a framework is needed to replace that of the human family—the basic cell of society—which is in crisis everywhere, including in Africa. Secularized schools and colleges are unable to provide it; Christian communities must be able to do so, but they will only succeed if they draw from the rich tradition of the Church. The institution that seems most suited to fulfill this role is the catechumenate. As a place of configuration with Christ, catechumenal initiation is indeed a place of both humanization and, inseparably, divinization.

The inculturated feature of this framework, for the Church in Africa, is the profound echo of traditional initiation rites still retained in African societies. Many well-informed African pastors have lamented for decades the spectacle offered by our "school-type" catechetical methods, by contrast with the intensity of the traditional initiation experience undergone by non-Christian young people and adults in the sacred grove.[3] Even though anthropological research has brought to light certain limitations of this traditional practice, especially the climate of fear in which it is conducted, there is still room to ask why the Church, in the same sociocultural setting, has not been able to put in place a Christian experience—of the perfect love that banishes fear—capable of bringing about a process of human maturing comparable to that observed in traditional initiation. My hypothesis is that in order to achieve this, catechesis needs to effect a re-centering of Christian initiation on the kerygma.

RECENTERING OF CHRISTIAN INITIATION ON THE KERYGMA

"Being Christian is not the result of an ethical choice or a lofty idea, but the encounter with an event, a person, which gives life a new horizon and a decisive direction" (Benedict XVI, *Deus Caritas Est* 1, quoted in *Africae Munus* 165). If there is one call that runs through the whole of Sacred Scripture, from the earliest writings to the last, it is undoubtedly the call to conversion. The image contained in the Hebrew verb שוב (*shuv*) is that of retracing one's steps, returning to the starting point. The preaching of the prophets up until the exile ceaselessly invited the sinful people to return to YHWH, in a relationship of righteousness (Amos 5:4–15; Micah 6:6ff.), rejecting idols (Hos 14:2ff.) and converting their lives (Isa 1:16–17.). In Jeremiah, in response to the inevitable catastrophe brought down on the people by their hardening in sin, God himself is presented as the one who will return (Jer 12:15) and bring his people back for a new covenant (Jer 31:18ff.). Conversion thus becomes a gift of God's mercy (Ezek 36:24–32).

The same prophetic zest is clear in the New Testament period leading up to Christ's first public manifestation, with John the Baptist's vigorous call to conversion to escape judgment (Luke 3:7ff.). His baptism signifies the will to return to God by turning away from sin (Mark 1:4ff.).

At the beginning of his preaching, Jesus himself takes up this theme: "The time is fulfilled, and the kingdom of God is at hand. Repent and believe in the gospel" (Mark 1:15). He thus links the going-back of conversion to faith in the gospel. This "good news" is about "Jesus Christ, the Son of God" (Mark 1:1). "There is no good news other than that of Jesus Christ: he is the essence of 'news' and the essence of joy. In Jesus Christ messenger and message are one. He is the one who proclaims, who has received the task of proclaiming the message from the Father. He is also the content of this proclamation, that which the Father has to announce to the world."[4] Thus the turning-around to give assent to this "good news" can only be the result of an event in which a unique encounter is produced, which sets out a new trajectory, gives a new meaning to life: the encounter with the person Jesus Christ.

It is this "time of grace" this "favorable time," that the Christian initiation catechesis given by the fathers of the Church included in the organization of the catechumenate with its threefold structure of "kerygma—initiation—mystagogy."[5]

In the structure of this initiation, the kerygma is the decisive moment, the moment of personal meeting with the Word of God that touches the person, overturns their life, induces them to change, to turn their life around completely. It is on that first movement that the fruitfulness of what follows seems to depend: it is then that everything is decided, that the person who is touched by God's grace is interiorly impelled to place their life at the Lord's disposal to carry out his loving plan. The moment of kerygma on the catechumen's path (or the call to become a Christian) thus leads to an experience of life that is in many respects very similar to the experiences of the prophets' vocations related by Holy Scripture.

The power for conversion possessed by the first kerygma announcement made by St. Peter on the day of Pentecost has the same radical nature as the voice that Saul of Tarsus heard on the road to Damascus.

Luke says that this Pentecostal proclamation brought about the conversion of three thousand people (Acts 2:21–24).

St. Paul's experience of turning his life around marked him so deeply that in his letter to the Corinthians he reminds his readers that the mission entrusted to him by Christ is first of all a mission to preach the kerygma: "Christ did not send me to baptize but to preach the gospel, and not with eloquent wisdom, lest the cross of Christ be emptied of its power" (1 Cor 1:17). And he illustrates this in the same letter (1 Cor 15:1–8).

Relying on this prophetic and apostolic tradition, the fathers of the Church laid great stress, in their catechesis, on the primordial importance of proclaiming the kerygma. For them, entry into the catechumenate was triggered by a radical conversion; something that the Church's catechetical practice seems to have lost track of as time went by. At the beginning of the last century, in the tide of the theological renewal that prepared the way for Vatican II, Josef Andreas Jungmann had already laid bare the cracks in a catechetical practice that was dominated by Scholasticism, when Christianity was broadly in the majority but had lost the inspirational drive of catechesis as practiced by the Church fathers. In a phrase that became famous, he said *Das Dogma sollen wir kennen, verkünden müssen wir das Kerygma*—we need to know the dogma, but we must proclaim the kerygma.[6] This disconnection from the kerygma continued even after the Council, with the invasion of the pastoral field by human sciences, and the noticeable replacement of the kerygma by *paraenesis*, or moral exhortation, in much catechetical practice. Roland Minnerath observed regretfully, "In 2014 the Episcopal Commission of Catechesis and the Catechumenate published a 'non-normative' document that 'tries to show why and how it is possible to open the door of the Church to converts to Christ, whatever their situation' (No. 9). I did not succeed in convincing the authors that judgment of a person's aptitude to receive baptism is done at the time of entering the catechumenate, and not at the following stage, that of the decisive call."[7]

There is a confusion of ideas here that needs to be raised: the proclamation of the kerygma—by "the Church in her missionary outreach" to "geographical and existential peripheries"—is addressed to everyone without exception; but Christian initiation can only be opened fruitfully to those who have already given their assent to the word they have received. That absolutely does not mean that the rest are left out in the cold. They too will be the object of the Church's pastoral solicitude, until the day comes when they open themselves to grace that is always coming in search of them in the figure of the Good Samaritan, who is none other than the Good Shepherd, ready to leave the ninety-nine sheep to find the one who is entangled in the brambles of human life. The immediate consequence here is to hold firmly to the statement that the *sacraments of the Church are sacraments of faith*: "The mission to baptize, and so the sacramental mission, is implied in the mission to evangelize, because the sacrament is prepared for by the word of God and by the faith which is assent to this word" (*Catechism of the Catholic Church* [CCC] 1122). This is what the Council fathers had already said: "The People of God are joined together primarily by the word of the living God...the preaching of the word is needed for the very ministering of the sacraments. They are precisely sacraments of faith, a faith which is born of and nourished by the word" (*Presbyterorum Ordinis* 4).

This useful distinction enables the Church not to obscure, in her pastoral work, the crucial moment of the proclamation of the kerygma, or to opt instead for widespread sacramentalization and moral instruction on Christian living that is not underpinned by *metanoïa*. The long-term results of that pastoral approach can only be disastrous, bearing fruits of radical secularism and rejection of the institutional Church.

However, the Church's magisterium has remained alert to this risk, often rowing against the current of certain approaches that take inspiration more from the human sciences than from the transforming force of the Gospel and its powerful grace. As far back as 1971, taking up the new impulses given by the Council documents, especially the Constitution *Dei Verbum*, and in conformity with *Christus Dominus* 44, the first *General Catechetical Directory* was produced. Even though the expression "kerygma" does not appear in it, the ministry of the word is presented as "the herald of the living tradition" that comes from the apostles and is developed in the Church with the assistance of the Holy Spirit (13).

In due course, the *General Catechetical Directory* of 1997, relying on the innovative impulse given by John Paul II's apostolic exhortation

Catechesi Tradendae (1979), clearly explained the kerygma in three significant instances:

- when it deals with the process of conversion in four steps: interest in the gospel, conversion following the proclamation of the kerygma, profession of faith, and journeying toward perfection (56);
- when it presents the four stages of the baptismal catechumenate of the Church fathers:
  - the precatechumenate, characterized as the locus of first evangelization leading to conversion and where the kerygma of the primary proclamation is explained;
  - the catechumenate properly speaking, the context of integral catechesis beginning with "the handing on of the Gospels";
  - a time of purification and illumination that affords a more intense preparation for the sacraments of initiation and in which the "the handing on of the Creed" and "the handing on of the Lord's Prayer" take place;
  - a time of mystagogy, characterized by the experience of the sacraments and entry into the community (88);
- when it presents, finally, the main aspects of the kerygma: the loving, active closeness of the Father, the gift of integral salvation, the announcement of God's justice (divine judgment and human responsibility), the inauguration of the kingdom in the person of Christ, the Church as the seed of the kingdom, and the consummation of history in Jesus Christ (102).

Benedict XVI, with the two synods he convoked on "The Word of God in the Life and Mission of the Church" (2008) and "The New Evangelization for the Transmission of Christian Faith" (2012) repeatedly recalled the importance of the kerygma in the new evangelization and catechesis:

> "Gospel" means: God has broken his silence, God has spoken, God exists. This fact in itself is salvation: God knows

> us, God loves us, he has entered into history. Jesus is his Word, God with us, God showing us that he loves us, that he suffers with us until death and rises again. This is the Gospel. God has spoken, he is no longer the great unknown, but has shown himself and this is salvation.[8]

Finally, Pope Francis, in his apostolic exhortation *Evangelii Gaudium* (2013), not only recalled the unbreakable link between evangelization and catechesis in the light of the culture of encounter, but also made the kerygma the main paradigm of catechesis:

> We must not think that in catechesis the kerygma gives way to a supposedly more "solid" formation. Nothing is more solid, profound, secure, meaningful and wisdom-filled than that initial proclamation. All Christian formation consists of entering more deeply into the kerygma, which is reflected in and constantly illumines the work of catechesis, thereby enabling us to understand more fully the significance of every subject which the latter treats. It is the message capable of responding to the desire for the infinite which abides in every human heart. (EG 165)

This constant presence of the kerygma throughout the catechumenal process and equally in the life of every disciple of Christ, which was then clearly set out in the new *General Catechetical Directory* (2020), especially in nos. 57–65, means that it is not simply one moment in a process, but a constitutive element that lies at its heart and runs through the whole of it. The inspirational kerygma that accompanies the entirety of Christian initiation transforms it into a genuine place of vocational journeying, in so far as it illuminates the inner structure of the baptismal vocation and works to bring it to life.

ENTRY INTO THE CATECHUMENATE AND VOCATIONAL JOURNEYING

In so far as embarking on the catechumenate is the consequence of a personal response to the Lord's call that has resonated in the depths of the person's life in the form of "Come, follow me," this catechumenal initiation, brought to life by the breath of the kerygma, can only be conceived of as a *sequela Christi*. It is a reliving of the experience of the Galilean fishermen, of Matthew the publican, and of the other disciples who, "immediately," left everything to follow Jesus of Nazareth. In this journeying in the Lord's footsteps, they have certainly begun to understand their life as a journey, a pilgrimage that will undoubtedly involve passages that are not yet clearly discerned, but which will take shape as the Lord's "Pasch" gets nearer.

What their walking together (*syn-hodos*) with the Lord begins to reveal to them is the existence of a "before" and "after" in their lives, from the moment when they consented to begin the journey. But in reality this changeover will be required of them at every moment, especially at times when they do not seem to understand the life or teaching of the Master anymore. Just as he did with the Galilean fishermen and the other disciples, he will be able to help them, as a skilled teacher, to continue on the journey: Matthew 16:8–11; Mark 9:32; Luke 2:50; 9:45; 18:34; John 8:27; 8:43; 10:6; 11:13; 12:16.

His disciples will realize, as they go along, that they have been drawn from the world—they are in the world, but no longer of the world (John 17:9–16). They will then need to learn *not to take this present world for their model, but to be transformed by a renewal of the way they think* (cf. Rom 12:2). The call that will be engraved for them on the heart of their synodal path with the Master will be a call to "*form our conscience*, to make it the object of a continuous conversion to what is true and to what is good" (John Paul II, *Veritatis Splendor* 64). They will experience little by little, through their Master's lessons of sovereign freedom, that in reality

> it is the "heart" converted to the Lord and to the love of what is good which is really the source of true judgments of conscience. Indeed, to "prove what is the will of God, what is good and acceptable and perfect" (Rom 12:2), knowledge of God's law in general is certainly necessary, but it is not sufficient: what is essential is a sort of "connaturality" between man and the true good. (VS 64)

Openness to this connaturality that John Paul II, in his anthropological approach,[9] found to be rooted in the virtuous dispositions of the human being, seems for the moment to be beyond their reach. Quite rightly, therefore, VS refers them immediately to the dispositions that grace alone infuses among the theological virtues (VS 64).

The time of initiation is a time when the disciples realize that something in their former life is dying—and this is what mystagogical catechesis will explain more eloquently—or that they are experiencing a real "expropriation" of self. In their journey in the Master's footsteps they no longer belong to themselves. But this process that, if it is taken seriously, is felt as a "one-way ticket," a burning of bridges, must reach its goal—the point where the human creature lets go completely, marked by the sacramental moment when the traveler becomes a "new creature": "If anyone is in Christ, he is a new creation; the old has passed away, behold, the new has come" (2 Cor 5:17). By following Christ in his passage through death, disciples are projected into a "living-for": their lives are no longer centered on themselves, but on Christ who died and was raised to life again for them (cf. 2 Cor 5:14–15). They are stripped of the "old nature with its practices" (Col 3:9) and dressed in "the new nature, created after the likeness of God in true righteousness and holiness" (Eph 4:24). With this new birth there also comes a "new world," a "new order": the old things give way to new. Incorporation into Christ thus becomes the *forma* of a new identity.

This incorporation is effected through the sacraments of Christian initiation, which in their unity and order reveal their trinitarian and paschal roots. In Peter's exhortation on the day of Pentecost, baptism in the name of Jesus Christ follows on conversion and is itself followed immediately by the gift of the Holy Spirit (Acts 2:38). Catechumens, who are sacramentally plunged into the death and resurrection of the Son, open themselves to the mystery of this Father-God whose love is expressed in the form of an absolute gift of self, to which the Son responds with an eternal act of thanksgiving (*eucharistia*) to the source that is none other than the original gift of the Father. Proceeding from both as their subsistent "we," the "Spirit of both," whose anointing the neophytes receive, opens them to the grace of the sacrament which will accompany them throughout their lives as pilgrims of faith: the *mysterium fidei* (the Eucharist). Everything is thus arranged in such a way that the Spirit received in baptism introduces the neophytes into an entirely Eucharistic life.

In this way, baptism is seen as the foundation of Christian identity, an identity that neophytes receive in the very heart of their existence, through the choice made on confronting the evil of their past lives (renunciation); the choice for the God of love who, in the death and resurrection of Christ and the gift of the Spirit, opens a new life to them (profession of faith).

This new life can be grasped as a covenantal existence: baptism is "a turning to God with a clear conscience" (1 Pet 3:21). But it is fundamentally "the act through which [Jesus Christ] commits his faithfulness to those who have given him their faith": God saves "through the resurrection of Jesus Christ" (1 Pet 3:21), "and this is affirmed in other terms by the doctrine of 'baptismal character' (DS 1609). We can thus see a structure of reciprocity governing the logic of the sacramental act. The intention of God in Christ is received by people who answer him in the Holy Spirit, with a view to building the Church. In baptism Christians receive their vocation. As the prayer accompanying the anointing with chrism states: 'Henceforth, you are one of His people, you are members of the body of Christ, and you participate in his dignity as priest, prophet, and king.'"[10]

> The sign of the Cross makes kings of all those reborn in Christ, and the anointing of the Holy Spirit consecrates them as priests, so that, except for the particular service of our ministry, all Christians who are spiritual and who have the use of reason may recognise themselves as members of this royal race and sharers in the priestly function. What is there, indeed, so royal for the soul as to govern the body in submission to God? And what is there so priestly as to vow to the Lord a pure conscience and offer the spotless victims of piety from the altar of his heart? (Leo the Great, *Sermo* 4, 1: PL 54, 149)

Following the fathers of the Church, *Lumen Gentium* specifies the elements of this triple function:

- the priestly function: "Christ the Lord, High Priest taken from among men, made the new people 'a kingdom and priests to God the Father.' The baptized, by regeneration and the anointing of the Holy Spirit, are consecrated as a spiritual house and a holy priesthood" (LG 10);
- the prophetic function: the holy people is prophetic through the supernatural sense of the faith, which is that of the people as a whole, clergy, religious, and lay faithful, for as long as it "adheres unwaveringly to the faith given once and for all to the saints" (LG 12), deepens its understanding of it, and becomes a witness to Christ in the middle of this world;
- the kingly function: Christ, the King and Lord of the universe, exercises his royalty by drawing all men to himself through his death and his Resurrection (cf. John 12:32); he made himself the servant of all, not coming "to be served but to serve, and to give his life as a ransom for many" (Matt 20:28). The people of God fulfills its "royal dignity" by living in accordance with this vocation to serve with Christ. For Christians, "to serve is to reign" (LG 36), especially "the poor and afflicted," in whom the Church "sees the image of its poor and suffering Founder" (LG 8).

Read in this way, the whole of Christian life is a baptismal life founded on the call to become "priest, prophet, and king." The gift of the Spirit given to the baptized is for their inner transformation, their sanctification, as Paul's theology illustrates (Gal 5:22; Rom 8:14). But this baptismal vocation also has a mission attached to it through which the baptized receive the strength of God, the Holy Spirit, as shown by Luke's theology.

Based on the internal structure of the baptismal vocation, the Holy Spirit, given "objectively and subjectively,"[11] will determine the specific forms of vocation, which it falls to the mystagogy of baptism to explain, at the same time as the meaning of the mysteries.

MYSTAGOGY AND SPECIFIC VOCATIONS

Traditionally, mystagogy was undertaken after baptism and with sufficient time to accompany the neophytes in their new life. The Church fathers produced a catechesis for it which explained, in particular, the mysteries of the rite of baptism and the demands on the life of the baptized person. In reality, this time of mystagogy, like the time of the kerygma, lasted for the whole lifetime of the baptized, because they needed to enter more deeply into their new life in Christ at every moment.

In this re-reading of what will become "the personal history of salvation" of each of the neophytes, the moment of the call (the time of the kerygma which will accompany them throughout their lives), can be seen as the moment that imprints their way of life on them, by making them discover their existence as a constant "response" to a "call" of love, which has always gone before them; the moment of (sacramental) initiation as the "material" moment in that it gives the "matter," the "content" of this life, which will be that of priest, prophet, and king. The Holy Spirit will take hold of this matter both "objectively" and "subjectively," to give a "form" by modelling states of life and specific vocations.

In the objective mode, two forms of life appear: one mainly oriented toward the Church and the other mainly toward the world. The one oriented toward the Church is the clerical form of life (sacred ministers); the one oriented toward the world is the lay form of life.[12] In the first, the priestly function, the prophetic function, and the royal function are exercised in a ministerial way toward the people of God; in the second, they are exercised for the life of the faithful themselves and their witness in the world.[13]

> The ministerial priest, by the sacred power he enjoys, teaches, and rules the priestly people; acting in the person of Christ, he makes present the Eucharistic sacrifice, and offers it to God in the name of all the people. But the faithful, in virtue of their royal priesthood, join in the offering of the Eucharist. They likewise exercise that priesthood in receiving the

> sacraments, in prayer and thanksgiving, in the witness of a holy life, and by self-denial and active charity. (LG 10)

The expression "ministerial priesthood," although occurring only once, in LG 10, as an alternative to "sacred ministry" (LG 13, 21, 26, 31, 32), brings out the full meaning of the vicarious nature of this priesthood, which really belongs to Christ alone, in that he is the sole high priest who effects the one eucharistic sacrifice and the remission of sins. Since "the Eucharist makes the Church," of which Christ is at one and the same time the only head and the only teacher, his priesthood recapitulates in himself the function of government and of teaching, and it is in this that the clergy participate as ministers.[14]

But this one priesthood of Christ is shared in another way, which differs from the first "in essence and not only in degree" (LG 10): the common priesthood of the faithful, or baptismal priesthood, to which the prophetic and royal witness of every baptized person must be intrinsically attached. This is the priesthood spoken of by Paul in the Letter to the Romans, when he invited disciples of Christ "to present your bodies as a living sacrifice, holy and acceptable to God, which is your spiritual worship" (Rom 12:1). And immediately afterward comes the prophetic injunction: "Do not be conformed to this world but be transformed by the renewal of your mind, that you may prove what is the will of God, what is good and acceptable and perfect" (Rom 12:2). This is followed by an exhortation to humility, followed in its turn by indications on the different functions in the Church. Even if in baptismal life disciples should be sanctified to the point where Christ attains his full stature in them, to the point where they can say with Paul, "It is no longer I who live, but Christ who lives in me" (Gal 2:20), their baptismal priesthood is not of the same order as the ministerial priesthood, which is ordered to the Church's hierarchical, institutional and sacramental structure.

In the subjective mode, meaning the ecclesial subject, understood not in the institutional and sacramental sense but in the sense of the faithful of Christ, in their life and their time of journeying behind Christ, the Holy Spirit has enriched the Church with two states of life: the consecrated state and the lay state (specifically, here, the married state).

Von Balthasar characterizes them as follows: "Both states of life touch the world and heaven, but the religious accomplish the movement of the mission of Christ who comes from heaven to earth to return to the Father, and the laity accomplish the movement of the world which, by virtue of grace, seeks heaven and, filled with the grace of Christ, returns to the world."[15]

The state of life of marriage, which is the "first vocation" in so far as it is a call written upon "human nature"[16] (Gen 1 and 2), is shown to be the foundation of everything in the life of Christian communities. Africa has not ceased to draw attention to what is at stake for the future of humankind concerning the divine institution of the family.[17] It is perhaps the continent that is suffering most severely from the fragmentation of the family unit. In a global vocational approach, the beauty of indissoluble marriage between one man and one woman, in accordance with God's design, needs to be shown forth once more to young people, because it is (and must remain) the "natural sacramental" expression of the irrevocability of God's love for humankind, as being designed to build "the domestic Church," which is the first setting for humanization and the experience of freely-given love. Wherever pastoral work for vocations promotes beautiful "vocations to marriage," beautiful vocations to the priesthood and the religious life also flourish.

Regarding the state of life of consecrated persons, *Lumen Gentium* states specifically,

> From the point of view of the divine and hierarchical structure of the Church, the religious state of life is not an intermediate state between the clerical and lay states. But, rather, the faithful of Christ are called by God from both these states of life so that they might enjoy this particular gift in the life of the Church and thus each in their own way, may be of some advantage to the salvific mission of the Church. (LG 43)

In this state of life, the three functions of priest, prophet, and king are adopted by way of vows: chastity or virginity (you did not want sacrifice or holocaust, but you have made a body for me), obedience (I come to do your will), and poverty (happy are the poor in heart, for theirs is the kingdom of heaven).

The consecrated life is one line taken by the search for the perfection of baptismal life, or life according to the Beatitudes. It is thus a sign and stimulus for all the other members of the Church in their following of Christ. It shows everyone that Christians have no abiding city here below but are pilgrims on the way to the heavenly Jerusalem of which the consecrated life aims to be a foretaste.

Thus, in the process of Christian initiation, the time of mystagogy becomes the time when the new Christians open themselves to spiritual fruitfulness, the work of the Spirit they received in baptism, who, working subjectively, infuses his various gifts and brings a diversity of charisms to flower in the heart of the Church for the sake of the coming kingdom. They begin to understand that no matter in what way the Holy Spirit works—objectively at the institutional and sacramental level, and subjectively at the level of charisms—he is pursuing one same mission: to build the Church, the Body of Christ, the mystery of communion, whose outstanding features are *leitourgia*, *martyria*, and *diakonia*.

WITHIN A TOTALLY MISSIONARY CHURCH, ALL HAVE A CALL

The Church's raison d'être is to continue the Redeemer's mission, because God's plan is for "all men to be saved and to come to the knowledge of the truth" (1 Tim 2:4). The Church only puts itself fully at the service of this plan when it becomes always more Church-as-communion, becoming ever holier through a liturgy directed to the glory of God, and through faithful witness and service, as an expression of the total gift of self. It assumes its identity most fully to the degree that it engenders children with an "ecclesial soul," who, in the course of their initiation, have discovered their spiritual organism—their vocation to build communion, to be priest, prophet, and king—and who are committed with regard to the world, in accordance with their state of life, to the sanctification of temporal realities, to the triumph of the truth and the coming of the kingdom of God.

In this shared ecclesial mission, each of Christ's faithful have their place and their specific role to play:

The lay faithful. The laity, by virtue of their consecration to Christ and the anointing of the Holy Spirit, are called to render to God "spiritual sacrifices acceptable to God through Jesus Christ" (1 Pet 2:5), through their married and family life, all their activities, their prayers and their apostolic undertakings, their daily work, and even the trials of life, endured in the Spirit of God. In this way they consecrate the world itself to God, giving the worship of adoration to God everywhere in the holiness of their lives (LG 34; cf. LG 10). Their prophetic witness to Christ, through their understanding of the faith and the attractiveness of speech that God gives them for proclaiming him in the ordinary conditions of the world (cf. LG 35), and their ministry of service toward the world, whose institutions need to be healed and brought into conformity with the rules of justice and the exercise of virtue—all of this places them at the very heart of the Church's mission. But it is above all in their married life and family life that the Church and society expect the best service from them. This Christian family life, enlivened by the gospel values, is the "first Church" and the "first city" to build.

Consecrated persons. The evangelical counsels and the perfection of charity are proposed to all of Christ's disciples. But there are some who are called to adopt them in a radical way. For these people their priestly oblation is manifested in the vow of chastity, their prophetic vocation in the vow of obedience, and the royal character of their vocation in the vow of poverty. Thus, they make a "more in-depth" consecration, rooted in their baptism and totally dedicated to God (cf. PC 5). They follow Christ more closely and give themselves to God whom they love more than anything or anyone else, thus announcing in the Church the glory of the world to come.

Some of them are called to follow this vocation in pure contemplation, separated from the world (the various forms of monasticism); others in the apostolate by visible witness and works (the apostolic religious life); and still others, in the heart of the world, with no distinguishing marks (the consecrated secular life). If one had to characterize these three forms of consecrated life by aligning them with the baptismal attributes, one might say that the contemplative life stresses the priestly dimension (pure oblation and praise), the apostolic religious life stresses the prophetic dimension, and the consecrated secular life stresses the royal dimension of service. Although these three dimensions are obviously present in the life of every consecrated person, this way of presenting the various forms of the consecrated life could provide food for thought.[18]

The clergy. "For the nurturing and constant growth of the People of God, Christ the Lord instituted in His Church a variety of ministries, which work for the good of the whole body. For those ministers, who are endowed with sacred power, serve their brethren, so that all who are of the People of God,...may arrive at salvation" (LG 18).

Unlike the other two states of life, the call to the priestly state is mediated through the Church. In the declaration that "one does not take the honor upon himself, but he is called by God, just as Aaron was" (Heb 5:4), the first phrase should be understood quite literally.

> No one can give himself the mandate and the mission to proclaim the Gospel. The one sent by the Lord does not speak and act on his own authority, but by virtue of Christ's authority; not as a member of the community, but speaking to it in the name of Christ. No one can bestow grace on himself; it must be given and offered. This fact presupposes ministers of grace, authorized and empowered by Christ. (CCC 875)

This point should be taken as an important element of a culture of vocation. We need to be able to explain to young people the fundamental difference existing between the two forms of calling in the Church: the call where the inner movement is of primary importance, and the call where what is of primary importance is the Church's mediation. The person concerned can, at the most, show good dispositions for the priesthood, but it falls to the Church alone to call men to this state of life, following Christ's command. "He called his disciples and chose from them twelve, whom he named apostles" (Luke 6:13).

The Church continues this act of the Lord's, in the Latin rite by taking candidates only from among those who have already felt a call to the "consecrated life" (chaste celibacy for the kingdom), and in the

Eastern rite, from among those who are already settled in one or other state of life (marriage or consecrated life). Since no one can claim to have a vocation to the priesthood unless the Church has confirmed it, the priestly ministry can never be a right. "The ministry in which Christ's emissaries do and give by God's grace what they cannot do and give by their own powers, is called a 'sacrament' by the Church's tradition" (CCC 875). "Intrinsically linked to the sacramental nature of ecclesial ministry is *its character as service*" (CCC 876). It also has a "*collegial character*" (CCC 877) and a "*personal character*" (CCC 878).

The distinctive element of this state of life is its very special connection with the Eucharist, the sacrifice that is to be perpetuated *in persona Christi Capitis*, who stands before his Body, the Church that he makes fruitful by his sacraments, as the *Sponsus in conspectus ponsa uae*. The anthropological realism and theological tenor of this spousal relationship between Christ and the Church at the heart of the eucharistic mystery is the basis of the principle maintained by the Catholic Church to confer the sacrament of holy orders only on *Viri*.

CONCLUSION

The objective of this paper is not to discuss certain aspects directly concerned with the fundamental theology of the priesthood, but to restore, starting from the particular context of Africa, the question of a vocational culture, in such a way as to provide food for thought in any other ecclesial setting. Christian initiation, in its threefold structure—kerygma, initiation, and mystagogy—has been shown to be the perfect framework for deploying that kind of vocational culture. The experience offered to catechumens enables them to discover human life as a "vocational existence": a call to natural life, a call to the new life in Christ, a call to a state of life, and a call to a specific vocation. This experience shows Christian life to be a "life in alliance," a constant invitation to respond to a call.

The vocational content that baptism confers on every Christian life—to be priest, prophet, and king—within an ecclesial community that possesses the whole of this triple function in its life of communion, liturgy, witness, and service, reveals the equal dignity of the baptized, and the equal depth of their baptismal responsibility for the mission of the Church in the world. The call to adopt one or other of the states of life, and the specific calls that may be heard from within it, are simply "forms," means used by the Lord within his Church to enable his faithful to attain the single purpose for which he created them: "to praise, revere and serve God."[19]

Christian initiation can only prepare people for this "choice" if the kerygma stage on their path is enriched so as to become its inspiration and lifeblood. The primacy accorded to the kerygma over moral exhortation is the basic answer not only to the crisis of vocations observable in many Christian communities, but also to the pathologies linked to deficient ways of living out a vocation (clericalism, worldliness of clergy, careerism, social promotion, legalism, moral judgmentalism, and the various scandals).

NOTES

1. E. M. Metogo, *Dieu peut-il mourir en Afrique ? Essai sur l'indifférence religieuse et l'incroyance en Afrique noire* (Paris-Yaoundé: Karthala-UCAC, 1997).

2. In Benin, where 40 percent of the population of 12 million are Christian, the Diocese of Cotonou alone counts 223 seminarians. In Burkina Faso (population 21 million, of whom 30 percent are Christian), one of the major seminaries (Koumi in Bobo-Dioulasso) has 129 candidates for the priesthood. In Guinea (population 13 million, 10 percent Christian), the Major Seminary in Conakry has 91 candidates for the priesthood. Not to mention Nigeria (population 206 million) where dioceses have over 1000 seminarians.

3. É. Adé, "Chemins d'initiation chrétienne de l'intellectuel communautaire. Implications culturelles de la conversion d'un Doyen d'âge," in *Une expérience africaine d'inculturation*, vol. 2 (Cotonou: Éditions du QIC, 1992), 198–238; cf. also Adé, "Le chemin de prière de l'intellectuel communautaire" *Revue Carmel* 48, no. 4 (1987): 305–12.

4. A. von Speyr, *Mark: Meditations for a Community* (San Francisco: Ignatius Press, 2012), 12.

5. Cf. R. Minnerath, "Pour une catéchèse au service de l'initiation sacramentelle," *Communio* 44, nos. 2–3 (March-June 2019) 13–25; here 14.

6. J. A. Jungmann, *Die Frohbotschaftundunsere Glaubensverkündigung* (Regensburg: F. Pustet, 1936), 60, quoted by U. Lorenzi, *L'héritage du renouveau catéchétique et le caractère performatif de la Parole en catéchèse* (doctoral thesis, Paris, 2007), 220.

7. Minnerath, "Pour une catéchèse," 15–16.

8. Benedict XVI, *Meditation during the First General Congregation of the XIII Ordinary General Assembly of the Synod of Bishops* (October 8, 2012). "The transmission of the Christian Faith consists primarily in proclaiming Jesus Christ, to lead people to faith in him.... 'At the heart of catechesis we find, in essence, a Person, the Person of Jesus of Nazareth, the only Son from the Father...who suffered and died for us and who now, after rising, is living with us forever.' To catechize is 'to reveal in the Person of Christ the whole of God's eternal design reaching fulfillment in that Person. It is to seek to understand the meaning of Christ's actions and words and of the signs worked by him.' Catechesis aims at putting 'people...in communion...with Jesus Christ: only he can lead us to the love of the Father in the Spirit and make us share in the life of the Holy Trinity'" (CCC 425–26, quoting *Catechesi Tradendae* 5).

9. It could be interesting to compare this viewpoint with Newman's teaching on conscience. Cf. H. Geissler, "La conscience est le premier vicaire du Christ," *Communio* 254, no. 6 (2017): 23–37.

10. De Clerck, "Baptism," in *Encyclopedia of Christian Theology*, ed. Jean-Yves Lacoste (New York: Routledge, 2005), 154.

11. I have borrowed this distinction from H. U. von Balthasar, *Theo-Logic III. The Spirit of Truth* (San Francisco: Ignatius Press, 2005), 307–411.

12. This distinction does not take into account the form of the consecrated life, which will be discussed later.

13. "What specifically characterizes the laity is their secular nature. It is true that those in holy orders can at times be engaged in secular activities, and even have a secular profession. But they are by reason of their particular vocation especially and professedly ordained to the sacred ministry" (LG 31).

14. Hervé Legrand, by contrast, finds this phrase inopportune, and he prefers to speak of "priestly ministry," which itself, in his view, is a dimension of the "pastoral ministry of presidency," "of which it forms a part" (H. Legrand, "Ministerial Priesthood," within the article "Priesthood," in Lacoste, *Encyclopedia of Christian Theology*, 1284–86.

15. H. U. von Balthasar, "*Et il appela à lui ceux qu'il voulait." Cinq contributions à une théologie de la vocation, Freiburg* (Johannes Verlag, 2014), 130. Cf. M. Ouellet, *Friends of the Bridegroom: For a Renewed Vision of Priestly Celibacy* (Irondale, AL: EWTN Publishing, 2019); A. Štrukelj, *Leben aus der Fülle des Glaubens. Theologie der christlichenStändebei Hans Urs von Balthasar* (Graz: Styria-Verlag, 2002), with a foreword by H. U. von Balthasar, 7–8.

16. I employ this traditional expression even though it needs semantic clarifications today.

17. Cf. among others: SECAM, *The Family, Our Future*. SECAM *Document for the Extraordinary General Assembly of the Synod of Bishops on the Family*, Accra 2014; *The Future of the Family, Our Mission*, SECAM Publications, Accra 2015.

18. The characterization given here is deliberately analogical to provoke reflection. As an illustration of the way each dimension is truly lived out in the other forms of consecrated life: (a) The prophetic dimension is very evident in the contemplative life: it is lived out by the radical way the world is set aside, which itself becomes witness. For the consecrated seculars, it is lived out above all by the witness of life; (b) With regard to the priestly dimension, the apostolic religious and the consecrated seculars offer God in their prayer the people they meet and the situations they go through in the world, for whom they offer themselves, not only for the sake of their own sanctification but also that of the world into which they are sent; (c) Regarding the royal dimension, the monastic cloister and the religious convent are places of humble service, real poverty and the manifestation of Christ's royalty. But what all are called to live out, certain people can show in ways that are particularly clear and evident.

19. Ignatius of Loyola, *Spiritual Exercises*, "Principle and Foundation," 23.

16

THE COMMON PRIESTHOOD AND THE SACRAMENT OF MATRIMONY*

Martha Olavarrieta de Gómez Serrano

ALL CHRISTIANS (*Christifideles*) have the same dignity. We are united by one vocation given by God through baptism, to be saints and to do apostolic works. Baptism makes us sharers in the mystery of Jesus Christ and in his saving mission as part of the prophetic, priestly, and royal people. The one priesthood of Christ is shared by the Church in two ways: the common priesthood of all the baptized, and the ministerial priesthood, which is shared by bishops, priests, and deacons ordained to ministry.[1]

Through our share in the prophetic mission and in the baptismal priesthood, each one of the baptized are called to provide a service to the Church and the world in organic cooperation between *Christifideles laici*—the lay faithful—and ordained priests, in an interchange of gifts, to work for the kingdom of God in mutual edification. We receive countless spiritual gifts, and it is our responsibility to respond fully to those gifts, which have been freely given to us by God. Our task is to "consecrate [our] life to serving [our] neighbors through preaching the Gospel."[2]

---

* Round Table "Women and Ministry. Status quaestionis."

A SYNODAL CHURCH

In 2015, at a commemoration of the Synod of Bishops held during the Synod on the Family, Pope Francis said that "it is precisely this path of synodality which God expects of the Church of the third millennium. What the Lord is asking of us is already in some sense present in the very word 'synod.' Journeying together—laity, pastors, the Bishop of Rome—is an easy concept to put into words, but not so easy to put into practice."[3]

In this paper, I will talk about the common priesthood in domestic life, and specifically about women's role of service in the Church.

What does serving the Church in married life mean? I will speak from my own experience.

Women always traveled alongside Jesus. They lent him a hand as mothers, sisters, and daughters, and he talked to them as such—for instance, the Samaritan woman, Martha, and Mary.

Like Jesus, priests in the exercise of their priestly ministry continue to meet many like Mary Magdalene, Veronica, and Martha and Mary on their way, and continue to recall Jesus's words to John standing at the foot of the cross: "Behold your Mother" (John 19:27).

Like the Blessed Virgin Mary, women have to continue taking on the missions God has given us in this life: like Mary Magdalene, giving Jesus hospitality and providing him with what he needs to accomplish his ministry; like Veronica, wiping the sweat from our Lord's face; like Martha, serving and attending to his guests; and like Mary, exercising motherhood in the faith toward many of their brethren who are priests. Always providing a great service filled with love.

Saying yes to God, responding to the ministry he has given us of transmitting physical life and supernatural life, must be a complete, serious commitment, and one that has many different facets. We women have been given different charisms, in consecrated life, in the laity, and in married life, the last of which involves the huge responsibility of being cocreators with God. As St. John Paul II said, because of our particular association with the mystery of life that germinates in us and is born of our womb, we have the mission of being guardians of humanity (cf. *Evangelium Vitae* 89). In each situation in our lives, we need to practice, in accordance with the position we have in the Church, for example, charity, synodality, the Church's witness of hope, the promotion of fraternity, and personal and community participation. As well as nurturing, in our homes, the vocation to the ministerial priesthood, and opening our homes up as places of respite and peace, in our little domestic and shared communities, to everyone who needs sheltering.

To me, specifically, God gave the mission of being wife and mother, so that my yes at the altar was wide-ranging and conscious. Together with my husband, Enrique, I discovered my mission step by step, with each new child, and with each wifely embrace. Thanking God for each of his blessings, I could not refuse him in what he was asking of me: an act of generosity and openness to life, not only by having the children he chose to give me, but by being available to the lives and needs of all those around me, even those whom I don't know. Many of those people, both priests and laypeople, have since told me how edified they were by our witness as a married couple and as a family. I think that this way of living out my vocation as mother and wife is also the best way to help our family to fulfill its mission of being a subject and responsible protagonist of evangelization.

God our Lord, throughout our journey through life as husband and wife, granted us the privilege of having great friends who were priests, with whom we were mutual witnesses on this journey, sharing anxieties, sufferings, and loneliness, but also joys and happiness; we accompanied and helped each other. We "journeyed together."

I was widowed thirteen years ago, and those same priests, our friends and brothers, have accompanied me in my widowhood, and continue to be a huge help to me and to my children today. If you don't have a friend who is a priest, look for one.

Saying yes to serving the Church was key for our own evangelization. We were evangelized in the first place by each of our nine children; and not only by them, but also in each of the services that we had the privilege of rendering in the Church. We never imagined that the yes that we said at the altar and endured throughout our lives, would, in fact, be the strength we needed for our own spiritual growth, or that it would enable us to take as our model the Holy Family, whose help in the growth, upbringing, and education of our children was beyond all reckoning.

We participated actively in different specific apostolates of the Church during the twenty-five years of our marriage, and that same participation continues to this day as I travel the solitary path of my widowhood—though not completely solitary, as today I travel more explicitly hand-in-hand with Jesus, always maintaining a very open attitude.

This apostolic service in the Church always meant contributing our own resources, time, and money, as missionaries in extremely poor indigenous communities; as members of commissions of our particular church; as representatives of that particular church in events with other local churches, and so on.

Through this testimony I would like to invite every baptized woman not to close the doors to Christ and to what he is hoping for from each of us as we develop our "feminine genius" in the service of the mission of the whole Church. We have great instruments—perhaps hidden talents that we have not yet discovered—that we can put toward the service of those who need them most; opening our homes to each Christ who is living in loneliness, sickness, or sadness, and letting them know that they have our family, which is their family in faith.

Let us not miss the opportunity offered to us by the terrible pandemic. We all went back inside our homes, where I am sure we have reflected much on our lives. It has been a time of great suffering and sadness, amid the illness and death of those closest to us, the ones we loved most. We have been on trial, our faith was called into question during this situation; we need to be a light, a lamp, a candle burning on every table in our homes. Without faith, all those times of sadness and suffering would have been meaningless. Let us share our experiences of faith and in accompanying Christ through all the sorrowful times.

We all need everyone else. It is not a question of waiting for the service that the priest will offer me—"the service I have a right to." The priest also has a "right" to receive service from me, because we are brothers and sisters in the faith, united by our common priesthood. Simon of Cyrene is the living example that Jesus wishes to give us in accepting help, service, from a brother or sister in the faith. And together, each from our own position in the Church, cooperating organically in the Church's mission and avoiding any kind of clericalism, let's carry out synodally and coresponsibly our witness of charity and our evangelizing mission, so that the world may have life in Christ.[4] Let us go out to meet those who need us most.[5]

NOTES

1. See Cardinal M. Ouellet, "Common Priesthood and Ministerial Priesthood: The Meaning of the Priestly Vocation," in *Friends of the Bridegroom: For a Renewed Vision of Priestly Celibacy* (Irondale, AL: EWTN Publishing, 2019).

2. J. Philippe, *Interior Freedom* (New York: Scepter Publishers, 2007), 101.

3. Pope Francis, *Speech at the Ceremony Commemorating the 50th Anniversary of the Institution of the Synod of Bishops,* October 17, 2015.

4. See E. Bueno, "El Camino Sinodal; la Iglesia tiene nombre de Sínodo," Aula de Teología, March 2018 (Spanish transcript: https://web.unican.es/campuscultural/Documents/Aula%20de%20estudios%20sobre%20religi%C3%B3n/2017-2018/5.%20El%20camino%20sinodal%20Eloy%20Bueno.pdf).

5. P. González, *La valentía de los misioneros protagonista de la presentación del Domund 2017,* October 17, 2017, www.diocesiscoriacaceres.es.

17

MINISTRIES, SERVICE, AND PROPHECY*

SISTER ALESSANDRA SMERILLI, FMA

MY REFLECTION BEGINS from the suggestion put forth by Michelina Tenace in her abstract: "Listen to what the Spirit suggests to the Church in order that the masculine and feminine face of humanity be turned back toward the kingdom." My perspective is that of the consecrated life, as a gift and service to the Church, to the body of the baptized. Pope Francis stresses that the distinctive characteristic of the consecrated is prophecy: "Radical evangelical living is not only for the consecrated: it is demanded of everyone. But the consecrated follow the Lord in a special way, in a prophetic way. I expect this witness from you. The consecrated should be men and women capable of awakening the world" (Meeting with the Superiors General, November 29, 2013).

THE PROPHECY OF CONSECRATED LIFE AND THE GIFT OF CHARISM OR CHARISMS

The charism, or rather the charisms (in the plural) within Christian tradition have at least two meanings. The starting point and the scriptural and foundational basis of every reflection on charisms is certainly the First

---

* Round Table "Women and Ministry. Status quaestionis."

Letter of St. Paul to the Corinthians (which is also the starting point for the basic definition of charisms), where Paul explains his ecclesiology, characterized by the presence of the Spirit that carries forth the Church through the bestowal of gifts—the charisms—that the various members of the Christian community receive for the common good.

Throughout the history of the Church, especially in the nineteenth century, the use of the expression *charism*, while remaining coherent with the Pauline source, was extended, and assumed a new meaning. It is used—thanks for the theological work of Rahner, Congar, and Balthasar—to indicate the great charismatic gifts received by the founders of orders and religious movements that have developed and brought the gospel message to maturation, charisms that are defined as "special graces" or "extraordinary" gifts, distinct from the "more simple and widely diffused" gifts (*Lumen Gentium* 12). It is possible to distinguish more "individual" charisms, connected to the specific task of a person, and "collective charisms" where the charism is at the origin of a new community or movement in the Church, whose members live in the same charism of the founder. From this perspective, which continues to move strictly within the Pauline meaning, the charisms are read in a dynamic context, as gifts through which the Spirit drives the Church forward toward the "fullness of truth," a truth that the charisms make even more visible and adapted to the times. A good theoretical framework for understanding the nature of charisms, and the charismatic economy, is that proposed by the theologian Hans Urs von Balthasar. The Swiss theologian, among the greatest of the twentieth century, describes the life of the Church as a dynamic between different "principles" or profiles that carry on and bring to life the ideal and typical experiences of several people who have lived alongside Jesus in his historical experience. In particular, for him the two foundational principles are the "Petrine" and the "Marian": the Petrine principle particularly emphasizes the institutional, hierarchical, juridical, and objective component of the life of the Church, while the Marian emphasizes its charismatic, popular, horizontal, and fraternal nature. The two principles, which in the final works of Balthasar were called "institutional" and "charismatic," were complementary for him and not in conflict with each other, but rather in a dynamic and discursive relationship. For Balthasar, the history of the Church can be told as the development and intertwining of these two coessential dimensions of the Church: the history of institutions and the history of charisms. This vision was taken up by John Paul II who, for example, spoke of the role and meaning of ecclesial movements:

> The new movements of spirituality are based on these "charismatic gifts" which, together with the "hierarchical gifts"—i.e., the ordained ministries—form part of the gifts of the Holy Spirit with which the Church, the Bride of Christ, is adorned. Charismatic gifts and hierarchical gifts are distinct, but also reciprocally complimentary. (*I Movimenti nella Chiesa*, Atti del II Colloquio Internazionale, Milan, 1987, 24–25)

For Balthasar, the history of the Church can be told as the development and intertwining of its two coessential dimensions: the history of institutions and the history of charisms, with a certain primacy of the feminine charism, as an icon of the Church which generates and cares for all the charisms.

Starting with these insights, I believe that there is material for reflection, free of prejudices, on new forms that can be given to ministeriality—not to bring women to the tasks and services that men now principally (or exclusively) perform, but to understand how the same tasks and services can be thought of in a new way, based on the covenant between men and women to which God has entrusted the earth.

18

DEACONESSES OF THE FIRST CENTURIES AND CONTEMPORARY MINISTRIES*

PROFESSOR MICHELINA TENACE

THE COMMISSION ESTABLISHED in 2016 by Pope Francis on the diaconate for women represented a surprise for the members called to participate: half of the commission, six of us, were women. It was an event that attempted to be internal to the theological reflection of the Catholic Church. It did not fail in its task. It has had repercussions, of which the first signs are becoming visible. (The *motu proprio Spiritus Domini* of January 1, 2021, speaks of the access of female persons to the ministry instituted by the lectorate and the acolyteship.)

Outside this lens of internal research, the task of the commission was understood in a reductive, improper way, as if it were trying to find historical arguments to restore a feminine ministry recorded with the word *deaconess* in the first centuries (in several letters by St. Paul and in other documents examined by the commission).

The task of the commission was to study. But the goal was not to restore, for at least two reasons connected to Scripture and Tradition: Scripture is not read to justify a school of thought; and the study of Tradition does not aim to reactualize something from the past. Scripture is read in the Spirit (revelation) and Tradition is read in the letter

* Round Table "Women and Ministry. Status quaestionis."

(history). The risk, otherwise, is to betray the novelty that the Spirit brings to history in every moment.

Deaconesses are mentioned in Scripture and are present in the tradition of the first Church. What can be deduced is the participation of women in the evangelization of charity for all, and the presence of women among the services (ministries) that may have been in contact with other women, especially where the exercise of modesty suggested it, especially at baptism and the unction of the sick.

The question posed today is therefore different: Is there a need to restore a service ministry? Why? Do we not perhaps need to ask ourselves, What ministry does the people of God need today?

Courage concerns the newness of today, not the restoration of something from the past. The attempt to recreate is anachronistic. The search for newness is prophetic because what is new keeps in mind the road of growth within cultural, social, and theological changes.

The first commission, which is dedicated to historical inquiry, has established a few incontestable facts. I outline three:

There were deaconesses in the first Church.
There was a real rite tied to this ministry.
The presence of deaconesses completely disappeared from the Latin Church.

The true success of the commission is in opening a path and having indicated an orientation in more directions:

The disappearance of deaconesses does not mean that women have disappeared from the Church.
The sanctity of women was recognized without any discrimination.
The *diaconia*, service, took place without any "established ministry."

Why, then, is there a need to reflect on the history of the ministries "not given" to women? Because this historical time of the absence of women from the ministries coincided with a "masculine-clerical" drift of the Church that has not let its true face shine with the new humanity in which men and women are vested with the same dignity as sons and daughters.

So, why is it so important and urgent to institute ministries for women? Not for a recognition of the dignity of women! But for a recognition of the true identity of the Church. It is the Church that needs women and should call them into service. It is in response to this call of the Church that women should respond yes and make their gifts fruitful for the good of everyone! If the Church does not call, a ministry risks being considered a right.

But service is not a right, it is a duty! The Church also responds to this duty to serve as Christ served through her hierarchical structure and should constantly ask, How can it best serve humanity in search of salvation, in the way that conforms best to the mandate of the teacher?

The scope of the discernment of the Church on the ministries of women is the good of the people of God, in very different geographical, cultural, and ecclesial contexts!

To not be a response too driven by an ideology (feminism, which has argued about rights too much), the reflection on ministries must turn to its source: baptism, where every vocation is born and flourishes.

The observation is made that a baptized person lacks nothing: having become a new creature in the death and resurrection of Christ, they are a participant in his priesthood, and therefore, part of the dignity of the body that continues to ensure the journey to the Father in history.

The dignity of the baptized person is the dignity of all people—men and women. Pope Francis often reminds us of this. Baptism is the undisputed source of the holiness of all people.

If we start anew from here, we will discover how to interpret service, and with regard to which ministries. In fact, dignity does not just concern priestly service: this is why it is a contradiction to think that conceding the priesthood to women would be a way of recognizing their dignity.

Service is determined by need, by the request, and by the urgency of charity. What do the men and women of today need? Salvation, witness, reconciliation, communion, formation, and fellowship. For this reason, the Church recognizes charisms or calls to "services" because "the building" is solid in charity.

Therefore, the question is not of recreating the deaconate of women; *it would be too little* if it were limited to repeating the functions possessed by the deaconesses known from history.

The issue is to do more: listen to what the Spirit suggests to the Church in order to recover the masculine and feminine faces of humanity toward the kingdom.

Respecting the vocation of each person without allowing diversity to be used one against another, but for the advantage of the one and the other. Otherwise, the "universal priesthood" risks remaining a fleshless expression, an illusion awaiting reality.

Or, another danger, the promotion of laypeople, and therefore of women, most of the time consists in making them enter into the shadow of the ministerial priesthood, as close as possible to the altar of eucharistic celebration!

A celebration that is considered the only worthy reality, because only there does "Christ act in person." The masculine man (not woman) Christ is a reality tied to the logic of the incarnation. The Savior, out of respect for the humanity that he wanted to assume, was born as a male child in whom the ancient covenant was inscribed through circumcision; to reveal the dignity of feminine humanity, he was born of a woman who, "full of grace" became the first redeemed person assumed into the heavens into the dwelling place of the Trinity.

It seems that the question of the ministries of women suffers from two reductions:

> the reduction of the dignity of each minister to the dignity of the ministerial priesthood;
> the reduction of the dignity of the ministerial priesthood and the priesthood of Christ to being "male."

This reduction does not correspond to faith: it is as a person of a human and divine nature that the Son, the second person of the Trinity, is our Savior. Salvation concerns everyone, men and women, as different people.

What is the reflection we are led to with this consideration of faith?

Man and woman are two realities that express a complementary diversity in respect to generation: according to their "gender," men "generate" and women "bring to the world." Thus, men and women participate symbolically in the one priesthood of Christ, who entrusted the Church to those who "generate" (in virtue of the ministerial priesthood) and to those who "bring to the world" (in virtue of the common priesthood) in reciprocal dependence and support.

The reflection on the ministries of women in the church cannot be separated from a renewed theology of the human person—an anthropology that considers male and female according to creation and vocation—and this anthropology of male and female must be fundamental to the reflection on ministries in the context of an ecclesiology of communion on a path of synodality.

I would like to conclude with the words of the title of a book by Bernard Pottier, one of the members of the commission. I will only add a question mark at the end of the title. *Le diaconatféminin. Jadis et bientôt*. I would say, The diaconate of women; in the past and soon? *Affaire à suivre!*

DAY THREE

CELIBACY, CHARISMS, AND SPIRITUALITY

February 19, 2022

19

ONE CALLED BY GOD

Homily

CARDINAL PIETRO PAROLIN

Eminences,
Dear brothers in the episcopate and the priesthood,
Dear brothers and sisters,

In these days you have reflected on the fundamental theology of the priesthood.

Now we find ourselves around the altar, which we could call the fundamental location of the reflection on the priesthood, as Pope Francis reminds us in his postsynodal apostolic exhortation *Beloved Amazon,* the priesthood "is a sign" of Christ, a

> wellspring of grace above all when he celebrates the Eucharist, the source and summit of the entire Christian life. That is his great power, a power that can only be received in the sacrament of Holy Orders. For this reason, only the priest can say: "This is my body." There are other words, too, that he alone can speak: "I absolve you from your sins." Because sacramental forgiveness is at the service of a worthy celebration of the Eucharist. These two sacraments lie at the heart of the priest's exclusive identity. (88)

I want to express gratitude to Cardinal Marc Ouellet for organizing the symposium on the fundamental theology of the priesthood, which has offered—drawing from the concrete experience of the bishops and the priests dedicated to local churches—further elements that can contribute to the elaboration of an organic thought around the ordained ministry, in the full perspective of the common priesthood of the faithful that is realized in the synodality of the Church.

Today's liturgical texts can also help us reflect on the fundamental theology of the priesthood. We priests, in fact, hear the words with which the Gospel passage on the transfiguration begins, just proclaimed, concerning us and describing our vocation: "Jesus took with him Peter and James and John, and led them up a high mountain apart, by themselves" (Mark 9:2).

The Lord took them with him. This is his design with us, expressed as a plan in the Gospel of Mark: "*And he appointed twelve, whom he also named apostles, to be with him, and to be sent out to proclaim the message, and to have authority to cast out demons*" (Mark 3:14–15).

The Lord leads us to the mountain, the place of the encounter with him, to take care of us (Gen 22:4), to look us in the eyes with love (Mark 10:21) and to speak to our heart (Hos 2:16), revealing to us everything that he has heard from the Father (John 15:15).

But the Lord proposes to us an uphill struggle, following him, to be his friends, and then to encounter him and his brothers, in a life offered and given in imitation of Christ.

Therefore, in a fundamental theology of the ministerial priesthood, we must first of all take as our premise, or rather as our first principle, the idea that the priest is one called by God, taken by him, grasped in his hands. The initiative, therefore, is always from God who calls, who takes us with him, who chooses disciples so that they will be with him, who are then apostles for a specific mission.

It is always healthy to turn spiritually to the origins of our vocation, to taste anew the beginnings of our road following Christ, to renew our first yes every day, to never forget who it is who wanted us with Him.

We are called, and Jesus repeats to us: "You did not choose me but I chose you. And I appointed you to go and bear fruit, fruit that will last" (John 15:16).

Another dimension, fundamental to the priestly identity, follows from the voice heard from Tabor: the priest is, and always remains, a disciple who "*learns every day to enter into the secrets of the kingdom of God, living a deep relationship with Jesus*" (RFIS 61). Therefore, as clergymen, we hear addressed to us in a particular way both the proclamation and the invitation expressed by the voice of the Father resounding from the mountain: "*This is my beloved Son: listen to him!*"

We should humbly cultivate the private belief that as "only in the mystery of the Word incarnate does the mystery of man find true light" (GS 22) so it is only in the listening to the Word of Christ contained in the Sacred Scriptures and mediated by the teaching and by the life of the Church through the centuries that we can understand and then live the gift and the mystery of our priesthood.

The words "This is my beloved Son" express the centrality of Christ in the life of the Church and especially in the existence of the priesthood.

Pope Francis, with prophetic words that have the flavor of synodality, mentioned that *the priest "is a contemplative of the Word and is also a contemplative of the people"* (EG 154); in fact, as St. Paul VI teaches, he learns along with all brothers to "*learn to read the message of God in events*" (EN 33).

The divine imperative "*Listen to him!*" therefore, includes an exhortation to humility, to patience, to sincere adhesion to God who is revealed in the Sacred Scriptures and who never ceases to make himself present in history for those who "listen to his voice" (cf. Ps 94:8).

In this light, we can understand the words that the Apostle James writes to those addressed in his letter, of which we have heard in the first reading: "Not many of you are teachers." In fact, Jesus says that "*You have one instructor, the Messiah*" (Matt 23:10) and "*you are all students*" (Matt 23:8).

The word of the priest draws "*clarity of thought and persuasive force at the source of the Word of the living God in the Gospel, meditated and prayed, rediscovered in the Crucified Jesus and in men, celebrated in sacramental gestures never reduced to pure rite.*"[1]

It is therefore always a "secondary" word that comes after that of God, passes through the mediation of Christ and, before being announced, dwells in the soul of the minister of God who has read it, assimilated it in prayer, and shared it with his brothers.

The famous passage from the first reading, on the power of "human" language, also makes us reflect on the heavy responsibility borne by the language of the priest: how many times Pope Francis has reminded us of the danger of what he calls "gossip"!

On the contrary, as we are called to listen to the beloved Son of the Father, priests hear the exhortation of the Apostle Paul addressed to them personally: "Let no evil talk come out of your mouths, but only what is useful for building up, as there is need, so that your words may give grace to those who hear" (Eph 4:29).

For this reason, "the priest is a man who, in the light of the Gospel, spreads the taste of God around him and gives hope to troubled hearts."[2]

In fact, he stands on the mountain with Jesus, and with Jesus descends from the mountain to meet men, especially the poor.

In fact, there is also the descent from the mountain, although it should be emphasized that the disciples, "on the plains" so to speak, do not remain alone, but Jesus is with them, descends with them, accompanies them and works with them (cf. Acts 11:21). In fact, Pope Francis tells us "it is only by remaining rooted in Christ that you can experience a joy that moves you to conquer hearts."[3]

Then there is also another element of the fundamental theology of the priesthood: the priest does not live an alternative between being with Jesus, apart from others, and being with his brothers. The priest is always with Jesus, even when he realizes a fundamental dimension of his own identity: living with his brothers, a characteristic especially particular to the diocesan priest, which the Second Vatican Council has called "*pastoral charity*" (PO 14).

This is why "we need to open up, to expand the horizon of ministry to the dimensions of the world, to reach out to every child of God whom he wishes to embrace with his love."[4]

May we be accompanied by Most Holy Mary, Mother of Priests and Queen of the Apostles. May her maternal love accompany every priest chosen by the Lord to continue, despite his poverty, to make him present in the world, in time and history, an instrument of redemption for him and his brothers.

Amen.

Basilica of Saint Peter

NOTES

1. Pope Francis, *Address on the Visit to the Tomb of Don Primo Mazzolari*, June 20, 2017.

2. Pope Francis, *Address to the Priests of the Community of San Luigi dei Francesi*, Rome, June 7, 2021.

3. Pope Francis, *Address to the Priests of the Community of San Luigi dei Francesi*.

4. Pope Francis, *Address to the Community of the Pontifical Lombard Seminary*, February 7, 2021.

20

THE NEED FOR A PRIESTLY LIFE

Introductory Address

Cardinal José Tolentino de Mendonça

THINKING OF THE morning of work that we have ahead of us, dealing with such important themes (celibacy, charism, and spirituality), I am reminded of two novels by Georges Bernanos where the protagonist is a priest. Beyond the details through which you can see that they are obviously novels tied to a certain era (*Under the Sun of Satan* was published in 1926 and the *Diary of a Country Priest* a decade later) there is at least one aspect—several others exist as well—but at least one aspect is central to both narratives, which continues to shed light on priestly life. The aspect is that whatever decisions they make, whatever crises or successes, or the impoverishment or fecundity of priesthood, these are never simply exogenous, external, sociological, or mundane factors. Instead, the determining factors are always endogenous and internal: it is the deep respiration of the real priestly life.

This is why it is not an indulgence to speak of the architecture of sanctity in us, but a necessity of the first order. Bernanos wrote in his *Diary of a Country Priest*, "Moralists happily consider sanctity to be an indulgence. It is a necessity. It is sanctity, it is the saints who maintain that inner life without which humanity would degrade to the point of death." The Church in all times, but especially now, has a desire for people fully centered in faith, who develop the questions and the tensions—even the most implacable—of the road in faith, people capable of a vital experience of God in all circumstances, who find in the gospel of Jesus their daily starting point for the impetus that they live out and put forward. And in the same way, the Church needs ministers who keep attentive watch over their own ministry, ordained ministers aware of what they are, and who interpret the complexity of history in the unwavering hope of Christ, proclaiming him with freedom and affection, with authenticity and creativity, to their brothers and sisters, the men and the women of today.

21

HOLINESS AND SACRED MINISTRY

A Theological-Canonical Perspective

CARDINAL GIANFRANCO GHIRLANDA, SJ

OBLIGATION TO STRIVE FOR HOLINESS

LET US BEGIN by referencing the Code of Canon Law 1983, which explains the spiritual and theological doctrine that the canons assume and contain.

Can. 276 §1 establishes,

> In leading their lives, clerics are bound in a special way to pursue holiness since, having been consecrated to God by a new title in the reception of orders, they are dispensers of the mysteries of God in the service of His people.

This duty, which is repeated in *Pastores Dabo Vobis* (PDV) 20,[1] relates to the fundamental obligation of all the faithful to conduct a holy life as stated in canon 210. It is an obligation of all the faithful that comes from the universal call to sanctity in the Church, the topic of the whole fifth chapter of *Lumen Gentium*, especially number 42. It was to the call to sanctity of all the baptized that Pope Francis dedicated his apostolic exhortation *Gaudete et Exultate* (GE) of March 18, 2018.[2]

The same Pope Francis in his opening address of this symposium on February 17, 2022,[3] said,

> We should never forget that each particular vocation, including that of Holy Orders, is a completion of baptism. It is always a great temptation to live *a priesthood without baptism*—and there are some priests "without baptism"—in other words, forgetting that our primary vocation is to holiness. To be holy means to conform ourselves to Jesus, letting our hearts thrill with his same sentiments (cf. Phil 2:15). Only when we strive to love others as Jesus does, do we make God visible and fulfil our vocation to holiness.

The same canon 210 contains the determination that the faithful should lead a holy life according to their condition, as holiness does not exist abstractly but is lived concretely in the faithful performance of the obligations that arise from the condition of each person's life, and therefore, specifically, from one's own charisms and ministries (cf. LG 41; 42).

Although all the faithful are called to carry out the perfection of charity and must strive for it (cf. LG 39), some are called by God to live the requirements of evangelical radicality as a stable rule of life. This is why, from an institutional perspective, forms of life are found in the Church that flow from a particular vocation, and therefore from a particular gift of the Spirit, which entail a particular duty in the search to carry out the perfection of charity.

The apostolic exhortation *Vita Consecrate* (VC), from March 25, 1996, nos. 18, 32, and 105,[4] repeating the doctrine of the Council of Trent[5] and the encyclical *Sacra Virginitas* of Pius XII of March 25, 1954,[6] affirms that, "as a way of showing forth the Church's holiness," it must be considered that with respect to the other states of life in the Church, the consecrated life has "an objective superiority," as does "the pre-eminence of perfect chastity for the sake of the Kingdom" in respect to marriage, as an assimilation of the life of the virgin Jesus, poor and obedient and an objective representation of this in the Church, in an eschatological perspective. And so, it must be considered, in virtue of the apostolic succession, that there is an objective superiority of the apostolic ministry in respect to all the other ministries of the Church, from which arises the objective need for a holy life. However, such an *objective* superiority that requires and sustains personal sanctity is one thing, while realized personal sanctity is another, because this can be excellent in any state of life.

Consequently, we can better understand the obligation of holy ministers, especially bishops (cf. can. 387), as laid out in the Code, to follow a particular path of sanctity (*ad sanctitatem persequendam peculiari ratione tenentur clerici*), as they are consecrated to God, in virtue of holy ordination as well as baptism, and they are stewards of the mysteries of God in the service of his people, as canon 276 §1 states explicitly. In fact, whoever assumes the ministry of helping others pursue sanctity is necessarily held by a stricter obligation to live out what he preaches to others in his own life (PC 12; 13; PDV 40).

I will first speak of the exercise of holy ministry as a place for the realization and nourishment of the holy minister, and then of the fact that this can only be realized in the faithful observance of the three evangelical councils in charity.

THE EXERCISE OF HOLY MINISTRY

Canon 276 §2 enumerates various obligations of the clerics to pursue perfection, or a holy life.

I will dwell on the first:

> In order to be able to pursue this perfection: 1) they are first of all to fulfill faithfully and tirelessly the duties of the pastoral ministry....

If holiness is not something abstract but is lived out concretely in the faithful fulfillment in charity of the obligations that are required from one's condition, it is clear that the chief way to follow a holy life, and a luminous manifestation and execution of the perfection of charity, can only be the faithful and tireless fulfillment on the part of a cleric with ministerial duties. The fulfillment of such a duty corresponds to the reason for which the search for holiness is demanded of clerics, being "stewards of the mysteries of God in service of His people" as the same canon enunciates.

Therefore, the exercise of ministry is the place—the existential situation—in which to pursue holiness.

As *Presbyterorum Ordinis* (12c) states, priests are not only personally sanctified through the exercise of their ministries, but their very sanctity contributes to the effective attainment of the ministry itself.[7] To see one's mission as the road to holiness means being contemplative also in action, and thus sanctifying oneself in the contemplation of how God acts in the world and in the Church through the responsible and generous exercise of one's ministerial mission (cf. GE 19; 26). What is said of priests clearly also applies to deacons and bishops.

Such focus on the pursuit of holiness is new in respect to the Code of Canon Law 1917 and is of primary importance, because all the other ways of nourishing spiritual life found in this same canon—Sacred Scripture, Eucharist, the Liturgy of the Hours, spiritual rites, mental prayer, the sacrament of confession, devotion to the Holy Virgin—are read in the light of the faithful and tireless fulfillment, in love, of the duties of pastoral ministry. In fact, such methods would not produce a nourishment of spiritual life if the holy ministers did not live out charity in giving themselves in the exercise of ministry, but these would only be formal, exterior acts. If you recall, Pope Francis underlined the fundamentally important difference for us between spiritual life and religious practice.

In *Pastores Gregis* (PG), October 16, 2003,[8] John Paul II resumes the discourse on holiness in relation to the bishops, but what applies to the bishops, mutatis mutandis, also has a particular application for priests.

According to John Paul II, the bishop, to avoid letting the functions he carries out be reduced to "to a merely organizational task," should have two reference points. First, "objective sanctification," accomplished by sacramental consecration, which communicates the Spirit, and then, "subjective sanctity" as a response to the objective. In subjective sanctity the bishop should continually advance through the exercise of the ministry. In fact, the "configuration to Christ" that is given with consecration "demands a lifestyle that manifests a 'being with him.'" In this way, charity is the soul of the ministry, through which he who exercises it "is in a sense the heart of the ministry of the Bishop, who is drawn into a dynamic pastoral *pro-existence* whereby he is impelled to live, like Christ the Good Shepherd, for the Father and for others, in the daily gift of self" (PG 11). We can remember here what Pope Francis said about closeness to God as one of the four foundational columns of sacerdotal life.

With priestly ordination, a gift of the Spirit is received (cf. 2 Tim 1:6), a charism, that of the spiritual paternity of the people of God (cf. 1 Cor 4:15), as an image of the Father (cf. LG 28d; PG 7). God consecrates in order to carry out the proper functions of the ministry, as an execution of that charism. It is the particular ontological configuration to Christ the priest, teacher, shepherd, and husband gained in ordination that determines the functions of sanctifying, teaching, and governing.

As with every other consecration in the Church, this is not simply an external deputation to the cult and in service of the deity, because God carries a consecration of the person as such, to which one must respond freely in a way conforming to the act of God. The only adequate response, as *Pastores Gregis* (13) suggests, is the dedication of oneself, in the sense of an offering of one's own life in the exercise of the ministry in a conformation to Christ, who gives his life on the cross (cf. PO 12b; PDV 20).[9] In Christ's offering of his life to the Father for the salvation of all humanity, the cross becomes an act of consecration par excellence, not for separation, but for communion with the Father and with all people. Christ fulfills his ministry on the cross: from his pierced side on the cross, Jesus generates the Church, of which he is the Bridegroom, in the signs of blood and water; the charism of spiritual paternity flows from the cross, a gift that the resurrection gives to those who are called to continue their ministry until the end of time. The charism of spiritual paternity and at the same time of the spousal love for the community is a gift of the resurrected Christ, but one that makes the signs of the cross visible. The lifestyle of the bishop, as well as that of the priest and the deacon, "imitates the *kenosis* of Christ, the poor and humble servant, so that the exercise of his pastoral ministry will be a consistent reflection of Jesus, the Servant of God" (PG 11; cf. PDV 23). Ministry is an *amoris officium*.[10] In his opening address of the symposium, Pope Francis said, "It is imperative to remember that the People of God are hoping to find *shepherds* in the style of Jesus. Not 'clerical functionaries' or 'professionals of the sacred.'"

In his address at the commemoration of the fiftieth anniversary of the institution of the Synod of the Bishops, while affirming that Jesus placed the apostolic college at the head of the Church, of which the Apostle Peter was the rock that should confirm his brothers in faith, Pope Francis says that "as in an inverted pyramid, the top is located beneath the base." The term "ministries" that is applied to the shepherds indicates that they are "the least of all." While serving the people of God, every pastor "becomes *vicarius Christi*," a vicar of that Christ who washed the feet of the apostles (John 13:1–15); in the same way the Successor of Peter is the *servus servorum Dei*.[11] Pope Francis says, "Become *vicarius Christi*." Certainly, the bishop is objectively vicar of Christ in virtue of the sacrament he receives, but subjectively he becomes even more so through the testimony he gives to the entire people of God in serving them. The shepherd has an authority in both doctrine and government that comes to him from the office that he is called to fulfill both through ordination and through the canonical mission that he receives, but in his ministry, he should grow in the authority that is given by his witness of life, offered by the total donation in service. His message and his government, if accompanied by moral authority, are certainly more easily accepted by the faithful, even though they still have their obligation to adhere to the ordinary magisterium and obey what the bishop commands.

The charism of spiritual paternity and spousal love is a permanent gift, tied to the sacramental character, through which the perpetuity of the subjective consecration of one's own person on the part of the holy minister is based on the perpetuity of divine consecration.

A functional mentality destroys pastoral charity because it attracts attention to the functions carried out and loses sight of the ontological dimension which is at the foundation of the functional dimension and the spiritual dimension that expresses it (cf. *Benedetto XVI* 55).

Pastoral ministry on its own requires an assimilation to Christ in the heart and the mind (cf. Phil 2:5–11; 1 Cor 2:16; 11:1), who is the principal author of the ministerial acts that the priest carries out, so that the pastoral charity of Christ becomes the form of his life (cf. *Benedetto XVI* 54). Therefore, if baptismal consecration is already in force, the holy minister, like every other believer, must live according to the spirit of the Beatitudes, by virtue of the consecration he receives with the sacrament of holy orders, and should strive for the full observation of the evangelical counsels, for a more faithful fulfilment of the ministry, in which his personal consecration is carried out, as a response to the gift of love received from God the Father. In this, he becomes a model for the various categories of the faithful working in his Church.

THE PRACTICE OF THE EVANGELICAL COUNSELS

As I hinted at above, a holy minister, by virtue of the consecration he receives with the sacrament of holy orders, is called to live the spirit of the Beatitudes in the observance of the evangelical counsels through the most faithful fulfillment of the ministry, in which his personal consecration is carried out, which is a response to the gift of love received from God the Father.

Vatican II, which in *Presbyterorum Ordinis* (15–17) covers obedience, celibacy, and the poverty of priests, does not speak of the evangelical counsels, but of the "more important virtues" for the ministry of the priesthood, in order not to confuse secular clergy with religious clergy.[12] John Paul II, however, in *Pastores Dabo Vobis* (27), speaks expressly of the evangelical counsels. They evidently should be lived according to the identity of the secular clergy.

This is to say that, even if the christological foundations are the same, there is a difference between the meaning and the observation of the evangelical counsels in the consecrated life and in the life of the diocesan clergy. All three evangelical counsels are essential to the consecrated life, as an assimilation to the form of life that Christ conducted on this earth, because it is meaningful in its objective value to all members of the Church, lay and clerics, who are thus called to the supreme eschatological values; not all three evangelical counsels are necessary to the life of the diocesan clergy, but, as we will see, only obedience for the three-tiered distinction of the very sacrament of ordination, through which the theological, spiritual, and pastoral opportunity for celibate chastity and poverty are related to the fulfillment of the ministry to which the priests are called, so that this ministry is not transformed into a functionalist vision, into a task to perform, but is rather a service. In the diocesan clergy the call to eschatological values is not primary but derived.

Jesus, in the moment that he offered his life on the cross, radicalized what he had announced and experienced throughout his life. The gift that comes to all the baptized from the Spirit through the resurrection of Jesus is the participation, as a requirement of baptismal life, in the values of chastity, poverty, and obedience, not in the renunciation of marriage, but in the free use of material goods and the full self-determination of one's own will. Living a life according to the commandments is already a path to sanctity (cf. LG, Ch. V). All the same, each precept, taken in its requirement for ultimate radicality, becomes a counsel when a person is called to continue the very mission of Christ as a service, to an assimilation to his being and action in the form of life that he lived on this earth, in the participation in his cross and resurrection.

The three evangelical counsels are based on the filial life of the Word incarnate, who gives himself totally to the Father in the Spirit, in an exclusive chaste love that becomes a renunciation of everything and obedience even unto death and death on the cross.

The life of virginity, poverty, and obedience was not something accidental or simply functional to the mission that he had to fulfill but was the visible and revealing earthly expression of his unique, unrepeatable relationship with the Father in the Spirit (cf. VC 16, 21, 22, 23, 24), through which we can in a sense say that Jesus could only be virginal, poor, and obedient. It would, in fact, be reductive to consider Jesus's virginity, poverty, and obedience only in their factuality. These three dimensions of his life express the unitarity and the totality of being a Son completely turned to the Father in the substantive love of the Spirit.

Divine life is trinitary in its gift; it is love as a total, unreserved gift. The Father giving himself from eternity to the Son in the substantive love that is the Spirit, he gives everything he is and everything he has, all the divine life, in what is therefore a total renunciation, so that the Son is the reflection of his glory and the object of all his delight (cf. Matt 3:17). The Son—in the same substantive love that is the Spirit—from eternity renounces everything he received from the

Father to completely return it to him (cf. John 1:1, 2). This infinite and exclusive love between the Son and the Father is not only expressed in renunciation, but also in reciprocal correspondence. In fact, without the Father there is no Son and without the Son there is no Father. So, the gift of love makes itself dependent. Trinitary life is the source of the chaste and exclusive love of Christ through the Father and for those who are sons of the one Father (cf. 1 John 5:1), of his renunciation into a radical poverty and his obedience as a total dependence on the will of the Father.

For this reason, the three classic counsels of perfect chastity in celibacy, poverty, and obedience express in a unitary way an attitude to life that unites with the divine filiation of the Word lived in Jesus Christ in a unique way. These are indeed founded on the filial life of the Word incarnate, who gives himself totally to the Father in the Spirit, in an act of chaste and exclusive love that becomes a renunciation of everything, and obedience to the very end, up to the death on the Cross (cf. Phil 2:5–8).

With a life that professes the evangelical counsels, as an act of love, as participation through the work of the Spirit in the sacrifice of Christ for the glory of the Father for the salvation of the world, the holy minister enters more deeply into the mystery of the life of Christ, who is a manifestation of the same intratrinitarian life. Given the uniqueness of trinitarian love and the life of Christ, the three counsels are three aspects of a single reality. It is not possible to be evangelically chaste without being evangelically poor and obedient; it is not possible to be evangelically poor without being evangelically chaste and obedient; and it is not possible to be evangelically obedient without being evangelically chaste and poor. True love, in fact, can only be renunciation and humility. It is only in this love that the ministry, as we have seen, will be a true service of love and therefore the place of the sanctification of the person who exercises it. In this sense the practice of the three evangelical counsels—of which those of celibate chastity and that of obedience have already been formally assumed with a promise in diaconal ordination—ensures that the secular cleric lives in a true consecration of his life.[13]

Obedience

Canon 273 reads thus:

> Clerics are bound by a special obligation to show reverence and obedience to the Supreme Pontiff and their own ordinary.

It is a very succinct canon, and so for the ends we have in mind, it is read in the light of Vatican II. Let us consider only a few texts.

Lumen Gentium (28a) gives us the sacramental foundation of obedience. Sacred orders are by their nature divided into three tiers: the episcopate, the presbyterate, and the diaconate. Given that it is the bishops who have the fullness of the sacrament of orders, priests and deacons are naturally their subordinates, although in the communion of the same sacrament (cf. LG 21b; 28a; PO 7c). Therefore, the deacons and the priests who enter the clerical state assume the obligation of respect and the need for hierarchical subordination which is intrinsic to the sacrament (cf. PO 7b; 15b). Obedience is an intrinsic need for the exercise of sacred ministry.

The very fact that the submission of the priests and the deacons to the bishop is intrinsic to the sacrament of orders ensures that the obedience of priests and deacons is required as an obligation. And so, it is legitimate to wonder if the obedience of clerics can be included in the category of the evangelical counsels, given that counsel is what is proposed for the free choice of the faithful.

The obedience of the holy ministers does not become mature, active, and responsible if it is not understood and experienced as an evangelical counsel in relation to the radicality of following Christ. In fact, one should distinguish between the canonical minimum required to fulfill the obligation of obedience and the dynamism of love which is proper to the evangelical counsels. It seems important to emphasize that there is a double source of the obedience of the sacred ministers:

1) One is objective, primary, of a sacramental and ecclesiological nature: the same hierarchical structure of the

sacrament of orders, from which derives the necessity of incardination and the jurisdiction that the bishop himself has over the clerics, and therefore the subjection of the latter.

2) Another is subjective, secondary, of a moral nature, tied to the assumption of the evangelical counsel of obedience, with the promise made at the time of diaconal ordination and renewed in priestly ordination.

The obligation for obedience itself primarily springs from the objective source, that of the sacramental and ecclesiological nature, through which a cleric would be obliged to be obedient, even if he did not make the promise in diaconal and priestly ordination. The promise is expressed and strengthened on a personal and moral level, being included in the evangelical dynamic of the radicality of following Christ, the will to be obedient that should already exist for objective and structural reasons intrinsic for the order that is freely received. The cleric makes the promise to reach a more mature freedom as a son of God in an ever-fuller conformation to Christ who was obedient even unto his death on the cross (cf. PO 15b). In this sense, the promise is the subjective and secondary source of the obligation.

Fundamentally, the relationship between the bishop and the cleric is played out in humility, the basis for the acceptance of the other and his reasons; both are challenged in their responsibility.

Here emerges the value of the spiritual dialogue that should develop between the bishop and the clerics, if the bishop wishes to effectively be a father for them, and the clerics to feel sustained in their ministry (cf. LG 28b; PO 7a).

The fundamental value that is experienced in obedience is that which is invoked in *Presbyterorum Ordinis* 15b and c: the spirit of faith in the conformation to Christ, obedience unto death on the cross, assuming his own feelings. Certainly, if the cleric has not internalized this fundamental value of the ministerial life, he will never manage to comply with a rule or a command by the bishop, if he does not deem the rule or command appropriate or useful, or if it simply does not correspond to his own perspective or desire.

Canon 273 says that the clerics are obliged to show "reverence (*reverentiam*) and obedience" to the Supreme Pontiff and their own ordinary. By "reverence," the canon refers to an internal act, but does not say anything about what it consists of. Therefore, to have a deeper understanding of what is meant by mature internal obedience, we must refer to *Presbyterorum Ordinis* 15b and c, which speaks of the "dedication of one's own will" and says that the clerics should be always "ready to submit to the decisions of those who rule the Church of God."

The conciliar decree depicts not only an obedience of the will as well as of judgment.

The obedience of the will is had when faith drives the will, as an internal act, to accept the law or to carry out the command, in an act of trust in God, who makes himself present mysteriously. With an act of the will, the cleric entrusts God with his own judgment and, even if he subjectively considers a command or law inappropriate or useless or damaging in concrete circumstances, or if it does not correspond with his own expectations, he freely adheres to them with an internal act of the will, letting himself be questioned by God, who in this concrete circumstance calls him to a deeper assimilation with Christ. With an act of his will sustained by faith, the cleric accepts the human mediation of the bishop and in any case the mediation of the circumstance that he is living in, believing that God still wants to pursue a good for him that he does not now see. This does not necessarily mean that the law or the command is immediately willed by God, because the bishop might also be wrong, but the cleric believes that the whole situation will certainly not escape the action of God, who calls him to enter a deeper communion with Christ and to assume behavior that protects ecclesial communion.

Also, the obedience of the will and of the judgment are had when the will, liberated through the grace of God from what could be an impediment in the search for all the reasons for the law or the command, inclines the intellect, as far as possible, to obey the law or the command. The cleric, then, conscious that even his valuation of reality can also be wrong, sets his judgment aside, thus making himself ready to adhere to the judgment of his superior. The whole dynamic of obedience of judgment is based on the real adhesion to the higher fundamental value of following Jesus, obedient even unto death and unto death on the cross, which is why the cleric puts aside his own judgment, because he believes that, for a greater good that he cannot now see, God enters mysteriously into the very judgment of the superior to make him achieve a good that is only accepted in faith and love. Here one enters deeper into the dynamism of the perfection of charity, in the adhesion to the supreme value in the redemptive sense of the offering of his own judgment and his own will, in full assimilation to Christ.[14] Given the unity of the three evangelical counsels, the obedience of judgment, which is the perfection of the evangelical counsel of obedience, goes hand in hand with the pursuit of the virginity of the heart, which is the fullness of celibate chastity, and of humility as poverty in the spirit, the foundation of material evangelical poverty, of which we will speak below.

It should be very clear that "obedience of judgment" does not mean not having judgment on things: rather, it is a part of the virtue of obedience to have one's own judgment, to present it to one's superiors if it differs from theirs, and to be ready to set it aside if they reaffirm their command. If one did not have one's own judgment, there would be nothing to set aside, and therefore the virtue of obedience would not be exercised, because it would be reduced to immature, purely executive obedience.[15]

It is fundamentally important to understand that one does not obey one's superiors as such, but God through human mediation. In fact, no human being can exercise dominion over the free will and judgment of another human being on their own, because freedom, will, and judgment are what gives us the likeness of God, and therefore are faculties that, given to us by God, belong to him and are restituted to him in the offering of oneself. The action of God, and therefore his will, is manifested in the principle of the incarnation through the human mediation of the bishop and therefore through the circumstances that constitute the fabric of life.[16] He submits his own will and his own judgment, recognizing that God is served mysteriously in the mediation of his superiors to fulfill his design of salvation that he has for each of us personally, calling us to life, even if this means that the will of the superior does not automatically correspond to the will of God in a concrete detail.[17]

The will of the superiors should not be loaded with an infallibility that it does not have and cannot have, as a human act, because one would become more easily exposed to the possibility of the instrumentalization and abuse by the superiors of the authority that they have received from God.[18]

In any case, both obstinate disobedience and conformist obedience are dangerous for the life of the Church and are refuted both by Vatican II and by the Code of Canon law, which require at least the obedience of the will, which is already evangelical, and open the perspective to that of judgment, which is the fullness of the evangelical counsel. In fact, in both conformist obedience and obstinate disobedience there is a situation of immaturity of the person. Such a situation has repercussions not just on the personal level, but also in ministerial pastoral action, where there will be at most efficiency, but not efficacy, as action will be taken without the evangelical spirit. The pastoral and apostolic efficacy of a cleric in the exercise of the ministry arises from authentically living and witnessing to the value of assimilation to Christ by following him. Such an assimilation does not exist in either conformist obedience or obstinate disobedience.

Only mature and responsible obedience, when this involves at least the internal act of the adherence of the will and eventually of the intellect in faith and in love, is the fruit of the decision of a personality who lives the evangelical value of obedience as a fruit of his ever-greater assimilation to Christ, which is his sanctification. It is the promise of obedience that leads to the dynamism of love of the evangelical counsel.

Celibacy

Canon 277 §1 is formulated thus:

> Clerics are obliged to observe perfect and perpetual continence for the sake of the kingdom of heaven and therefore are bound to celibacy which is a special gift of God by which sacred ministers can adhere more easily to Christ with an undivided heart and are able to dedicate themselves more freely to the service of God and humanity.

The canon, based on *Presbyterorum Ordinis* (16), establishes the obligation of clerics to observe perfect and perpetual continence for the kingdom of heaven. From here, the canon derives the constraint of celibacy, which is considered a particular gift of God. Such a gift is seen as a way in which the holy ministers can adhere more easily to Christ with an undivided heart and are enabled to dedicate themselves more freely to the service of God and man. Celibacy, then, is the heart of the spiritual perfection of the priest and makes him grow in ministerial pastoral charity.

As *Presbyterorum Ordinis* (2c) states, "Priests, by the anointing of the Holy Spirit, are signed with a special character and are conformed (*configurantur*) to Christ the Priest in such a way that they can act in the person of Christ the Head ('*in persona Christi Capitis*')." Therefore, the relationship of convenience between celibacy and the holy minister, reaffirmed by *Presbyterorum Ordinis* 16b, springs from the adhesion to Christ with an undivided heart in virtue of consecration to him with a new and excellent title (*nova et eximiaratione*). The conformity to Christ that this brings ensures that the priest does not simply carry out a professional service, but pursues the mission of Christ himself, carried out in his person, which requires the fullest dedication.

From a terminological perspective, canon 277 could be unclear, because it seems that the first, direct object of the obligation is perfect, perpetual continence, which implies celibacy as a consequence. In diaconal ordination, however, celibacy is promised,[19] which necessarily entails perfect and perpetual continence for the kingdom of heaven.

The Directory *Benedetto XVI* (80) expresses the obligation more clearly: "This (celibacy), as a particular charism and gift of God, requires the observance of perfect and perpetual continence for the Kingdom of Heaven, because the holy ministers can adhere more easily to Christ with an undivided heart and dedicate themselves more freely to the service of God and man."

The canon, then, can generate confusion between continence and chastity, which is why to understand it well, it must be said that the object of the obligation is celibate chastity, which is lived in perfect and perpetual continence.

Therefore, it should not fall into the equivocation, as often happens, and hold that the content of the obligation of ecclesiastic celibacy is simply not to enter into marriage and not to use the genitalia.

Because the celibate deacon can live the gift of service of the people of God and the priest and the bishop can live that of spiritual paternity and spousal love in Christ, according to the ministry received in ordination (cf. PO 16b), they should have reached the sufficient maturity for the integration of the dynamic components of their own affectivity and sexuality in a disposition to oblative love, so that celibacy is not lived in a repressive way, as mortification and negation, because fidelity to this would be based on voluntarism and not on the gift of self in the ministry. This would make celibate ministers, as Pope Francis says, "bachelors" with all the passions of "bachelors." However, one should certainly bear in mind meanwhile that the full integration of the virtue of chastity in the dynamism of sexuality is a process that lasts one's whole life, as an orientation to the future is an indication of maturity, for the realization of values which are adhered to and identified with for the realization of an existential plan.[20]

Regarding the sources for the obligation of celibacy, before and after the CCL 1917, the authors generally maintain that the obligation of celibate chastity arose not only from ecclesiastical law, but also from a solemn vow tacitly and freely made in the subdiaconal ordination, an ordination in which celibacy was then assumed.[21] Canon 132 §1 in the CCL 1917, then, seemed to maintain this position, claiming that all sins, without distinction between external and internal, committed by a major cleric (bishop, priest, deacon, and subdeacon) against chastity entail sacrilege. What is proper to a vow, a promise made directly to God, is that it is obligatory by virtue of religion (cf. can. 1191 §1). The simple promise, however, made to the Church or to the ecclesiastical authority, does not entail sacrilege because it is not obligatory by virtue of religion.[22]

To respond to the question, whether a vow is made implicitly or not at the time of ordination, let us see what we can learn from the Second Vatican Council.

The Council never speaks of the vow of celibacy, but of the law of celibacy, and one can note that the conciliar acts have not adopted the opinion that believes a vow is at least implicit on the part of the major clerics (cf. OT 10a; PO 16c).[23]

Then, proceeding by degrees, we must first say that the obligation of celibacy is an obligation of positive right, established by the positive law of the Church, and therefore not demanded by the nature of holy ministry itself.

The documents of the recent popes and the Dicasteries of the Holy See, while insisting on the fact that the spirit with which celibacy is assumed should be that of a free will to offer oneself to God, nevertheless speak of the law of celibacy rather than a vow as the source of the obligation of ecclesiastical celibacy.[24]

According to the encyclical *Sacerdotalis Caelibatus* (14), celibacy is the way in which full dedication to God is expressed and corroborated and therefore it should be said that, in respect to the law, the primary source of the obligation is the exclusive, perennial, and total choice of the one love of Christ as an act of consecration of oneself to God and to the Church. The law simply supports this choice.[25]

Presbyterorum Ordinis 16c, confronted with the dilemma of the obligatory nature of the law and freedom in the assumption of celibacy, in confirming the legislation of the Latin Church, insists, on the one hand, on the nature of the gift of celibacy generously (*libenter*) granted by the Father, and on the other hand, the freedom of embracing celibacy, appreciating it as a gift wonderfully (*praeclarumillud donum*) granted by the Father. One can legitimately hold, in the light of the doctrine of the Council on the charisms, that *Presbyterorum Ordinis*, speaking of a gift granted by the Father, even if the term "charism" isn't used, means this reality. Finally, it is in this relationship with the gift that the Church in the Spirit has the certainty that the Father gives to those who are called to ministerial priesthood, and the grateful recognition for this on the part of the person who receives, it that causes the priest's adherence to the law set down by the Church (cf. OT 10a).

Pastores Dabo Vobis 29 makes an important clarification on the ecclesiastical law on celibacy:

> Inasmuch as it is a law, it expresses the Church's will, even before the will of the subject expressed by his readiness. But the will of the Church finds its ultimate motivation in the link between celibacy and sacred ordination, which configures the priest to Jesus Christ the head and spouse of the Church. The Church, as the spouse of Jesus Christ, wishes to be loved by the priest in the total and exclusive manner in which Jesus Christ her head and spouse loved her. Priestly celibacy, then, is the gift of self in and with Christ to his

> Church and expresses the priest's service to the Church in and with the Lord.[26]

The law of celibacy is not presented as a mere disciplinary disposition of the Church. It finds its deepest motivation in the conformation of the priest to Christ the head and the spouse of the Church, which, for this reason, is loved in a way similar to how it loved Christ: in a total and exclusive way.

Canon 277 §1 and the more recent documents from the popes and the Dicasteries of the Holy See[27] insist on the fact that celibacy is a gift of the Spirit, and therefore a charism, which pushes a person called to holy ministry to choose celibacy as a condition of consecrated life in service of God and the Church. This is a charism that is accepted by the Church as a requirement for the admission into holy orders.[28]

The Directory *Benedetto XVI* (90) a summarizing text, expresses itself thus:

> For these reasons, the ecclesiastical law on one hand confirms the charism of celibacy, showing how it is intimately connected with the holy ministry in its double dimension of relationship with Christ and with the Church; on the other hand, it protects the freedom of the person who assumes it. Then the priest consecrated to Christ with a new and excellent reason, should be very aware that he has received a gift necessitated by a precise juridical obligation, from which the moral obligation of observance derives. This obligation, freely assumed, has a theological character and is a sign of the reality of spousal love that occurs in sacramental ordination. With this, the priest acquires that spiritual, but real, paternity, which has a universal dimension and is made concrete in a particular way in the encounters with the community entrusted to him.[29]

Celibacy, then, better expresses the configuration or conformation to Christ, Spouse of the Church, through whom the ministry of the celibate cleric acquires a greater efficacy, partly because it better expresses without doubt that reality of assimilation in the spousal love that is carried out in the same sacramental ordination.[30]

Although not assumed with a vow and not being established as was done in canon 132 §1 CCL 1917, sacrilege through the sins against the obligation assumed still can be held, since, given that celibacy has on its own a character of consecrating the whole person to God, grave violations against this obligation are expressions of a will to retract the consecration itself, and can only be seen as sacrilege, since they directly involve the relationship wherein the whole person belongs to God in the dimension of celibate gift, and therefore involve the very act of being consecrated to God.

Therefore, to summarize, we can say that the obligation of ecclesiastical celibacy has its source: primarily, in the gift of the Holy Spirit, or the charism, given in connection with the bestowal of holy ministry through the ties of convenience with this (cf. PDV 29); secondarily, in the free response of love with the assumption of the evangelical counsel of celibacy through the public promise at the moment of diaconal ordination as a strengthening of the desire for consecration to the ministry with an undivided heart and public commitment in front of the Church; and finally, in canon 277 §1, canonical institutionalization of the bond of theological, spiritual, and pastoral convenience that the Church, guided by the Spirit, creates between celibacy and sacred orders, which sustains the exercise of the charism.

Consequently, this is not just about juridical obligation, but primarily moral obligation, which concerns theological order, as it derives from the special relationship that is established between the man called to celibacy by God and the same God when he calls him to permanent diaconal ministry in celibacy or to priestly ministry in the Latin Catholic Church.

We should remember that perpetual and perfect chastity does not exclude sexuality as a dynamism in the person, who, ordained to a chaste life, finds his fulfillment in oblative love, but excludes the exercise of sexuality in its genital expression: therefore, besides marriage, all autoerotic acts, and every kind of sexual-genital relationship with another person of the same or of the other sex.

This is the moral, canonical minimum of observation of the obligation of celibacy. For particularly grave violations, penal sanctions intervene, as in the cases laid down in canons 1394 §1[31] and 1395,[32] up to dismissal from the clerical state (cf. can. 290, 2°).

All the same, the dynamism of the evangelical counsel of celibate chastity, which is delineated canonically in 277 §1, goes well beyond this moral and canonical minimum. Perfect celibate chastity, in fact, because it is the realization of sexuality in oblative love, participation in the love of God, is not only the exclusion of genital expression, it is not just continence, but integration of one's affectivity in the gift of oneself to God and to others.[33]

Il presente sussidio 47 specifies that celibacy "should never be a negation or an escape, but a sublimation of sexuality" as one renounces genital function, conjugal love and human paternity, and renounces these "for the love of the kingdom of Heaven." One should note that the document explicitly comprehends in its content on the obligation of ecclesiastical celibacy the renunciation of human paternity as a prerequisite for spiritual paternity, which is the content of the charism of priestly ministry and is an expression of the total gift of oneself that is proper to the dynamism of love.[34] Natural spousal love and paternity necessarily restrict the "being for others" in a predominant way, between the limits of the natural family; spiritual spousal love with the Church and supernatural spiritual paternity, instead, open to a love that does not come from blood and flesh, but from God, love that on its own opens, without preclusion and exclusivity, to everyone who God puts on the path of the exercise of ministry. This opening is an anticipation of what will be, in eschatological finality, the condition of all saved people in Christ (cf. Matt 22:30). In fact, the renunciation of natural paternity is a living testament to faith in the final resurrection, as it is a sign that a person does not realize himself by perpetuating himself in posterity but transcends his historical realization into the hope of a full communion with God and all those saved in Christ.[35]

The dynamism of the evangelical counsel, understood as an ever-fuller conformation to Christ the virgin and the spouse of the Church, also leads one to the virginity of the heart.

Presbyterorum Ordinis 16b seems to speak indistinctly of the virginity or celibacy observed for the kingdom of heaven, as if identifying the two things. In *Pastores Dabo Vobis* (29), John Paul II thus explains the relationship between chastity and virginity:

> In virginity and celibacy, chastity retains its original meaning, that is, of human sexuality lived as a genuine sign of, and precious service to, the love of communion and gift of self to others. This meaning is fully found in virginity which makes evident, even in the renunciation of marriage, the "nuptial meaning" of the body through communion and personal gift to Jesus Christ and his Church which prefigures and anticipates the perfect and final communion and self-giving of the world to come: "In virginity or celibacy, the human being is awaiting, also in a bodily way, the eschatological marriage of Christ with the Church, giving himself or herself completely to the Church in the hope that Christ may give himself to the Church in the full truth of eternal life."

There is a difference between *virginity* and perfect chastity in consecrated celibacy. Celibate chastity, as an evangelical counsel (cf. PDV 27; 29), a gift of the Spirit, attempts and should attempt its full realization in the virginity of the heart, of which physical virginity is a sign and protection. If for some reason physical virginity is not present, it does not mean that celibate chastity cannot or should not strive for the virginity of the heart. It is the dynamism of love that leads a person who is truly chaste in celibacy to this virginity, whatever his physical condition.

Physical virginity only indicates the total and exclusive gift to God if it is offered in love, because only in love is physical virginity also the virginity of the heart, which is signified and protected by physical virginity. Physical virginity lived in the virginity of the heart indicates the donation of oneself to God from birth, lived in the eschatological hope of the fullness of communion with God and with all those saved in Christ. All the same, the path toward the virginity of the heart, which is the perfection of charity, is in no way closed to someone who no longer possesses physical virginity. In fact, the virginity of the heart is the fulfillment of that total purity of the heart that wants, and always looks for ever fewer things to desire and search for only God, and thus find the fullness of one's realization as a person. As a fulfillment of the beatitude of the pure of heart to whom it is promised to see God (cf.

Matt 5:8), virginity of the heart is at the apex of a path of total liberation from the passions and the renunciation of earthly desires, to arrive at a full union with God, through an ever-fuller conformation to Christ the virgin.[36] This is a spiritual path in which all the dimensions of the person are implicated. A path of progressive psycho-affective maturation corresponds to this, brought about using all human means that can contribute to this maturation, and sustained by the action of grace. Pureness of heart is to look for and love God in all things and all things in God.

Virginity of the heart must be coupled with radical poverty in total abandonment to God and a full obedience to his will.[37] This path of holiness can only lead to a greater fecundity of ministry.

Love, as a peculiar gift of grace, conforms to Christ, and pushes the chaste celibate person toward the virginity of the heart to implement it in an ever-greater response of love. It is this dynamism of love that ensures that the ministry is not carried out as a role, composed of a combination of functions, but as an sacrifice of life not only in celibacy, but also in obedience and poverty, counsels which must also inform the life of the holy minister (cf. PDV 27–30; can. 273; 282; 286).

This type of life—lived in such a way as to be a sign—that leads to the dynamism of the virginity of the heart as the fullness of all the three evangelical counsels, necessarily requires a special vocation and a special grace, which have the character of consecration on the part of God and to which the person can only respond freely, consecrating themselves into the totality of the gift of their person, through—as we have seen—the faithful and tireless exercise of the ministry (cf. can. 276 §1). This is the "undivided heart" of which St. Paul speaks (1 Cor 7:32–34) and to which *Presbyterorum Ordinis* 16b, canon 277 §1 and various other documents that address the question refer to.

Sacerdotalis Caelibatus (15) preserves the practices of the first centuries of the Church, which admitted married clerics, although later with the obligation of continence, and the discipline of the Eastern Churches.[38] At the same time, however, we should say that if celibacy is a charism, a gift of the Spirit, and the Church, through the experience of many centuries slowly became aware of the theological, spiritual, and pastoral convenience, to establish the requirement of the charism of celibacy those who are called to the holy ministry of the permanent diaconate, the priesthood, and the episcopate of the Latin Church, and of the episcopate of the Eastern Church as well, then this must be in virtue of that ministerial power that Christ gave to the Church, under the guidance and inspiration of the same Spirit who gives the gift of ministry as well as celibacy.[39]

A cleric who perceives celibacy as "a tribute that is paid to the Lord" to be ordained, and not, instead, as a "gift that is received from his mercy" would remain in permanent immaturity and experience perhaps insurmountable difficulty in observing it and therefore great damage to the ministry.[40]

Poverty

Canon 282 §1 expresses itself thus:

> Clerics are to foster simplicity of life and are to refrain from all things that have a semblance of vanity.

While celibate chastity is assumed with a public promise in diaconal ordination and obedience both in diaconal ordination and again in priestly ordination, poverty is not assumed with any promise, and therefore we can say that it is not formally publicly assumed.[41]

However, because clerics imitate and follow Christ in their ministry, although they are not obliged to embrace material poverty with a sacred obligation, they should live in a spirit of poverty, cultivating a simplicity of life and refraining from everything that has a semblance of vanity.[42]

We can start by saying that in a certain sense, poverty is included as a necessity in creation itself. In fact, all goods are from God, as he is the Creator, and humanity is only his beneficiary. Humans can use all goods in dependency on God, as a gift from God. Humans are the true owners of nothing. All the same, original sin leads to an autonomous and disordered use of the goods of creation, through which they are considered a possession until they are placed above God himself. This is because, fundamentally, the relationship between creature and Creator is distorted. Jesus, with the redemption enacted by him, redeems the use of goods from the dominion of sin. Therefore, the obligation for a correct relationship between material goods and a sober life in solidarity with the poorest concerns all Christians (cf. can. 222). It is within this fuller perspective that the obligation seen in canon 282 §1 is considered, wherein the clerics are called to a witness that is meaningful both for those who lack necessities as well as for those who indulge in an unbridled consummation of goods.[43]

Because what is required by canon 282 does not stay in a vacuum but is made concrete in the life of the holy minister as a search for sanctity and dedication in the ministry, the Council and the Code descend to specific determinations of how he should live poverty.

Above all, in general, he should use temporal goods only for those ends that are in line with the Gospels and the will of the Church (cf. PO 17b), then, in a more specific way, he must use (*destinent semper*) the strictly ecclesiastical goods, those which belong to a public entity in the Church, like the parish church or the diocese, for those ends for which the Church legitimately possesses goods, such as the preparation of the divine cult, the dignified maintenance of the clergy, the sustenance of the works of the apostolate and of charity, especially for the poor (cf. PC 17c; can. 1254 §2). From this derives the need for a completely transparent witness in the administration of the goods of the Church, where one is accountable to God and one's brothers, especially to the poor (cf. PDV 30).

As for personal goods, which are not ecclesiastical goods and are left to the free disposal and administration of the priest, the following should be considered: (1) those that arise from the fulfillment of an ecclesiastical office, like that of a parish priest, parochial vicar, or any other office in the diocese, for example in the diocesan curia; (2) those originating in the patrimony of the priest (family goods, inheritance, donations *intuitu personae*) or from his activities (publications of his writings); and (3) those coming from savings.

While for the use of goods of the second and third type, reference is made to what is generally indicated on the use of temporal goods, namely, that they should follow the Gospels and what the Church requires, and to the voluntary poverty that a person might wish to choose,[44] for the first type we have canon 282 §2, which is a specification of what is stated in §1.

Canon 282 §1 is too synthetic and rather general, which is why what it indicates should find a concrete specification in reference to habitation, means of transport, vacations, dress, and so on (cf. *Benedetto XVI* 83).[45] Leaving to the responsibility of the individual the concretization of a simplicity of life detached from everything with a semblance of vanity, clearly taking into account the circumstances of time and place, the canon should be read in the light of *Presbyterorum Ordinis* 17 and other documents of the Holy See.[46]

Presbyterorum Ordinis 17a, for the correct use of material goods in conformity with the will of God, calls for spiritual discernment on the part of the priest, which must take place based on an acquired freedom from every disordered preoccupation, and therefore on the basis of trust in the providence of God, who grants the goods necessary for ministry as a gift.

The decree, then, invites priests to embrace voluntary poverty, precisely because there is no formal promise of poverty on their part. This means that clerics are invited to go beyond the canonical minimum indicated by the discipline of the Church to enter into the dynamic of love of the evangelical counsel, which leads to conformation to Christ to be able to be ready to carry out ministry and to witness poverty to the people of God.

The conformation is to Christ, who, as the conciliar text says, "though he was rich yet for your sakes became poor, so that by his poverty you might become rich" (2 Cor 8:9). Therefore, the poverty that Christ lived has a redemptive value for us, because it has made us rich with the goods of salvation. As we have already said when we spoke of the evangelical counsels in general, Christ's making himself poor is a sign and expression of that renunciation that as the second person of the Trinity from all time is essential to his being a Son, receiving everything from the Father, everything he is and everything he has, to eternally restore it to the Father. This renunciation is part of the *kenosis* of Christ (cf. Phil 2:6–8). The holy minister is invited to live those same sentiments that were of Christ Jesus (cf. Phil 2:5). Without this abasement, which is a renunciation of all, because it is the renunciation of his divine omnipotence and transcendence, neither obedience nor virginal love would have been possible for Jesus.

The minister's participation in the renunciation and poverty of Christ assumes a salvific dimension because it has an apostolic character in the very assumption of the authority of sanctity that assimilation to Christ gives to whoever continues his ministry.

Presbyterorum Ordinis 17e adds a meaningful specification:

> Led by the Spirit of the Lord, who anointed the Savior and sent him to evangelize the poor, priests, therefore, and also bishops, should avoid everything which in any way could turn the poor away. Before the other followers of Christ, let priests set aside every appearance of vanity in their possessions. Let them arrange their homes so that they might not appear unapproachable to anyone, lest anyone, even the most humble, fear to visit them.
>
> The reference to the habitation that the Conciliar Decree makes, so that the priest's style of life would be exemplary for all the faithful, can be indicative for other determinations, like the type of car, the way of dressing, the use of electronics, the acquisition of books, holidays, the search for more rewarding ministries, etc.[47]

All the same, here we are not only looking at a sociological kind of poverty, which is simply a lack of material goods, but evangelical poverty, which is a poverty chosen freely, even if it is not always formally assumed with some kind of holy obligation (a promise, vow, or oath), for the kingdom of heaven, just like participation in the spiritual and material poverty of Christ. Spiritual poverty is primary, and this is what material poverty should be based on. Without spiritual poverty, material poverty would not be evangelical; without material poverty, spiritual poverty would be empty. Because evangelical poverty is a participation in the trinitarian love which indissolubly unites the Father and the Son in the one Spirit, it must be the result of a choice made in love rather than simply a social condition, and it cannot be separated from the other two evangelical counsels.

Spiritual poverty postulates a profound dependence on God. Christ, in fact, just because he has nothing of his own, but has received everything from the Father, depends on the Father in everything (cf. John 17:2, 6b–8, 22–24). For this reason, spiritual poverty consists of that attitude of the soul that recognizes God as the Creator and Savior, the giver of all goods, material and spiritual, and recognizes oneself as unworthy of these gifts given freely by God. Evangelical poverty finds its apex, as I stated above, in the path to the virginity of the heart that is the tendency of the soul to search ever-less for goods and center oneself ever more on the one, most beloved good, which is God (cf. PDV 30). Virginity of the heart, like purity of the heart, is the progressive acquisition of the capacity to see and love God in all things and to love all things in God.

This is why the poor in spirit are blessed, because for them the kingdom of heaven is already here (cf. Matt 5:3). They know how to recognize that everything they have, however little or however much, is freely given from God. In this way God himself, the supreme good, is the source of their happiness, which only God, by participation in his kingdom, can give. Beatitude consists in putting the source of happiness only and uniquely in God.

In this way, the free renunciation of material goods becomes a visible manifestation and a support for spiritual poverty and the confident abandonment to the providence of God (cf. Matt 6:25–34). Depending on God, man makes himself truly free from the slavery of the search for human security, and gives himself more generously to God and to his neighbor. In the renunciation of material goods, as an act of submission and reliance on the providence of God, the holy minister shows that he dies to himself and to the pretense of saving himself with human means, and participates in the resurrection of Christ. Evangelical poverty thus assumes a eucharistic dimension, because it is participation in the paschal mystery.

This is the prerequisite for pastoral ministry to be carried out in the spirit of service and generosity: whoever is conscious of having received everything freely from God is disposed to give freely (cf. Matt 10:8; Acts 8:18–25; PO 17d; *Benedetto XVI* 83). *Pastores Dabo Vobis* 30 affirms,

> It is true that "the workman deserves his wages" (*Lk* 10:7) and that "the Lord commanded that those who proclaim the Gospel should get their living by the Gospel" (*1 Cor* 9:14), but it is no less true that this right of the apostle can in no way be confused with attempts of any kind to condition

> service to the Gospel and the Church upon the advantages and interests which can derive from it. Poverty alone ensures that the priest remains available to be sent wherever his work will be most useful and needed even at the cost of personal sacrifice. It is a condition and essential premise of the apostle's docility to the Spirit, making him ready to "go forth," without being weighed down or bound by ties, following only the will of the Master (cf. *Lk* 9:57–62; *Mk* 10:17–22).

Poverty is seen in strict connection with willingness and therefore obedience. This is confirmed by the obligation to accept and faithfully fulfill any kind of assignment which the ordinary entrusts (cf. can. 274 §2). All this also includes the renunciation of any kind of search for a career, charges, or honors, that would condition one's availability for any kind of ministry (cf. *Benedetto XVI* 83) and a total renunciation of what Pope Francis described as "spiritual worldliness" in *Evangelii Gaudium* 93–97.

As for the goods that come to the cleric when he carries out an ecclesiastical office, we have canon 282 §2, which specifies,

> They are to wish to use for the good of the Church and works of charity those goods which have come to them on the occasion of the exercise of ecclesiastical office and which are left over after provision has been made for their decent support and for the fulfillment of all the duties of their own state.

The canon, almost literally referring to *Presbyterorum Ordinis* 17c, exhorts (*impenderevelint*) the clerics, provided with the goods that come to them on the occasion of the exercise of an ecclesiastical office for their honest maintenance and for the fulfillment of all the tasks connected with their own state,[48] to use what they can spare for the good of the Church and the works of charity. *Presbyterorum Ordinis* 17c specifies "especially for the poor," which is not, however, repeated by the canon. Besides, the Conciliar Decree concludes, "Therefore ecclesiastical office should not be treated as a way to make money, nor should the income that derives from it be used to augment the substance of one's own family. The priests, therefore, without being in any way attached to riches, should avoid every greed and abstain from every kind of business." Unfortunately, the CCL 1983 does not include the first part of this text.

The canon speaks of the "superfluous" (*bona quae supersunt*) in relation to the "honest maintenance" (*honesta sustentatio*). This involves two concepts that can only be defined in relationship with concrete spatial-temporal situations.

The cleric, then, adopting the Church's preferential choice for the poor, without excluding anything from the annunciation and from the gift of salvation, is called, on the model of Jesus and based on the social doctrine of the Church, to pay particular attention to and share with the poor, the weak, the small, the sinners, the marginalized. All this, then, with a prophetic attitude when faced with the rich in an opulent, consumerist society and with the poor, because they know how to live their material poverty so that it is united with a spiritual poverty (cf. PDV 30; *Benedetto XVI* 83). All this requires the creation of a "culture of solidarity" to accommodate the individual "poor," and also to operate to change those realities which generate more poverty, to the advantage of those who become ever richer at the expense of the poor.[49]

But what is the source of the obligation of giving superfluous things to the poor or to pious causes,[50] which was already found in canon 1473 CCL 1917?

It is good to bear canon 222 in mind. Reading canon 282 §2 in the light of this canon, we can see a certain contradiction, because canon 222 §1 concerns all the faithful, and therefore clerics as well, and generally lays down the obligation (*obligatione tenentur*) of aiding the necessities of the Church and the works of charity, and §2 specifies the obligation of §1 with the obligation (*obligatione tenentur*), mindful of the commandment of the Lord, to "assist the poor with one's own income" (*ex propriis reditibus pauperibus subveniendi*). In canon 222, no distinctions are made among the sources of income, while regarding the source of the income, canon 282 §2 only refers to what is received on the occasion of the exercise of an ecclesiastical office, and for the goods that should be intended for the good of the Church and works of charity, therefore to the poor, only refers to the superfluous. From this, we can deduce that the cleric who does not have an ecclesiastical office in a strict sense, but any other duty or function received from the ordinary would not be held to canon 282 §2, which seems absurd. Canon

385 §1 CCEO, in fact, rightly extends the obligation to the superfluous of whatever was received not only on the exercise of an office, but also of a ministry or a function (*occasione exercitii officii, ministerii vel muneris ecclesiastici*). If we do not take into consideration that canon 282 §2 should be read in the light of canon 222, or if canon 282 §2 is interpreted as overriding canon 222, we would arrive at the conclusion that while laypeople are held to a real duty, the clerics are not, because giving the superfluous for the good of the Church and for the works of charity, therefore to the poor, is left to their good will (*ad bonum Ecclesiae opera que caritatis impenderevelint*).[51] This seems rather absurd if the clerics who, through the very ministry they exercise, should give witness to holiness, and therefore also to solidarity in charity. The thing appears even more incongruent if we consider that the invitation to sustain the good of the Church and the works of charity is limited to the superfluous in respect to the incomes coming from the exercise of ecclesiastical office, because a significant personal patrimony that a cleric might have independently would not fall under what was established in canon 282 §2. All the same, he should not use these goods at his pleasure because he should only use them according to canon 282 §1, that is, leading a simple life devoid of anything that might taste of vanity, but this could only be materialized in solidarity with the needs of the Church and the works of charity, therefore with the poor. In my opinion, canon 282 §2 should be considered a specification of canon 222, which, we should observe, regarding the poor with one's own income, makes reference to the commandment of the Lord (*praecepti Domini memores*). So, we can deduce that, as for all the faithful the duty to aid the poor with one's own incomes is a divine law, so is the disposition contained in canon 282 §2 to be understood as a duty of divine law, which binds by virtue of religion, charity, and justice, for which the cleric who, after having provided for his own honest maintenance[52] and the fulfillment of all the duties of his own state,[53] would sin gravely if he did not fulfill this obligation.

CONCLUSION

The title of this speech might seem a little strange to some. Consider the holiness of those who are called to sacred ministry, starting from the Code of Canon Law. Instead, we have been able to see how, starting from the canons themselves, we can derive a rich theological and spiritual doctrine. Clearly, the canons, through their very synthetic formulation, cannot unfold a complete theological and spiritual discourse, but we have seen that they offer elements that unexpectedly stimulate deep understanding and open onto a theological and spiritual dimension. In the apostolic constitution *Sacrae Disciplinae Leges*, which promulgated the CCL, John Paul II affirmed that this was an attempt to translate the doctrine of Vatican II in canonical language, for which it should be considered complementary to Vatican II itself.[54] At the same time, given that the CCL is part of the tradition of theological reflection of the Church, the canons contained within it should necessarily be interpreted in the light of the documents of the magisterium, subsequent to their promulgation.

Canon 276 states that the first duty of a cleric, to achieve the sanctity required by being oneself a minister of the mysteries of God, is to faithfully and tirelessly carry out the duties that arise from the ministry itself. This position opens (in its novelty in respect to the CCL 1917) a theological-spiritual perspective that is sourced not only from Vatican II but from the entire tradition of the Church. In fact, St. Paul tells us, "Think of us in this way: as servants of Christ and stewards of God's mysteries. Moreover, it is required of stewards that they be found trustworthy" (1 Cor 4:1–2).

NOTES

1. Cf. *AAS* (1992): 677–81; *Enchiridion Vaticanum* (EV) 13/1154–1553.
2. Cf. *AAS* 110 (2018): 1111–61.
3. Cf. https://www.vatican.va/content/francesco/it/speeches/2022/february/documents/20220217-simposio-teologia-sacerdozio.html.
4. Cf. *AAS* 88 (1996): 377–486; EV 15/434–775.
5. Cf. Sess. 24, *de sacram. matr.*, can. 10.
6. Cf. *AAS* 46 (1954): 176.
7. Cf. Congregazione per il Clero, Dir. *Benedetto XVI*, February 11, 2013, Città del Vaticano 2013, no. 89; EV 29/112–359.
8. Cf. *AAS* 96 (2004): 825–927; EV 22/665–963.
9. In *Pastores Gregis* 13 we read, "The spiritual journey of the Bishop coincides, from this perspective, with that pastoral charity which must rightly

be considered the soul of his apostolate, as it is of the apostolate of priests and deacons. Here it is not only a matter of an *existentia* but indeed of a *pro-existentia*, that is to say, of a way of living inspired by the supreme model of Christ the Lord and which is spent totally in worship of the Father and in service of neighbor. The Second Vatican Council rightly states that pastors, in the image of Christ, must carry out their ministry with holiness and zeal, with humility and fortitude, "which, fulfilled in this way, will be for them an excellent means of sanctification." 63 No Bishop can fail to realize that the summit of Christian holiness is the crucified Christ in his supreme self-oblation to the Father and to his brothers and sisters in the Holy Spirit. For this reason configuration to Christ and a share in his sufferings (cf. *1 Pet* 4:15) becomes the royal road of the Bishop's holiness in the midst of his people." Emphasis in original.

10. Augustinus, *In Io. Ev. tract.* 123, 5; *PL* 35,1967, cited in *Pastores Dabo Vobis* 23 (nt. 52) and in *Pastores Gregis* 11 (nt. 44).

11. Cf. *AAS* 107 (2015): 1142; EV 31/ 1669.

12. Cf. *Acta Synodalia* (*AS*) IV/VI, 399.

13. Cf. J. Beyer, "De seminario diocesano *recentiora quaedam quaesita*," *Periodica* 82 (1993): 86–88.

14. Cf. Ignatius of Loyola, *Spiritual Exercises*, nos. 353; 365.

15. St. Ignatius of Loyola, in the famous letter to the Jesuits of Portugal on March 26, 1553, describes three levels of obedience: the first, which consists only in executing what has been commanded, but does not reach the value of the virtue of obedience; the second, which consists not only in execution, but also in the effective conformity of one's will with that of the superior and already reaches the virtue of obedience (cf. no. 5); and the third, "in which there is not only the unity of wills, but also the same sentiments with one's superior, submitting one's judgment to his in the measure in which the devoted will can incline intelligence" and this is obedience as the "entire and perfect oblation of one's self" (no. 7). The fact that for St. Ignatius the obedience of judgment does not a priori exclude the use of the intellect and therefore each judgment of the situation by the Jesuit, is demonstrated by what he affirms at the end of the letter: "This does not exclude that if something were to present itself differently from how the superior sees it, and after having prayed, it seemed opportune in respect and in obedience to God, to need to manifest your opinion, you could not. But if in this you wish to proceed without suspicion of self love and personal judgment, you must remain available (*indifferenti*) before and after having expressed your opinion, not only to undertake or leave the execution of the thing in question, but also to approve and consider as better whatever the superior orders" (Ignatius of Loyola, *Gliscritti*, 785–94). Rather, in the letter to the whole Company of Jesus on May 29, 1555, St. Ignatius admits that a Jesuit can present even more than once, over time, the good reasons he believes he has, even if the thing had already been decided once or twice by the superior (cf. *Gliscritti*, 794–95).

16. The Congregation for the Institutes of Consecrated Life and the Societies of Apostolic Life, in the Instruction *Faciem Tuam, Domine, Requiram*, of May 11, 2008, on the service of authority and obedience, at no. 11 affirms, "One remains devoted to the Lord when sensing in some way his presence in human intermediaries…when one has the courage to cast the nets on the 'strength of his word' (cf. Luke 5:5) and not only from solely human motivations; when one chooses to obey not only God but also others, but in every case, for God and not for others." In his *Constitutions*, St. Ignatius writes, "Genuine obedience considers not the person to whom it is offered but Him for whose sake it is offered: and if it is exercised for the sake of our Creator and Lord alone, then it is the very Lord of everyone who is obeyed" (EV 25/349–448). The reference is to no. 84 of the *Constitutions of the Company of Jesus, General Examen* in Ignatius of Loyola, *Gliscritti*, 416.

17. This is how Jesus prays in Gethsemane at the first moment: "My Father, *if it is possible, let this cup pass from me*; yet not what I want but what you want!" (Matt 26:39); "Abba, Father, for you all things are possible; remove this cup from me; yet, not what I want, but what you want" (Mark 14:36); "Father, if you are willing, remove this cup from me; yet, not my will but yours be done" (Luke 22:42); in a second moment: "My Father, if this cannot pass unless I drink it, your will be done" (Matt 26:42). In both moments it is always the disposition of Jesus's soul to do the will of the Father, and therefore to adjust his will to that of the Father, but in the first moment he asks to be free from the cup that is presented to him, while in a second moment he adheres to it with his whole being, both in his will and in his intellect, because he sees the necessity of drinking the cup for the fulfillment of the salvific design of the Father. For this reason, Jesus submits to the judgement of the Sanhedrin and the judgment of Pilate, recognizing it as the human mediation of the salvific will of the Father, but this does not change the fact that the judgement of the Sanhedrin is sacrilege while that of Pilate is unjust and opportune.

18. The Instruction *Faciem Tuam, Domine* states, "Reverence for the will of God keeps those in authority in a state of humble seeking, so that their acting conforms as much as possible to that holy will. St. Augustine reminds us that the one who obeys always fulfils the will of God, not because the command of the authority necessarily conforms to the divine will, but because it is the will of God that is obeyed by the one who is in charge. But those in authority, on their part, must search assiduously with the help of prayer, reflection, and the advice of others for what God really wills. Otherwise, instead of representing God, superiors risk putting themselves carelessly in God's place" (12).

19. Cf. *Pontificale Romanum* 213.

20. Cf. M. Szentmártoni, "Celibato per il Regno dei Cieli e maturità della persona," *Periodica* 83 (1994): 251–52; 254–55; 258.

21. Cf. F. X. Wernz and P. Vidal, *Ius canonicum*, II, Pontificia Universitas Gregoriana, Rome, 1934, 145–46.

22. For the whole topic, see J. Ferreira Pena, *O celibato, "peculiare Dei donum" aosclérigos (can. 277, §1°)* (diss. Doct. Fac. Iur. Can. Pont. Univ. Gregorianae), Rome, 1993, 84–96.

23. Cf. *AS* IV/VII, 217.

24. Cf. Paul VI, *motu proprio Sacrum diaconatus ordinem*, June 18, 1967, II.4, in *AAS* 59 (1967): 697–704; EV 2/1368–1406; Paul VI, encyclical letter *Sacerdotalis Caelibatus*, June 24, 1967, nos. 7, 14, 17, 36, 37, 42, in *AAS* 59 (1967): 657–97; EV 2/ 1415–1513; Secretary of State, circular letter *L'année qui vien*, Feb. 2 1969, in EV 3/791–95; Id., *Letter to Card. Villot*, Feb. 2 1970, in *AAS* 62 (1970): 98–103; EV 3/1958–71; Synod of Bishops (1971), Doc. *Ultimis Temporibus*, Nov. 30 1971, II.I.4c, in *AAS* 63 (1971): 898–922; EV 4/1135–1237; John Paul II, letter *Novo Incipiente*, April 8, 1979, no. 9, in *AAS* 71 (1979): 393–417; EV 6/1287–1328.

25. *Ultimis temporibus* states, "Because of the intimate and manifold convenience of pastoral office and celibate life, the law remains in effect: in fact, he who freely desires *total availability*, which is the distinctive note in this office, accepts celibate life just as freely. The candidate should understand this form of life not as an *external* imposition but rather as the manifestation of his free gift which is accepted and ratified by the Church through the bishop. In this way, the law becomes a safeguard and protection of liberty, through which the priest gives himself to Christ does so, therefore, as a 'light yoke'" (c). *Presbyterorum Ordinis* 16b also speaks explicitly of convenience and not of a relationship of necessity between the ministerial and celibate priesthood.

26. Emphasized in the text.

27. Cf. Paul VI, encyclical letter *Sacerdotalis Caelibatus*, June 24, 1967, no. 15; Congregation for Catholic Education, Or. ed. *Il presente sussidio*, April 11, 1974, no. 47; John Paul II, letter *Novo Incipiente*, April 8, 1979; John Paul II, postsynodal apostolic exhortation *Pastores Dabo Vobis*, March 25, 1992, no. 29; Congregation for the Clergy, Dir. *Benedetto XVI*, February 11, 2013, no. 80.

28. If celibacy is a charism, a gift of the Spirit, and the Church, which has through its experience of many centuries slowly become aware of the theological, spiritual, and pastoral convenience, establishes the charism of celibacy for those who are called to holy ministry, this can only be in virtue of the same ministerial power that Christ has given to the Church under the guidance and inspiration of the same Spirit, which makes a gift of both ministry and celibacy (cf. Synod of Bishops [1971], Doc. *Ultimis Temporibus*, November 30, 1971, II.I. 4c).

29. Emphasis ours. It should be noted that this text speaks explicitly of the "charism of the celibate," as does Or. ed. *Il presente sussidio*, no. 47.

30. *Sacerdotalis Caelibatus* primarily gives a christological reason of convenience between holy ministry and celibacy: this is a gift of love from God that

man responds to in love to be assimilated to Christ the virgin (cf. 19–25). From this arises a eucharistic-ecclesiological reason: "acting in the person of Christ, the priest unites himself most intimately with the offering, and places on the altar his entire life, which bears the marks of a holocaust" (29). The pastoral reason depends on both of these reasons: in virtues of this last consecration to Christ, celibacy, beyond that given in the sacrament, the priest can have, even in the practical field, the greatest efficacy and a better psychological attitude in the continual exercise of perfect charity, in a greater freedom and availability to all (cf. 32). For a deeper study of the encyclical letter *Sacerdotalis Caelibatus*, see P. Emeka Aroh, *Priestly celibacy: a gift and a commitment (can. 277 §1). Adaptation to Igbo culture. Nigeria*, Tesi Gregoriana. Serie Diritto Canonico 99, Rome, 2014, 117–25.

31. "Firmo praescripto can.194 §1, no.3, clericusmatrimonium, etiamciviliter tantum, attentans, in suspensionemlataesententiaeincurrit; quod si monitus non resipuerit et scandalum dare perrexerit, gradatimprivationibusac vel etiam dimissione e statu clericali puniripotest."

32. §1. "Clericusconcubinarius, praetercasum de quo in can.1394, et clericus in alio peccato externo contra sextumDecalogipraeceptumcum scandalo permanens, suspensionepuniantur, cui persistente post monitionemdelicto, aliaepoenaegradatim addi possuntusque ad dimissionem e statu clericali. §2. Clericus qui aliter contra sextumDecalogipraeceptumdeliquerit, si quidemdelictum vi vel minis vel publice vel cum minore infra aetatemsedecimannorumpatratumsit, iustispoenispuniatur, non exclusa, si casus ferat, dimissione e statu clericali." The Congregation for the Doctrine of the Faith with the letter *Ad Exsequendam* of May 18, 2001, raises the age to 18 years for the configuration of the crime of pedophilia, reserved for the Tribunal of the Congregation for the Doctrine of the Faith, and establishes that for this crime the statute of limitations starts on the day that the minor reaches 18 years of age (cf. *AAS* 102 [2010]: 785–88; EV 20/715–724). The *Normae de Gravioribus Delictis* establish that, as regards the crime against the sixth commandment on the part of a cleric, a person less than 18 years is equal to the person who habitually has an imperfect use of reason (cf. art. 6 §1, 1°), also including among the *delicta graviora* the crime of child pornography, which is the acquisition, possession or distribution by a cleric of pornographic images of minors under the age of 18, for purposes of sexual gratification, by whatever means or using whatever technology (art. 6 §1, 2°) (cf. *AAS* 102 [2010]: 419–31; EV 26/1871–1921).

33. Celibacy therefore constitutes a path of—also affective—maturation in the integration of sexuality as the dynamism of the person in an oblative love, a road that clearly constitutes a duty in the "holding-together the dissonant factors in oneself." Szentmártoni, "Celibato per il Regno dei Cieli," 262–63.

34. This imposition is also found in *Benedetto XVI* 80, according to which the spiritual paternity that arises from the renunciation of natural paternity and included in the assumption of celibacy has a character of universality, as it cannot

be exclusive, but is not unreal for this reason, because it becomes concrete in the confrontation with the community entrusted to the pastor.

35. In *Novo Incipiente*, John Paul II states that the Catholic Church connects the gift of celibacy with the priestly vocation "because celibacy 'for the sake of God's kingdom' is not only an eschatological sign but also has great social importance in our present life for the service of God's people. The priest's celibacy makes him a 'man for others,' although in a way different from that of the man who through conjugal union with a woman likewise becomes, husband and father, a 'man for others,' especially within the home and family, that is, for his wife and, with her, for the children to whom he gives life."

36. Cf. *Catechism of the Catholic Church*, nos. 2342; 2343; 2345.

37. *Pastores Dabo Vobis* (27) closely connects the three evangelical counsels of obedience, chastity, and poverty.

38. Refer to *Presbyterorum Ordinis* 16a for the legitimacy of the eastern practices.

39. Cf. Synod of Bishops (1971), Doc. *Ultimis Temporibus*, November 30, 1971, II.I.4c.

40. Cf. Congregation for Catholic Education, Or. ed. *Il presente sussidio*, April 11, 1974, no. 16.

41. During the discussion in the council hall, there were people who proposed that the secular cleric should be ready to make a promise of poverty at diaconal ordination (F. Franić) (cf. AS IV/IV 803) and others who thought it should occur at priestly ordination (E. Florit) (cf. AS IV/V 20), but as can be seen, the proposal was not taken into consideration and the *Relatio* al *textus emendatus* speaks only of voluntary poverty (cf. AS VI/VI 401). The Commission for the reform of the Code did not address the question.

42. Cf. Synod of Bishops (1971), Doc. *Ultimis Temporibus*, November 30, 1971, II/II, 4. In the first edition, the canon was introduced thus: "Spiritu paupertatis ducti," a reference that was unanimously suppressed, but no reason was given, at least in the acts of the Commission (cf. *Communicationes* 16 [1984] 193; 14 [1982] 80). A reference, however, is found in can. 385 §1 *CCEO*.

43. Cf. A. Zambon, "Il presbitero e i beni materiali: un rapporto scontato? Alcune riflessioni a partire dal can. 282 §1," *Quaderni di Diritto Ecclesiale* 17 (2004): 86.

44. Cf. A. Zambon, *Il consiglio evangelico della povertà nel ministero e nella vita del presbitero diocesano*, Tesi Gregoriana, Serie Diritto Canonico 52 (Rome, 2002).

45. Cf. In the past, proclamations against the greed of clerics, bishops, and priests were given at the Council of Chalcedon (a. 451; can. 22), the Nicene Council (a. 787; can. 19), the Fourth Council of Constantinople (aa. 869–870; can. 19), the Third Lateran Council (a. 1179; can. 13 e 14); the Fourth Lateran Council (a. 1215; can. 66), the Council of Trent (aa. 1545–1563; sess. 24, de ref.,

can. 6; sess. 21, de ref., can. 1); against the use of luxurious clothes, ornaments of the body and other luxurious ostentation at the Second Nicene Council (can. 16), the Second Lateran Council (can. 4), the Fourth Lateran Council (can. 16), the Council of Vienna (aa. 1311–1312; decr. 9), the Council of Constance (a. 1415; Sess. 43, de ref. eccl.), the Council of Trent (Sess. 22, de ref., can. 1 e 6); against the enrichment of one's family at the Second Nicene Council and the Council of Trent (Sess. 25, de ref., cap. 1); against the entitlement to opulent treatment on the occasion of canonic visits, the Fourth Council of Constantinople (can. 19), the Third Lateran Council (can. 4); cf. ZAMBON, *Il consiglio evangelico della povertà*, 141–45.

46. The CCL 1983 does not make any reference to witness, something which, as we will see, the Council had referred to the revision of the Code. It refers simply to dress (can. 284), but not to dwelling place. Cf. ZAMBON, *Il consiglio evangelico della povertà*, 120–23.

47. Cf. ZAMBON, "Il presbitero e i beni materiali," 106–9.

48. In *Presbyterorum Ordinis* 17c this is included explicitly as a requirement (*adhibeant*). Can. 282 §2 is formulated differently, but in fact this too puts forward as a requirement supporting oneself honestly and the fulfillment of all the duties one is held to in the use of such goods.

49. Cf. ZAMBON, *Il consiglio evangelico della povertà*, 194–201.

50. Pious cause is the destination of the goods, either with an *inter vivos* act or a *mortis causa* act, to a supernatural end which is that of the Church. "Pious" is said because the motivation, the intention of the one disposing of the goods, is religious. Cf. V. DE PAOLIS, *I beni temporali della Chiesa* (Bologna: EDB, 2016), 224–26.

51. Cf. ZAMBON, *Il consiglio evangelico della povertà*, 233.

52. Clearly, by honestly supporting oneself, the savings that are necessary to provide for the eventualities of illness and old age are included. This also depends on the mechanisms that the state may make available.

53. This includes equitable retribution for people in the service of the cleric.

54. Cf. *AAS* 75/II (1983): XI-XII; EV 8/628; 630.

22

PRIESTHOOD AND CELIBACY

Father Emilio J. Justo

CELIBACY IS ONE of the questions that have come up constantly in the history of the Church. In times of crisis for the Church, and when ecclesial renewal is being sought, it is a recurring theme. This will probably continue to be the case in the future. It is a permanent topic that needs to be thought through in the light of certain basic themes and helps us to discuss certain key aspects of Christian life, the ordained ministry,[1] and the proclamation of the gospel in every age.

THE QUESTION OF CELIBACY

Current criticisms of obligatory celibacy for priests follow the same lines as at other times in the past: it is not in the Bible, it has pagan roots, its aim is control, it was not always a constant in the history of the Church, the Eastern rites ordain married men, it reduces the number of vocations, it separates those responsible for the community from ordinary life and ordinary people....It is argued that, if ordained ministers were married, they would be closer to their communities and so would be able to fulfill their ministry more effectively and satisfyingly. Further arguments are specifically related to our own times, referring to the anthropological understanding of sexuality, a social transformation of the meaning of sexual relations, and the tragic scandal of child abuse. Legitimate and enlightening arguments are mixed with others that are highly questionable.[2] Undoubtedly, the psychological, social, and educational matters connected with celibacy are fundamental to a proper understanding of priestly celibacy and need to be tackled seriously and in depth. There are also historical and canonical aspects, discussion of which has borne fruit over the last decades, and enriched reflection on the whole subject.

Celibacy is a complex subject involving many different aspects. Basically, the connection between priesthood and celibacy is a deeply theological matter. What is at stake is the way the ordained ministry is understood, and consequently, the way the Church is understood. The apostolic ministry belongs to the structure of the Church, as a sacrament that builds the Church. Discussion of it needs to include the ecclesial context and affects the way the Church is understood—its nature, its structure, and its mission in the world. Celibacy is not an accident of priestly life; it has to do with the understanding of what the Church is and what the ordained ministry means within it. And the way the ministry is lived out in the Christian community affects to some degree the way Christian life is understood. Therefore, the question of celibacy is connected to the theology of the ordained ministry, the ecclesial community, and Christian living. And that also applies when people propose that the law of celibacy should be abolished: what is decisive is the way the sacrament of holy orders is understood, and the ecclesial configuration that is intended.

At the same time, the question of celibacy relates to the understanding of marriage. The celibacy of ordained ministers presupposes a theology of matrimony and a high value set on married life. The proposal to ordain married men affects the way marriage is understood—and would also necessitate a discussion of the meaning of the sacrament of matrimony and its possible connection with the ordained ministry. This would be helped by a study of the theological perspective of the Eastern churches in relation both to priesthood and to marriage.

The present study focuses on the theological relationship between the ordained ministry and celibacy, starting from the way it has been understood in history, and presenting the theological foundation for this relationship. Finally, it attempts a tentative theological exploration, as a basis for further discussion, of whether celibacy belongs to the sacrament of holy orders.

THE ORDAINED MINISTRY AND CELIBACY IN HISTORY

The whole journey of the Church has been marked by a connection, in different forms, between the ordained ministry and the celibacy or continence of ministers. It is not a uniform connection, but certain emphases and predominant tendencies are discernible.[3]

The Law of Celibacy

It is commonly thought that evidence for what is known as the law of celibacy dates back to the twelfth century, when in 1139 the Second Lateran Council declared marriage contracted by ordained ministers to be invalid. For centuries before this point, such a marriage had already been considered illicit, and in fact, clergy had been forbidden to marry; now it was declared invalid. It was not in fact about a law of celibacy in the sense of not ordaining married men, but rather about the fact that, in line with the whole tradition of the Church, men who were ordained could not afterward get married. At around the same time came the publication of Gratian's *Decretum* (c. 1142), which includes legislation in which the obligation of continence for the clergy was assumed. There was a progressive imposition of the rule that all those who were going to be ordained had to promise to live in continence.[4] Obviously, the need to make that promise favored the ordination of celibate men.

The legislation of the Middle Ages is in line with the approach to celibacy during the Church's first millennium, in which there are references to the subject and legislative rulings. Many ordained ministers were married and it was taken for granted that marriage was no obstacle to being ordained.[5] But some fourth-century legislation shows that sexual continence was required of those who were ordained. Canon 33 of the Council of Elvira (c. 305) states, "It has been decided to totally prohibit bishops, priests and deacons, all clergy who exercise ministry, from having relations with their wives and begetting children."[6] The Council of Carthage (419) stated that this was a teaching from the apostles that had been followed in previous centuries: "It has been duly understood that the holy Pontiffs, the priests of God and also the Levites, meaning those who are at the service of the divine sacraments, must observe perfect continence so that they may obtain simply what they ask for from God. This, which the apostles taught and which antiquity itself observed, we too maintain."[7]

To guarantee continence, specific guidelines are given on the women with whom ministers can live. Canon 3 of the Council of Nicaea had previously laid it down that members of the clergy could have a "woman companion," provided that she was "a mother, a sister, an aunt, or people who are beyond all suspicion."[8] It is taken for granted that married men can be ordained and that they do not have to live alone; but they are asked for sexual continence. This canon may reflect the insistence of some authors that the priest should separate from his wife to guarantee continence; but others declare that the ordained minister must not abandon his wife. St. Leo the Great affirms that married affection should be retained but without marital relations.[9]

The specific ways in which these rulings were followed varied considerably. The fact that the requirement of continence for priests had to be restated may show that it was not practiced perfectly, and legislation in the fifth to seventh centuries reflects a variety of opinions on the way married sacred ministers should live. The Second Council of Trullo (691) legislated on the question of celibacy for the Eastern Church, which distinguished between bishops on the one hand, and priests and deacons on the other.[10] In no case was marriage permitted after ordination. The norm previously assumed in principle and with different shades of emphasis for all clergy, was applied in general terms to bishops: sexual continence after ordination and, if they were married, separation from their wives. This rule meant that bishops tended to be chosen from among celibate men. Priests and deacons, if they were married, continued normal marital relations after ordination, observing sexual continence temporarily in preparation for liturgical service.[11]

What is known as the law of celibacy, then, relates to sexual continence; in other words, married men were ordained as a matter of course, but for a large part of the Church's tradition, ordained ministers were required to observe perfect perpetual continence. This allows us to see that the life of ordained ministers who were married was perceived as a special case. It was possibly even more demanding than celibacy, because it implied a relationship with the subject's wife, and a way of living sexuality, that were unusual and to a certain degree scandalous. There was certainly a danger of Encratism, which was combated by emphasizing the dignity and value of marriage. And from another angle, we may see a connection between this requirement of continence, and the call of Jesus to leave everything behind, even one's own family, to follow him (cf. Luke 9:23–26; 14:25–27). In the light of this direction clearly being taken by the legislation, what are the reasons for the requirement of continence on the part of ordained ministers?

Theological Reasons in the Patristic Period

The main reason for the requirement of sexual continence on the part of ordained ministers relates to the exercise of their ministry. Celebrating the sacraments requires purity for the sake of worship, the service of God. In the Old Testament, this purity did not refer principally to sexuality, but to holiness. The people needed to be holy in order to be able to serve God, who is holy (cf. Lev 11:44–45). The priests had to remain holy for their service in the temple (cf. Lev 21:21–22), and here were included all the norms of purity, mainly connected with food and ethical behavior. Within this broad sense of purity, which is a reflection of the holiness of God, sexual continence is included; the priests lived in the temple during their time of service and were therefore separated from their wives during this time (cf. 2 Cor 23:8; Luke 1:8–9).

In the patristic period, this connection between priestly service and purity was taken up and transformed by the new reality of the Christian priesthood. If Christ's priesthood is existential, and therefore permanent, then sexual continence has to be perpetual; if Christ's sacrifice is personal, then the self-sacrifice of the priest is connected to the whole person and also affects his conjugal life.[12] According to St. Jerome, the bishop's mediatory mission requires a form of life that includes a "chastity of its own," connected with the exercise of ministry, which is centered on prayer and accompanying people:

> But if laymen are commanded to abstain from intercourse with their wives for the sake of prayer, what is one to think of a bishop, who will daily offer spotless victims for his own sins and the people's?...And so, just as gentleness, patience, sobriety, moderation, abstaining from profit, hospitality, too, and kindness, ought to be found in a bishop in particular, and in an eminent way by comparison with the laity,

> so also a unique chastity and, so to speak, a priestly purity [*pudicitia sacerdotalis*] should be found in the bishop, so that he not only keeps himself from the unclean act but even from the glance of his eye and from straying in his thoughts. Let his mind be free to confect the body of Christ.... Let the bishop also be "abstinent," not only, as some think, from lust and from the embrace of a woman, but from all disturbances of the mind. Let him not be incited to wrath; let not sadness cause him to be dejected; let not fear scare him away; let him not be carried away by excessive merriment. Now abstinence is listed by the apostle among the fruits of the Spirit. And if it is demanded of everyone, how much more of the bishop, who ought to bear the vices of sinners with patience and gentleness: "console the faint-hearted, endure the weak," "render to no one evil for evil," but "overcome evil by good."[13]

These indications for bishops show that the exercise of ministry implies a form of life suited to their mission, which obviously includes different aspects. So, the requirement of perpetual continence refers us back to the understanding of the ordained ministry itself, which gives that requirement a specific form, and situates it within the totality of the life of the minister, who has to take care of all its various aspects.[14] The fathers stress mediation between God and humanity. The minister is a mediator, in union with Christ the Mediator. This mission of mediation demands total personal commitment. Continence expresses this total commitment to God and is a means to achieve its purpose. This approach starts from St. Paul's idea that continence facilitates prayer (cf. 1 Cor 7:5) and greater personal consecration to God (cf. 1 Cor 7:32). Therefore, it is understood that celibacy and continence are in harmony with the meaning of the priesthood as mediation between God and humanity.

The patristic writings constantly stress the superiority of virginity over marriage, because of its total consecration to God and because of its eschatological significance. Virginity is an appropriate form and a clear and fruitful sign of total love of God and self-surrender "for the kingdom of heaven" (Matt 19:12). Nevertheless, the fathers show high appreciation of the dignity and greatness of marriage, and also defend it against Encratism, which rejected sexuality, the body, and marriage.

As we have seen, then, in the first millennium, celibacy in the strict sense was not compulsory for ordained ministers. However, stress was laid on the need for sexual continence for the exercise of sacramental mediation between God and humankind. Ministers were asked for a special approach to marital relations, whether temporarily or in perpetuity. This points toward celibacy in the strict sense of not being already married or getting married, because a marriage in which the couple renounced sexual relations and children is something of an anomaly. Admittedly, some of the motives behind this were ambiguous and appear to reflect a negative view of human sexuality. What was known as ritual purity or purity for the sake of worship has a healthy theological meaning but may hide attitudes that are inconsistent with anthropology correctly understood. Anthropological and theological study is needed to unmask such motives and attitudes and throw light on the reasons underpinning the right way to practice priestly celibacy.

THEOLOGICAL FOUNDATIONS OF PRIESTLY CELIBACY

Clearly, the ordained ministry is specially linked to continence and hence to celibacy. What are the theological reasons that have led to the maintaining of this link, in one form or another, down through the ages? In short, what is the theological foundation of priestly celibacy?

"Many-Faceted Suitability"

Vatican II taught clearly that perfect, perpetual continence "is not demanded by the very nature of the priesthood," although "celibacy has a many-faceted suitability for the priesthood."[15] Two aspects of tradition are here being maintained in balance: the ordained ministry does not absolutely exclude marriage and it is possible to be a priest when married; but the priesthood has a special affinity with celibacy and what it signifies, and this is why celibacy is appropriate for ordained ministers and the law of celibacy is maintained in the Latin Church.

This appropriateness is shown in different aspects, not only theological but also spiritual and pastoral. However, it is not based mainly on practical or functional reasons; it is based on theological reasons that connect celibacy with what the apostolic ministry means for the Church and for the priest himself. This is why St. John Paul II said that "it is especially important that the priest understands the theological motivation of the Church's law on celibacy."[16] There are theological reasons for different aspects of chastity, like total self-giving to God and identification with Christ the Bridegroom and with his Church; but the reasons for priestly celibacy are shaped by the sacrament of holy orders. The sacramental configuration of the ordained minister has consequences for his personal life and is the basis of his ministerial celibacy. The recent magisterium and theology emphasize the christological, ecclesiological, and eschatological dimensions of ministerial celibacy.[17] What follows is a reflection on some aspects of the theological dimensions of celibacy.

Identification with Christ

The mission of the ordained minister presupposes personal, ontological, and existential identification with Christ, sharing in his evangelizing mission:

> For the whole priestly mission is dedicated to the service of a new humanity which Christ, the victor over death, has aroused through his Spirit in the world and which has its origin "not of blood, nor of the will of the flesh, nor of the will of man but of God" (*Jn* 1:13). Through virginity, then, or celibacy observed for the Kingdom of Heaven, priests are consecrated to Christ by a new and exceptional reason. They adhere to him more easily with an undivided heart. (PO 16)

Jesus brought about a new humanity in himself and inaugurated the eschatological age in the world. His humanity is complete and full, the model and destiny of all men created in him (cf. Col 1:16). This new humanity of Jesus means the fullness of life, which is accomplished in the loving gift of himself to God the Father and to humankind. He is life (cf. John 6:35; 14:6), he gives life (cf. John 7:38; 10:10), and his life is the achievement of the plenitude of human being. Thus his love for men is the gift of the eternal love of God to this world. His love, to the extreme of giving up his life, offers the fullness of humanity in the world, the eschatological achievement of God's love. Identifying oneself with Jesus implies loving as Jesus does and fulfilling in one's own life the form of humanity that Jesus brings.

The christological reason for celibacy includes at its root the eschatological dimension, not only as a sign of the future life but mainly as the personal realization in history of the greatest love that irrupted into the world. This love means service to others (cf. Mark 10:45; John 13:1–20), giving one's life for one's friends (cf. John 15:9–17), and forgiving one's enemies (cf. Luke 6:35–36; 23:34). This love of Jesus is lived out in marriage; but being conformed to Christ and consecrated to the pastoral ministry are expressed in a special way by identifying one's life with the way he actually loved, by being celibate as he was. Love for Jesus and passion for the kingdom fill one's life to such an extent that they imply a radical option, leaving no room for any other; this is why there are people who do not get married (cf. Matt 19:12).[18] If the apostolic ministry configures a man with Jesus as head and shepherd, it has an affinity with celibacy, because celibacy signifies consecration with Jesus to the apostolic mission and the configuration of one's own life to the life that Jesus lived.

In this christological and eschatological meaning of celibacy as personal identification with Christ and total consecration to the apostolic ministry, we can see that celibacy is theologically appropriate for the ordained ministry, though not absolutely necessary. It seems that celibacy is the state that most adequately achieves identity with the historic form of Jesus's love and with the mission of the apostolic ministry.

Ecclesial Configuration of the Ministerial Life

The pastoral mission of ordained ministers entails a special relationship with the Church: they are dedicated to serving for the sake of building up the Church and of the growth of the Christian community. Identification with Christ's mission engenders a special link with the Church, with total commitment and self-surrender to the Church and to the life of the Christian community. This ecclesial commitment has been presented as a spousal gift of self.[19] Identification with Jesus brings with it union with his Church, whose head and spouse he is and for which he gave himself and gave up his life. The ordained minister unites himself to the Church and surrenders himself totally to serving it. This full self-surrender is spousal in its form and implies a type of exclusivity. For this reason, the celibate life is the most adequate expression of commitment to the Church and the pastoral mission of building up the Christian community.

The ecclesial dimension of celibacy implies that in the Christian community the ordained minister loves and is loved. He is not called to loneliness but to communion and to the mission of generating communion. The community in which the ordained minister lives out his dedication is a source of fruitfulness for himself also. Johann Adam Möhler emphasized this community and family aspect of priestly life.[20] The greatest spiritual problem for many priests probably does not lie in their renunciation of marriage and a family of their own, but the lack of a living Christian community in which to dedicate themselves, in which to be loved as a celibate person, in which to be valued for their ministry. Christian communities need ministers who are totally dedicated to their ministry, with evangelical faithfulness and pastoral love; ministers need living communities in which to minister and be loved. Ministers also need the love of the Church in the concrete form of their Christian community, in which they can share their lives and receive the gifts of affection, care and company from others. The ecclesial community belongs to the identity of the priestly life.

This ecclesial dimension of celibacy presupposes an ecclesiological understanding of the sacrament of holy orders.[21] Ordained ministers are in the midst of the Church and at the service of the Church to shape it not according to their personal life but according to him who is the head of the Church. Configuration with Jesus brings with it an ecclesial form for the ordained minister, in the service of the Church and according to the needs of the Church. As against individualistic and narcissistic tendencies, celibacy is a form of life that should shape the lives of ministers, from the standpoint of the ecclesial community and for the service of others.

A Form of Loving

Ecclesial celibacy has a christological basis, meaning, and form. It needs to be understood beginning from Jesus himself and his life, from his personal mystery, and to be personally configured with him. It is not therefore, fundamentally, a renunciation or state of remaining single or remaining continent: it is a way of loving and being loved, which has to be shaped by a personal relationship with Christ and in order to love others.[22] The Church understands that celibacy is "an incentive to charity, and is certainly a particular source of spiritual fecundity in the world" (LG 43; cf. PO 16). If it is not understood as a human way of loving and is seen mainly as a renunciation of marriage and family, it will be difficult to understand its meaning, and to live by it. The celibate person does not renounce love; he loves in a different way from married people. Celibacy is a way of loving in which there is true human fulfillment and a true expression of sexuality. Therefore, it does not mean the amputation of something human but a fully human way of living. If a person does not love, he is not celibate, because celibacy is a way of loving other people. Love for Jesus and the Church also involves love for the people one lives with, works with, and meets.[23]

This way of loving is alternative and complementary to marriage.[24] Someone who is celibate, and especially an ordained minister, expresses feelings, shares his life with others, performs acts of charity and help for others, shows solidarity with everyone and especially the poor and the unloved, aims for everyone to be included in the community, favors the freedom that includes people without producing dependency.... Living in celibacy means loving, in a different way from marriage, but in a very real and human way.[25]

The life of Jesus, who is celibate, sheds light on this way of loving. That shows the need for a theological consideration of Jesus's celibacy. Jesus's way of loving, his emotions, his sexuality, his feeling, and his commitments all shaped his human life.[26] An adequate understanding of priestly celibacy demands a theological study of Jesus's way of loving. Christian spirituality pursues identification with the whole of Jesus's humanity, because the whole of his life is theologically relevant and important. Loving in a celibate way, Jesus is fully human, and therefore he includes all human beings and identifies himself with them. He is in solidarity with those who are married because he loves in a fully human way, and married people find in him their model for the way to love one another in marriage. Meanwhile the apostolic ministry configures the subject especially to the mission of Jesus as head of humankind and the Church, so that loving in celibacy harmonizes with the mission of bringing into being a new race of humanity in communion.

SACRAMENTAL MEANING OF CELIBACY

It may be seen that there is a theological foundation for speaking of the appropriateness of celibacy for the apostolic ministry. The next point aims to offer a theological exploration of whether celibacy may be an existential element of the sacrament of holy orders.[27]

Sacramental Representation of Christ—Head and Shepherd

The sacramentality of the apostolic ministry is centered on the representation of Christ as head and shepherd of the Church (cf. PDV 14–15).[28] Bishops, and priests in communion with their bishop, make Christ sacramentally present in this dimension of his personal mystery. By their ordination, ministers are configured to Christ the Shepherd who loves by giving his life for humankind and by that love brings a community to birth.

This sacramentality presupposes the humanity of the ordained minister who represents Jesus sacramentally in his own identity and with his personal life. He is the sacrament of Jesus precisely in his personal singularity, not by being diluted or changed into something different, but by configuring his personal life with Jesus. The sacramentality maintains his difference from Jesus, whom he represents. Precisely by being different, he makes Jesus truly present in the midst of the Church, because he is personally his sacrament.[29]

This difference from Jesus, whom he represents, is evident in the acts of preaching the word, celebrating the sacraments, and guiding the community, because the word of God, the gift of Christ's paschal mystery, and his pastoral love are made present by the minister's speech and actions. Jesus becomes present and acts in the measure in which the minister acts, being himself and carrying out his ministry with his own personality. This suggests that the fact of being Christ's sacrament demands an existential configuration of the whole person, who has to be a sacramental sign. This aspect of the minister's sacramentality is especially notable when he presides at the eucharistic liturgy. The person who says "This is my body" is the minister, but he represents Christ and it is Christ who gives himself up sacramentally and who says it to the community that is celebrating the Eucharist. The minister is not showing his own body but the body of Christ, who is the one who is received in the Eucharist. But because he represents Jesus sacramentally, when he says "This is my body," the minister must also configure his body with that of Jesus, and give himself up personally to the community like Jesus and with him. Jesus's self-giving and his style of life also become present through the self-giving and style of life of the person who represents him sacramentally. Thus, the sacrament of holy orders, with its special connection to the Eucharist, generates a way of living and a state of life.[30] The ordained minister is not Christ, but he represents him sacramentally, and so conforms his life with Christ. That ministerial life, a eucharistic life in a special way, takes shape in the practicing of Jesus's pastoral charity.[31]

Pastoral Charity

In connection with the sacramental representation of Christ, John Paul II explains that "priests are called to prolong the presence of Christ, the one high priest, embodying his way of life and making him visible in the midst of the flock entrusted to their care" (PDV 15). The ordained minister represents Jesus in "his pastoral charity" (cf. PO 14; PDV 22–23). This pastoral charity means a love that is concerned for people, knows them and makes itself known to them, cares for and protects them, brings community into being and fosters communion, seeks out the lost and helps those in difficulties; it is the love of someone who gives up his life as a gift and thus gives life to others (cf. Jer 23:1–3; Ezek 34; Ps 23; John 10:1–18). This pastoral love of Jesus becomes real and living in the community through the sacrament of holy orders. Therefore, the person who receives this sacrament must configure his life with Christ in order to love like him and with him, and to serve like him and with him.[32] And the way Jesus loved was in celibacy, in which the pastoral charity belonging to the apostolic ministry takes concrete form.

One aspect of Jesus's love is its spousal dimension. This spousal character of God's love and Christ's self-sacrifice for his Church is shown sacramentally in marriage, which belongs to the theological identity of the Church. In the sacrament of holy orders, however, it is Jesus's pastoral love that is shown sacramentally. This "pastoral charity" involves a special bond with the Church and a way of relating to and loving people as Jesus did (cf. PDV 22).

Existential Form of the Sacrament

As has been stressed, celibacy is essentially a way of loving and not simply a discipline or mere absence of sexual relations. Celibacy and marriage are two different and complementary ways of loving. Christ's love took the form of celibacy. Those who sacramentally represent Christ as head and shepherd and make his pastoral love present must love as he loved so that the sacrament signifies truthfully.[33]

Just as other sacraments possess specific human forms, the apostolic ministry possesses Jesus's way of loving, which we can call celibacy. The sacraments configure a person's existence, presupposing certain forms of life and enabling them. They are related with faith and with the actual lives of those who receive them.[34] Thus, the sacraments of Christian initiation presuppose personal conversion and living according to the gospel; the sacrament of penance involves the conversion of the sinner, who repents and lives on God's path; the anointing of the sick is received in a situation of personal suffering endured in union with Jesus's cross; the sacrament of marriage involves the love between husband and wife. Every sacrament gives form to a sacramental existence. The sacrament of holy orders signifies the representing of Christ as head and shepherd and therefore it configures the subject's life to the way Christ the shepherd loved. This pastoral way of loving is expressed in the celibacy of the minister, which has a conformation of its own, stemming precisely from pastoral charity.[35]

Loving like Jesus, the ordained minister makes the pastoral love of Jesus present—Jesus who gives his life for love and thus brings to life a community whose head he is. The sacramental representation of Jesus in the apostolic ministry has an essential reference to the Christian community, in which the ordained minister represents Christ as its head, that is, as its foundation and source of its life, as its shepherd and Lord. The figure of the ordained minister cannot be understood without reference to Jesus's pastoral love, of which he is the personal sacrament, and without the community of Jesus, in which he represents him sacramentally. And thus, he loves his brethren in the community like Jesus and with Jesus.

Can it be maintained that celibacy belongs to the reality of the sacrament of holy orders in terms of the existential form of the sacrament? The sacramental dynamic includes a human element in which Christ's mystery is made present. To make the pastoral love of Christ who brings into being a living community sacramentally present, the recipient of the sacrament of holy orders loves like Christ whom he represents: that is, he loves in a celibate way. Thus, the celibacy of ordained ministers is linked to the sacramental condition of their ministry and the Christian community that gives that sacramental ministry its meaning.

To take another angle, the sacraments are a manifestation and realization of the Church. Both marriage and, in its own way, celibacy belong to the structure of the Church, which is a Bride because it is united to Christ, Mother because it gives the life of faith, and Virgin because it maintains the faith in fidelity to the Gospel (cf. LG 64). Married love signifies a sacramental realization of the being of the Church. Celibacy is a sign of the eschatological destiny of humankind, and of a personal bond with Jesus who was celibate; a sign that is expressed especially clearly in the apostolic ministry. The sacramental expression of virginity within the Church may be recognized in the celibacy of those who exercise the apostolic ministry, sacramentally representing Christ, head and shepherd of the Church.[36] Thus it may indeed be held that celibacy belongs to the sacramental sign of the ordained ministry as the human way of loving in which Jesus's pastoral love is made present.

CONCLUSION

This theological exploration of whether celibacy belongs to the sacrament of holy orders leaves some important aspects open. Among them, a basic field for reflection is this sacrament's unity and diversity in the episcopate, the priesthood, and the diaconate, and how this unity and diversity affect the subject of ministerial celibacy. It would be necessary to go deeper into the relationship of marriage with Jesus's way of loving. Thinking about celibacy would also be helped by continued reflection on Jesus's emotional life and its theological and ecclesiological meaning. It will always be necessary to consider the anthropological, psychological, educational, moral, and pastoral aspects, which to a certain extent underlie theological reflection on celibacy and can enrich it. Study of the question from the viewpoint of canon law is indispensable to gain a deeper understanding of the canonical meaning of celibacy and its various aspects and possibilities.[37]

The Church does not currently teach that celibacy necessarily belongs to the sacrament of holy orders, but I consider that it harmonizes with the Church's understanding of the apostolic ministry. There are aspects that can be successively discovered as the understanding of faith and tradition grows. In the current discussion, I am not requesting a declaration that priestly celibacy is essential to the Christian faith, or that the law of celibacy is part of divine law. I have aimed to look more deeply at celibacy's theological link with the sacrament of holy orders. There are clear reasons why it is appropriate, but perhaps they are not quite sufficient for making celibacy obligatory. In other words, perhaps the law of celibacy needs to be based on weightier theology in order to be upheld in its full strength.

Living in celibacy involves difficulties and dangers; but, like every way of loving, it is a source of fruitfulness for the person concerned and for others. The apostolic ministry represents Christ sacramentally in the middle of the ecclesial community. Like Christ and with Christ, ordained ministers must love to the extreme of giving up their lives. In this christological, ecclesial, and sacramental sense, it can be truly said that there is a strong link between the sacrament of holy orders and celibacy.

NOTES

1. I will be talking about the ordained ministry, the apostolic ministry, the priesthood, priests, and ordained ministers, without making any clear distinctions. All these terms refer, with differing shades of emphasis, to the sacrament of holy orders, whose connection with celibacy is the subject being looked at here. The present discussion of holy orders and celibacy may serve as a basis for further studies of the exact relationship of celibacy to the episcopate, to the priesthood, and to the diaconate.

2. Cf. H. Wolf, *Zölibat. 16 Thesen* (Munich: Beck, 2019). Although I do not share the book's approach or many of its ideas, I am grateful to the author for this clear and well-reasoned presentation of the main reasons against celibacy.

3. Cf. L. Hödl, "Die *Lex continentiae*. Eine problemgeschichtliche Studie über den Zölibatin," *Zeitschrift für Katholische Theologie* 83 (1961): 325–44. R. Gryson, *Les Origines du célibat ecclésiastique du premier au septième siècle* (Gembloux: Duculot, 1970). A. M. Stickler, "El celibato eclesiástico. Su historia y sus fundamentos teológicos," *Scripta Theologica* 26 (1994): 13–77. C. Cochini, *Les Origines apostoliques du célibat sacerdotal* (Geneva: Ad Solem, 2006). G. Denzler, *Die Geschichte des Zölibats* (Freiburg: Herder, 2016).

4. Cf. Hödl, "Die *Lex continentiae*," 339–43. Stickler, "El celibatoeclesiástico," 38–42. Cf. A. M. Stickler, "The Evolution of the Discipline of Celibacy in the Western Church from the End of the Patristic Era to the Council of Trent," in *Priesthood and celibacy*, ed. J. Coppens (Milan: Ancora, 1971), 503–97 (orig. ed. *Sacerdoce et célibat: Études historiques et théologiques* [Louvain: Peeters, 1971]).

5. At the end of his document on chastity Tertullian states that many ordained men also practiced continence, which implies that it was not compulsory, but he also states that there had been celibate priests ever since the first centuries. "How many men and women who live in continence are to be found in the ecclesiastical orders, who preferred to espouse themselves to God, who have restored the honour of their flesh, who are called children of that time, here and now, dying to the concupiscence of desire and to all that which cannot be admitted into paradise?" Tertullian, *De exhortatione castitatis* 13 (PL 2, 930A).

6. Quoted by Cochini, *Les Origines apostoliques*, 184.

7. Cochini, *Les Origines apostoliques*, 296.

8. Cochini, *Les Origines apostoliques*, 211.

9. "In order that their wedlock may become spiritual instead of carnal, it behooves them not to put away their wives but to have them as though they had them not, whereby both the affection of their wives may be retained and the marriage functions cease," Leo the Great, *Letter 167 to Rusticus* (PL 54, 1204A). St. Gregory the Great includes the wife among the women with whom the ordained minister may live, in a chaste relationship. "We desire that the priests who abide in Corsica shall be forbidden to have any connection with women, unless it is a mother, or a sister, or a wife, towards whom chastity should be observed." Gregory the Great, *Epistola* 52 (PL 77, 515A).

10. Cf. Cochini, *Les Origines apostoliques*, 431–46.

11. In the Latin Church this has applied since Vatican II to "permanent deacons," though with no reference to continence. Cf. Vatican II, *Lumen Gentium* (LG) 29.

12. "A layman, or any believer, cannot pray unless he abstains from sexual intercourse. Now a priest must always offer sacrifices for the people: he must therefore always pray. And if he must always pray, he must always be released from the duties of marriage." Jerome, *Adversus Jovinianum* I, 33 (PL 23, 257B). "You know that the ministerial office must be kept pure and unspotted, and must not

be defiled by conjugal intercourse; you…who have received the gifts of the sacred ministry, with pure bodies, and unspoiled modesty." AMBROSE OF MILAN, *De officiis ministrorum* I, 50 (258) (PL 16, 97B–98A).

13. JEROME, *Commentariorum in epistolam ad Titum* I, v. 8–9 (PL 26,568D. 569A. 569B-C).

14. Cf. CROUZEL, "Celibacy and Ecclesiastical Continence in the Early Church: The Motives Involved," in COPPENS, *Priesthood and Celibacy*, 451–502.

15. *Presbyterorum Ordinis* (PO) 16.

16. *Pastores Dabo Vobis* (PDV) 29.

17. PAUL VI, *Sacerdotalis Caelibatus*, June 24, 1967, 17–34. John Paul II, *The Theology of Marriage & Celibacy: Catechesis on Marriage and Celibacy in the Light of the Resurrection of the Body* (Liverpool: Pauline Books & Media, 1986). M. THURIAN, "Fondazione teologica del celibato sacerdotale," in *Solo per amore. Riflessioni sul celibato sacerdotale*, ed. C. SEPE and M. PIACENZA (Turin: Paoline, 1993), 48–59. T. MCGOVERN, *Priestly Celibacy Today* (New York: Scepter, 1998), 117ff. M. HAUKE, "Die Verbindung zwischen Amtspriestertum und Zölibat. Eine theologische Bestandsaufnahme," *Forum Katholische Theologie* 27 (2011): 1–30. T. WOJTAL, *Come Cristo Sposo della Chiesa. Aspetti dogmatici del celibato sacerdotale* (Siena: Cantagalli, 2015), 253–348. G. SELIN, *Priestly Celibacy: Theological Foundations* (Washington, DC: Catholic University of America, 2016), 105–66. A. ARANDA, "La encíclica *Sacerdotalis caelibatus* cincuenta años después," in *El celibato cristiano. Una vida plena y fecunda*, ed. J.-L. CABALLERO (Madrid: Palabra, 2019), 75–108.

18. Cf. E. SCHILLEBEECKX, *Celibacy* (New York: Sheed and Ward, 1968).

19. Cf. PO 16. PDV 29. WOJTAL, *Come Cristo Sposo della Chiesa*, 284–91. L. TOUZE, *L'avenir du célibat sacerdotal et sa logique sacramentelle* (Paris: Parole et Silence, 2009), 75–220. L. TOUZE, "Las edades del celibato: madurar con, por y en Cristo. Estudios recientes sobre la teología del celibato sacerdotal," *Scripta Theologica* 50 (2018): 99–119; 107–13. M. OUELLET, *Friends of the Bridegroom: For a Renewed Vision of Priestly Celibacy* (Irondale, AL: EWTN Publishing, 2019).

20. See J. A. MÖHLER, *The Spirit of Celibacy* (1828; repr., Chicago: Hillenbrand Books, 2007), 69–74. "The profound joy to be derived from being honoured and loved as the father of a whole community as you carry them all within your heart, watch over the growth of the scattered divine seed, and see fruits for heaven ripen under your hands—that is something which can only be appreciated by those who see it or experience it for themselves.…Love is the measure of love. It is in the nature of things that the person who divides his heart between a wife and a community simply cannot expect to receive the same degree of warmth and tenderness of feeling from the community as the one who is exclusively devoted to them. The more excellent the pastor of souls, the more inward his relationship to the community, the more comprehensive and the fuller his delight," 70.

21. Cf. G. Richi Alberti, *In sinu Populi Dei. Espiritualidad presbiteral tras los pasos del Vaticano II* (Madrid: Universidad San Dámaso, 2015), 68–100. M. Marini, *Il celibato sacerdotale. Apostolica vivendi forma* (Siena: Cantagalli, 2005), 11–58.

22. "Celibacy is renunciation. But that renunciation is only the reverse side of an affirmation, because a life cannot be built only on a renunciation. The personal experience of the love of Christ has to be what motivates every option for celibacy for the sake of the kingdom of heaven.... Everything depends on a living relationship with Christ. Just as every inter-personal relationship lives by personal contact, so too does the relationship with Christ." K.-H. Menke, "Das sakramentale Amt in der Kirche," in *Aktuelle Herausforderungen des kirchlichen Weiheamts*, ed. C. Ohly, S. L. Conrad and R. Hangler (Regensburg: Pustet, 2020), 103.

23. In a novel by Emilia Pardo Bazán published in 1887, the curate of Ulloa explained why he avoided seeing a particular person too much by saying, "If someone marries, it is right and good for him to love his children above all things, after God; but a priest, and especially a parish priest, has to be a father to all his sheep, because that is his office...and not love any one person in particular, in order to be able to love all of them, and love them not in himself but in Christ, who is his true model." E. Pardo Bazán, *La madrenaturaleza* II, chapter 15 (Eng. ed. *Mother Nature* [1887; repr., Lewisburg, PA: Bucknell University Press, 2010]).

24. On the meaning and experience of ministerial celibacy as love, one of the best and most enlightening reflections is that of J. M. Uriarte, *Celibacy: Anthropological, Spiritual and Pedagogical Considerations* (Maliaño: Sal Terrae, 2018, 2015). Cf. A. Cencini, *Por amor, con amor, en el amor. Libertad y madurez afectiva en el celibato consagrado* (Salamanca: Sígueme, 2001). K. Berger, *Der Zölibat. Eine theologische Neubegründung* (Heiligenkreuz: Be&Be, 2012). S. Guarinelli, *El celibato de los sacerdotes. ¿Por qué elegirlo todavía?* (Salamanca: Sígueme, 2015). C. Griffin, "The Anthropological Witness of Celibacy," *Scripta Theologica* 50, no. 1 (2018): 121–38.

25. "Virginity and marriage are, and must be, different ways of loving. For 'man cannot live without love.'" Pope Francis, *Amoris Laetitia*, March 19, 2016, 161.

26. Cf. A. Amato, *Il celibato di Gesù* (Vatican City: Libreria Editrice Vaticana, 2010). S. Voorwinde, *Jesus' Emotions in the Gospels* (New York: T&T Clark, 2011). E. Durand, *Les émotions de Dieu. Indices d'engagement* (Paris: Éditions du Cerf, 2019). F. García Martínez, "Me has dado un cuerpo...Jesucristo y el cuerpo humano," *Ciencia Tomista* 148 (2021): 47–79.

27. There are some studies arguing for this sacramental approach, although they do not entirely match what is being set out here. Cf. J. Galot, "Sacerdoce et célibat," *Nouvelle revue théologique* 86 (1964): 114–36. D. Massimino, "Il carattere teologico-sacramentale del celibato sacerdotale alla luce del recente magistero,"

Divinitas 61 (2018): 169–92. M. del Pozzo, "La *ratio* e le esigenze della castità sacerdotale nella società secolarizzata," *Annales theologici* 34 (2020): 59–90.

28. *Pastores Dabo Vobis* speaks of configuration with Christ as head, shepherd, servant and spouse. What is most clearly emphasized is that priests fundamentally represent Christ as head and shepherd. On the sacramentality of the ordained ministry, cf. Menke, "Das sakramentale Amt in der Kirche," 85–108. G. Greshake, *Ser sacerdote hoy. Teología, praxis pastoral y espiritualidad* (Salamanca: Sígueme, 2003), 121–79 (new ed. *Priester sein in dieser Zeit: Theologie—pastorale Praxis—Spiritualität* [Würzburg: Echter, 2005]). S. del Cura Elena, "Sacramentalidad del ministerio ordenado: alcance teológico y relevancia espiritual," *Revista española de Teología* 70 (2010): 293–332. A. Cordovilla, *"Como el Padre me envió, así os envío yo." Teología y espiritualidad del ministerio apostólico presbiteral* (Salamanca: Sígueme, 2019), 135–75.

29. On the idea of sacramentality cf. K.-H. Menke, *Sakramentalität: Wesen und Wunde des Katholizismus* (Regensburg: Pustet, 2012), 74–125.

30. Cf. L. Trujillo Díaz, "Secularidad: espiritualidad, estilo y estado," in Comisión Episcopal del Clero & Comisión Episcopal de Seminarios y Universidades, *Presbiterado y secularidad* (Madrid: EDICE, 1999), 135–79.

31. "Pastoral charity, which has its specific source in the sacrament of holy orders, finds its full expression and its supreme nourishment in the Eucharist" (PDV 23). Cf. Selin, *Priestly Celibacy*, 144–51.

32. On the theological and spiritual meaning of pastoral charity cf. J. M. Uriarte, *Ministerio presbiteral y espiritualidad* (San Sebastián: Idatz, 1999), 53–77. J. M. Uriarte, *Visibilizar a Cristo Pastor. Cuatro rasgos de la espiritualidad sacerdotal* (Maliaño: Sal Terrae, 2021), 33–68.

33. "The requirement of chastity on the part of the minister is not linked to the choice or virtuous decision of the subject, but to the dignity of the sign. The importance of the sacrament of holy orders (considering its derivation and orientation to the Eucharist) is such that it demands a full, complete conformation of the person in terms of enabling and offering." Pozzo, "La *ratio* e le esigenze della castità sacerdotale," 70.

34. Cf. International Theological Commission, *The Reciprocity between Faith and Sacraments in the Sacramental Economy* (Vatican City: Libreria Editrice Vaticana, 2021).

35. Cf. Uriarte, *Celibacy*, 109–25.

36. A consideration by Möhler on Christian love in marriage and in celibacy points in this direction: "But now in Christianity the highest can be attained without marriage, as Christ and Paul said and as both showed in their lives, so the necessity of celibacy was given along with the possibility. All phenomena that are *possible* through the Christian principle *must* become a reality. All the attacks on celibate priesthood amount to nothing, simply because celibate priesthood is in fact a necessity. This is the most profound reason for the fact that ascetics and

then monks made their appearance with the beginnings of the Christian Church. Abstracting from the fact that the priestly state tends of itself to celibacy, celibacy became established only in the priestly order because whereas the monastic orders may disappear—as in the greater part of Germany—there are always priests in the Church." Möhler, *The Spirit of Celibacy*, 82. Cf. H. U. von Balthasar, *Ensayos teológicos* IV, *Pneuma e institución* (Madrid: Encuentro, 2008), 305–16.

37. Cf. Redazione di QDE, "Il celibato: solo una legge? Alcune recenti riflessioni sul fondamento del celibato ecclesiastico," *Quaderni di diritto ecclesiale* 34 (2021): 295–322.

23

MINISTERIAL PRIESTHOOD AND CONSECRATED LIFE

BISHOP PAOLO MARTINELLI, OFM, CAP.

THE RELATIONSHIP BETWEEN the ministerial priesthood and consecrated life is a long one in the history of the Church. It has passed through several phases, between harmony and moments of tension.[1] The relationship involves two fundamental aspects: on one hand, the interaction between these two vocational forms; and on the other hand, the singular figure of the priest who belongs to an institution of consecrated life, in particular, the "religious priesthood."[2]

Ministerial priesthood and consecrated life are two different states of life which were originally tied to the mystery of the person of Christ, the supreme priest of the new alliance, who lived his mission obedient to the Father, poor and chaste. We consider them two vocations of "special consecration" in reference to the *fundamental person, the faithful,* fully initiated into Christian life (baptism, confirmation, and Eucharist).

In this presentation, we primarily limit ourselves to defining some problems and perspectives that have emerged recently in relation to consecrated life and ministerial priesthood and indicate some observations on the figure of the priest religious as an emblematic condition wherein ministerial priesthood and religious consecration coincide in the same person.

MINISTERIAL PRIESTHOOD AND CONSECRATED LIFE AND THE STATES OF LIFE OF THE CHRISTIAN

As far as the first category is concerned, it is important to observe how, from a perspective of modern history, the relationship between ministerial priesthood and consecrated life can be seen paradoxically through the relationship of these forms of life with the lay state and the sense of the common priesthood of the faithful. For this reason, it is important to refer to some events in modern history that have called into question the relationship between the different vocational forms.[3]

Key Questions at the Beginning of Modernity

Not coincidentally, at the beginning of the sixteenth century, at the Protestant Reformation,[4] starting with the principles of "sola Scriptura," "sola fide," and "sola gratia" calls into question the traditional Christian states of life, not recognizing the sacramental nature of priestly orders[5] and the religious monastic state, connected to the practice of the evangelical counsels that were understood to acquire merit before God through a *votum*.[6] Consequently, baptismal priesthood was radically emphasized. The same reference to the cultic character of the Christian experience and of the priesthood tends to transform itself with a prophetic character, more closely tied to the preaching of the word than to the celebration of the eucharistic sacrifice.

In its detailed work, the Council of Trent reaffirmed sacred Tradition, apostolic succession, the necessity of the priesthood characterized by a specific sacrament, that of orders. From the subsequent theological reflection, the theme of the baptismal priesthood was not particularly emphasized, given the substantially antihierarchical use that arose from it, carried out by the Protestant Reformation. While in the Roman Catechism, there is some discussion of an "interior priesthood," in the chapter dedicated to the ordained priesthood, the theme is, however, not taken up again.[7] Along with this, in the same Council's decree on marriage, canon 10 affirms the traditional "excellence" of virginity over marriage; it is recognized in its sacramental value.[8]

This situation was further complicated by the complex process of secularization,[9] which has the division between the Reformation and the Catholic Church as one of its fundamental causes, since the unity of the European conscious regarding faith was no longer present, and indeed the Christian universalism experienced during the previous centuries was put into crisis. Thus, *new universal projects emancipated from faith*[10] emerged, elaborated *etsideus non daretur*, to dominate over Christian confessions, now in open conflict among themselves.

Here, one should first note the great cultural transformation of the very word *lay*,[11] which went from indicating the simple believer, a member of the people of God, to designating someone who moves independently from the Christian faith, if not in contrast to it. The concepts of the "world," "human nature," "freedom," and "reason" along with the sense of history, grow ever distant from the Christian value.

In responding to the provocation of modernity, Catholic theology could not completely avoid assuming the categories of the position that it wished to combat. This fate, as is well-known, is described by the studies of de Lubac on the question of the supernatural.[12] The Jesuit theologian shows how the Catholic position to save the supernatural character of the Christian faith has often risked excessively separating grace from nature, giving origin in theology to extrincism.[13] Because of this process, we progressively see an overshadowing of the *baptismal subjectivity of the Christian layperson*, increasingly understood in passive terms.

This is also the time when a certain clericalization of the consecrated male life will develop, emblematic of this is how culturally capable religious people are mainly only introduced in ecclesiastical studies, almost always in view of holy orders, with a growing weakness of the figure of the religious and not clerical "brother," which in certain ways remains in our day.[14] According to a provocative affirmation by von Balthasar, in the modern age we witness the formation of religious people who are "experts in the supernatural"[15] with a substantial lack of nonpresbyteral "professionality," unlike in the past. In the same years, Romano Guardini made the same observation for the entire Church, which "became increasingly poor in secular content, limiting itself in an increasingly exclusive way to a purely religious doctrine and practice."[16]

Successive Developments

Emblematically, starting at the beginnings of the twentieth century, we find some attempts on the part of the specially consecrated vocations to reestablish a connection with the lay condition. On the part of the clerical state, this dynamic moves in at least two directions: chiefly to promotion of an "apostolate of laypeople" in the places where clerics can no longer arrive, not yet as an expression of Christian laity, but as an extension of the cleric where he no longer has access because of secularization.[17] And second, the desire of the priest to assume lay tasks in the first person also arises: the most emblematic case in this direction is the movement of the worker priests, which fully concerns religious priests as well.[18]

In the category of consecrated life as well, strongly characterized up to that moment by "separation" from the world, an approach to the lay condition takes place with the birth of the *secular Institutes*, recognized by the Church in 1947, with the *Provida Mater Ecclesia* and the specifications of the succeeding *motu proprio Primo Feliciter* (1948): to live the evangelical councils in the secular condition,[19] thus showing at the same time their anthropological and baptismal pertinence.

Together with these directions that were taken, one should note a certain tension between ministerial priesthood and religious life, which occurred throughout the twentieth century, from its very beginnings. First of all, we should notice the tension implied by the movement of the promotion of spirituality of the diocesan cleric (which linguistically tried to overcome the term *secular cleric*) as the highest possible grade of spirituality, as Cardinal Mercier, the Belgian primate, said in 1918, because it was founded directly by Christ while the religious orders were founded by mere men, most of them were saints. While the spirituality of the orders could appear partial and mostly pursued for personal perfections, the spirituality of the diocesan cleric would in a certain sense include all spiritualities and be the pursuit of sanctity not for oneself but for others, those in pastoral care.[20] Consequently, they resumed and amplified elements of the priestly spirituality elaborated earlier by De Bérulle in reference to the total sacrifice of oneself implied in the exercise of priestly ministry, referring to the Eucharist.[21]

A few authors have reacted to such affirmations. We remember that of von Balthasar, along with other religious theologians like J.-H.

Nicolas and L. Bouyer. Some refer to the logical and chronological precedence of "following" in respect to the ministerial task, beyond the fact that elements of the spirituality of the diocesan cleric mentioned seem, in reality, to be taken from the spirituality of the religious orders. Balthasar, as well, not without a certain controversy, notes that if the higher spirituality was that of the diocesan cleric, then Most Holy Mary and all women would remain excluded from evangelical perfection.[22]

The Second Vatican Council

The road continues, particularly with the great novelty of the *theology of the laity*, which tries to value the state of the Christian who lives in the world not as a substitute of the cleric, but with his own "secular" temperament,[23] through which his own sanctity is pursued, not "despite" the world, but really sanctifying the world and ordering it to the kingdom of God. This will be the position held by the Second Vatican Council, specifically in the fourth chapter of *Lumen Gentium* and in the decree *Apostolicam Actuositatem*.

To this is added the meaning that was already born before Vatican II of ecclesial aggregations that point to the rediscovery of baptismal and familiar spirituality as well as that which comes from the charismatic dimension of the Church.[24]

Considering the entire conciliar event, now sixty years after its beginning, its true inheritance seems to be the *theology of the faithful*.[25] This is clear from the affirmations on the *common priesthood*:[26] the theme of chapter II of *Lumen Gentium*, which precedes chapters III on the hierarchy, IV on the lay Christian, and VI on the religious. Besides, in chapter V, the *universal vocation to holiness for all the faithful* is affirmed: sanctity, discipleship, conformity to Christ, and the same eschatological character are related to the faithful and to the people of God before being related to a particular state.[27] It is, then, significant that the same evangelical counsels are discussed by *Lumen Gentium* in chapter V (39, 42), earlier than in chapter VI, *De Religiosis*, rediscovering their baptismal value.[28]

It should be further noted that religious life in the conciliar texts is essentially defined by the profession of the evangelical counsels, accepted by the authority of the Church, a state that is different from the hierarchy of the Church (LG 44). *Perfectae Caritatis* affirms that such a form of life "constitutes a complete state of the profession of the evangelical counsels" (PC 10). This makes it clear that it refers to the recovery of the identity of the consecrated life on its own and not as it refers to a role or the sacrament of ordination.[29]

From the perspective of priestly life, the conciliar reflection seems to be concentrated particularly on the ministeriality of ordination, with particular reference to the *figure of the shepherd* who cares for souls.[30] In this sense, the conciliar text does not seem to focus on the relationship between priesthood and consecrated life in such a way as to recover the specific identity of the religious person around the evangelical counsels and that of the priest around ministeriality in reference to the local Church and "pastoral charity." It is still interesting that the practice of the evangelical counsels is held to be decisive for the priest as well, as is stated in *Presbyterorum Ordinis* 15–17.[31] The circularity between the different states of life, starting with the unique baptismal vocation, is reiterated successively with particular clarity by *Christifideles Laici* 55: the dignity of every baptized person is in the ecclesiology of equal communion; every state of life is essential for each other, since each expresses in a particular way what is essential for everyone.

From this position, however, a new set of problems arises that particularly concerns consecrated life. In fact, chiefly emphasizing the pastoral commitment of the priest ("in the care of souls") and specifying the fact that lay life presents a possibility for real, full sanctification, in the postconciliar reflection, the question is posed on *the meaning of the consecrated life in relation to baptism*. The most significant risk seems to have been and still is in certain aspects that of understanding consecrated life merely as an optional variant of the common baptismal vocation.[32] Life according to the evangelical counsels would, in this minimalist perspective, certainly be a gift to the Church, but not essential, simply desirable.[33] It is clear that the magisterial documents after Vatican II never embraced this leveling position.[34] From here, the current debate is born on the theological identity of the consecrated life and its ecclesial placement.[35] How to recover this specific element of the consecrated life without losing the great conciliar enrichment around the baptismal vocation and the sacerdotal figure who cares for souls?

The Charismatic Dimension (*Iuvenescit Ecclesia*) and Spousal Love

At this point, it is useful to add to the relationship between the ministerial priesthood and consecrated life the doctrine around the charismatic dimension of the Church, rediscovered by Vatican II and developed by the reflection on the pontifical magisterium from St. John Paul II to Pope Francis, which has found its complete expression in the letter of the Congregation for the doctrine of the Faith, *Iuvenescit Ecclesia* (2016).[36]

The text's focus is on the "co-essentiality" of the relationship between hierarchical and charismatic gifts. From this perspective, it is easy to place the ministerial priesthood in the category of hierarchical gifts, tied to the sacrament of holy orders, and the consecrated life in the charismatic dimension of the Church. The relationship between the ministerial priesthood and consecrated life appears as a paradigmatic model of relationship between hierarchical and charismatic gifts. In this context, we should not forget that it was St. Paul VI in *Evangelica Testificatio* (1971) who spoke explicitly of the religious life in charismatic terms, coining the expression "charism of the founder," which would be instructional in the spiritual theology of the following decades.[37]

The charismatic dimension of the Church was taken up by the Council, primarily in chapter II of *Lumen Gentium*, dedicated to the Church as the people of God, in reference to the prophetic *munus*. The people of God is a prophetic people because it possesses the *sensus fidei* and is animated by charisms.

In this circumstance, it is not necessary to recall the neglect of the theme of charisms in the history of the Church; the term, while copiously present in the New Testament, especially in the Pauline letters, fell into wide disuse by the subapostolic era. In the history of the Church, the question of the charisms is associated with the question of the "spiritual people," which, in different ways and in different ages, grew distant from the ecclesial community and its institutions (authority, sacraments, canonical scriptures) by virtue of a presumed direct relationship with God through the gift of the Spirit.[38] In a certain sense, despite these difficulties, consecrated life has kept the knowledge of the charismatic gifts active in the Church, even in the periods of the strongest institutionalization.

The formulation in *Lumen Gentium* 12, which shows that at the origin of the hierarchical and charismatic gifts there is the action of the same Holy Spirit, is of great importance. The Holy Spirit "sanctifies and leads the people of God and enriches it with virtues...not only through the sacraments and the ministries of the Church but...distributes special graces among the faithful of every rank. These charisms, whether they be the more outstanding or the more simple and widely diffused, are to be received with thanksgiving and consolation."[39]

Although Vatican II does not use the expression *charism* to identify the religious life, when it describes the state of life composed of the profession of the evangelical counsels, it does remind us that "though it does not concern the hierarchical structure of the Church, nevertheless, it undeniably belongs to its life and holiness" (LG 44), in fact recognizing it in the charismatic dimension, as the *Evangelica Testificatio* (1971) and *Mutuae Relationes* (1978) later affirm.

Describing consecrated life in terms of the charisms seems for many to expose it to an importance it possesses, while not being constitutive of the ecclesial mystery. The same forms of consecrated life are rather different from each other; many institutes arise in different times, spread, and are then extinguished. Should the consecrated life be something that can never be renounced by the Church? To this question, *Vita Consecrata* responds first when, commenting on *Lumen Gentium* 44, it states that "the idea of a Church made up only of sacred ministers and lay people does not therefore conform to the intentions of her divine Founder, as revealed to us by the Gospels and the other writings of the New Testament" (VC 29).

In unequivocable terms, Benedict XVI reminds us that "the various religious families—from monastic life to the religious congregations and societies of apostolic life, from secular institutes to the new forms of consecration—have had their origin precisely in history, but consecrated life as such originated with the Lord himself who chose this form of virginal, poor and obedient life for himself. For this reason consecrated life can never be absent or die out in the Church: it was desired by Jesus himself as an irremovable part of his Church" (November 5, 2010).

Therefore, it is not the individual forms of consecrated life that are essential to the Church, but the witness to an obedient, poor, and chaste form of life, because this was founded by Christ Himself, who thus lived and realized his redemptive mission as a human. And therefore, also, consecrated life should refer to the person of Christ before those of the founders.

The doctrine of the coessentiality of the hierarchical and charismatic gifts becomes strict at this point, referring to the ministerial priesthood and the consecrated life. With this, one wishes to avoid two barren figures in the life of the Church: contraposition and juxtaposition. If hierarchical and charismatic gifts derive from the same Spirit, they cannot be related in terms of competition or opposition; in the same way they can also not be conceived of in a sterile parallelism where the priests fulfill their pastoral ministry while consecrated persons follow the activities proper to their own charism. Coessentiality indicates that hierarchical and charismatic gifts need each other to be themselves.

Following *Iuvenescit Ecclesia*, one can state that the task of the ordained ministry is that of guaranteeing that what the christological event has realized is offered unconditionally to the freedom of the believer, through the celebration of the sacraments (starting with the centrality of the Eucharist), the annunciation of the word, and pastoral guidance; the task of the charismatic gift, which is realized paradigmatically in the consecrated life, is to receive that gift, to accept it, to make it fertile, and "restitute" it in terms of the witness of one's life (cf. *Iuvenescit Ecclesia* 13–17).

More specifically, the ministerial priesthood has the task of representing the "objective" of Christ, starting with the eucharistic celebration, a memorial of the body given, and the blood spilled: consecrated life has the task of representing the "subjective" of Christ, the human form of his poor, chaste, and obedient existence, which at the same time constitutes the paradigmatic response of the Church to her Bridegroom.

If the ministerial priesthood is put in the category of the *exitus*: in other words, to the christological grace that reaches the believer from the Most Holy Trinity here and now, the consecrated life, and with it the entire charismatic dimension of the Church is in the category of the *reditus*, the "restitution," the spousal and loving response that makes the gift of the Spirit fertile. Clearly, hierarchical and charismatic gifts belong to each other, the gift is transmitted in order to be accepted and made fruitful.

The charisms, and in particular consecrated life, are the gifts that the Spirit gives to his Bride in order that she know how to accept fruitfully the gift that Christ the Bridegroom makes of himself to the Church. In *Vita Consecrata*, John Paul II justly states that this spousal dimension of consecration is especially incarnated in the consecrated woman (VC 34) as a peculiar expression of the "Marian principal" compared with the "Petrine principal" in reference to the ministerial priesthood.[40]

This coessential vision also has clear pastoral implications that affect even the details of the local Church. In fact, if it is true that one of the characteristics of consecrated life is universality, it is still just as true, as *Iuvenescit Ecclesia* mentions, that this does not indicate any "disincarnated dislocation" (21). The Church in its totality is always experienced through concrete immanence in a particular Church, the portion of the people of God around their bishop.

With this view, Pope Francis, recently turning his attention to consecrated people in a major Italian archdiocese, affirmed that "diocesanity" should be considered characteristic of the consecrated life (Genoa, May 27, 2017).[41] In fact, it would be a mistake to think that the diocesan life only concerns the cleric incardinated in the diocese and not also consecrated persons; in fact, they are called to contribute to the spirituality of the diocese, expressing their charismatic patrimony in this context.

Ultimately, the coessentiality of the ministerial priesthood and consecrated life in the local Church as well, reinterpreted in terms of spousal love, asks the bishop and his presbytery to fully welcome the presence of the consecrated in their being and their work; however, the consecrated life can only offer the dioceses in which it is included its own original specific contribution, by supporting the pastoral indications of the bishop (*Iuvenescit Ecclesia* 19–23).

The "Sacerdotal" Value of the Evangelical Counsels

Finally, the relationship between the ministerial priesthood and the consecrated life can be explored from the perspective of the Christian priest in his globality. Here, I would like to call on a suggestive theological idea of von Balthasar's,[42] which I would describe as a "sacerdotal" vision of the evangelical counsels themselves, which in my opinion allows us to understand this form of life in the original relationship between the priesthood and the common priesthood of the faithful.

In short, the institution of the Eucharist and the total offering that Christ makes of himself to the Father for the salvation of the world are made possible by the very fact that his freedom possesses the form of perfect availability, represented by the evangelical counsels.[43] The unconditional adhesion to the will of the Father, who asks the Son to take the place of the sinner on the cross, is possible because his freedom is offered perfectly through love from the very beginning. Here the priesthood of the new and eternal alliance is founded. In this radical offering of himself, Christ is present as priest, victim, and altar, as the perfect coincidence of the one who offers and the reality offered, thus transcending the Old Testament priest: chastity, poverty, and obedience here come to describe the form of the subjective priesthood, that is, the spontaneous, free, and total gift of himself in love.[44]

Jesus Christ "*is a priest insofar as he erects in himself the unity of ministry and love*."[45] In him, the ministerial aspect is not something different from his subjective dedication of love.[46] The common (baptismal) priesthood and the ministerial priesthood (the sacrament of holy orders) represent the two necessary modalities for participation in the one priesthood of Christ. *Among all the faithful, the subjective aspect and the objective ministry can never perfectly coincide.* They *only* coincide in the person of the Word incarnate, making himself obedient even unto death on the cross (Phil 2).

Because man on his road is imperfect, it is necessary that in the life of the Church there be an objective priesthood that consents to the effective proposition of the gift of Christ in his perfection in an unconditional way. In this sense as well, the ministerial priesthood is ordered to the common priesthood (LG 10).

The *sacerdotal dimension of the evangelical counsels* shows the form of life of Jesus, his obedient, poor, and chaste freedom, who offers his life to us absolutely. For this reason, the evangelical counsels express, in a certain sense, the essence of the new priesthood of Christ: *the irreversible and perfect offering of his own life through love*. The state of the counsels also becomes a paradigm in the Church in the form of exercising the baptismal priesthood. In this perspective, the evangelical counsels all indicate how a man can put himself into the hands of God and bear witness to the gospel.

This clearly also corresponds to the Marian willingness, from the yes of Nazareth to the yes under the cross, which accepts the total sacrifice of the Son as the true lamb, sacrificed since the foundation of the world (1 Pet 1:19; Rev 13:8). The willingness of the Bride to the unconditional gift that the Bridegroom makes of his body is expressed in this way.

In this perspective, both the priest and the layperson find a representation of the form of the christological and Marian freedom of our redemption in the evangelical counsels. *The ordained priesthood* will always imply an essential total personal dedication, but its primary task is that which is predominantly ministerial. The *form of the counsels*, however, is predominantly representative and can never do without reference to the objective priesthood of the sacrament of holy orders.

THE FIGURE OF THE PRIEST RELIGIOUS

This reflection can shine a new light on the oft-debated figure of the priest religious, which also possesses a rather turbulent history as has been well documented in different recent studies.[47] It should be borne in mind that this is a notable reality in the Church; in fact, around a third of the priests in the Church belongs to institutes of consecrated life, and in the youngest Churches they are the great majority of ordained ministers. The possibility of understanding the priest religious identity in a harmonic way, in my opinion, is possible through the coessentiality of hierarchical and charismatic gifts and by the "priestly" dimension of the counsels.[48] It finds itself regularized by the itinerary established by the specific charism of the institute, that can have an emphasis that is predominantly "from ministerial to representative" or "from representative to ministerial," according to the predominantly lay or clerical character of the institute, from its chiefly contemplative or apostolic disposition.

Furthermore, it is good to point out a problem detectable in the priest religious today: it is that regarding the unity of the life that should characterize him.[49] If, on the one hand, there is no clarity on the relationship between the ordained ministry and consecration itself, through the evangelical counsels, we run the risk of living the priesthood with the religious essence made somewhat parenthetical. On the other hand, we can be exposed to the risk of making the ministerial priesthood itself parenthetical in the moment when one's "consecratedness" is lived according to one's own charism in common fraternal life. The most recent magisterium of the Church invites us to overcome this dichotomy. Let us start with several considerations of the ecclesial teachings and then look at several theological positions on this topic.

The Recent Magisterium of the Church

Vatican II largely seems to stay quiet on the figure of the priest religious, giving many people the impression of considering that the fundamental image of the priest is the one of the diocesan priest caring for souls, even if, even if the final version of *Presbyterorum Ordinis* does not fulfill the request of many of the Council fathers to refer this document "especially" to the diocesan priests in the title of the document.[50]

It is interesting that, in 1966, the day after the end of Vatican II in a conversation with the Major Superiors of the orders and religious congregations of Italy,[51] Pope Paul VI said that, even if the consecrated life was founded on the profession of the evangelical counsels,

> in the life of the Church, religious profession has been associated with the priesthood.... The union in the same person, consecrated religiously, which offers him absolutely to God, and of the sacerdotal character, particularly configures the person to Christ who is both Priest and Victim.

The holy pope paradoxically notes that "it was certainly not the idea of the Council to remove the raison d'être from the Priesthood of those Monks who exercise it almost exclusively in the celebration of the Mass, because...it is always an act of Christ and of his Church, even when it is not possible for the faithful to be present" (PO 13).[52]

Paul VI speaks of a "special connection between the two consecrations":

> The special connection that exists in these Institutions between the religious profession and the priestly ministry has the consequence that 'the whole religious life of their members should be inspired by an apostolic spirit and all their apostolic activity formed by the spirit of religion. (PC 8)

On the background of this intervention, it seems that the statements of the document *Vita Consecrata* (1996) are also fitting, nothing that "the priest who professes the evangelical counsels is especially favored in that he reproduces in his life the fullness of the mystery of Christ, thanks also to the specific spirituality of his Institute and the apostolic dimension of its proper charism. In the priest, in fact, the vocation to the priesthood and the vocation to the consecrated life converge in a profound and dynamic unity" (VC 30). And this remains true even when such a priesthood is not expressed in the explicit caring for souls.[53]

Some Paradigmatic Positions

Now we see some interpretive lines of the priest religious that emerged after Vatican II. The relationship between "consecrated life" and "ministerial priesthood" possesses rather different modalities according to the charism to which it refers. From this, we can also understand why one speaks of *religious priests* or *priests religious* according to the charismatic modality of regulating the relationship between ministerial priesthood and religious consecration.[54] All the same, in a general sense, it seems that there are three paradigmatic forms of relationships that I will take the liberty of reviewing very briefly.

When the Priest Taking Care of Souls Is the "Paradigm" of the Priestly Life

Recognizing the theological change of Vatican II with *Presbyterorum Ordinis*,[55] some authors claim that the kind of priest who best incarnates the meaning of the ministerial priesthood is the one taking care of souls, understood as the diocesan priest. While recognizing that there are at least four concrete forms of the exercise of the ministerial priesthood (the diocesan and regular priest, the priest taking care of souls and not taking care of souls), the most complete figure would be the diocesan priest taking care of souls. With the Council, one would pass from a "sacral" and cultic vision of the priesthood to a vision of "ministeriality" innervated by the "pastoral charity" that is expressed in the annunciation of the word, in the celebration of the sacraments, and in pastoral guidance. This model would have been introduced by the fact that Vatican II centers on the local Church. In this view, the priest religious would incarnate in himself two states of life while sacrificing something of the one or the other identity. In any case, the suspicion arises that, in this vision, the priest religious is weakly configured in the diocese, simply as an *auxilium cleri*.

Being a Religious Priest as a Peculiar Charism in the Church

Other positions[56] maintain that religious persons should chiefly develop a theology of the ordained ministry as experienced in the state of consecrated life. The priesthood of religious persons would represent a specific charism in the Church, distinct from that of the diocesan priest. In this sense, the charismatic identity of the priest religious would not be

> recognized in the daily life of the particular Church owed to a tendency which is the fruit of a deliberate choice of the same Church: that of centering the ecclesial and pastoral life on the particular Church entrusted to the secular priest and limiting the contribution of the priest religious to the parochial administration, in practice. This tendency drives the religious cleric to rival the secular cleric in the exercise of ministry....In ecclesial practice the differences between the secular cleric and the religious one are equalized in favor of a unilateral diocesan sense, which is justified under the motto of the promotion of the pastoral unity of the particular Church, thus laying aside the charism that arises from the associative communitary dimension of the group of religious ministers.[57]

The charism of the priest religious would seem to express a specific aspect of the sacramentality of the Church that should be further recognized, maintained, and integrated in ecclesial life. This provocative position would, on the one hand, help the priest religious to cultivate his specificity; on the other hand, it would perhaps risk separating the two forms of the ministerial priesthood too much, with notable pastoral consequences, opening onto a vision that juxtaposes the two forms of the ordained ministry.

The Positive Sense of a "Lack of Distinction"

Finally, there is a contribution particularly expressed in the thought of Cardinal Velasio de Paolis[58] that deserves mention. He noted that it is not meaningless that the Code of Canon Law does not pose the problem of the relationship between the diocesan or secular priest or the priest religious; all the same, the paradigm of the ministerial priesthood does not lie in the direction of the diocesan priest taking care of souls. At the base of this concept, there is no longer a leveling of the priest religious to the figure of the diocesan priest; rather, there is a certain priestly consideration in the consecrated life, as such, if contemplated from the christological perspective:

> The profession of the evangelical counsels is also a configuration to Christ, but not as a priest and the head of the Church, but as the Only-Begotten Son of the Father has called us brothers and sisters to live as he himself has lived. But it should not be forgotten that in Jesus, the evangelical life is only the other side of the same coin of his reality as the highest priest of the Father, who has redeemed the world through his sacrificial offering, sanctifying men and restoring them to their dignity as sons: evangelical life and the high priesthood of Jesus coincide in the total belonging to the Father and willingness for mission. In Jesus, before being a role, priesthood expresses his very nature as the only-begotten son of the Father, totally dedicated to the glorification of the Father and the sanctification of men.[59]

To this end, the author recommends the recentering of the Christian priesthood on the Letter to the Hebrews. As "the priesthood does not change the nature of religious life, characterized by the profession of the evangelical counsels, so religious life does not change the nature and uniqueness of the priesthood as a configuration to Christ the Head," in the knowledge that "consecrated life is an optimal condition for fulfilling the priestly mission; the priesthood requires total belonging to the Lord, which is well expressed in the consecrated life through the profession of the evangelical counsels, which allow a perfect adherence to Christ and to his mission. The priesthood finds its fulfillment and its crown in the profession of the evangelical counsels."[60]

A Forward-Looking Synthesis

From this perspective, it is not wrong to think that all the priests who work in a diocese are like the "diocesan" priests and comprise a single presbytery surrounding the bishop. The priest religious, rather than being preoccupied with combining two identities, should recognize that it is life itself as a vocation that is to unite his existence radically. *In the lens of life as a vocation, the priest religious should recognize and live the charism of his own institute and the ministerial priesthood as coessential.* In this sense, consecrated life and priesthood constitute a dual unity in the priest religious.

In a certain sense, the priest religious remembers in the Church what should be essential to every priestly life and every baptismal existence, the total dedication of oneself in discipleship to Christ. At the same time, the priest religious remembers that, although priestly existence is expressed specifically in caring for souls, it still does not have a lesser meaning if it is lived within a monastic tradition or in a pastoral dimension that is different from that of the diocesan cleric. Every vocation, in fact, even the most hidden and contemplative one, is never for itself, but expresses the mission of the Church. In this way, valorizing the spiritual patrimony of the charism of his own institution, the priest religious can experience that living priestly life allows him to deepen his own religious consecration, and that the practice of the evangelical counsels finds a specific expression in the exercise of the priestly mission.

The witness of the priest religious in living his own priesthood, concretely belonging to a religious community, also seems foundational to us, showing the importance of common life in the exercise of the ministry, avoiding an individualistic understanding of pastoral action.

In any case, the fact that the Second Vatican Council and the succeeding magisterium have affirmed that *the priest religious also belongs to the unique presbytery of the diocese* (*Christus Dominus* 28, 34) indicates the right path: the priest religious should exercise his priestly mission, characterized by his own charismatic identity, in service of the local and universal Church. However, the bishop should fully recognize that the priest religious is a member of his unique priesthood, thus recognizing that *pluriformity in unity* that makes the Church a living organism, capable of valorizing all the differences that the Holy Spirit arouses within it, for the glory of God and for the good life of all people.[61]

CONCLUSION

At the end of this journey, I would like to recapitulate everything I have said in a simple expression: history and the problems that we have seen teach us that the relationship between ministerial priesthood and consecrated life, understood in the singular figure of the priest religious, will be more fertile in the degree that they are more greatly determined by communion and mission: priests, consecrated people, and priest religious are complementary and coessential modalities for living the mandate of Christ, recognized as the priest, shepherd, and Bridegroom of the Church.

The Holy Spirit, wise director of salvation history to realize fully the entire pre-established design of the Father, acts in the hierarchical and charismatic gifts, because the redemption of Christ is offered unconditionally in every time and in every place, generating a loving response and a fertile witness.

Ministerial priesthood and consecrated life are indivisibly vocations of special consecration in favor of the faithful people of God, a priestly, prophetic, and regal people, a people of pilgrimage, sign and beginning of the kingdom, until its full manifestation, when God will be all in all (cf. 1 Cor 15:26).

NOTES

1. Cf. J. C. R. Garcia Paredes, *Teologìas de las formas de vida cristiana. I: Perspectiva Històrico-Teològica* (Madrid, 1996); P. Martinelli, "Sull' 'essenzialità'

(o 'necessità') della vita consacrata nella Chiesa per il mondo. Note per una ricerca che continua," *Religiosi in Italia* 346 (2005): 32–46.

2. What we will say can be analogically referred also to the members of societies of apostolic life, and, making the necessary proportions, also to priests belonging to secular institutes, even if normally they should be entirely considered as members of the diocesan clergy of the diocese where they are incardinated.

3. Cf. P. Martinelli, *Vocazione e forme della vita cristiana. Riflessioni sistematiche*, prefazione del cardinale Angelo Scola (Bologna: EDB, 2018).

4. Cf. G. Canobbio, F. Dalla Vecchia, and G.P. Montini, eds., *Gli stati di vita del cristiano* (Brescia: Morcelliana, 1995).

5. Cf. A. Maffeis, *Il sacerdozio universale dei fedeli secondo Lutero. Valenza critica e implicazioni ecclesiologiche di una dottrina*, in Canobbio, Dalla Vecchia, and Montini, *Gli stati di vita del cristiano*, 123–52.

6. Cf. E. Ferasin, *Matrimonio e celibato al Concilio di Trento* (Rome: Lateran University Press, 1970).

7. Cf. *Catechismo Romano*, 284: "As Sacred Scripture describes a twofold priesthood, one internal and the other external, it will be necessary to have a distinct idea of each to enable pastors to explain the nature of the priesthood now under discussion. Regarding the internal priesthood, all the faithful are said to be priests, once they have been washed in the saving waters of Baptism. Especially is this name given to the just who have the Spirit of God, and who, by the help of divine grace, have been made living members of the great High-priest, Jesus Christ."

8. Cf. DS 1810.

9. Cf. F. Botturi, *Universale, plurale, comune. Percorsi di filosofia sociale* (Milan: Vita e Pensiero, 2018).

10. Cf. P. Hazard, *La crisi della coscienza europea* (Milan: Il Saggiatore, 1968); W. Pannenberg, *Cristianesimo in un mondo secolarizzato* (Brescia: Queriniana, 1990).

11. Cf. G. Canobbio, *Laici o cristiani? Elementi storico-sistematici per una descrizione del cristiano laico. Seconda edizione riveduta e ampliata* (Brescia: Morcelliana, 1997).

12. Cf. De Lubac, *Surnaturel* (Paris, 1946) and the subsequent explicative works *Le mystère du surnaturel* (Paris, 1965) and *Augustinisme et théologie moderne* (Paris: Aubier, 1965), cf. also the specific studies by G. Colombo, *La ragione teologica* (Milan: Glossa, 1995) and *Del Soprannaturale* (Milan: Glossa, 1996).

13. A certain transposition of the inherent problems regarding states of life can be found in the underlining of the *separation between precepts and counsels,* which would be strongly contested by illuminism, in a vehement way, especially by Immanuel Kant. Cf. M. Konrad, *Precetti e consigli. Studi sull'etica di san Tommaso d'Aquino a confronto con Lutero e Kant* (Rome: Lateran University Press, 2005).

14. Cf. Congregation for Institutes of Consecrated Life and Societies of Apostolic Life, *Identità e missione del fratello religioso nella Chiesa. "E tutti voi siete fratelli" (Mt 23,8)* (Vatican City: Libreria Editrice Vaticana, 2015).

15. Cf. H. U. von Balthasar, *Der Laie und der Ordensstand* (Einsiedeln: Johannes Verlag, 1948); see also by the same author, "Das Ärgernis der Laienorden," *Wort und Wahrheit* 4 (1951): 485–94.

16. R. Guardini, *La fine dell'epoca moderna. Il potere* (Brescia: Morcelliana, 1984), 94.

17. Cf. Balthasar, *Der Laie und der Ordensstand.*

18. The phenomenon was particularly intense in France: cf. M. Margotti, *Preti e operai: la mission de Paris dal 1943 al 1954* (Turin: Paravia, 2000).

19. Cf. M.T. Cuesta Polo, *Istituti secolari*, in *Dizionario teologico della vita consacrata*, ed. A.A. Rodriguez and J.M. CanalsCasas, Italian ed. T. Goffi and A. Palazzini (Milan, 1994), 866–82. G. Moioli, "'Consacrazione' e 'secolarità': problema degli istituti secolari o problema ecclesiologico?" in *Gli istituti secolari nella chiesa oggi*, ed. A. Oberti (Rome, 1979), 11–51.

20. Cf. D. Mercier, *La vie intérieure. Appel aux âmes sacerdotales. Retraite prêchée à ses Prêtres* (Brusells, 1918). See also G. Thils, *Le clergé diocésain* (Bruges: Desclee De Brouwer, 1942). Mercier, *Nature et spiritualité du clergédiocésain* (Bruges: Desclee De Brouwer, 1946).

21. Cf. G. Moioli, *Scritti sul prete* (Milan: Glossa, 1990).

22. Cf. the above cited: Balthasar, *Der Laie und der Ordensstand.*

23. Cf. Y.-M. Congar, *Per una teologia del laicato* (Brescia: Morcelliana, 1967).

24. Cf. on this theme M. Camisasca and M. Vitali, eds., *I movimenti nella Chiesa negli anni '80. Atti del 1° Convegno Internazionale. Roma 23–27 settembre 1981* (Milan: Jaca Book, 1982).

25. Cf. A. Scola, *Laici nella Chiesa*, in AA.VV., *I laici e la missione nella Chiesa* (Milano, 1987), 47–65, G. Colombo, *La "Teologia del laicato": bilancio di una vicenda storica*, in AA.VV., *I laici nella chiesa* (Leumann, 1986), 9–27; AA.VV., *Il laicato. Rassegna bibliografica in lingua italiana, tedesca e francese* (Vatican City: Libreria Editrice Vaticana, 1987). G. Angelini and G. Ambrosio, *Laico e cristiano. La fede e le condizioni comuni del vivere* (Turin: Marietti, 1987); Canobbio, *Laici o cristiani? Elementi storico-sistematici*; M. Vergottini, *Il testimone cristiano. Congedo dalla teologia del laicato* (Bologna: EDB, 2017).

26. Cf. D. Vitali, *Popolo di Dio* (Assisi: Cittadella Editrice, 2013).

27. Regarding the eschatological temperament of the faithful, consider the seventh chapter of *Lumen Gentium.*

28. Cf. D. Vitali, *Lumen Gentium. Storia, commento, ricezione* (Brescia: Studium, 2012); G. Philips, *La Chiesa e il suo mistero. Storia, testo e commento della Costituzione Lumen Gentium* (Milan: Jaca Book, 1982).

29. The attempts to recover the lay temperament of religious life present in some orders, who seek to free themselves of an excessive clericalization of their members, gladly refer to this section of the Council.

30. Documentation in E. Castellucci, *Il ministero ordinato* (Brescia: Queriniana, 2002).

31. Besides what we have already noted regarding *Presbyterorum Ordinis*, one must read *Pastores Dabo Vobis* on this point (27–30). In the importance of the evangelical counsels for the life of a priest, one can also understand the meaning of the Roman tradition regarding celibacy. Cf. M. Ouellet, *Amici dello Sposo. Per una visione rinnovata del celibato sacerdotale* (Siena: Edizioni Cantagalli, 2019).

32. Cf. P. Martinelli, ed., *Custodi dello stupore. La vita consacrata: Vangelo, profezia e speranza* (Milan: Glossa, 2017.

33. Cf. G. Canobbio, *La vita consacrata nelle esortazioni apostoliche postsinodali. Dalla Christifideles Laici ad oggi*, in AA.VV., *Chiesa Locale, vita consacrata e territorio: un dialogo aperto* (Rome, 2004), 43–60.

34. We think of the affirmation of the "objective excellence" of virginity contained in the post-synodal document *Vita Consecrata* (18, 32) or to its essentiality in the life of the Church (29).

35. For an interesting comparison between two texts on this topic: L. Oviedo, *Vivere o sopravvivere? I francescani e la vita consacrata in un mondo che cambia* (Assisi: Porziuncola, 2007) and E. Bianchi, *Non siamo migliori. La vita religiosa nella Chiesa, tra gli uomini* (Magnano: Qiqajon, 2002). Cf. P. Martinelli, "La teologia della vita consacrata: alcuni punti chiave," *Vita Consecrata* 44 (2008): 404–19.

36. Cf. the monographic issue of *Revista Española de Teología* 77 (2017) dedicated to the document *Iuvenescit Ecclesia*. See also the summary in P. Martinelli, "I carismi nella vita e nella missione della Chiesa. Una lettura della Lettera *Iuvenescit Ecclesia*" (2016), *Rivista del Clero* 6 (2018): 465–80.

37. Cf. P. Martinelli, "L'esortazione apostolica di san Paolo VI "Evangelica testificatio" a cinquant'anni dalla sua promulgazione," *Notiziario dell'Istituto Paolo VI* 82 (2021): 58–76. On this expression, also see F. Ciardi, *I fondatori uomini dello Spirito. Per una teologia del carisma del fondatore* (Rome, Città Nuova, 1982).

38. If there has always been a shadow of diffidence with respect to the "spiritual people," one however cannot deny that the sense of charisms has remained present in the Church, although with different linguistic expressions: think for example of the classic medieval distinction between *gratia gratis data* and *gratia gratum faciens.* On this topic see I. Biffi, *Mirabile medioevo*, La costruzione della teologia medievale (Milan: Jaca Book, 2009), 43–76.

39. The formula will become even more stringent in *Apostolicam Actuositatem*: "By having received these charisms, even the simplest, arises for each believer the right and the responsibility to exercise it for the good of men and the edification of the Church" (AA 3).

40. The Marian principle and the Petrine principle are expressions of the ecclesiology elaborated by von Balthasar. See in particular his essay, *Sponsa Verbi. Saggi teologici*, II (Brescia: Morcelliana, 1972).

41. Cf. https://www.vatican.va/content/francesco/it/speeches/2017/may/documents/papa-francesco_20170527_consacrati-genova.html.

42. For the following see Balthasar, *Gli stati di vita del cristiano*; cf. Martinelli, *Vocazione e forme della vita cristiana*, 349–68.

43. Our author is very aware of the fact that the three counsels as such are explicated only in the second millennium of Christian history, with John de Matha (Trinitarians) and St. Francis of Assisi. This is not an objection if one grasps the original meaning of the counsels as the form of christological freedom. Christ's life is in effect in every way determined by the mission of the Father, who sends him into the world to recapitulate all things in himself and to reconcile all in his blood poured out on the cross (cf. Col 1; Eph 1).

44. "In so far as the perfect love of the Son possesses as its interior forms poverty, virginity, and obedience and thanks to these it become a sacrificial offering, these forms are nothing other than the foundation of his priesthood. In fact the Lord is priest in no other way than becoming, by offering actively, the passive sacrificed victim." Balthasar, *Gli stati di vita del cristiano*, 218.

45. Balthasar, *Gli stati di vita del cristiano*, 219.

46. "The one and the other thing, the active gesture of availability to let himself be sacrificed and the consequent passive being sacrificed, form in the interior attitude of the Son a unity which in both its phases is equally perfect." Balthasar, *Gli stati di vita del cristiano*, 218.

47. Cf. in summary U. Sartorio, "Il religioso presbitero. Una figura ecclesiale da riconsiderare," *La Rivista del Clero Italiano* 11 (2021): 769–85; R. ZasFriz de Col, *Il presbitero religioso nella Chiesa. Saggio storico-teologico d'interpretazione* (Bologna: EDB, 2010); E. Castellucci, "I religiosi presbiteri nella Chiesa. Excursus storico," *Sequela Christi* 2 (2009): 86–119. Conferenza Italiana Superiori Maggiori (a cura di), *Il religioso presbitero nella Chiesa oggi; Atti del Seminario di studio* (Rome, May 31, 2005), Il Calamo; Ch. Raab, *Understanding the Religious Priesthood: History, Controversy, Theology* (Washington, DC: The Catholic University of America Press, 2021).

48. In the understanding that this cannot constitute an overcoming of the polarity between objective priesthood (ministry) and subjective priesthood (oblative dedication of one's self) in the life of the Church.

49. Cf. P. Martinelli, "L'unità della vita spirituale del religioso presbitero," *Sequela Christi* 34 (2010): 78–95.

50. Cf. *Acta Synodalia* IV/7, 114–15: "2 - Rogant non pauci Patres (139) ut titulus Decreti sit 'De ministerio et vita Presbyterorum speciatim dioecesanorum'. Rationes allegantur quia schema non agit de sacerdotio qua tali, sed de sacerdotibus dioecesanis et nonnisi analogice de illis qui in ministerio inserviunt,

et quia quae dicuntur de spiritualitate Presbyterorum exclusivevalent de sacerdotibus dioecesanis, non vero de religiosis, qui habent spiritualitatem propriam. R. - Cum de ministerio Presbyterorum quaestio sit, et de vita eorum uti exigitur ab ipso ministerio, declarationes schematis reapsevalent de omnibus Presbyteris, qui in ministerio partem habent; ceterum Presbyteratusordinatur ad ministerium, ita ut per sevaleant declarationes de omnibus Presbyteris, qua tenus de facto in ministerio partes habent." (With thanks to Msgr. Richi Alberti for the indication of this text.)

51. The text can be found at the address: https://www.vatican.va/content/paul-vi/it/speeches/1966/documents/hf_p-vi_spe_19661118_superiori-maggiori.html.

52. This affirmation seems to relativize the emphasis of the priest in care of souls, in the strict sense the pastor or assistant pastor, as if it represented the exhaustive ideal of the priest. It is interesting that this reference to the objective value of the eucharistic celebration, often put into question in the postconciliar debate, has instead always been taken up in the magisterial and canonical affirmations, all the way to the postsynodal exhortation *Sacramentum Caritatis.*

53. In fact, "Of incommensurable value is the contribution given to the life of the Church by the religious priests who are fully dedicated to contemplation. Especially in the eucharistic celebration they carry out an act of the Church and for the Church, to which the unite the offering of themselves, in communion with Christ who offers himself to the Father for the salvation of the whole world" (VC 30).

54. Cf. A. Montan, "Il religioso presbitero nella Chiesa oggi," in *Il religioso presbitero nella Chiesa oggi. Atti del Seminario di studio*, ed. Conferenza Italiana Superiori Maggiori (Rome, May 31, 2005), Il Calamo, 10.

55. Cf. Castellucci, *I religiosi presbiteri: aspetti storici ed elementi teologici*, 39–90.

56. Cf. R. ZasFriz de Col, *L'identità ecclesiale del religioso presbitero*, 91–119.

57. R. ZasFriz de Col, *L'identità ecclesiale del religioso presbitero*, 111–12.

58. Cf. De Paolis, "Il presbitero religioso e il presbitero secolare oggi," 121–52.

59. De Paolis, *Il presbitero religioso e il presbitero secolare oggi*, 137–38.

60. De Paolis, *Il presbitero religioso e il presbitero secolare oggi*, 144–45. See also the profound and well-known reflections of A. Vanhoye, *Sacerdoti antichi e nuovo sacerdozio* (Torino-Leumann: Elledici, 1985); A. Vanhoye, *Mistero di Cristo e vita del cristiano* (Rome: ADP, 2004).

61. On pluriformity in unity, see A. Scola, *Educarsi al "pensiero di Cristo" (1 Cor 2,16)* (Milan: Centro Ambrosiano, 2015), 68–70; A. Scola, *Dio ha bisogno degli uomini. Preti per il terzomillennio* (Milan: BUR, 2016).

24

PRIESTHOOD

A Ministry in Service of God's People

Cardinal Kevin Farrell

I WOULD LIKE to extend my cordial greetings to all the participants in the symposium and to the speakers whom I will introduce later. I wish also to extend my heartfelt thanks to Cardinal Ouellet and the organizers of the event for the invitation to moderate this concluding session of the symposium, in which we will reflect upon "priestly spirituality in the contemporary world and its relation to the evangelizing mission." I will not dwell on this theme at this time as you will hear three interventions on this theme scheduled for this afternoon. The moderators of the various sessions of the symposium, as prefects of various departments of the Roman curia, have been asked to deliver a brief message on the theme of the symposium: the priesthood in its relation to the baptismal vocation of all the faithful.

The connection of the priesthood to other states of life, especially to the lay faithful, is a topic that touches me very closely, having been called by the Holy Father to preside over the dicastery that deals with the laity, the family, and the promotion of life.

In all the areas of our dicastery's work, we seek to promote the vocation and coresponsibility of the laity in the life and mission of the Church. Our commitment is aimed at consolidating that change of mentality, which was initiated by the Second Vatican Council; fifty years later, we still struggle to understand that the laity are an essential part of the Church.

The missionary activity belongs to them as baptized members of the Church, catechesis and announcing the gospel pertains to them, the task of bearing Christian witness in society pertains to them… and they must also hold offices of governance and responsibility in the Church. For this reason, it is not enough to say, "The laity must serve the Church," or even "The laity must have roles in the Church." It is more correct to say, "The laity are the Church."

One need only reflect on the fact that, from the very beginning of the Church's life, the gospel has spread throughout the world thanks to the laity! This is what happened in Rome: the first missionaries were probably simple laymen and -women, families, who spread their Christian faith in the capital of the empire and formed an initial community, quite diversified and cosmopolitan, even before the arrival of Peter and Paul. Therefore, we must not look at the Church from a hierarchical or sociological perspective and consider the laity in a relationship of subordination with respect to priests and religious; it is more correct to view the Church as a body (the Mystical Body of Christ), where all are members of the same organism, even if with different functions, and all are equally important in ensuring the life of that Church.

Of all the baptized present in the Church, the vast majority are laypeople. Without the laity there is no Church. This strong emphasis on the importance of the laity is in no way intended to diminish priests; on the contrary, it contributes to enhancing their value and to re-establishing a clear identity for them. The sacrament of holy orders, in fact, is not in function of individual salvation, but is conferred for the building up of the Church. A characteristic of the priestly vocation is to enhance the divine life that the Jesus Christ has given to all the baptized.

The ordination to the priesthood is essential and indispensable in the Church precisely because it is a guarantee of the divine origin of what is received in the sacraments and in preaching and, to varying degrees, in governance as well. The charism of priests is precisely that of being "instruments of Christ." The priestly ministry assures the faithful that what they hear in the preaching is the word of life, which comes from divine revelation—not just human words—and that what they receive through the sacraments is a true communication of divine life—not just empty ritualism—and that all the activities of the Christian community, carried out in communion with the pastors and with all the other faithful, contribute to strengthening and increasing the Body of Christ that is the Church. In the letter *Iuvenescit Ecclesia* a beautiful expression is used in this regard: "The hierarchical gifts proper to the sacrament of Orders, in its diverse grades, are given so that the Church as communion may never fail to make to each member of the faithful an objective offer of grace in the sacraments, and so She may offer both a normative proclamation of the Gospel and pastoral care" (IE 14). Ordained ministers have the task of ensuring the perpetual bestowal of grace within the Church. Priests, within this spiritual organism that is the Church, are visible and effective instruments of Christ the head who, in a stable and continuous way, nourishes the Body, giving himself to his Church, to nourish it, build it up, and make it grow in unity.

From this we can understand the different ways in which ordained ministers and the lay faithful participate in the one priesthood of Christ. They are two different types of emphasis, which are not mutually exclusive: priests participate in the priesthood of Christ above all to nourish and sanctify the Church—the lay faithful participate in the priesthood of Christ above all with regard to the world—in order to transform it and bring the kingdom of God into it.

In closing, this is the message I would like to deliver as part of this common reflection we have on the priesthood.

Both in theological reflection and in the concrete formation of seminarians, greater emphasis should be placed on the constitutive reference of priests toward the lay faithful, the people of God: ordained ministers represent Christ who nourishes his Church. Their whole mission is to lead the baptized to live fully as God's children, to cherish the new nature that Christ has given them, to attain a mature faith and to discover and joyfully experience their vocation, whether it be to marriage or to other states of life.

All the joy of a priest and his personal gratification lie in "giving life" to his lay brothers and sisters, that is, in communicating to them the divine grace of which he is a conveyor, thus seeing them "blossom" spiritually. When, however, a priest begins to seek his own fulfillment elsewhere, detaching himself from his lay brothers and sisters and from their spiritual life, seeking other personal, social, emotional, or affective gratifications, little by little his priesthood becomes "sick," it weakens, and can even become "corrupt."

The true face of the Catholic priesthood is represented in the words and life of Jesus himself, the origin and model of every priest.

Jesus no longer calls the disciples "servants" but "friends" because everything he has heard from the Father, he has made known to them (cf. John 15:14); a little earlier he also says, "I have told you these things so that my joy may be in you and your joy may be complete" (John 15:11). Jesus wanted his disciples to share his own joy; he wished to share with them the most precious thing he had: he introduced them to that relationship of sonship with the Father that is at the root of his being, and is the source of his joy. This should also be the true joy of every priest, the center of his vocation and ministry.

Thank you for your attention. I will now move on to introduce the first of the speakers.

25

CHALLENGES OF PRIESTLY FORMATION TODAY

FATHER GASPAR HERNANDEZ PELUDO

IN HIS CLOSING speech at the International Symposium on the new *Ratio* Pope Francis, taking inspiration from Jeremiah 18, beautifully described priestly formation as a "going down into the potter's workshop" where God the potter, "patient and merciful," shapes in candidates the features of Christ the shepherd, through the various formators, "on the wheel" that is the people of God.[1] All formation, including priestly formation, is an ongoing dialogue between faithfulness and newness; in our case, between faithfulness to the apostolic priesthood instituted by Christ and crystallized by the Tradition of the Church, and the newness of its concrete embodiment in every age. Along these lines, the Church historian H. Jedin, after studying the development of the figure of the priest from Trent to Vatican II, concludes:

> There is certainly a doctrine on the priesthood that is valid for always, but there is no ideal figure of the priest that is valid for always. The ideal figure of the priest must be oriented to the tasks that are faced by the Church at a given time and in a particular situation.[2]

Hence the need to take a new approach to the question posed by St. John Paul II at the beginning of *Pastores Dabo Vobis*: "How can we form priests who are truly able to respond to the demands of our times and capable of evangelizing the world of today?" (PDV 10).

In our days, however, we are witnessing something new: not only the content, method, and instruments of formation are in crisis, but the very concept of formation itself. Today's postmodern culture, in the words of the then Cardinal Bergoglio, is characterized by "liquefaction of forms," prioritizing the lived experiences that mix, blur, or transform them. "Formation presupposes a process," but today everything is open to change, and what predominates is an "a-historical" understanding of time as merely several unconnected "moments." Formation implies building an identity and strengthening the sense of belonging, but today multiple identities are vaunted (e.g., gender ideology) for "deconstructed" man, and fragmented belongings for "dissociated" man. We are living through a crisis of institutions and objective mediations, while formation implies precisely *institutio* according to its Latin etymology. Formation is suspected of extrinsicism, generalization, and passivity by contemporary man, who absolutizes autonomous freedom, his own individuality and "making himself" *tamquam homo Deus*.[3]

Hence, the first and greatest challenge is to rediscover the *genuine meaning of the Christian understanding of all formation*. According to biblical anthropology, man was created to be called. His vocation is not something added on to his nature; he is what he is called to be. If the priestly vocation is a divine "gift," as the title of the new *Ratio* has it, formation belongs to man's free response, which this gift enables and requires.[4] "The formation of future pastors," concluded the future pope, "aims to have them 'configured with Christ the Good Shepherd,' and this implies a renewal of faith that Christ is the one who 'forms,' renewing trust in grace, certain that the priestly form does not depend on the world but is a gift of the Spirit, accepted and cultivated faithfully. This applies to all times, beyond the fact that society and our cultural environment have a clear concept of formation itself or that the concept is in crisis."[5]

Current challenges for priestly formation abound, and are of many different kinds, depending on geographical location, cultural context, ecclesial context, and the ever more widely varying profiles of candidates; they surpass the modest limits of the present paper. Besides, many of them have been dealt with in documents authorized by the universal Church and local Churches in recent decades,[6] including the recent *Ratio Fundamentalis Institutionis Sacerdotalis* (2016) (RFIS). So based on that document, my own experience of formation, and the reflection shared with other rectors in my country in drawing up our *Ratio Nationalis*,[7] I would like to present four of these challenges that correspond to the four principles set out by Pope Francis in *Evangelii Gaudium* for building "the common good and peace in society" (EG 222–37), principles that harmonize strikingly with the four criteria given by the theologian Y. M. Congar in his classic work, *True and False Reform in the Church*.[8] Church reform down through history has always been linked to the renewal of priestly formation (cf. *Optatam Totius* [OT] 1), urged by the current pope under the criterion "pastoral conversion in a missionary key" (cf. EG 27–33). That will be the fifth challenge that I will discuss.[9]

THE CHALLENGE OF INTEGRAL FORMATION

It is not only society that is conflictual, but every human person; maturing as a human being consists of reconciling conflicting elements in the self, little by little. As against the complexity, dispersion, and fragmentation of subjects that is characteristic of our culture, integral formation is one of the great challenges of training for the priesthood, as indicated in the new *Ratio*. It points out two dangers to be avoided: overly simplistic or erroneous visions of the priesthood and emphasizing certain dimensions of formation or models of priesthood to the detriment of others (cf. RFIS 92). In line with this, we could point to three aspects related to the challenge of integral formation.

In the first place, *an integral theological understanding of the priesthood*. The priestly identity is the basis and the purpose of formation (cf. RFIS 30–34). And so, PDV 11 states that knowledge of the nature and mission of the ministerial priesthood is an "essential presupposition," the "surest guide and incentive" for priestly training and for pastoral work for discerning vocations. Now that in a sense what has been called the "priestly identity crisis" of the immediate post-Council decades has been overcome, one of today's challenges, besides the permanent one of how to translate the essential features of that identity into daily life, is how to deepen understanding of its pneumatological character as a specific dimension of the theology of the priesthood, by virtue of which the priest also acts "in the strength of the Holy Spirit."[10] This would help to harmonize more closely the christological and ecclesiological dimensions of the priestly ministry, avoiding absolutizing one or other of them. It would set the theology of the ministry more firmly within the trinitarian mystery and its relationships. It would show more clearly how the ministerial priesthood is rooted in the baptismal priesthood. Finally, it would in its turn enable a greater integration of the sacramental identity, the ministry, and the life of priests, since it is the Spirit of Christ himself who "configures" them to his being, "empowers" them to act, and "enlivens" them with his whole life.[11]

A second aspect would be the *integration of priestly models or images in the exercise of ministry*, the place of sanctification and consequently of being conformed with Christ for the priesthood (cf. PO 12–13). Msgr. E. Castellucci highlights three great "models" or "metaphors" "from *Presbyterorum ordinis* to today" following the *triamunera Christi*: the sacral-worship model, the prophetic model, and the pastoral model.[12] However, what can be observed currently is on the one hand a return to a sacral-worship model of the ministry that predominated before the Council, sometimes in reaction to present-day secularism; and on the other hand the risk of "functionalizing" it, by limiting it to liturgical celebrations or to the "managing" of several communities because of the steadily dwindling number of priests.[13] My current theme is the challenge of returning, with the legitimate stresses and modifications, to the integral vision of the exercise of the *triamunera* the Council presented to us as three dimensions of the one single ministry, rooted in the sacrament of holy orders. The concept of the ministry based on evangelization—speaking of the "priestly service of the gospel," in the words of Rom 15:16 (cf. PO 2: *sacro Evangelii munerefungentes*)—and of "presiding" meant that the order and relationships of the *triamunera* could be dynamically set forth.[14] Thus the ministry of priests that is initiated with the announcing of the gospel *receives its force* from the eucharistic sacrifice as the effective realization of that announcement, and *is oriented* to the whole Church, redeemed humanity, being offered to God as a universal sacrifice in Christ (cf. PO 2; 4–6).

This global vision of the ministry must have consequences for formation *for* the priesthood and *in* the priesthood. First it must start from prayerful meditation on the word, which "forms" the priest, making him a "witness" who is inseparable from the message, and not merely a mechanical transmitter. The word is actualized in the sacrament, and the Eucharist is the "center and summit" of the priest's life and ministry and, therefore, of his formation. Thus, J. Ratzinger concluded, the Eucharist is the "school of right living" and pastoral love, of the gift of self in Christ, and so "All priestly formation must be measured by this standard."[15] What is more, all the stages of the process of formation could be designed on the model of the various parts of the eucharistic celebration. A celebration that, using the image employed by Cardinal Kasper, culminates by impelling the faithful to "come down to the plain" of human life (cf. Luke 6:17) to make this love a reality and give it to the world.[16]

The third aspect of integration refers to the different elements of formation. Set out in *Optatam Totius*, these were developed in more detail in *Pastores Dabo Vobis*, in the following order: human, spiritual, intellectual, and pastoral formation (cf. PDV Chapter V, 43–59). Today each of these elements offers challenges in formation, which there is no time to discuss now. I would just like to underline the way the new *Ratio* stresses the *challenge of transversality* between them all, because they "interact simultaneously in the *iter* of formation and in the life of ordained ministers" (RFIS 89), and thus contribute toward integrated formation. Each element sheds light on another, making it grow greater, and overcoming reductionisms in understanding it.[17]

In this way the human formation is conceived as "the necessary, dynamic basis" for the rest, since grace does not supplant nature but presupposes it, purifies it, and perfects it. In view of the deep anthropological crisis we are experiencing, which often results in weak, fragmented characters, this dimension is more and more vital and, according to many people should be the "key to a new concept for formation."[18] The *spiritual life* is the "center" of the dimensions of formation, because it "configures" the heart to that of Christ the shepherd and should help to cultivate, on the basis of the shared Christian initiation spirituality, the specific spirituality of a diocesan priest, understanding of which has deepened especially in recent decades,[19] and can be enriched with other charisms in the service of communion (cf. RFIS 71).[20] In this interaction the *intellectual dimension*, without losing rigor and solidity, which are if possible all the more necessary now, when "lack of truth is the major disease of our age,"[21] cannot be restricted to academic studies (in the faculty or theological center) but must be integrated into the whole project of formation so that it feeds the spiritual life (sapiential theology) and lights up pastoral action (the pastoral nature of theology).[22] In this sphere, the application of the criteria indicated by Pope Francis in the apostolic constitution *Veritatis Gaudium* for the renewal of ecclesiastical studies, particularly the principle of "cross-disciplinarity" within an "organic" concept of these studies, is a further great challenge. Finally, the *pastoral dimension* is the "goal" that orients and should "permeate thoroughly" all formation (cf. OT 4; 19–21) and, according to some specialists, should be the "basic criterion" of reform; this pastoral formation should be "shepherding," in the then Cardinal Bergoglio's words, not limited to "intellectual training" during initial formation, but a "major instrument of vocational discernment" even in the seminary.[23]

Following *Optatam Totius*, the new *Ratio* sets Christ himself as the "center of convergence" at which all the dimensions of formation interact.[24] Thus "the educational endeavor helps seminarians to bring all aspects of their personality to Christ, in this way making them consciously free for God and for others. In fact, it is only in the Crucified and Risen Christ that this path of integration finds meaning and completion; all things are united in him (cf. Eph 1:10), so that '*God might be all in all*' (cf. 1 Cor 15:28)" (RFIS). The dynamism that draws candidates toward this "center" is *pastoral charity* as a sacramental grace of the Spirit in ordination. That is the "inner principle and dynamism capable of unifying" the life and ministry of priests (cf. PO 14; PDV 23; RFIS 69), and it should also do the same throughout the process of formation, both when preparing to receive ordination and as a disposition for exercising the priestly ministry.

In this way, the priestly ministry can be seen to be, in Dianich's words, a "charism of totality"[25] that "unifies competence and transparency, professionalization and sacramental image....In the case of the priests what matters is acting on the basis of what one is, and living on the basis of what one is and the way one acts."[26] That is what integral formation means.

THE CHALLENGE OF THE DISCIPLE'S PATH

Present-day society tends to "dominate spaces" and reduce time to the "present moment," losing the long perspective of history. The challenge, then, is to initiate processes. The seminary is a "space," but it needs to be opened up to the dynamism of time, thus favoring growth—including by learning lessons from times of crisis (cf. RFIS 96). Here we have another great challenge (the process element) that corresponds to the "note" of the unity of priestly formation.[27] The *Ratio* presents formation as one single journey by the disciple called to be a shepherd, begun at baptism and throughout the whole process of initiation, discerned initially in vocational pastoral work, intensified during the initial formation, sealed by the sacrament of holy orders, and continuing afterward for the whole of the priest's life.[28] Formators are invited to a change of paradigm in the work of formation today, replacing the automatic process of passing exams or going from one year to the next in inertia, with the process of assimilating what has gone before and advancing in growth (the principle of spirality or progressive accumulation; cf. RFIS 57–58). St. Gregory the Great, as quoted by Bede, recalled this principle when speaking of evangelization: "It is impossible to clear everything out of their untutored minds at one stroke, since a person who aims to climb to a high place goes up by degrees or steps, and not by leaps."[29]

This step-by-step character of formation is based on discipleship as its key. Discipleship is not only a stage in initial formation, but a real dimension of the priest's life. Cardinal Stella points this out:

> Discipleship is the distinctive note of priestly identity, which the *Ratio* aims to set as the itinerary for the whole of every priest's life....The priest is a permanent disciple journeying in the school of the Teacher, and he is constituted a shepherd and guide for the people only in so far as he leads the way in following the same path as his Lord.[30]

Discipleship expresses priests' ministerial identity: "ministers of him who is the Head" (PO 12, 1), *ministers* of the *magister* (cf. Matt

23:10); and it implies *docibilitas* (RFIS 45) as "permanent availability to God's will" (RFIS 56; 80) and hence implies a relationship with time that is part of his identity. The vocation is not something instantaneous; it is given and lived out in time.[31] The new names of the stages of initial formation suggest that it should be organized on the model of the steps of the formational path that Jesus followed with the Twelve.[32]

Discipleship refers, in its turn, to the baptismal call. The *Ratio* repeatedly stresses that the vocation to the priesthood is set "within the wider realm of the baptismal vocation" (RFIS 12), since "the unity and dignity of the baptismal vocation precede any differentiation in ministry" (RFIS 31). What is more, it belongs to the ministerial priesthood to be at the service of the common priesthood, in which—to take another angle—it also participates. The priest, as an ordained subject, stands "before the Church" manifesting Christ sacramentally as the source of all grace; but as a baptized subject he is always "in the heart of the Church," receiving God's gifts with all the faithful. This principle of "contemplation" or "receptivity" derived from baptism is the condition for making progress along the journey of formation as an ever-growing response to the baptismal grace which will afterward be expressed specifically as the grace of holy orders. Deepening in understanding of this relationship and its consequences for the ministry and life of priests is another current challenge singled out by a number of recent studies.[33] One way of meeting this challenge could be to plan out the stages of initial formation by taking the process of initial Christian formation as a paradigm to be relived in the specific vocation to priestly ministry, and at the same time stressing the vocational dimension of the process of Christian initiation as a reliable measure of its successful accomplishment.[34]

The concept of priestly formation as one single path starting from baptism raises the challenge of vocational pastoral work within the context of the common Christian vocation and the various vocations in the Church,[35] as well as its relationship with seminary formation.[36] Chapter II of the *Ratio*, together with minor seminaries and other traditional places for nurturing vocations, contains an invitation to look for "new approaches and...creative pastoral initiatives" (RFIS 18). The increasingly heterogeneous character of candidates in terms of age, life experience and background, the diminished numbers of seminarians, and the relatively frequent fact of candidates proceeding from other seminaries or centers of formation, make it necessary to draw up and share appropriate, rigorous, objective guidelines for selection and discernment, as well as sufficient accompanying, before admitting a candidate to the seminary.

From another angle, in order to understand the whole drift of the one formational process, I think it is important to take particular care of the first, propaedeutic period (because it goes straight to the aim of the whole process, assessing the option for the priesthood)[37] and of the last one, of "vocational synthesis" (because it favors a "synthesis" between discipleship and configuration with Christ in the concrete pastoral experience within a community). OT 11 said that the purpose of initial formation was to provide "in a certain sense, an initiation into the future life which the priest shall lead (*quaedam initiatio sit futurae vitae a sacerdote ducendae*)."[38] Because, as St. John Paul II beautifully expressed it, there is not just a vocation *to* the priesthood, but a vocation *within* the priesthood that demands ongoing formation as a constant response to grace (cf. PDV 70, 9). Just as initial formation has its stages, ongoing formation has stages of its own, or rather "ages," as the spiritual classics put it.[39] To raise awareness, motivate, and prepare seminarians for this ongoing formation in the priesthood is a challenge that has still to be met. Some people think that the current model makes too sharp a dividing line between initial formation (very intensive, stressing the spiritual and academic aspects) and ongoing formation (in which commitment to pastoral service impedes development of the other dimensions of formation). Thus, the challenge is to include in initial formation an experience that is closer to their future life and ministry. Because "to be with him" and "to be sent out to preach" (Mark 3:14), even though with differing emphases at each stage, have to go hand in hand both in initial and in ongoing formation.[40]

THE CHALLENGE OF PERSONALIZATION

Another feature of postmodern culture is disconnectedness from reality, which is reduced to interpretations and ideologies that impoverish it. The digital world is not merely an instrument of communication;

it actually modifies people's characters so that we risk escaping into virtual reality, and this leads to mass marketing, uniformity in thinking, and polarization of attitudes.[41] Realities, however, are more important than ideas, and in our case this raises the challenge of personalizing priestly formation. "There is no structure that forms automatically; people are required. And in Christianity everything is a personal matter. Jesus came in person to train his disciples. He came to teach us in person the Spirit of a law that alone was not enough."[42] The challenge of personalized formation, in my view, has at least three offshoots:

Personalization as "adaptation," in the first place, to the demands of the socioeducational setting and the concrete reality of the local Church. For this reason the *Ratio*, apart from its necessary application in each *Ratio Nationalis*, indicates that in order to draw up the official integral scheme of formation, or formation itinerary, it is necessary to take into account the seminarians' cultural background, the pastoral reality of the diocese, and its "tradition of formation" (RFIS 10). But in the second place adaptation means starting from the "'concrete' human person" (RFIS 93) with his character, life story, and particular stage in the formational process. This challenge has never before been so great as it is now because of differing ages, backgrounds, personal histories and spiritualities. PDV pointed to the need to bring together "a clear statement of the goal to be achieved" and its requirements, and "attention to the 'journeyer,' that is, the individual person," with "wise flexibility," which "does not mean compromising" but is an expression of "true love and a sincere respect for the person" (PDV 61). Although the *forma Christi Pastoris* is one, each person is called to achieve it in a different, unique way. Hence no two processes are alike. All training for the priesthood has an element of "craftsmanship."[43]

Personalization as internalizing. The real challenge of personalization is located at a still deeper level: it needs to transform the person's inner core. This is why the new *Ratio* speaks of formation for internalization, to counteract two frequent dangers that characterize externalization: the mere outward appearance of virtuous habits, or obedience or purely formal observance of rules; in other words, to counteract certain "priestly styles" marked by what the Holy Father calls "spiritual worldliness."[44] An author has written that one of the "obsolescences" of the traditional model of seminary formation was that it was ruled by the modern ideal of the "Vitruvian man,"[45] with the danger of a purely external imitation of an ideal figure. Without renouncing the ideal, the challenge of formation is to help the actual self to emerge, with its strengths and gifts, weaknesses and inconsistencies, in order to be formed on that basis; so that the real subject, who is "principally and primarily responsible" (RFIS 82) for his own formation, as the *Ratio* rightly stresses,[46] can achieve, with the help of grace, a creative, serene synthesis of all of them (cf. RFIS 28–29).

It could be said that in this field there is a similar problem to the one encountered by sociologists of religion, on Christian initiation: the religious experience has changed the *Denkform* of our contemporaries to such an extent that if evangelization does not reach the core of the person, there will be no "effective religious socialization."[47] So, indeed, we will not achieve any "effective priestly formation" if that formation does not reach and transform the candidates' *Denkform*, the deepest core of their feeling, thinking, wanting, loving—in biblical terms, their "heart," the place of the covenant between God's will and the human will. This is the sense in which St. Paul speaks of building the "inner man" (*τὸνἔσωἄνθρωπον*) by contrast with the outer man who is crumbling away day by day (cf. Rom 7:22; 2 Cor 4:16; Eph 3:16). This path to interior life—nourished especially by a continual relationship with Christ—is not self-centeredness. On the contrary, it impels the seminarian to "go out of himself" toward God and others (cf. RFIS 29), and, working from the inside outward, progressively forms a priestly lifestyle (cf. RFIS 131). With this internalization the priest will be able to "drink from his own well," as St. Bernard recommended his student Pope Eugene, and to explain and apply the word for his contemporaries on the basis of his own experience.[48]

Personalization as all-encompassing appropriation. Finally, personalization means making the vocation to the priesthood one's own, in one's whole person and all one's time. This is what makes it radically different from any profession or job; and it involves overcoming the dichotomy between "priestly identity" and "self-fulfillment," between "public life" (where I act as a priest) and "private life" (as the place of my freedom). "Perhaps," said a wise Spanish rector, "the key to the sacrifice that the priest as such shares and receives in the Eucharist is that he surrenders his whole life, including the private realm, in order to be made into the public man of the history of salvation."[49] Today the private realm of the "cell" in the seminary or the priest's "house," rather than being a place of focus, helping toward internalizing, can be a place of danger leading to dispersion by seeking compensations and entering an uncertain virtual world. An all-encompassing understanding of the priestly vocation brings with it the challenge of teaching candidates to live according to the evangelical counsels joyfully in real life. The evangelical counsels are closely interrelated, like a "song in three-part harmony,"[50] and are livable and fruitful in the broader setting of total self-surrender to the apostolic life, with Jesus and like Jesus.[51] Hence the importance of presenting these topics (e.g., the celibate life, the meaning of obedience, austerity of life) honestly and positively in the process of formation, not passing over them in silence or overspiritualizing them.[52]

The best instrument for personalization is *formational accompanying*, which has a large element of mystagogy.[53] This means a vision of the formator first and foremost as an accompanier, not an "armed guard" for the fulfillment of officially prescribed rules, or a "supervisor" for the smooth running of machine parts in a mass-production process. The accompanier is like the "vocational axiological mediator of identification" who, in a certain way, personally incarnates the priestly ideals that he is proposing, thus exercising true fatherhood and motherhood.[54] Accompanying needs to be integral—though naturally each formator will provide it according to his specific competence—and based on mutual trust and openness to the light of the Spirit.[55] Cardinal Bergoglio emphasized the challenge of personal accompanying through the formational processes, and the need for closeness, being attentive to the crucial times when candidates may feel impelled (interiorly or from outside) to dissolve forms.[56]

The goal of accompanying is *discernment*, which, like all formation, must be constant. This is another of the key words, according to Cardinal Stella, of the new *Ratio*:

> Anyone who follows the path of the Gospel and submerges himself in the life of the Spirit overcomes both ideological approximation and a rigorist approach, discovering that life's processes and situations cannot be classified accord-

> ing to inflexible schemas or abstract norms, but that they have to be understood through listening, dialogue and the interpretation of the motions of the heart....The main challenge that the *Ratio* also tries to present is suggested to us by Pope Francis: forming pastors who are "prudent in discernment."[57]

The *Ratio* presents the challenge of making the candidates into "men of discernment," that is, not "passive" subjects (who allow themselves to be discerned by others) but "active" seekers of God's specific will, letting themselves be confronted and consoled by the mediations of the Church. What they need to do is acquire a "deep spiritual style" in order to read their own lives, the world and the events of their ministry "in the light of the Gospel" with the eyes of the good shepherd (cf. RFIS 43). This vocational discernment will thus form the basis for "pastoral discernment" (RFIS 120) and must always be understood as a "path of freedom" that brings out the best in a person and makes him flourish.[58] Only when it is understood and lived in that way will discernment in the formational process help consolidate the candidate's free choice to surrender himself finally and permanently to the Lord in exercising the priestly ministry in the Church.[59]

THE COMMUNITARIAN AND ECCLESIAL CHALLENGE OF FORMATION

Together with internalizing, the new *Ratio* requires formation "for communion," because, in practice, what is most at risk in the interior life today is fraternity. The South Korean philosopher Byung-Chul Han has described the digital community as a "swarm" or cluster of isolated individuals,[60] with multiple loyalties, identifying with "microgroups" (e.g., the woke culture) without feeling part of a broader whole, of human brotherhood.[61] This individualism also marks today's candidates for the priesthood. Unlike the patristic period, many candidates today manifest an understanding of vocation characterized by "self-candidature," which stresses the subjective side: feeling called by God, and risk seeing the seminary, or contribution by the Church, only as a checkpoint or a toll-barrier on their road to achieving the goal of ordination.[62] For this reason, community and ecclesiality are always a living challenge.

The identity of the priest, rooted in the mystery of the Trinity and the ecclesiology of communion, is essentially relational. "The ordained ministry has a radical 'communitarian form' and can only be carried out as 'a collective work'" (PDV 17). Thus in PO, the ministry is not only seen on the basis of the *triamunera*, but also on the basis of the relationships that compose it. So the new *Ratio* presents the community not merely as the *humus* in which the priestly vocation is born, grows, and matures, and not even as one among several dimensions of formation, but as a "note" of formation, that is, "the environment in which the aforementioned dimensions come together and interact, and where they attain to mutual harmony and integration" (RFIS 90). In other words, the community "forms."

The *Ratio*, in line with OT 4, considers that "the most suitable context" for community life during initial formation is the major seminary, just as for ongoing formation it is the family of the presbyterate (cf. RFIS 90, 2; 79). But here appears the first challenge, as was indicated in the closing act of the symposium on the new *Ratio*:

> The question arises whether the seminarian and the priest truly live in a community setting, or whether they are alone among others; community life is not always meaningful and relevant. Here we have a great formational challenge: we cannot continue to form priests who think of themselves as solitary ministers at the head of a structure, but...priests who recognize in their relationships with God, with their bishop, with the presbyterate and with the People of God, a distinctive feature of their own identity.[63]

From this major challenge several others are derived:

a) For community life to be meaningful and relevant, *living communities of formation* are needed. This raises the question of the viability of some seminaries that have very small numbers of candidates. RFIS 188, 1 gives the criteria for a "sufficient and sustainable community": a sufficient number of students and formators dedicated to the task; a good teaching body for high-quality education; and economically sustainable. Otherwise, it recommends setting up an interdiocesan seminary, or sending seminarians to the seminary in another diocese. Nevertheless, there are in fact different kinds of reluctance to make progress in that direction. The decisive criterion has to be guaranteeing solid formation for the candidates in a living community, as well as bishops and those responsible for priestly formation working in communion.

b) Meaningful community life also means taking care of *community accompaniment*—another new aspect presented by the new *Ratio* (cf. RFIS 50–52)—to create an environment that favors the priestly vocation in a family atmosphere, where candidates learn from actual experience the meaning of the relationships they will afterward forge in their ministry (with the bishop, the presbyterate, and the people of God), thus combining the roles of filiation, fraternity, and fatherhood as befits a priest, who is called to be father and brother, while always remaining a son.[64] A special challenge is to initiate awareness, appreciation and practice of priestly fraternity. Priestly fraternity, which originates in the sacrament, is the first form of pastoral charity and the best setting for ongoing formation. "If the seminary is the presbyterate in embryo, the presbyterate is the seminary of ongoing formation."[65] Along these lines, it is necessary to emphasize a more "presbyterial," and not just "priestly," spirituality,[66] in order to live in the awareness of "we," the priests who "exercise, with the bishop, one single priestly ministry for the sake of mankind." This awareness should be shown in specific ways of living that fraternity, not limited to priests they are friends with, as is indicated in RFIS 77–78, developing what is said in PO 8. E. Brancozzi points to a paradox of our seminaries: they spend years forming candidates for community life, but once they are ordained they will lead an individual and solitary existence.[67] Be that as it may, forming candidates for the community life of priests, in its multiple possible forms, is a key challenge not only for reasons of quality of life, psycho-affective balance or pastoral effectiveness, but above all because of the relational nature of the ministry, the spiritual life of priests, and the credibility of their witness.

c) Finally, a genuine formational community is not closed in on itself. It needs to be open to "welcoming and engaging with various groups, for instance families, consecrated persons, young people, students, and the poor" (RFIS 52, 2). This openness to other ecclesial communities, to the life of the diocesan Church and people's real problems, will enable formation to be rooted in real life.[68] Additionally, having healthy friendships in the seminary and the presbyterate but also outside them will help the priest to acquire human and therefore ministerial maturity.[69]

Linked to the challenge of communitarianism, there is also the awareness and intense experience of being part of a diocese. The new *Ratio* recalls this at various points, in connection with the fact that many candidates have no real bond with the diocesan Church, coming from other dioceses (and sometimes other countries), religious orders or movements. Membership in and dedication to a particular Church, as taught in PDV 31–32, is not merely a canonical bond mediated by incardination, but an essential element of the identity and spirituality of the priest, as being fully dedicated and consecrated to a particular Church, with its history and pastoral tradition, within a presbyterate headed by a bishop, and only within it and from it, open to the universal mission (cf. PO 10).[70]

The other challenge linked to the ecclesial dimension of formation is *coresponsibility*. Chapter VI of the new *Ratio*, about "the Agents of Formation," lists them in detail, beginning from the principle set out in PDV 65, 1 that "the Church as such is the communal subject which has the grace and responsibility to accompany those whom the Lord calls to become his ministers in the priesthood," and specifically the diocesan Church, all of whose members "share responsibility for priestly formation at different levels and according to different ways and competencies" (RFIS, 127). An important aspect is the *communitarian dimension of those agents*: of the priests in the presbyterate and with the bishop; of the formators on the formational team; of the seminarians in their community; of teachers and specialists within the broader "formative community."[71] It also points out the responsibility of (the candidates') families, the communities or movements they come from, specialists, consecrated persons, and women.[72] However, the challenge still exists of how to *apply this coresponsibility effectively and creatively*, with participation not being limited to the technical or official level but operating in the context of the ecclesial vocation and throughout the whole of the formation journey. The same could be said, in a way, of the presbyterate and Christian communities, whose participation in formation should not be restricted to applying for information when a candidate enters the seminary or for ordination. The task needs to shift, as E. Brancozzi explains, from delegating responsibility for formation to just a few people, to being coresponsible as a Church—sharing responsibility with everyone, each in our own role, but based on the shared mission derived from our one baptism.[73] In the exercise of the coresponsibility to which we are called by RFIS, G. Schneider sees an "interesting change of perspective": the seminary's task is not only to clarify and cultivate the vocation to the priesthood but to root it more positively in the plurality of vocations and services within the Church.[74]

The coresponsibility practiced by the agents will form the candidates during their initial formation and for their future ministry. It will help them to become fully aware of what it means to be one of the baptized, and to experience and value the equality of everyone as a path of discernment and maturing in their vocation. It will prepare them for a new style of presidency, by which they stand at the head of Christian communities, stimulating more synodal forms and structures, and new ways of exercising authority and taking decisions.[75] From this awareness of the state of the baptized ("with you I am a Christian") they will be able to live out their specific priestly vocation as "service" ("for you I am a priest"), and not only in the spiritual sense, but as recognition, promotion and integration in communion, of the different vocations, charisms, and ministries raised up by the Spirit in the Christian community so that each person can find their place in the shared evangelizing mission of the Church.[76] This is the best remedy for all kinds of clericalism and forms of domineering over the flock (cf. RFIS 33–34) and an important way to prevent the lamentable abuses of different kinds.[77]

THE CHALLENGE OF MISSION

Together with the challenges already described there is one last one that the pope, from the start of his pontificate, has recalled as the yardstick of renewal of pastoral practice in the Church and, accordingly, the formation of the Church's pastors: missionary conversion (cf. EG 27–33). The Second Vatican Council presented the priesthood within a missionary ecclesiology. Therefore *the real challenge of priestly formation today*, over and above all discussions of ways and means, is to return to a form of ministry inspired by the apostolic lives of Jesus and his disciples, which involves greater evangelizing and apostolic dynamism for priests and for the whole of the Church.[78] Thus the new *Ratio* proposes, as the fourth "note" of formation, missionary drive, "the goal and the horizon of all formation. Mission is another thread that binds (cf. Mark 3:13–14), animates and gives life to the dimensions already mentioned. It allows the priest, who has been formed humanly, intellectually, spiritually, and pastorally, to live his ministry fully" (RFIS 91). Pastoral work and mission are inseparable, but mission contributes dynamism, life, fullness, a permanent "going forth." Mission is part of the priest's identity within a missionary Church, the "universal sacrament of salvation" (LG 48, GS 45; AG 1). There is a beautiful Latin liturgical hymn that sums up this challenge of the missionary pastor: *qui bonum, pastor optime, dumservas, quaerisperditum*.[79]

To tackle this challenge, it is necessary to enter more deeply into the *secularity of the priest* as an essential dimension of his mission and spirituality.[80] This secularity clearly has nothing to do with secularism or with "spiritual worldliness." The world does not need "confirmation" by the Church; what it needs is "transformation" in accordance with the kingdom.[81] But currently the opposite temptation is apparent in some people: to tackle the pastoral crisis in the face of growing secularization and pluralism by reverting to a sacral concept of the ministry that sees the world with mistrust and from a distance, and sees the Church as a "beleaguered city" in the midst of it. It is necessary to take up the teaching of PO 3 about the controverted position of priests in the world; a picture that forms an inseparable diptych with that in PO 2 which presents the nature of the priesthood in the mission of the Church. Like the Son, like the Church, priests are "anointed" to be "sent" into the world (cf. John 10:36). Their "segregation" in a certain sense "amidst the people of God" does not mean "separation" but total consecration to God and the salvation of men. In the beautiful words of St. Pope Paul VI in *Ecclesiam Suam* (63), quoted in note 20 of PO 1, "The fact that we are distinct from the world does not mean that we are entirely separated from it. Nor does it mean that we are indifferent to it, afraid of it, or contemptuous of it. When the Church distinguishes itself from humanity, it does so not in order to oppose it, but to come closer to it."

The secularity of the Church and its priests is based on the mystery of the Incarnation and the apostolic witness, and the key to understanding it and living it is mission.[82] God chose to save humankind by becoming man and *modo humano*, assuming, purifying, and elevating what is human. Secularity is rooted, then, in the humanity of the priest but also in the sacramentality of holy orders, insofar as it is a sacramental representation in the Church and to the world of the newness of Christ's priesthood that, unlike the former priesthood, is characterized by merciful closeness and the giving of one's life for everyone.[83] That is the final question asked in the rite of ordination to the priesthood: "Do you resolve to be united more closely every day to Christ the High Priest, who offered himself for us to the Father as a pure sacrifice, and with him to consecrate yourselves to God for the salvation of all?"[84]

Therefore the challenge of priestly formation is to *nurture and cultivate a spirituality* which, with the patience of the sower and the dovelike wisdom of the gospel (cf. Matt 10:16), can express the prophets' criticism of the world, not being conformed to its mentality (cf. Rom 10:2), with openness and respect toward it,[85] since in the "field of the world" and in the heart of man alike, there has been planted both the "wheat" of God and the "cockle" of the evil one (cf. Matt 13:24–30, 36–43). The true mission is to open oneself to a "critical and trusting" dialogue with the world, seeking points of contact with the gospel and its fulfillment in Christ. Dialogue is inseparable from witness. It has to avoid reducing theological matters to humanitarian matters, and it should employ explicit testimony rather than implicit testimony, because in the current context the latter does not necessarily lead to the former. "This explicitness," remarked B. D. de la Soujeole, "should not be a defensive attitude toward secularized society (negative positioning), but rather should express a positive attitude, offering something new that may motivate people."[86] In short, the aim is to form candidates to be able to carry out a "creative apologetics" as Pope Francis exhorts us in EG 132, revealing Christianity as invitation and protreptics,[87] which, starting off from the present state of reason and science, can show the credibility of the faith in the attractive beauty of its truth. This requires broad, solid intellectual formation that can respond to cultural challenges.

And if, as PO 10 states, the priestly ministry "shares in the universality of the mission entrusted by Christ to his apostles," the missionary challenge in its turn involves forming candidates who are open to the universal Church and prepared to carry out a universal ministry, that is, "for everyone." This means training for a change in approach, turning from "a pastoral ministry of mere conservation" (centered on the priest and the *triamunera* and aimed at the Christian faithful) toward "a decidedly missionary pastoral ministry" (EG 15; broader, centered on the community presided over by the priest and, while not neglecting the faithful, aimed at the lapsed, Christians of other denominations, religious seekers, the indifferent, and atheists). Focusing pastoral ministry on one or other of these two ways influences the ministers' psychology. The first leads to discouragement at the way the faithful sink lower according to Church criteria; the second opens hope on seeing the immense harvest lying ahead, based on the trust that God has already done the sowing (cf. Matt 9:37–39). This approach requires a *new image of the priest* marked by humanity, closeness and mercy, with a mode of speech that asks questions rather than gives orders, consoles rather than asserts.[88] This is the image of the "shepherd who smells of the sheep" as Pope Francis repeats, in a Church that is a "field hospital" for wounded humanity.[89] In this regard Cardinal Kasper said recently that "we need priests who do not merely manage shortages well or badly (*Mangelverwalten*); we need priests with a pioneering spirit…a new foundational generation of priests" who will shape the future (*Zukunft gestalten*) with daring, availability and joy.[90] And that generation should be trained from the initial formation, cultivating their apostolic fervor, empowering their evangelizing creativity, and offering them tried and tested paths of missionary pastoral work.

CONCLUSION

In the light of the challenges set out above the question may arise as to which is the most appropriate ordinary model for priestly formation today. The recently published commentary on the decree *Optatam Totius* by the Italian theologian S. Panizzolo concludes as follows:

> Today, more than twenty-five years after the publication of *Pastores dabo vobis* and fifty since *Optatam totius*...it seems opportune...in a historical and ecclesial context that is so different from those times, not just to concentrate on partial aspects of priestly formation, but also to ask ourselves about the validity of the overall approach. The basic question that some are raising, and which would need to be the subject of wide-ranging debate and a synodal response at several levels, is whether seminaries, as they are configured, are even capable of fulfilling the purposes for which they were instituted.[91]

The question is not new. It was raised in the postconciliar period, and tackled using various different methods, with uneven results. The Church's teaching and rules up until the new *Ratio*, based on centuries of experience, insisted on the indispensability of the major seminary not only as a time and a space but, above all, as a "formative community on the journey," that enabled the Church to recreate the intense formative experience of the Twelve gathered around Jesus.[92] This ideal, however, as PDV explains, has taken many diverse forms and undergone many vicissitudes as a human institution. So, the apostolic exhortation is a stimulus to finding a way of fulfilling the ideal that is "faithful to the Gospel values from which it takes its inspiration, and able to respond to the situations and needs of the times" (PDV 60, 3). The typology of current candidates is certainly very varied; the Council offered us a rich profile of the identity and spirituality of the priestly ministry; and the Church urges us not to delay in strengthening the community and giving new impulse to missionary drive. In this field, as in many others in the life of the Church, what is afoot is not a break with past ways but "reform in continuity." In different publications and in some local Churches proposals have been made and new models of formation are being initiated, integrating positive elements from the heritage received.[93] Drawing up a new *Ratio Nationalis* in each country based on the new *Ratio Fundamentalis* can be—and is being—a providential opportunity for discernment and renewal, and a practical exercise of ecclesial and episcopal communion. The challenge, as a German book title puts it, is "new concepts for an old institution,"[94] trusting, as Origen said, that the "new wine" can also renew the old wineskins (cf. Mark 2:22).

While maintaining the centrality of the seminary, different models and integral formational itineraries can be proposed, bearing in mind the challenges noted. Notable ones are the personalization of processes, given candidates' heterogeneity; guaranteeing greater homogeneity between initial formation and ongoing formation; the close relationship between initial formation and the diocesan vocational pastoral work; ensuring a community that is sufficiently large and lively to be able to be formative, with well-formed formators dedicated to this task; the openness of the educational community to other ecclesial communities, entities and vocations/ministries; effective coresponsibility of the different ecclesial agents according to their competence, in the formational journey; interdiocesan and national cooperation in priestly formation; and above all, the criterion of making "mission" the key to all pastoral formation. Formation *for* the priesthood needs to be joined by formation *in* the priesthood, with careful "pastoral work for priests" in which priests are the object, offering them, under the bishop's responsibility, projects, instruments, and opportunities for integral ongoing formation and the practical, joyful experience of priestly fraternity.

Let us return to the presentation by the then Cardinal Bergoglio referred to at the outset of this paper. He maintained that in his judgment, the heart of priestly formation according to PDV was not the dimensions or the environment, but the protagonists, or rather, the one main protagonist, of whom the other agents are "co-protagonists" and necessary coworkers: the Holy Spirit, who engraves on those who are called the "form" of Christ the priest, head and servant, shepherd and bridegroom. A properly formed priest is a jewel cut by the Holy Spirit. Ultimately, then, *the challenge of priestly formation is, now and always, a spiritual challenge*: to enable the candidate to actively let himself be "shaped" by the Spirit, by uniting himself more closely every day to Christ the priest and shepherd, in order, "through him, with him and in him," to serve the Church and the world for the glory of God the Father (cf. PO 2, 5).

In the middle of the Second World War, Romano Guardini sketched in his autobiography, with prophetic vision, an ideal of the seminary and priestly formation, and concluded, "All of this *may sound like a Utopia*, but in my opinion it is not. And even if it were, it should not be forgotten that Utopias have been the most effective forces in human history because they express the forms of perfection to which man believes it is worthwhile aspiring."[95]

Speaking of the multiple challenges of priestly formation and how to tackle them may seem like a utopia. But it is time for new creativity in priestly formation. In the light of faith, challenges are opportunities. Let us aspire to these "forms of perfection" despite living in times of the "liquefaction of forms"!

NOTES

1. Pope Francis, Speech to the participants in the International Congress organized by the Congregation for the Clergy, October 7, 2017; Congregation for the Clergy, *Il dono della vocazione presbiterale. Convegno Internazionale sulla* Ratio Fundamentalis Institutionis Sacerdotalis October 4–7, 2017 (Vatican City, 2017), 3–6.

2. H. Jedin, "Das Leitbild des Priesters nach dem Tridentinum und dem Vaticanum II," *Theologie und Glaube* 60 (1970): 102–24, here 121.

3. Cf. Y. N. Harari, *Homo Deus: A Brief History of Tomorrow* (New York: Vintage, 2016 [Hebrew orig. 2015]).

4. St. Paul describes Christian formation in parental terms: "My little children, with whom I am again in travail until Christ *be formed* [μορφωθῇ] in you!" (Gal 4:19). The passive "be formed" is a divine passive indicating the action of the Spirit who is modelling the features of Christ, and it implies an active allowing of himself to be shaped (*docibilitas*, cf. Isa 54:13; John 6:47) on man's part in order to achieve, in the specific vocation to which he is called, the fullness of the image engraved on him from the beginning. Cf. A. Scola, *Atraídos por Cristo. Reflexiones sobre la formación sacerdotal*, Biblioteca Autores Cristianos (Madrid,

2017); A. Cencini, *Los sentimientos del Hijo* (Salamanca: Sígueme, 1996), 196–97; RFIS 45. The relationship between the shared baptismal vocation and the specific way it is fulfilled in a particular vocation could be illustrated by an analogy with the dynamics between *imago* and *similitudo* in patristic anthropology. Cf. V. Grossi, *Lineamenti di antropologiapatristica* (Rome: Borla, 1983).

5. J. M. Bergoglio, "Priestly Formation Today," in *In Your Eyes I See My Words: Homilies and Speeches from Buenos Aires*, vol. 3, *2009–2013* (New York: Fordham University Press, 2020), 68–81, here 69.

6. In the Spanish sphere, see Conferencia Episcopal Española, *La formación sacerdotal. Enchiridion. Documentos de la Iglesia sobre la formación sacerdotal (1965–1998)* (Madrid, 1999); Conferencia Episcopal Española, *La formación sacerdotal permanente. Documentos de la Comisión Episcopal del Clero sobre PDV* (Madrid, 2004).

7. Conferencia Episcopal Española, *Formar pastores misioneros. Plan de formación sacerdotal. Normas y orientaciones para la Iglesia en España* (Madrid: Editorial Edice, 2020).

8. Y. Congar, *True and False Reform in the Church* (Collegeville, MN: Liturgical Press, 2010 [orig. *Vraie et fausse réforme dans l'église*, 1950]).

9. On the current challenges of formation in relation to the four notes in the RFIS ("one, integral, grounded in community and missionary in spirit"), cf. J.C. Patrón Wong, "Les défis actuels de la formation des prêtres. Intervention pour le centenaire du Séminaire des Carmes, November 25, 2019, conférence pour les 100 ans du Séminaire des Carmes," *La Croix*, December 6, 2019; J. C. Patrón Wong, G. Austin and Farrer, *La formación de seminaristas y sacerdotes. Impulsos desde la* Ratio Fundamentalis Institutionis Sacerdotalis (Santander: Sal Terrae, 2021).

10. Cf. S. del Cura Elena, "En la fuerza del Espíritu Santo: dinamismo pneumatológico y espiritualidad sacerdotal," *Theologica* 45 (2010): 59–92; G. Hernández Peludo, "Ministerio del Espíritu y ministros del Espíritu. La dimensión pneumatológica del ministerio ordenado," in *Deus semper maior. Teología en el horizonte de su verdad siempre más grande*, ed. G. Tejerina and J. Yusta (Salamanca: Secretariado Trinitario, 2021), 1077–1111.

11. Cf. PDV 15; 27; 33. The RFIS contains frequent references to the pneumatological dimension in the process of formation for configuration with Christ: see RFIS 35, 43, 46, 68, 69, 125.

12. Cf. E. Castellucci, "Il ministero presbiterale da *Presbyterorum ordinis* ad oggi," in *Incontro Vescovi ed esperti Triveneto*, January 7, 2010. For a more extended discussion, cf. Castellucci, *Il ministero ordinato*, 4th ed. (Brescia: Queriniana, 2014), 209–88.

13. Cf. G. Como, "Non è bene che il prete sia solo. Il decreto *Presbyterorum ordinis* e la condizione attuale dei presbiteri," *Scuola Cattolica* 43 (2015): 273–98, 286–89; W. Kasper, "Priesterwerden und Priesterseinheute," in *Priesterseinheute.*

Leben-Berufung-Sendung, ed. G. Austin (Stuttgart: Matthias-Grünewald-Verlag, 2019, 17–19.

14. Cf. E. Castellucci, "*Presbyterorum ordinis.* Introduzione e commento," in *Commentario ai documenti del Vaticano II*, ed. S. Noceti and R. Repole, vol. 4 (Bologna: EDB, 2017), 295–474, 360–63; Castellucci, "Il ministeropresbiterale...," 23: "The announcement of the gospel appears, therefore, as the all-inclusive category of the apostolic ministry which also includes the sacramental-ritual dimension and the building up of the community. There exists a kind of 'presidency in the announcement' that appears to include both presiding at the Eucharist and presiding over the community"; Castellucci, "Mutamenti del minister nel corso della storia," *Archivio Teologico Torinese* 19 (2013): 278–301, 297–301. Along these same lines, Joseph Ratzinger also stresses the priority of evangelization in PO: cf. J. Ratzinger, "Life and Ministry of Priests," in Congregation for the Clergy, *Priesthood: A Greater Love*, 1997, 117; and on the meaning of presidency, Ratzinger, *Die Letzte Sitzung Periode des Konzils* (Köln: Bachem, 1966), 65–66.

15. J. Ratzinger, "Preparation for Priestly Ministry," in *A New Song for the Lord: Faith in Christ and Liturgy Today* (New York: Crossroad Herder, 1997) (available online at: http://www.clergy.asn.au/wp-content/uploads/journal/the_priest_2002_nov.pdf; cf. Koch, "Lebensform und Dienst des Priesters und Feier der Eucharistie," 48–73; R.M. Woelki, "Das Mysterium der Eucharistie. Seele der ganzen priesterlichen 'formatio,'" *Seminarium* 3 (2005): 751–801.

16. Cf. Kasper, "Priester werden," 17. In this way the categories "evangelization" and "presiding" are not restricted to the ministry of the word but embrace the *triamunera* according to an integral concept of Christian sacramentality that includes word, sacrament and life-community.

17. Cf. Genn, "Das Seminar Ausbildungsprogramm," 37–55, 43: "Ausbildung bzw. Bildung kann man dann als 'ganzheitlich' qualifiziert werden, wenn zeitlichesNacheinander und Gleichzeitigkeit gewissermaβen wie in einer Matrix ineinandergreifen und jede Ausbildungsphase von allen Dimensionen bestimmt ist, und jede Dimension in jeder Phase in unterschiedlicher Akzentsetzung vorkommen muss. Das matrixförmige Ineinander von Phasen und Dimensionen ist ein hervorragendes Mittel, die ganzheitliche Ausbildung darzustellen." ("Formation or education can then be described as 'holistic' if temporal succession and simultaneity interact to a certain extent as in a matrix, so that each phase of formation is determined by all dimensions, and each dimension must appear, with different emphasis, in each phase. This matrix-like interaction of phases and dimensions is an excellent way of offering holistic formation.") The interaction of the different dimensions prevents human formation from falling into "scientific relativism," spiritual formation into neo-Pelagianism or neo-Gnosticism, intellectual formation into abstraction or syncretism, and pastoral formation into activism or functionalist impatience. By contrast, the "Marian character of

affective-community formation" prevents "Pharisaic hardness," causing "the spiritual dimension to take flesh" while "the pastoral dimension does not lose tenderness." Bergoglio, "Priestly Formation Today," 77 and 79.

18. Cf. C. Hess, "Das Geschenk der Berufung annehmen—Herausforderungen und Chancen der Priesterausbildung in Deutschland," in *Das Geschenk der Berufung zum Priestertum. Zur Zukunft der Priesterausbildung*, ed. C. Ohly, S. Häring, L. Müller and W. Rees, KB 18 (Berlin, 2020), 42–55, 27–28. Hess offers a dogmatic reason: the whole person of the ordained priest is called to represent sacramentally the risen one who is present, not to replace someone who is absent (cf. G. Greshake, *The Meaning of Christian Priesthood* [Dublin, 1988]). In this regard it is significant that there is a growing emphasis on human formation in the magisterial documents after the Council, especially based on PDV. Cf. J. San José Prisco, *La dimensión humana de la formación sacerdotal. Aproximación histórica, aspectos canónicos y estrategias formativas* (Salamanca, 2002); San José Prisco, "La formación sacerdotal en su dimensión humana," in *Teología del sacerdocio XXXI. El don de la vocación sacerdotal a la luz de la* Ratio Fundamentalis (Burgos, 2020), 211–50.

19. In the Italian sphere cf. among others M. Semeraro, *Il prete, uomo in servizio* (Trani, 1982); Semeraro, *Ministero generativo. Per una pastorale delle relazioni* (Bologna, 2016); G. Moioli, *Scritti sul prete* (Milan: Glossa, 1990); F.G. Brambilla, *Esse pretti, oggi e domani. Teologia, pastorale, spiritualitá* (Milan, 2008); E. Castellucci, *Il ministero ordinato*, 330–33; Castellucci, "Il presbitero nel 2000: uno sguardo alla teologia," *Seminarium* 4 (2000): 785, highlighting "diocesanity." "Stable" dedication to the particular Church is stressed more by secular diocesan priests, while "openness" from the particular to the universal Church is stressed more by the religious; cf. M. Costa, *Traidentità e formazione. La spiritualità sacerdotale* (Rome, 1999). In the Spanish sphere, cf. Comisión Episcopal del Clero, *Espiritualidad sacerdotal. Congreso* (Madrid, 1990); Conferencia Episcopal Española, *Formar pastoresmisioneros*, no. 189.

20. Cf. Martinelli, *Vocazione e forme di vita cristiana* (Bologna, 2018). It should be noted that the spirituality of the diocesan priest has some specific features of its own and cannot be considered as an "empty container" that needs to be "filled" with other spiritualities belonging to religious orders, movements, or associations (cf. E. Castellucci, "Il presbiteronel 2000: uno sguardo alla teologia," *Seminarium* 4 [2000]: 785). Upon this common basis, it can afterward be modified and enriched by other charisms raised up by the Spirit for the edification of all.

21. Ratzinger, "Preparation for priestly ministry," 8.

22. Cf. PDV 55; CEI, *La preparazione al sacerdozio ministeriale. Orientamenti e norme* (15 August 1971), no. 162. On the pastoral character of theology as a constitutive factor of spirituality, cf. R. Guardini, *Vom Sinn der Kirche* (Mainz-Paderborn, 1965), 19; and personal appropriation: cf. K. Rahner, "Sobre la

actual formación teórica de los futuros sacerdotes," *Escritos de Teología* VI (Madrid, 1967), 145–59.

23. Cf. E. Brancozzi, *Rifare i preti. Come ripensare i Seminari* (Bologna, 2021), 131–58; 126–29; 162–68.

24. Cf. S. Panizzolo, "*Optatamtotius.* Introduzione e commento," in *Commentario ai Documenti del Concilio Vaticano II*, ed. S. Noceti and R. Repole, vol. 4 (Bologna, 2017), 191–294, 245. The process of human maturing (without undervaluing the help of psychology and other sciences) has "Christ, the perfect man as its model and source" (RFIS 93). Candidates' spiritual life is built up by adhering to Christ "as friends in intimate companionship," living out the paschal dynamism and seeking Christ in everything and everyone (cf. OT 8). OT 14 points to the mystery of Christ as the unifying principle of ecclesiastical studies. "Our Lord Jesus Christ, teacher, priest, and shepherd" is the model at which the formation of shepherds of souls should aim (cf. OT 4).

25. Cf. S. Dianich, *Teologia del ministero ordinato: una interpretazione ecclesiologica*, 3rd ed. (Rome, 1993).

26. F. Cases Andreu, "Continuidad y novedad en la Ratio Fundamentalis sobre la formación sacerdotal," in *Teología del sacerdocio XXXI. El don de la vocación sacerdotal a la luz de la "Ratio Fundamentalis"* (Fonte, Burgos 2020), 21–50, 40.

27. Cf. RFIS, Introduction, no. 3 and chapter IV ("Initial and Ongoing Formation").

28. Cf. RFIS 81 (PDV 71); 3.

29. Bede, *History of the English Church and People*, I, 30 (Letter to Mellitus).

30. B. Stella, "Benvenuto e presentazione delle linee generali della Ratio Fundamentalis Institutionis Sacerdotalis," in Congregation for the Clergy, *Il dono della vocazione*, 12. The theme appears in various passages in the RFIS: 3; 54, esp. note 91 with the quotation from Pope Francis; 60.

31. Cf. L. Trujillo, "La formación sacerdotal como tarea permanente," *Teología del sacerdocio XXXI*, 161–210.

32. Since the initial formation is described as *Christum ad modum apostolorum sequi* (PDV 42), it could be structured according to the stages followed by Jesus's disciples in the Gospels: the *attractio Christi* or first calling (the propedeutic stage); the *sequela Christi* with the rest of the disciples around Galilee (the disciple stage); the *imitatio Christi* through the specific instruction given by Jesus to the Twelve, oriented toward the paschal mystery (the stage of configuring); and the *missio apostolorum*, being sent out with the authority of the risen one (the stage of vocational synthesis).

33. PO 2, 2 includes the sacrament of holy orders among the sacraments of initiation. Cf. B.D. de La Soujeole, *Prêtres du Seigneur dans son Église* (Fribourg, Suisse 2009); S. del Cura Elena, "La vocación al sacerdocio ministerial en

el marco de la vocación cristiana," in *Teología del sacerdocio XXXI,* 51–107; C. Delarbre, "La double identité sacerdotal du prêtre selon la doctrine du Concile Vatican II sur l'Ordre," *Bulletin de littérature ecclésiastique* 113 (2012): 275–90; G. Richi, *In sinu populi Dei. Espiritualidad presbiteraltras los pasos del Vaticano II* (Madrid, 2015).

34. Cf. Pope Francis, speech to the symposium, "Toward a Fundamental Theology of the Priesthood," February 17, 2022: "Each particular vocation... is a completion of baptism." See also C. M. Martini, *La vocación en la Biblia. De la vocación bautismal a la vocación presbiteral* (Salamanca, 2013), who offers a vocational formational journey based on the stages of Christian initiation, relating them with each of the four Gospels: catechumenal (conversion, Mark); illuminatory-baptismal (community, Matthew); confirmational (testimony, Luke); eucharistic-priestly (John, which he characterizes as a synthesis of responsibility and contemplative simplifying).

35. This is done by the programmatic document *New Vocations for a New Europe (In Verbo Tuo...): Final Document of the Congress on Vocations to the Priesthood and to Consecrated Life in Europe* (Vatican City: Libreria Editrice Vaticana, 1998); *Final Document of the Synod of Bishops on Young People, Faith and Vocational Discernment,* 2018, especially 77–90; Pope Francis, apostolic exhortation *Christus Vivit,* March 25, 2019, 248–77.

36. In many dioceses the seminary is also the place of reference for the diocese's vocational pastoral work. In the German field, G. Schneider even proposes that the seminary should be made into a "spiritual center for the diocesan vocational pastoral work" where, living together with the seminarians, there can be other people who are interested in the vocation to the priesthood, but also other students with different ecclesial vocations, all enriching each other on their specific paths. Cf. G. Schneider, *Auslaufmodell Priesterseminar? Neue Konzepte für eine alte Institution* (Herder, 2016), esp. 113–30. For an evaluation of this proposal, see n94 below.

37. In the RFIS the propaedeutic period is presented somewhat ambiguously. On the one hand, it states that it is an "indispensable phase" and lists it among the stages of initial formation, implying that it is part of the whole process of the major seminary; but on the other hand, it states that its purpose is to see whether candidates should continue on to training for the priesthood or embark on a different path in life, making a "careful selection of candidates for Major Seminary" (RFIS 60), and it recommends that candidates should live as a separate community and have their own formators. Cf. G. Schneider, "Keine geschlossene Sonderwelt. Die neue Grundordnung für die Priesterausbildung gibt Impulse," *Herder Korrespondenz* 4 (2017): 27–31, 30.

38. Cf. RFIS 79; 86–87.

39. RFIS 83–85, speaking of the stages of ongoing formation, points to the specific challenges raised by each of them, especially in RFIS 84; Comisión

Episcopal para el Clero, *Sacerdotes día a día. La formación permanente integral* (Madrid, 1995). Cf. De La Soujeole, *Prêtres du Seigneur*, 227–46.

40. Cf. Castellucci, "Saggiointroduttivo," in Brancozzi, *Rifareipreti*, 13; De La Soujeole, *Prêtres du Seigneur*, 82–83: it would be a mistake to focus on receptiveness only during the initial formation and on action only in ongoing formation. Granted that greater care is normally taken of the integral nature of formation in initial formation, there continues to be a risk of sometimes reducing ongoing formation to mere theological or pastoral updates.

41. Cf. RFIS 97–100; Pope Francis, apostolic exhortation *Christus Vivit*, 86–90; encyclical *Fratelli Tutti*, October 3, 2020, 42–50.

42. Bergoglio, "Priestly Formation Today."

43. In this respect, G. Schneider speaks of an "inductive concept" of seminary formation. Cf. Schneider, *Auslaufmodell Priesterseminar?*, 131–33.

44. Cf. RFIS 41–42; EG 93–97.

45. Cf. Brancozzi, *Rifare i preti*, 118–20.

46. Cf. RFIS 53; 130; PDV 69 says that ultimately formation is also "self-formation."

47. Cf. G. Uríbarri Bilbao, "La ruptura entre la fe y los sacramentos en la iniciación cristiana: perplejidades y caminos," *Pastoral Litúrgica* 360 (2018): 13–38; G. Uríbarri Bilbao, "Retos de la cultura plural actual a la Iglesia para su reforma misionera," *Revista Catalana de Teología* 43, no. 2 (2018): 263–301.

48. Cf. Ratzinger, "Life and ministry of priests," 118ff.; Benedict XVI, speech to parish priests of Rome, February 26, 2009.

49. Trujillo, "La formación sacerdotal," 194.

50. Cf. S. Guarinelli, *Los consejos evangélicos. Notas psicológicas y espirituales de un canto a tres voces* (Salamanca: Sígueme, 2017); J. M. Uriarte, *El celibato. Apuntes antropológicos, espirituales y pedagógicos* (Sal Terrae, Maliaño, 2015).

51. The "slave" (*δούλος*) unlike the "servant" (*διάκονος*) has made the whole of his life into a service to the Father and to his brethren. Cf. H. Schürmann, *Im Knechtsdienst Christi. Priesterliche Lebensform* (Freiburg, 1985); E. Bianchi, *Ser presbíteros hoy* (Salamanca: Sígueme, 2015), 57–66.

52. Cf. Hess, "Das Geschenk der Berufung," 53–54: "For the personalised appropriation of a priestly form of life, it is totally indispensable to talk about the theme of the celibate form of life and tackle it productively. This is the basis for expounding positive reasons for this form of life, that the candidate for the priesthood must himself lay solid rational and emotional foundations for in positive ways." Cf. Kasper, "Priester werden," 19 (celibacy and priestly form of life as all-embracing).

53. In priestly formation, as in pastoral theology, there has also existed a more doctrinal model that emphasized the goal, the objectives of formation; followed in the postconciliar period by a more "experiential" model that took account of the "starting point," the life experiences and personal situation of each

candidate. But both models neglected the "journey"; hence the need for "sapiential mediation," combining the ideal and the real situation, in which the formator is called to be a "mystagogue." Cf. J. C. Carvajal Blanco, *Evangelizadores al servicio del Espíritu* (Madrid: PPC Editorial, 2018); L. Vives, "La formación sacerdotal en su dimensión pastoral," *Teología del Sacerdocio XXXI*, 338–45.

54. Cf. Congregation for Catholic Education, *Directives Concerning the Preparation of Seminary Educators* (Rome, 1993), 33; Sánchez Manzanares, "La formación sacerdotal como camino de configuración con Cristo," *Teología del Sacerdocio XXXI*, 140–43.

55. Cf. RFIS 44–49. Although a proper distinction must be made between the accompaniment provided by the spiritual director and that provided by other formators, in accordance with the Church's tradition of keeping the internal and external forums separate, the emphasis given by the new *Ratio* to integral formational accompaniment favors personalization, preventing parallel processes and avoidance of formative confrontation.

56. Cf. Bergoglio, "Priestly Formation Today."

57. B. Stella, *El don de la vocación presbiteral* (Madrid, 2017), appendix, 212–13; G. Hernández Peludo, "Discernimiento y acompañamiento de la vocación al sacerdocio ministerial," *Teología del Sacerdocio XXXI*, 347–91.

58. Cf. Pope Francis, apostolic exhortation *Christus Vivit,* 257, 295; XV General Assembly of the Synod of Bishops, *Final Document of the Synod of Bishops on Young People, Faith and Vocational Discernment*, 2018, 77–78.

59. Ratzinger, in "Life and Ministry of Priests," by contrast with the "temporary priesthood," shows how permanence belongs to the basic structure of the Christian faith, as well as to the decision taken by man, who is open to eternity. The sacramental character expresses the eternal sealing of this decision as the surrender of freedom to God who is always faithful.

60. Cf. B.-C. Han, *In the Swarm: Digital Prospects* (Cambridge, MA: MIT Press, 2017).

61. See the analysis made by Pope Francis in chapter 1 of his encyclical *Fratelli Tutti*, 9–55.

62. Cf. Brancozzi, *Rifare i pretii*, 27; 120ff.

63. Congregation for the Clergy, *Il dono della vocazione*, 155. Cf. Pope Francis, speech to the symposium "Toward a Fundamental Theology of the Priesthood," February 17, 2022, speaking of the "four forms of closeness" that priests need to cultivate.

64. Cf. B-D. De la Soujeole, *Paternités et fraternités spirituelles* (Paris: Éditions du Cerf, 2021).

65. Trujillo, "La formación sacerdotal como tarea permanente," 191.

66. Cf. Castellucci, "Il ministero presbiterale da *Presbyterorum ordinis*"; G. Frausini, *Il presbiterio. Non è bene che il vescovo sia solo* (Assisi: Cittadella, 2007).

67. Cf. Brancozzi, *Rifare i preti*, 116; 171–73.

68. Cf. *Final Document of the Synod of Bishops on Young People, Faith and Vocational Discernment*, 2018, 164.

69. Cf. A. Cordovilla, *Como el Padre me envió así os envío yo. Teología y espiritualidad del ministerio apostólico presbiteral* (Salamanca: Sígueme, 2019), 260–61.

70. Cf. Como, "Non è bene," 275; E. Castellucci, "Il presbitero nel 2000: uno sguardo alla teologia," *Seminarium* 4 (2000), 785; Richi Alberti, *In sinu populi Dei*, 98 with reference to universality.

71. Cf. RFIS 139; 127.

72. Cf. RFIS 145–51.

73. Cf. Brancozzi, *Rifare i preti*, 159–62.

74. Cf. Schneider, "Keine geschlossene Welt," 30. The same is proposed by the apostolic exhortation *Amoris Laetitiae*, 203; or the *Final Document of the Synod of Bishops on Young People, Faith and Vocational Discernment*, 2018, 164; 124.

75. Cf. del Cura Elena, "La vocación al sacerdocio ministerial," 68–69.

76. Cf. Como, "Non è bene," 291–92; A. Borras, "Ministerio presbiteral y derivas clericales," in G. Tejerina and J. Yusta, *Deus Semper Maior*, 1047–61.

77. The cases of sexual abuse, abuse of power, and abuse of conscience, have damaged the credibility of the proclamation and the effectiveness of priests' evangelizing mission; dealing with them is unquestionably a challenge *to* the priesthood and *in* the priesthood. They have been tackled with courage and clear guidelines by the pope and other Church organisms. Together with the problem of psycho-affective maturity and the integration of sexuality into the celibate life, these abuses frequently have at their root the notion of authority as "dominion" over the other, sometimes based on a broad, false interpretation of acting *in persona Christi*, and not as "service" that is able to bring forth autonomy and freedom and so make each Christian grow (*auctoritas* comes from *augere*) "to the measure of the stature of the fullness of Christ" (Eph 4:13). Cf. C.J. Scicluna, H. Zollner, and D.J. Ayotte, eds., *Abuso sexual contra menores en la Iglesia. Hacia la curación y la renovación* (Santander, 2012); A. Cencini, *¿Ha cambiado algo en la Iglesia después de los escándalos sexuales? Análisis y propuestas para la formación* (Salamanca, 2016); S. Fernandez, "Towards a Definition of Abuse of Conscience in the Catholic Setting," *Gregorianum* 102, no. 3 (2021): 557–74.

78. Cf. Cordovilla, *Como el Padre me envió*, 245ff.; del Cura Elena, "La sacramentalidad del sacerdote," 93–94.

79. "Scientiarum Domino," *Liturgia Horarum*, vol. III, Feria IV, Of. Lect. II.

80. Cf. Comisión Episcopal del Clero, *Presbiterado y secularidad. Simposio* (Madrid: Edice, 1999); Cordovilla, *Como el Padre me envió*,177–89.

81. Cf. J. Ratzinger, *Ministers of Your Joy* (London: St Paul's Publishing, 2005), 125. Along the same lines, Benedict XVI spoke of the Church's need to become "unworldly": cf. Benedict XVI, Speech at the Meeting with Catholics

Engaged in the Life of the Church and Society, Freiburg, September 25, 2011; J. Erbacher, ed., *Entweltlichung der Kirche? Die Freiburger Rede des Papstes* (Freiburg: Herder, 2012).

82. Cf. Richi Alberti, *In sinu populi Dei*, 82–89.

83. Cf. Cura Elena, "La secularidad del presbítero desde la sacramentalidad," in Comisión Episcopal del Clero, *Presbiterado y secularidad*, 89–125.

84. *The Roman Pontifical. Rites of Ordination* 124.

85. Cf. Hess, "Das Geschenk der Berufung," 54–55.

86. Cf. De La Soujeole, *Prêtres du Seigneur*, 226; for the whole of this paragraph, cf. 217–26.

87. Cf. O. González de Cardedal, *Invitación al cristianismo. Experiencia y verdad* (Salamanca: Sígueme, 2018).

88. Cf. De La Soujeole, *Prêtres du Seigneur*, 163–216 ("Prêtre pour tous"). On the need to move from an "organizational" pastoral ministry (linked to the classic "locations" of evangelization) to a "generative pastoral ministry" that moves to the threshold between the Christian vocation and the human vocation, see recent theological studies in French (cf. C. Théobald, *Urgences pastorales. Comprendre, partager, réformer* [Montrouge: Bayard, 2017]), German (cf. C. Hennecke, *Gottes Design entdecken—was der Geist den Gemeinden sagt: Theologie und Praxis einer gabenorientierten Pastoral* [Würzburg: Echter Verlag, 2017]), English (cf. M. Moynagh, *Church in Life: Innovation, Mission and Ecclesiology* [London: SCM Press, 2017]), Italian (cf. Carrara, *Forma ecclesiae. Per un cattolicesimo di popolo oggi: per tutti, anche se non di tutti* [Milan: Glossa, 2017]), or Spanish (A. Join-Lambert, "Nuevos lugares eclesiales para regenerar la Iglesia en Europa," *Salmanticensis* 68 [2021]: 251–63).

89. Cf. Brancozzi, *Rifare i preti*, 145–158.

90. Kasper, "Priesterwerden," 19–21.

91. Panizzolo, "*Optatam Totius.* Introduzione e Commento," 213.

92. Cf. OT 4; PDV 60–61; RFIS 90, 1; F. Rýpar, "L'indispensabilità del Seminario Maggiore," *Seminarium* 3 (2005): 595–635.

93. Cf. Brancozzi, *Rifare i preti*, especially Castellucci's proposal in his "Saggio introduttivo," 7–19. Although Brancozzi says that "seminaries, taken individually, are obsolete institutions for the formation of priests" since they "treat the healthy" and do not manage to "heal the sick," he nevertheless recognizes that there is no other, better alternative which would be "valid, available and shared universally" (131) and for this reason he speaks of an "effective renewal" of seminaries, and points to some possible paths such a renewal should take (cf. chapter 8, 159–78).

94. G. Schneider, *Auslaufmodell Priesterseminar? Neue Konzepte für eine alte Institution* (Freiburg: Herder, 2016). Schneider concludes by expressing his conviction that seminaries are not an "outdated model" (*Auslaufmodell*) but a model for the future (*Zukunftsmodell*) if use is made of their potential "for innova-

tive concepts of priestly formation." His proposal, over and above combining the seminaries in one diocese to achieve a sufficient formational community, is a seminary based on the inductive concept (starting from the candidates' previous situations) as the spiritual center of the diocese's vocational pastoral ministry, where different ecclesial vocations live together, each with their own lifestyle, like a series of concentric rings. Although this model does emphasize the priestly identity in relation to the other vocations in ecclesial communion, what it lacks is the cultivation of the specific goal of the formational community of the seminary (forming pastors with an identity, spirituality and mission of their own in the Church) as described in PDV 61.

95. R. Guardini, *Apuntes para una autobiografía*, Madrid 1992, 133 (orig. *Berichte über mein Leben. Autobiographische Aufzeichnungen*, Düsseldorf, Patmos Verlag, 1984).

26

PRIESTHOOD, REDEMPTION, AND THE MISSIONARY SPIRIT

Chiara Amirante

IN THE SETTING of this encounter, rather than giving a presentation about the ministerial or baptismal priesthood—since we have some great theologians to do that—I would like to share with you something of my and many people's discovery of how important it is to live the baptismal priesthood, on the basis of my personal experience of thirty years' deep immersion in the hells of thousands of young people, people living in the peripheries, the margins, what I call "the hell of the streets," in the deserts of our metropolises.

I would like to entrust to you the tears of so many of them, tears I store up as a precious treasure, as a cry that has pierced my heart to the core, but that unfortunately often goes unheard.

I would then like to highlight, in the light of my lived experience of these people of the night who have become my new extended family, some of the main poisons that are literally ravaging the new generations, and some of the challenges of our time, which call on each of us personally to discover and live out the beauty of the Christian vocation to holiness, by all conforming ourselves to Christ the king, priest and prophet, each in our own state of life, aware of the intrinsic relationship and distinction that exist between the priesthood of the faithful and the hierarchical priesthood.

Finally, I would like to propose some possible responses that we are called to give as a Christian community, if we don't want to betray our own vocation.

When, thirty years ago now, I began to go through the streets by night, to the "hottest" districts in my city, I could never have imagined meeting a set of people in such a deathly state—young people in despair, with nobody taking any interest in them, right here in Rome, at the heart of Christendom.

Thirty years ago, I could never have dreamed that this very set of people, living amid drugs, alcohol, prostitution, violence, and crime, could turn, thanks to a transforming encounter with the risen Christ, into a set of over seven hundred thousand knights of the light, who have committed themselves to living the gospel in a radical way.

Today, many of them go round the very same streets where they lived, to give witness to God's love, the fullness of joy of the risen Christ, trying in their turn to be always ready to listen, so as to respond to the cry of so many others who are marginalized, living in the peripheries today.

In *Evangelii Gaudium*, Pope Francis says, "Each individual Christian and every community is called to be an instrument of God for the liberation and promotion of the poor, and for enabling them to be fully a part of society. This demands that we be docile and attentive to the cry of the poor and come to their aid....If we, who are God's means of hearing the poor, turn deaf ears to this plea, we oppose the Father's will and his plan" (EG 187).

Pope Francis speaks very forcefully. If we don't feel personally involved in the cry of the poor, we are opposing God's will! I think that on seeing the great challenges presented to us in today's society, it becomes more and more urgent for all of us to make a renewed commitment to start listening deeply to the cry of the little ones.

Often, however, we fail to recognize the new kinds of poverty that characterize our time. And so, the inarticulate cry of so many people is mostly left unheard and unanswered. It was this desire to listen to all of it, especially to the cry of those I call the "people of the night," that led me when still very young to resolve to go through the streets at night, to meet many of our brothers and sisters who are living in extreme poverty and need.

And that was how I discovered that there are many new poor, who may not be homeless, but are desperately hungry for love. Others may have a good house but feel alone, feel homeless, perhaps in the middle of a crowd. Others are apparently free, but in fact, are imprisoned on death row by the terrible chains of new addictions. Many of them wear designer clothing but are stripped of their dignity, abused, battered, and scarred to the depths of their hearts.

When I began to travel through the deserts of our city, I did not imagine I would find such a huge set of young people ravaged by substance abuse, sex addiction, alcoholism, perversions, gambling, eating disorders, abuses, and the multiple allurements of the consumer society, the deadly poisons of relativism, hedonism, and consumerism.

So many young people, tricked by the offers of the false prophets of the world, have tried to find happiness in pleasure, money, and image, but have only reaped sadness, depression, despair, hell, and death! So many have been compelled to sell their bodies to unscrupulous abusers! So many are reduced to living skeletons, in the mirage of artificial paradises that imprison the soul until it falls mortally sick! So many children are robbed of their innocence! So much loneliness, suffering, despair, and so much too much indifference!

I have tried to listen for the cry of Jesus, crucified, abandoned, which is repeated in the cry of each of the little ones, each of the poor. And that cry has pierced my heart to the core.

On seeing the many fearful bloodsuckers, hellish mafias that imprison the people of the night, I asked myself, "But what can I do?" I was only a young girl. I always felt very strongly the desire to share the joy of the risen Christ with those brothers and sisters who were in despair.

But I had the impression that committing myself to evangelizing in the deserts of our cities, among the marginalized, among young people living among drugs, violence, perversions, prostitution, and crime, among young people in situations of dire poverty, runaways, immigrants, teenage mothers, was an impossible challenge.

Then I started to listen for another cry: the cry of love of the Man-God, who is still journeying through the deserts of our cities today, and tells us continually, "Love one another, love one another as I have loved you" (John 13:34). "This is my commandment, that you love one another as I have loved you. Greater love has no man than this, that a man lays down his life for his friends" (John 15:12–13).

That engraved on my soul, in letters of fire, the conviction that love is stronger, love conquers, love makes impossible things possible, love can restore hope even to someone badly wounded by life's scourges, someone who has been laid low by despair. Love is all-powerful: it can turn darkness into light, bring flowers to bloom in the deserts. Love has overcome death. Love works miracles, because "God is love" (1 John 4:8).

The command "Love one another as I have loved you" moved me still more deeply. And like that, my heart made new with the tears caused by the cry of the people of the night, I looked at the "man of sorrows...acquainted with grief...; one from whom men hide their faces, he was despised, and we esteemed him not....But he was wounded for our transgressions, he was bruised for our iniquities....With his stripes we are healed" (Isa 53:3.5).

Then I understood in a completely new way that the love that Christ came to teach us and that opens us to the horizons of the good news of life in heaven, eternity, is not a love that can be limited to giving alms to the poor—though that too is valuable—but it is a love that makes its own each of our sufferings, each of our sorrows!

Christ loved us to the extreme of making our cry his own. He plunged to the depths of our hell for love, he endured death's cold embrace, and conquered it! He who is love, the most beautiful of the sons of men, let himself be disfigured to transfigure all suffering, to make his divine beauty shine forth in us.

And it is in that same love that Jesus has shown us the path to the fullness of joy: "These things I have spoken to you, that my joy may be in you, and that your joy may be full. This is my commandment, that you love one another as I have loved you" (John 15:11–12).

And so, I tried to commit myself wholeheartedly, always, to make my own the cry of our brothers and sisters, to take their sufferings, their pain, on myself, to witness to as many people as possible the fullness of joy of the risen Christ.

From the very first encounter I discovered that often just a little love, a simple act of listening, is enough to rekindle hope in someone who has lost all hope. As I listened to so many people's stories, I understood straight away that when a brother or sister is suffering and feels trapped in the claws of hell, we can't limit ourselves to a mere act of charity.

In Rome's Stazione Termini district, where I went, there were several volunteers who took it in turn to bring sandwiches, hot tea, clothes, and so on. You need to stop and listen deeply to the cry of that brother or sister of ours, through whom Jesus himself is still saying to us, "I thirst; I am thirsty for *your* love" (cf. John 19:28).

We need to set ourselves to listen to the greatest poverty that afflicts both the poorest countries and those that are labeled "affluent." Poverty of love is the poverty of those who have never experienced love, who have not known God's love, who live in the hells of separation from their brothers and sisters and from God; the hells that are the fruit of sin, and "the wages of sin is death" (Rom 6:23).

Many of our first encounters with our brothers and sisters on the streets wounded my heart and left deep marks burnt into it. The encounter with Viria, sold by her brother into the cruel, enslaved prostitution ring; shut into refrigerated containers, often raped, terrorized by being branded with cigarette burns to warn her against trying to escape....

The encounter with Maria, who for seventeen years had been forced to drink the blood of animals and take part in ritualistic black masses with atrocious violence perpetrated on children.

The encounter with Mauro, a handsome Arab boy about six and a half feet tall, reduced to a skeleton by a drug habit, who told me, "You know, I've been living on the streets for twenty years, and you're the first person who has ever stopped and asked me how I am."

The encounter with Claudia, a sixteen-year-old who helped a friend escape from a prostitution ring, and then was forced to watch her friend having her skin sliced all over with knives before being fed to pigs.

The more I went through the streets at night, the more deeply my heart was engraved with the certainty that only an encounter with the one who came to heal ruined hearts, to proclaim freedom to captives, to give us the joy of the resurrection, could restore life to these brothers and sisters in death.

That was how I got the idea of a welcoming community in which to offer the gospel as a rule of life. Naturally, I was terrified at the thought; I realized that for a young woman of twenty-six without much money or any relevant professional training—my degree was in political science—the idea of setting up a house and living there with young people off the streets who are seen as dangerous by everyone, was sheer madness. But I knew that everything is possible for God.

In the Stazione Termini district, I often had the impression I was standing before a valley of dry bones, and I admit that because I had so little faith, I found it very hard indeed to believe that those bones could come back to life. Today, I want to testify to the fact that I have witnessed the wonderful miracle described in Ezekiel 37:10—"The Spirit breathed from the four winds upon the dead to revive them. The Spirit entered into them, they came back to life, and formed a great army."

In March 1994, in total abandonment to God's providence, the first New Horizons (Nuovi Orizzonti) community came into being, and over the years I can truthfully state that I have seen thousands of young people with the worst imaginable past experiences, rebuilding themselves in the light of love and passing from death back to life.

Right from the start, I proposed to all the young people we gathered off the streets, most of them unbelievers, anticlerical, even angry with God, to try and take the gospel as our only way of life, committing ourselves to live by it together and, as far as possible, quite literally. The fruits surpassed all expectations.

Out of this was born a path to knowing oneself, healing the heart, and learning the art of loving, based on the word of God, the prayer of the heart, the discovery of the powerful action of the grace of healing in the sacraments. Thousands of people in over seventy countries take part in it today.

For the past thirty years, I have witnessed every day, with renewed astonishment, the miracle of the resurrection repeated in the lives of an immense crowd of people who were travelling in darkness and lived with death in their hearts. It is the Holy Spirit who brings life where there is death, inflames hearts with his fire, and kindles zeal for evangelization.

When I began, alone, at night, I could never have imagined that thousands of young people who were living amid violence, their lives derailed, in criminality, drugs, and prostitution, thanks to the discovery of God's love, the action of the Holy Spirit, and a pathway to healing of the heart based on the gospel, could become in their turn witness to joy and resurrection among their peers.

I could never have imagined that they would commit themselves systematically to evangelization projects. In just a few years, from those people of the night, Our Lord did indeed raise up a new nation. As I said before, over seven hundred thousand "knights of the light" have committed themselves to live by the gospel in a radical way, and take love to people who have never known it; take heaven to those who are living in hell; take the joy of the resurrection to as many people as possible.

Today, thousands of people all around the world follow via the Web the "Word of Light" project in which we pledge together to live a word from the gospel of the day, so that God who makes all things new can renew our lives, and the whole world, with the amazing revolution of the gospel.

Many more centers and evangelization projects have opened, thanks to the efforts of many young people who have been helped. Today there are 231 refuge centers, training centers, counseling centers, hostels, social rehab centers, where people listen and offer preventive care, genuine foster families....There are over a thousand service teams committed to the new evangelization in different areas: welcoming, support, guidance, prevention, awareness raising, international cooperation, social services, media and communications, training in culture, economics and work, spirituality and prayer, entertainment and animation.

And there are six "Heaven Cities," little villages offering lodging and training for international volunteering and evangelization, being established. As well as that, very many evangelization projects have been set up, both ordinary and exceptional, like the mission to the streets and now the mission to the beaches during the summer.

In the missions to the streets, over a hundred missionaries, many of whom have had personal experience of drugs, alcohol, prostitution, prison, and homelessness, commit themselves to spend a week, day and night, going round the hottest areas, the places where young people gather, trying to share with as many people as possible the fullness of joy that only Christ can give us. Each time the fruits of grace are incredible.

So, in the light of this lived experience, I would like to sketch some of the challenges that represent a personal call to each of us. The data are honestly more and more alarming. Different forms of dependency and malaise among young people are on the increase. About 80 percent of the adolescents we meet, even in schools in the most prosperous areas, present at least one of the worrying symptoms that characterize the new forms of poverty in young people today.

Substance abuse, alcohol abuse, anorexia, bulimia, depression, psychic disorders, Internet addiction, gambling...sickness, perversions, different kinds of bullying at different levels, with violence, are all growing. The family is increasingly under attack. Gender theory is proposed with violence, actually imposed in many countries, taking dangerous forms in schools.

Sex addiction is affecting a growing number of people, with terrible effects on their lives. You only need to consider the worrying spread of enslaved prostitution, pedophilia, and abortions. WHO data records 56 million abortions every year—realize that the total number of people killed in the Second World War was 45 million.

People point to the growth of sexual abuse and its dire consequences. In one year, 150 million small girls and 73 million small boys have been subjected to forced sexual relations (UNICEF data). Twenty-nine percent of adults say that they were sexually abused in childhood, and over 30 percent of the young people we speak to have experienced this. Another challenge is the increase in addiction to the Internet and other social media; data show that we spend six hours on the Internet every day on average. This means that for adolescents, and people in general, the line between the real world and the virtual world is becoming progressively more blurred, with all the psychological and social problems that brings.

Something else that is on the increase is the incidence of developmental neuropsychological disorders, worsened by the pandemic. Recent UNICEF data are alarming, showing that one in seven adolescents present mental health problems. In Italy, developmental neuropsychological disorders affect 20 percent of children and adolescents. During the pandemic, despite all the attention paid to physical health, that figure has been neglected.

Further challenges include violence against women, which increased rapidly during the pandemic—over 70 percent of women have suffered violence; 150 million children are living on the streets worldwide; world poverty, with another 150 million people in the world suffering from hunger, and about one in nine people not having enough to eat.

Regarding migration, we know that many young people are forced to emigrate to escape from hunger and war, and go to Western countries in search of work, but often become victims of organized crime.

Regarding ecology, the fragile balances of our common home are subjected to increasingly burdensome and aggressive pressures by economic interests that seem not to want to look at the clear, traumatic consequences of heedless exploitation of our planet's natural resources.

Then there are the many new diseases caused by the progressive poisoning of the environment in which we live; the pandemic with all its economic, psychological, and social effects: terrorism, conflicts, selfishness....And now we have the crisis, which we need to pray for, in Ukraine, with so many arsenals throughout the world ready to explode at the first sign of change.

These are just some of the alarming data relating to the terrible challenges that we are called to face up to with a great sense of responsibility.

We are now living through a third world war with millions of deaths, not only physical ones but also invisible deaths to which we often pay no attention. The culture of death and terror affects us even more violently, and we should not underestimate the danger of the many false ideologies that continue to poison minds and hearts daily, wreaking havoc on upcoming generations.

Faced with all these challenges, we as Christians are called, individually and personally, to respond. Let's try to single out some of the causes of this.

The lived experience of these past years, in contact with many young people, even from good families, who display more worrying signs of *malaise*, has led me to believe that all of this is the fruit of the many poisons that the younger generations are feeding on unawares.

Until a few years ago, identity was a secure construction where continuity and consistency were not being constantly called into question. Today, however, young people are at the center of processes of negotiations in which they often find themselves choosing alone. Over a day, we ingest many poisons without even realizing it.

There is a growing sense of *relativism* where there is no longer any dividing line between what is right and what is wrong. Everything can be done because that's what everyone does.

Dangerous heresies are spread and claimed as major progress, when in fact, while pretending to defend people's rights they are undermining the ethical foundations of society.

Consumerism and the throwaway culture are steadily poisoning us, including relationships, and inflicting deep, catastrophic wounds. There is a growing *hedonism*: we have crossed over from what is right to what suits me, with an exponential increase in alcohol use, drug taking, and many kinds of addictions.

There is also a sense of *narcissism* where image is always more important than who people really are. The need to feel that they are the center of attraction no matter what, nurtured and sharpened perhaps by excessive use of the Internet and social networks, becomes dangerously obsessive and compulsive, especially in the younger generations.

There is also an *exaggerated rationalism* whereby people only believe in what they can see and what can be scientifically demonstrated, but humans cannot live without love. What is more fundamental, and at the same time more impossible to pin down, than love? Rather, we find *individualism*: competition is taking over cooperation and solidarity to an increasing extent.

In a society that boasts of 24-hour worldwide interconnectedness, what we see is a growing difficulty in real communication. Young people are more alone, lonelier, even amid thousands of people. There are too many attempts at what Pope Frances calls ideological colonialization, powerfully driven by the false prophets of the prince of this world, often in influential pressure-groups.

It is urgently necessary for us all to increase our sense of responsibility in the face of the many challenges of the third millennium and intensify at every level our efforts to achieve holiness, communion, the new evangelization, and to deal with the new challenges that the world of young people offers so forcefully.

I am absolutely convinced that if we intensify our efforts to propose great ideals to young people for them to commit their lives to—genuine relationships, the possibility of playing a leading role in building up a civilization of love by living out the gospel in a radical way—they will show themselves able to respond enthusiastically, using the great potential that characterizes them.

My limited experience over these past years confirms this. Thousands of young people who were living on perversion, alcohol, drugs, or sex addiction, are now spending their lives in the service of those in hardship and are committing themselves wholeheartedly to witnessing to the joy of the risen Christ.

What I have just described, as experienced by me personally and as the missionary journey of the many people who have answered the call to a specific charism, recognized by the Church in the Nuovi Orizzonti/New Horizons community, includes the discovery of the common baptismal priesthood, the call to holiness for everyone, in different states of life.

Consecrated first in baptism, then as laypeople who take on commitments of poverty, chastity, obedience, and joy; in celibacy; those who live a shared life in little fraternities; those who are in the world, those who are married; and others in the hierarchical priestly ministry; all of them have chosen to consecrate themselves to God as "little ones of joy" in the name of our consecrated brethren.

The discovery of the common baptismal priesthood, the active role of all *Christifideles*, all of Christ's faithful, in the Mystical Body that is the Church, is one of the most outstanding fruits of the Second Vatican Council. Providentially, it introduced a process of interaction and coresponsibility into the very heart of the Church. The ecclesiology that the Council wanted to overcome was essentially built on the authority and sacral nature of the hierarchical priesthood, assigning a merely marginal role to the laity.

The rediscovery of the centrality of the trinitarian mystery of God and the relaunching of an ecclesiology of communion contributed to the rediscovery and enhanced understanding of the priesthood of all the baptized. There has been, as we all know, a truly Copernican revolution in the Church's self-awareness, but at the same time there has been clear intervention by the Holy Spirit, aimed at overcoming the worn-out contrast between clergy and laity, through a rediscovery of the ontological communion that comes from baptism and professing the one same faith.

In any case, it has meant that the reading of human life as a priestly life, more than fifty years after the Second Vatican Council, and despite authorized pronouncements by the magisterium, has not yet made a breach in the mentality or usual vocabulary of the people of God.

For most people, the priesthood simply means the ministerial priesthood, and it is difficult for the baptismal priesthood to find its own proper location in in the self-awareness and praxis of our Christian communities. Not infrequently, the exercise of the baptismal priesthood is reduced to a clericalization of laypeople, robbing the notion of its true essence.

The priesthood of the faithful, clearly based on Scripture, has been forgotten in the course of time because of a pyramidal view of the Church that set hierarchy and laity on different levels. For centuries, the irreplaceable function of the ordained priesthood has been highlighted to the detriment of the priesthood of the faithful, which was not formally denied but reduced in value to a mere metaphor.

Within the one people of God, the baptismal priesthood and the ministerial priesthood are inseparable. The common priesthood achieves its full value within the Church thanks to the ministerial priesthood, while the ministerial priesthood exists solely for the sake of the exercise of the common priesthood. Bishops and priests are indispensable for the life of the Church, but they are also called to live the very same common priesthood to the full, and as such they need the ministerial priesthood.

"With you I am a Christian; for you I am a bishop," said St. Augustine. The ministry of priests, and therefore of bishops, precisely because it is a ministry, that is, service, is in function of the common priesthood. It is not my job to talk about the developments in modern theology on the baptismal priesthood. I would just like to offer a humble witness of my experience, of how I have discovered personally, and how I try to live, my vocation as a Christian to be a priest in Christ.

And to show how we try to live out this aspect of our Christian vocation in practice, within the Nuovi Orizzonti/New Horizons community, which has sprung from one of the many charisms bestowed by the Holy Spirit in our time and recognized by the Church. Considering the very arduous challenges of this particularly dramatic time we are living in, it is urgent to intensify our shared effort to achieve a deep, effective conversion of the whole Christian community, centering on some of the constitutive points of our vocation: the call to holiness, communion, docility to the Holy Spirit, continuous prayer of the heart, joy, and living by the gospel in a radical way. "This is the will of God, your sanctification" (1 Thess 4:3). The seriousness of the challenges we face reminds us strongly of the heart of our Christian calling: holiness.

More than ever, the world needs saints. In this world that is dying for lack of love, we need to let ourselves be truly renewed in depth by God's love to live by his love, testify to it, and take it to so many people who have never known love. The world does not need doctors, theologians, philanthropists, preachers, and pastoral and social projects. In the face of these incredible challenges, they are just not enough! They are not sufficient! What is urgently needed are saints.

What is needed are people who are crazily in love with God, inflamed with the fire of the Spirit, rooted in the gospel, people who can rekindle the longing for heaven that is present in the heart of every human person. What is needed are pastors and Christians who are credible because they have been deeply, radically renewed by their encounter with the risen Christ, and have an ongoing, progressively deeper living experience of closeness to him, with him, who is love; who can help others discover the beauty of Christian life, the meaning of the words "on earth as it is in heaven" (Matt 6:10), by which we are called to live.

"Be holy, for I your God am holy" (cf. Lev 11:45). "This is the will of God, your sanctification" (1 Thess 4:3). If we don't aspire to holiness, we are outside God's will.

"Perfectly made one": another response that we can give to these challenges. The spirituality of communion: "As you, Father, are in me and I in you, that they also may be in us, so that the world may believe that you have sent me" (John 17:21). "By this all shall know that you are my disciples, if you love one another" (John 13:35).

There are so many wounds, factions, and divisions in the Mystical Body of Jesus that is the Church! There is so much rivalry, envy, and jealousy in our ecclesial communities! How many regulations, prescriptions, rules, precepts, and duties! But how little heart! We have forgotten that the heart of the law is love, and that this is the new commandment that Jesus left us: "Love one another," and he has loved us with immeasurable love, to the extreme of giving up his life for us, giving himself always, totally, to each of us in the Eucharist.

If we gather in his name, the risen one becomes present among us: "Where two or three are gathered in my name, there am I in the midst of them" (Matt 18:20). And it is he who draws us to himself, who makes our hearts burn with his joy; it is he who makes all things new, who always renews our life and that of the ecclesial community to which we belong.

And many young people who first came to the New Horizons community with death and despair in their hearts, when they take their testimony of resurrection to other young people, always emphasize that what most impacted them in the community has been finding young people who all loved each other wholeheartedly. Love is the only weapon capable of opening a breach in a heart that has been hardened by life's scourging.

Only if we live in trinitarian communion, "perfected" in the unity to which we are called, will all those who meet us be able to be converted. "Perfectly made one so that the world may believe." And also, "Do not grieve the Holy Spirit" (Eph 4:30). Be docile to the action of the Spirit, and to charisms. It is beautiful to let ourselves be deeply affected by the words that the risen Christ offers to his disciples when he appears to them in the upper room. "Jesus said to them again, 'Peace be with you. As the Father has sent me, even so I send you.' And when he had said this, he breathed on them and said to them, 'Receive the Holy Spirit'" (John 20:21–22).

It is wonderful to discover that we are called to be, like Jesus, a gift of the Father's love to the world: "As the Father has sent me, even so I send you." But to be able to respond fully to that vocation we need to receive the Holy Spirit.

Only if we receive and welcome the Holy Spirit do we learn to walk according to the Spirit every day, fulfill God's plan for us completely, and become witnesses to the truth in this world that feeds on lies.

We can pass over from superficiality to depth, we can contemplate and bear witness to "what no eye has seen nor ear heard, nor the heart of man conceived" (1 Cor 2:9). And these things are what God has prepared for those who love him, what "God has revealed to us through the Spirit" (1 Cor 2:10). We can pass over from passions to a passion for the kingdom and evangelize effectively: "You will be clothed with the power of the Holy Spirit who will come down upon you, and you will be my witnesses" (cf. Luke 24:48, 49).

Another response to the challenges that confront us is continuous prayer of the heart, unceasing prayer. In most of our Christian communities, we can see how it has been forgotten that constant prayer is God's will for every Christian, whatever our vocation. We are all called to be contemplatives, that is, to live deeply immersed in communion with God, so that everything that we then do and live through and are, can spring forth from our contemplation!

Priests and religious perhaps do their best to recite the Liturgy of the Hours every day, but how much of that time is truly prayer, a time of communion with God? Many Catholics are content to go to Sunday Mass sometimes, to say some little half-distracted prayer, especially in times of difficulty. But even when they pray often, they get distracted. In short, we are still very far from living immersed in continual prayer of the heart.

We have forgotten that only one thing is necessary: to stay at the feet of the teacher, to listen to his words, to let ourselves be guided by him. In these times, which are so hard for all our great family, humankind, there is an urgent need for contemplatives who, enlightened by the Spirit, can read the signs of the times and act with wisdom and discernment to renew the world, to build the civilization of love. We often pride ourselves on achieving many important things but forget that only if we remain firm in life can we produce fruit. Because without Jesus we can do nothing (cf. John 15:5).

Everything that we say, do, live through, decide, and are, ought to spring from continuous prayer of the heart, from our remaining in God, so that it is he who works in us.

Another response that we can give, and should give, of conversion as a Christian community, is to rediscover the heart of our Christian vocation, which is joy: being witnesses to the joy of the risen Christ! That is the radical nature of the gospel! In a world that continues to persecute happiness through the many suggestions of the prophets of the father of lies, which in fact lead to death, there is an urgent need for witnesses of the fullness of joy that is given to us only by the risen Christ.

Too often we present a Christianity made up only of cross, mortification, and suffering, but don't testify with our lives that the cross is a step toward the manifestation of the glory of the resurrection. We don't put into practice the secret that Jesus has given us: that his joy may be in us and our joy may be full. "Remain in my love. If you keep my commandments you will abide in my love, just as I have kept my Father's commandments and abide in his love. These things I have spoken to you, that my joy may be in you, and that your joy may be full" (John 15:10–11).

The joy of the risen Christ is infectious; it frees and converts the heart. The heart of each man and woman is imprinted with a thirst for that inexpressible, glorious joy that awaits us in heaven. When our heart sees that joy shining in the eyes of someone who is living in communion with the risen One, we recognize it and desire to have it too.

We need to discover the radical nature of the Gospel that characterized the early Christian communities. We need to live by God's word as literally as possible, so that the joy of the risen Christ can shine out in our hearts and rekindle the longing for heaven, the desire for a new life, renewed by God's love, in so many people who are imprisoned by hell, by the death of the soul.

And it is more urgent than ever to intensify our effort to respond effectively to Pope Francis's continual invitations to move from a pastoral approach of hoping to a pastoral approach of encounter, with clearly defined goals:

- Increase our efforts toward a new, integral formation process for lay Christians, that will make them capable of listening more deeply to the silent cry of so many people.
- Rediscover joy as a constitutive characteristic of the Christian vocation, and our responsibility for testifying about it. Reinvigorate the initial proclamation of the gospel, by finding different modes of evangelization. Apply the means of the new evangelization, discovering the great possibilities that exist for shouting the gospel from the rooftops. Be present and active where the fate of the upcoming generations is being decided: culture, politics, communications, and economy.

- Establish communication at the diocesan and parish levels between all the various ecclesial bodies, to increase communion among the different groups, associations, and movements. Renew and revitalize communication systems in the areas of prevention, awareness raising, and evangelization, starting with formation in the parishes, seminaries, theological institutes, and the various ecclesial communities.
- Integrate the initial proclamation with pastoral care so that they work in synergy, and a bridge is built between the streets and the ecclesial community, paying particular attention to the development of the new evangelization in the parishes and the various ecclesial bodies through the restoration of a pastoral approach of the initial proclamation.

And so, we conclude. When over thirty years ago, I started going through the streets at night in Rome's "hottest" districts, I did so in the awareness that it was my duty to take the joy of the risen Christ and Christian hope even to those who were living in indifference and despair.

I had received the gift of understanding that each of us, united to Christ by baptism, are called to give our own life to others by being available to make Christ's gift of himself present in our time. In those first days my activity was only a response to a calling, not an easy one to understand in those years, in the context I was living in. But little by little I understood that it had a deep theological reason, a priestly value derived from baptism.

Each act of a baptized person that is performed in consonance with incorporation into Christ, and even more, therefore, each act of evangelization, each act of charity, each commitment to helping raise up human beings from their physical and mental sufferings—all of these are priestly acts, spiritual sacrifices that are pleasing to God through Jesus Christ. It follows that just as Christ's priestly action, taking his mission as a whole, is not limited to the sacrifice of the cross, so too, the priestly dignity of the baptized extends to every sphere of life.

So, we need to let ourselves be addressed personally, enter into crisis, make ourselves uncomfortable by this holy unease. Let us ask the Holy Spirit to brand our hearts, and the heart of every Christian, with St. Paul's words: "If I preach the gospel, that gives me no ground for boasting. For necessity is laid upon me. Woe to me if I do not preach the gospel!" (1 Cor 9:16). We need to let Our Lord write his desire in letters of fire: "Be holy because I the Lord am holy" (Lev 11:45).

I will take this opportunity to say that in our little New Horizons community a small seminary came into being, training men for the priesthood, and straight away we felt how important it was that it should include the post of a woman formator. The reason was that the specific features of a woman's charism—welcoming, listening, empathy with suffering, which are typical of motherhood—are also essential in the priesthood.

We proclaim Mary as Queen of Apostles, and the gospel says that "Jesus lived under their authority," so Jesus was formed in the school of Joseph and Mary. We have seen that it is also important for priests to have a Marian figure, as well as a priestly figure, present in their formation. For a long time, it was my mother who formed the priests, and now there is another woman formator, and I must say that it has been a source of great riches. Part of that has been the capacity to listen, which is more typically feminine, but which I believe is essential to the priesthood, because there is no love if one cannot listen.

Sometimes priests make the mistake of thinking that they need to preach all the time, but they don't understand that many more people are won over by being listened to, because then they feel loved. That's why I think the feminine presence is very important as well as attention paid to the Church's Marian charism. In fact, we urgently need to recover Mary's role within the Church.

27

THE JOY OF MISSION

Cardinal Luis Antonio G. Tagle

AS WE COME to the conclusion of the symposium, we renew our thanks and congratulations to the organizers, especially His Eminence Cardinal Marc Ouellet, whose initiative and perseverance have inspired us all.

You, dear participants, have been gifted with much teaching and wisdom from the Holy Father and our speakers these past days. Most of you probably desire to go now to a quiet space to internalize and pray over what you have heard. So, I have decided to offer a light and hopefully a brief reflection on the topic, "The Joy of Mission." Let me start by sharing two experiences.

During the Synod of Bishops on the Youth, the bishops in our English-language working group asked some youth representatives about their friends' or peers' impression of the Church. One of them said, "The experience of my friends of the parish is that of priests who are angry, impatient, negative, and unapproachable. They criticize persons during homilies and talk always about rules. So, after the mass, my friends go to the Bible services of other Christian groups to encounter Jesus." I was shocked and saddened to hear this, but at the same time, was glad to have been challenged by the youth. The other experience happened during the celebration of Catechetical Month in the diocese, attended by children, their parents, and catechists. Instead of giving a conference I interviewed some children about what they have learned in catechism classes. Many of them gave wonderful answers that must have affirmed the catechists. But one girl raised her hand. I asked her what her significant experience of her catechist was, to which she answered, "Quiet! Quiet! Quiet!" Then the girl sat down.

These experiences prompted me to reflect on joy in the lives of the baptized and lay and ordained ministers. Even in ordinary life there are many reasons why we feel tired, empty, and joyless. But I ask myself, Is it possible that one reason for the loss of joy in a baptized person or a minister of the Church is the lack or weakening of the sense of mission? Without a commitment to mission, the priesthood of the baptized, consecrated life, and the ministerial priesthood are deprived of joy. Why? Because the priesthood of Christ is intrinsically linked to his mission.

THE PRIESTHOOD OF CHRIST IN THE LETTER TO THE HEBREWS

According to the author of the letter, Jesus's unique priesthood, which surpasses and fulfills all other forms of priesthood, is a priesthood of a holy life, a life that is sacrifice (*sacer* or set apart and *facere* to make: to make holy) and therefore, pleasing to God. There are two main components to Jesus's priesthood and sacrifice of a holy life. The first is his total obedience to the Father who sent him. Hebrews says, "On coming into the world, Jesus said, 'Sacrifice and offering you did not desire, but a body you have prepared for me. Holocausts and sin offerings you took no delight in.' Then I said, 'As is written of me in the book, I have come to do your will, O God'" (Heb 10:5–7). The second element is Jesus's communion with and compassionate mercy toward sinners. The letter says,

> Jesus, [who] was made for a little while lower than the angels, that through God's gracious will he might taste death for the sake of all men and women. Indeed it was fitting that when bringing many children to glory, God...should make their leader in the work of salvation perfect through suffering. He who consecrates and those who are consecrated have one and the same Father. Therefore he is not ashamed to call them brothers and sisters. (Heb 2:9–11)

The priesthood of Jesus is completely missionary and continues to be so for he intercedes eternally for his brothers and sisters before the Father in the heavenly sanctuary. This is the priesthood that Jesus shares with all the baptized, and on the foundation of baptism, with all ministries and states of life in the Church. Jesus's priesthood is a holy missionary life.

PARTICIPATING IN THE MISSIONARY PRIESTHOOD OF CHRIST

It is not surprising that Jesus called disciples to be with him and to be sent by him as his witnesses. During his public ministry and after his resurrection, Jesus called his companions, students, or followers so that he could send them as witnesses. Discipleship and mission are intrinsically linked to each other as evidenced in New Testament texts. "He appointed Twelve that they might be with him, and he might send them forth to preach and to have authority to drive out demons" (Mark 3:14–15). Jesus said to his disciples, "It was not you who chose me, but I who chose you and appointed you to go and bear fruit that will remain" (John 15:16). We are glad to hear the words, "As the Father loves me, so I also love you. Remain in my love" (John 15:9) and "Peace be with you. As the Father has sent me, so I send you" (John 20:21). The ones Jesus loves are the ones he sends. When Jesus sent the disciples, he promised that the Holy Spirit would accompany them. "When the Advocate comes, whom I will send you from the Father, the Spirit of truth that proceeds from the Father, he will testify to me. And you also testify because you have been with me from the beginning" (John 15:26–27). We are in awe of having been called to belong to Jesus and to share in his mission. It is the joy, not of creating or promoting one's own project, but of participating in God's plan in the missions of Jesus and of the Holy Spirit. It is the joy, not of inventing one's message, but of proclaiming what one has heard, seen, looked upon, and touched of the word of life (1 John 1:1–4). It is the joy, not of boasting of one's knowledge of the Lord, but of humbly being led by the Holy Spirit's testimony to Jesus. It is the joy, not of being obsessed with achievements, but of gratitude to him who makes weak disciples strong by his grace. We wish every baptized Christian would experience the joy of being a disciple missionary. Without a vibrant friendship with Jesus, mission easily becomes a burdensome work, performed by "missioners" who feel more like slaves than witnesses to the good news. But without mission, discipleship might become a lifeless prison.

I met a former student of mine in the country to which his religious superior had sent him. From the conversation I learned that in the village where he ministered, there was only one Catholic. Feeling sorry for him, I asked if he were not frustrated that after almost fifteen years of religious and seminary formation, he would have only one parishioner. With a serene smile he said, "That one Catholic is my flock. I will give to him all of my love and energy." Mission gives a baptized and an ordained minister zeal and joy.

We need to add immediately that while Jesus called his disciples by name, in a uniquely personal manner, he also called them to be with other disciples. He sent them on mission with other missionaries. Discipleship forms community, which in turn becomes the womb that begets other disciples. Mission forms community, which in turn becomes the flame that fires up other missionaries. According to the First Letter of John, the proclamation of the word of life by a disciple missionary to a listener has for its purpose, "so that you too may have communion with us; for our communion is with the Father and with his Son, Jesus Christ. We are writing this so that our joy may be complete" (1 John 1:3–4). The Christian community began in a simple manner by which a disciple shares Jesus to a listener who, upon receiving Jesus, forms a bond of communion with the proclaimer. But that fellowship between two or three persons is indeed a communion with the Father and with Jesus. Simple human interaction or conversation centered on the word of life that fosters unity needs to be encouraged in our time, especially in families, schools, workplaces, recreation centers, hospitals, social media, and simple gatherings of friends. We also need to emphasize the proclamation of the word in dialogue with all the nations, cultures, and tongues of the world. The communion of the Christian community is not meant only for smooth personal and working relationships. It is essential to authentic discipleship and missionary witness. Jesus prayed this way: "I pray not only for them, but also for those who will believe in me through their word, so that they may all be one, as you, Father, are in me and I in you, that they also may be in us, that the world may believe that you sent me" (John 17:20–21). The unity of the Father with Jesus, whom he sent, must be mirrored in the unity of those sent to proclaim Jesus. In our contemporary world, beset with nationalist and ethnic divisions, discrimination, armed conflicts, and inequality, the communion of disciple-missionaries from different walks of life and nations testifies to the truth of Jesus. The risen Lord clearly stated, "Go therefore, and make disciples of all nations" (Matt 28:19). Disciples from their nations will go to other nations and as one community of diverse nations, they will go together to all human, social, cultural, economic "spaces" in the spirit of dialogue centered on the word. The joy of priestly mission springs from the conviction that Christians belong to each other and to all human beings because we belong to Jesus. It is the joy, not of independence, but of relationships. It is the joy, not of self-contentment because I am already a disciple, but of caring for others. It is the joy, not of self-sufficiency, but of coresponsibility. It is the joy, not of lording it over others, but of journeying with them. It is the joy, not of group or national superiority, but of mutual respect, appreciation, and enrichment. We wish Christians could ignite this joy in a world grown tired of individualism, suspicion, and fear of the other. When destructive and dehumanizing competition enters the Christian community and its mission, the whole world becomes a lonelier and darker place. May the groanings of despair rising from all corners of the world turn into a symphony of joy through the communion of hearts and voices of the disciple missionaries of Jesus Christ from all the nations!

I met a Filipino woman working as a babysitter here in Italy. She admitted that every time she prepares the meals for the two Italian children under her care, she wonders who is preparing the meals of her children in the Philippines. This is the daily cross of a migrant parent. To my surprise and consolation, she added, "But when I look at the two beautiful Italian children before me, I promise that I would give them the love that my own children deserve." This disciple-missionary mother bridges families, nations, and cultures.

PRIESTHOOD, MINISTRY, AND MISSION

I served as seminary rector for many years. The words I addressed to the bishop during the ordination of a deacon or a presbyter always struck me. "Most Reverend Father, holy Mother Church asks you to ordain this, our brother, to the responsibility of the diaconate or priesthood." The ordaining bishop responds, "Do you know him to be worthy?" My response, according to the rite: "After inquiry among the Christian people and upon the recommendation of those responsible, I testify that he has been found worthy." The bishop closes by saying, "Relying on the help of the Lord God and our Savior Jesus Christ, we choose this, our brother for the Order of the Diaconate or Priesthood." The community says, "Thanks be to God" or applauds. Those who have attended many ordinations might consider this opening rite as a formality. But it contains a spirituality and theology that the Church has kept sacred for centuries.

Let us dwell on some details. The rite is clear that it is not the person to be ordained that asks for ordination. It is the holy Mother Church that asks the bishop to ordain a person. No one can call oneself, present oneself, and apply for ordination. No one declares oneself as worthy of ordination. It is the discernment of the Christian people and those responsible that establishes the worthiness of a person for ministry. The bishop openly declares that, ultimately, the Church relies on the help of the Lord God and Jesus Christ in accepting someone to ordained ministry.

Without denying the profoundly personal aspect of the baptismal calling and calling to ministry, we should not forget the essential role of the Church in discerning and calling someone to ministry. If discipleship and ministry become purely personal pursuits of self-fulfillment, there will never be joy but only apprehension caused by self-promotion and competition. Deepening the ministerial and missionary aspect of baptismal discipleship would enrich the discernment of vocations to ministry and states of life.

We can also revisit the role of the Church community and its leaders and their criteria in discerning the needs of the community for ministers for our times in the spirit of Acts 1:15–26 (the choice of Matthias to replace Judas Iscariot); Acts 6: 1–6 (the institution of the ministry of the Seven in response to the needs of the Greek-speaking widows); and Acts 13:1–3 (the setting aside of Barnabas and Saul by the Holy Spirit through the prophets and teachers in Antioch). Some of the criteria they used were the Scriptures, the emerging pastoral needs, respect for the ministry specific to each one, and the qualifications required by the ministry, to name a few. They prayed, fasted, and allowed God to act through them (e.g., casting of lots). No one presented oneself as a candidate. The Church called them.

I suppose all of us here are baptized and are in some form of ministry or state of life, I would ask you to recall how you got where you are? Did you apply for the "position"? Were you called and commissioned by the Church? Calling oneself, presenting oneself, obeying oneself, and sending oneself where one chooses to go make people anxious, not joyful. May the joy of the Lord be your strength. Go in peace!

LIST OF CONTRIBUTORS

Father Édouard Adé
Catholic University of West Africa
Father Gabriel Richi Alberti
Saint Damasus Ecclesiastical University, Madrid
Chiara Amirante
Founder and President of "Nuovi Orizzonti" (New Horizons)
Father Jean-Robert Armogathe
Académie des Inscriptions et Belles-Lettres
Father Serge-Thomas Bonino, OP
Pontifical Academy of St. Thomas Aquinas (Angelicum)
Father Philippe Capelle-Dumont
French Catholic Academy
Father Piero Coda
International Theological Commission
Sister Alexandra Diriart, CSJ
Pontifical John Paul II Institute
Cardinal Kevin Farrell
Prefect of the Dicastery for the Laity, Family and Life
Cardinal Gianfranco Ghirlanda, SJ
The Dicastery for the Laity, Family and Life
Cardinal Lazzaro You Heung sik
Prefect of the Dicastery for the Clergy
Father Emilio J. Justo
Pontifical University of Salamanca
Cardinal Kurt Koch
Prefect of the Pontifical Council for Promoting Christian Unity
Father Dominic Legge, OP
Pontifical Faculty of the Immaculate Conception, Washington, DC

Bishop Paolo Martinelli, OFM, Cap.
Auxiliary Bishop of Milan
Cardinal José Tolentino de Mendonça
Archivist and Librarian of the Holy Roman Church
Cardinal Marc Ouellet
Prefect of the Congregation for Bishops
Cardinal Pietro Parolin
Secretary of State of His Holiness
Father Gaspar Hernandez Peludo
Rector of the Seminary of Avila/Faculty of Theology Pontifical University of Salamanca
Cardinal Arthur Roche
Prefect of the Congregation for Divine Worship and the Discipline of the Sacraments
Martha Olavarrieta de Gómez Serrano
Former Member of the Pontifical Council for the Family
Sister Alessandra Smerilli, FMA
Secretary of the Dicastery for Promoting Integral Human Development
Father Benoît-Dominique de la Soujeole, OP
The University of Fribourg, Switzerland
Cardinal Luis Antonio G. Tagle
Pro-Prefect of the Dicastery for Evangelization
Professor Michelina Tenace
The Pontifical Gregorian University
Cardinal Giuseppe Versaldi
Prefect of the Congregation for Catholic Education
Father Robert Vorholt
University of Lucerne